Prose Readings

Impressions and Ideas

Prose Readings

Impressions and Ideas

Edited by

William M. Sale, Jr.

Cornell University

Rinehart & Company, Inc.

New York

Second Printing, July 1958
Library of Congress Catalog Card Number: 58-7999

Preface

The prose here collected is intended to represent the kind of reading that a reasonably intelligent person will find interesting provided that his range is not exceptionally narrow and provided that he is not in pursuit of special or somewhat esoteric material. If the criterion of selection has been applied successfully, then these pieces of prose represent the kind of reading that cannot be comprehended by a student at a hasty and superficial glance. Too often, I think, anthologies are prepared on the mistaken assumption that the college student should read what he cannot fail to understand and readily imitate. Such pieces of prose often fail to gain the student's respect, and they do not engender the instructor's enthusiasm when he is faced with the task of explicating them to a class. Upon the instructor's response to an assignment depends much of the profit for the student.

However many standards we may choose to apply in judging the excellence of prose, we are, I think, generally agreed that good writing is distinguished by the author's discovery of a significant subject in the raw material that he finds before him. Some of the authors in this collection have come upon their subjects by reflecting upon the relations discovered in their observed experience. Others have reflected on the relations among a set of facts or a group of ideas. But whether the material is the consequence of impressions or of facts or of ideas, the subject in the material is found only when a significant relation or set of relations is found. In the first essay in this book, for example, we see that Clarence King has encountered in California a family that has pushed westward from Pike County, Missouri. In this material lie a half dozen or more subjects, some of which are undoubtedly pretty trivial. For Clarence King, the family from Pike represents the social disintegration that was as much a consequence of the pioneering spirit as was the heroic conquest of new territory. King has seen in his material a relation that others might fail to see, a relation between what he calls "that brave spirit of Westward Ho!" and the retrogression that sometimes attends uprooted humanity.

Once the author has discovered his subject, he must then hit upon a plan of presenting his material so that we, as readers, will make the same discovery. The student as reader must consider the author's plan of presentation, for in this plan lies the course that the author hopes the reader's mind will take. As writer the student must learn to provide such a plan for his reader. But as writer he should be made constantly aware of the importance of finding a subject in his material, for no amount of skill in ordering material will compensate for the student's failure to have discovered an interesting relation among the impressions or ideas that are to be his raw material. Students often consume an incredible amount of their own time and an instructor's time in writing pretty well what isn't really worth writing at all, and in reading pieces of prose in which the relations are about as fresh and exciting, for example, as those between an increase in automobiles and an increase in traffic problems, or between the alumni of a college and an exaggerated emphasis on an athletic program.

To discover a subject of one's own or to find the subject that an author of some maturity has found is not an altogether easy task. But little progress can be made until the attention of the student is focused and his resources challenged. In focusing a student's attention upon such important matters as these, he can be encouraged to see that all speaking and writing, whether by amateurs or professionals, results from looking at what we may call a given A in order to be able to say that this A is like a given B in spite of differences, or that the A is different from the B despite similarities. In the waking hours of any day we have to record many of these similarities and differences. When our use of language is advanced enough for us to say, "Those are scrambled eggs," we are able to note almost instantaneously that what lies before us on a plate (A) is like various sorts of cooked eggs (B) with a difference in appearance that we have learned to call "scrambled" and by which we distinguish this appearance from appearances that we have learned to call "boiled," "poached," and so forth. Good writing differs not in kind from "Those are scrambled eggs," but it differs in degree. No one is prepared to discount the value of the language skill that enables us to identify scrambled eggs, but if in reading and in writing we continue to detect only similarities and differences of this order, then a whole universe, material and immaterial, will remain *terra incognita*. We must have some practice in looking long enough and steadily enough at a given A in order to say that it is like or unlike a given B in a way or ways that at least *we* have previously not noted. A good piece of writing offers us a hitherto unperceived relation or relations in a hitherto unachieved unity.

Each of the essays in this book has been preceded by a brief headnote, designed to identify the author, and footnotes give the name and publication date of the book or periodical from which each selection has been taken. No questions have been appended, because in the main such questions are merely rephrasings in a variety of ways of the essential questions: What is the author's subject (the "controlling idea")? In what ways does the ordering of the parts (sentences, paragraphs, sections) contribute to our discovery of the subject? What does a given part contribute? How is a given part relevant? Why start with a given part? Suppose he had put this part before another part, what then? Why this word? this phrase? To what does he allude here? And must we recognize this allusion, if we are fully to understand what he is writing about? The ingenuity exercised in phrasing these essential questions often suggests in a misleading fashion that we must shift our focus as we move from one piece of writing to another.

These pieces of prose were not selected with any kind of grouping in mind. But with a list in hand, I discovered that they could be loosely grouped provided that the subdivisions did not have to be conventionally named, or representative of all of man's important concerns on this planet, or illustrative of the so-called forms of discourse. I found, for example, that I had without premeditation selected a group of essays in which the authors may be said to have reflected on man after observing—more or less accurately, more or less seriously—the doings of animals. I have grouped these essays, but I would be hard put to describe them more accurately than I have just done. My experience has been that essays chosen to fill out a group or to illustrate a form of writing frequently do not quite fit or are frequently inferior except insofar as they do fit. The groups here established can readily be ignored, but if we are to be concerned with similarities and differences, it may be profitable to encourage students to find and to try to describe the differences among pieces of writing similar enough to justify the loose grouping of the table of contents. Relations that cross these group lines will of course occur to a resourceful instructor.

I am appreciative of the advice of my colleagues, William R. Keast and Arthur Mizener, and must acknowledge the kindness of Winston Hannesson in the preparation of my text.

WILLIAM M. SALE, JR.

Cornell University
Ithaca, New York
February, 1958

Contents

Prose Readings

Impressions and Ideas

I

Clarence King

The Newtys of Pike

Clarence King (1842-1901), a distinguished geologist of the last century, was active in the organization of the United States Geological Survey and served as its first director. A. J. Liebling in The New Yorker *("The American Golconda," November 16, 1940) provides a lively account of King's exposure of a great diamond fraud in 1872. Henry Adams in* The Education of Henry Adams *records his friendship with King, of whom he said that "with ordinary luck he would die at eighty the richest and most many-sided genius of his day." The scene of the essay which follows is the Sequoia district of the southern Sierras, which King himself first discovered.*

Our return from Mount Tyndall to such civilization as flour-ishes around the Kaweah outposts was signalized by us chiefly as to our *cuisine*, which offered now such bounties as the potato, and once a salad, in which some middle-aged lettuce became the vehicle for a hollow mockery of dressing. Two or three days, during which we dined at brief intervals, served completely to rest us, and put in excellent trim for further campaigning all except Professor Brewer, upon whom a constant toothache wore painfully—my bullet mold failing even upon the third trial to extract the unruly member.

It was determined we should ride together to Visalia, seventy miles away, and the more we went the more impatient became my friend, till we agreed to push ahead through day and night, and reached the village at about sunrise in a state of reeling sleepiness quite indescribably funny.

At evening, when it became time to start back for our moun-tain camp, my friend at last yielded consent to my project of climbing the Kern Sierras to attempt Mount Whitney; so I parted

From *Mountaineering in the Sierra Nevadas*, first edition, 1871.

from him, and, remaining at Visalia, outfitted myself with a pack
horse, two mounted men, and provisions enough for a two weeks'
trip.

I purposely avoid telling by what route I entered the Sierras,
because there lingers in my breast a desire to see once more that
lovely region; and failing, as I do, to confide in the people, I fear
lest, if the camp I am going to describe should be recognized, I
might, upon revisiting the scene, suffer harm or even come to
an untimely end. I refrain, then, from telling by what road I found
myself entering the region of the pines one lovely twilight evening, two days after leaving Visalia. Pines, growing closer and
closer, from sentinels gathered to groups, then stately groves, and
at last, as the evening wore on, assembled in regular forest, through
whose open tops the stars shone cheerfully.

I came upon an open meadow, hearing in front the rush of a
large brook, and directly reached two campfires, where were a
number of persons. My two hirelings caught and unloaded the
pack horse and set about their duties, looking to supper and the
animals, while I prospected the two camps. That just below me, on
the same side of the brook, I found to be the bivouac of a company
of hunters, who, in the ten minutes of my call, made free with
me, hospitably offering a jug of whisky, and then went on in their
old eternal way of making bear stories out of whole cloth.

I left them with a belief that my protoplasm and theirs must
be different, in spite of Mr. Huxley, and passed across the brook
to the other camp. Under noble groups of pines smouldered a
generous heap of coals, the ruins of a mighty log. A little way
from this lay a confused pile of bedclothes, partly old and half-
bald buffalo robes, but, in the main, thick strata of what is known
to irony as comforters, upon which, outstretched in wretched awk-
wardness of position, was a family, all with their feet to the fire,
looking as if they had been blown over in one direction or knocked
down by a single bombshell. On the extremities of this common
bed, with the air of having got as far from each other as possible,
the mother and father of the Pike family reclined; between them
were two small children—a girl and boy—and a huge girl, who,
next the old man, lay flat upon her back, her mind absorbed in
the simple amusement of waving one foot (a cowhide eleven)
slowly across the fire, squinting, with half-shut eye, first at the vast

shoe and thence at the fire, alternately hiding bright places and darting the foot quickly in the direction of any new display of heightening flame. The mother was a bony sister, in the yellow, shrunken, of sharp visage, in which were prominent two cold eyes and a positively poisonous mouth; her hair, the color of faded hay, was tangled about her head. She rocked jerkily to and fro, removing at intervals a clay pipe from her mouth in order to pucker her thin lips up to one side and spit with precision upon a certain spot in the fire.

I have rarely felt more difficulty in opening a conversation, and was long before venturing to propose, "You seem to have a pleasant camp spot here." The old woman sharply, and in almost a tone of affront, answered, "They's wus, and then again they's better."

"Doos well for our hogs," inserted the old man. "We've a band of pork that make out to find feed."

"Oh! How many have you?" I asked.

"Nigh three thousand."

"Won't you set?" asked madam. Then, turning, "You, Susan, can't you try for to set up, and not spread so? Hain't you no manners, say?"

At this the massive girl got herself somewhat together and made room for me, which I declined, however.

"Prospecting?" inquired madam.

"I say huntin'," suggested the man.

"Maybe he's a cattle feller," interrupted the little girl.

"Goin' somewhere, ain't yer?" was Susan's guess.

I gave brief account of myself, evidently satisfying the social requirements of all but the old woman, who at once classified me as not up to her standard. Susan saw this, so did her father, and it became evident to me in ten minutes' conversation that they two were always at one, and made it their business to be in antagonism to the mother. They were then allies of mine from nature, and I felt at once at home. I saw, too, that Susan, having slid back to her horizontal position when I declined to share her rightful ground, was watching with subtle solicitude that fated spot in the fire, opposing sympathy and squints accurately aligned by her shoe to the dull spot in the embers, which slowly went out into blackness before the well-directed fire of her mother's saliva.

The shouts which I heard proceeding from the direction of my camp were easily translatable into summons for supper. Mr. Newty invited me to return later and be sociable, which I promised to do, and, going to my camp, supped quickly and left the men with orders about picketing the animals for the night, then, strolling slowly down to the camp of my friends, seated myself upon a log by the side of the old gentleman. Feeling that this somewhat formal attitude unfitted me for partaking to the fullest degree the social ease around me, and knowing that my buckskin trousers were impervious to dirt, I slid down in a reclining posture with my feet to the fire, in absolute parallelism with the rest of the family.

The old woman was in the exciting dénouement of a coon story, directed to her little boy, who sat clinging to her skirt and looking in her face with absorbed curiosity. "And when Johnnie fired," she said, "the coon fell and busted open." The little boy had misplaced his sympathies with the raccoon, and having inquired plaintively, "Did it hurt him?" was promptly snubbed with the reply, "Of course it hurt him. What do you suppose coons is made for?" Then, turning to me, she put what was plainly enough with her a test question: "I allow you have killed your coon in your day?" I saw at once that I must forever sink beneath her standard, but, failing in real experience or accurate knowledge concerning the coon, I knew no subterfuge would work with her. Instinct had taught her that I had never killed a coon, and she had asked me thus ostentatiously to place me at once and forever before the family in my true light. "No, ma'am," I said; "now you speak of it, I realize that I never have killed a coon." This was something of a staggerer to Susan and her father; yet as the mother's pleasurable dissatisfaction with me displayed itself by more and more accurate salivary shots at the fire, they rose to the occasion and began to palliate my past. "Maybe," ventured Mr. Newty, "that they don't have coon round the city of York"; and I felt that I needed no self-defense when Susan firmly and defiantly suggested to her mother that perhaps I was in better business.

Driven in upon herself for some time, the old woman smoked in silence until Susan, seeing that her mother gradually quenched a larger and larger circle upon the fire, got up and stretched herself, and giving the coals a vigorous poke swept out of sight the quenched spot, thus readily obliterating the result of her mother's precise and prolonged expectoration; then, flinging a few dry boughs upon the fire, illumined the family with a ruddy blaze and sat down again, leaning upon her father's knee with a faint light of triumph in her eye.

I ventured a few platitudes concerning pigs, not penetrating the depths of that branch of rural science enough to betray my ignorance. Such sentiments as "A little piece of bacon well broiled for breakfast is very good," and "Nothing better than cold ham for lunch," were received by Susan and her father in the spirit I meant—of entire good will toward pork generically. I now look back in amusement at having fallen into this weakness, for the Mosaic view of pork has been mine from infancy, and campaigning upon government rations has, in truth, no tendency to dim this ancient faith.

By half past nine the gates of conversation were fairly open, and our part of the circle enjoyed itself socially—taciturnity and clouds of Virginia plug reigning supreme upon the other. The two little children crept under comforters somewhere near the middle of the bed and subsided pleasantly to sleep. The old man at last stretched sleepily, finally yawning out, "Susan, I do believe I am too tired out to go and see if them corral bars are down. I guess you'll have to go. I reckon there ain't no bears round tonight." Susan rose to her feet, stretched herself with her back to the fire, and I realized for the first time her amusing proportions. In the region of six feet, tall, square-shouldered, of firm iron back and heavy mold of limb, she yet possessed that suppleness which enabled her as she rose to throw herself into nearly all the attitudes of the Niobe children. As her yawn deepened, she waved nearly down to the ground, and then, rising upon tiptoe, stretched up her clinched fists to heaven with a groan of pleasure. Turning to me she asked, "How would you like to see the hogs?" The old man added, as an extra encouragement, "Pootiest band of hogs in Tulare County! There's littler of the real sissor-bill nor Mexican racer stock than any band I have ever seen in the state. I driv the original outfit from Pike County to Oregon in '51 and '52." By this time I was actually interested in them, and joining Susan we passed out into the forest.

We walked silently on, four or five minutes, through the

woods, coming at last upon a fence which margined a wide circular opening in the wood. The bars, as her father had feared, were down. We stepped over them, quietly entered the enclosure, put them up behind us, and proceeded to the middle, threading our way among sleeping swine to where a lonely tree rose to the height of about two hundred feet. Against this we placed our backs, and Susan waved her hand in pride over the two acres of tranquil pork. The eye, after accustoming itself to the darkness, took cognizance of a certain rigidness of surface which came to be recognized as the objects of Susan's pride.

Quite a pretty effect was caused by the shadow of the forest, which, cast obliquely downward by the moon, divided the corral into halves of light and shade.

The air was filled with heavy breathing, interrupted by here and there a snore, and at times by crescendos of tumult, caused by forty or fifty pigs doing battle for some favorite bed-place.

I was informed that Susan did not wish me to judge of them by dark, but to see them again in full light of day. She knew each individual pig by its physiognomy, having, as she said, "growed with 'em."

As we strolled back toward the bars a dusky form disputed our way—two small, sharp eyes and a wild crest of bristles were visible in the obscure light. "That's Old Arkansas," said Susan; "he's eight year old come June, and I never could get him to like me." I felt for my pistol, but Susan struck a vigorous attitude, ejaculating, "S-S-oway, Arkansas!" She made a dash in his direction; a wild scuffle ensued, in which I heard the dull thud of Susan's shoe, accompanied by, "Take that, doggone you!" a cloud of dust, one shrill squeal, and Arkansas retreated into the darkness at a businesslike trot.

When quite near the bars the mighty girl launched herself in the air, alighting with her stomach across the topmost rail, where she hung a brief moment, made a violent muscular contraction, and alighted upon the ground outside, communicating to it a tremor quite perceptible from where I stood. I climbed over after her, and we sauntered under the trees back to camp.

The family had disappeared; a few dry boughs, however, thrown upon the coals, blazed up, and revealed their forms in the corrugated topography of the bed.

I bade Susan good night, and before I could turn my back she kicked her number eleven shoes into the air and with masterly rapidity turned in, as Minerva is said to have done, in full panoply.

Seated upon my blankets next morning, I beheld Susan's mother drag forth the two children one after another, by the napes of their necks, and, shaking the sleep out of them, propel them spitefully toward the brook; then taking her pipe from her mouth she bent low over the sleeping form of her huge daughter and in a high, shrill, nasal key screeched in her ear, "Yew Suse! Get up and let the *hogs* out!"

The idea thrilled into Susan's brain, and with a violent suddenness she sat bolt upright, brushing her green-colored hair out of her eyes, and rubbing those valuable but bleared organs with the ponderous knuckles of her forefingers.

By this time I started for the brook for my morning toilet, and the girl and I met upon opposite banks, stooping to wash our faces in the same pool. As I opened my dressing case her lower jaw fell, revealing a row of ivory teeth rounded out by two well-developed "wisdoms" which had all that dazzling grin one sees in the show windows of certain dental practitioners. It required but a moment to gather up a quart or so of water in her broad palms and rub it vigorously into a small circle upon the middle of her face, the moisture working outward to a certain high-water mark which, along her chin and cheeks, defined the limits of former ablution; then, baring her large red arms to the elbow, she washed her hands and stood resting them upon her hips, dripping freely, and watching me with intense curiosity.

When I reached the towel process, she herself twisted her body after the manner of the Belvedere torso, bent low her head, gathered up the back breadths of her petticoat, and wiped her face vigorously upon it, which had the effect of tracing concentric streaks irregularly over her countenance.

I parted my hair by the aid of a small dressing glass, which so fired Susan that she crossed the stream with a mighty jump and stood in ecstasy by my side. She borrowed the glass, and then my comb, rewashed her face, and fell to work diligently upon her hair.

All this did not so limit my perception as to prevent my watching the general demeanor of the family. The old man lay back at his ease, puffing a cloud of smoke; his wife, also emitting volumes of the vapor of "navy plug," squatted by the campfire, frying certain lumps of pork and communicating an occasional spiral jerk to the coffee-pot, with the purpose, apparently, of stirring the grounds. The two children had gotten upon the back of a contemplative ass, who stood by the upper side of the bed quietly munching the corner of a comforter.

My friend was in no haste. She squandered much time upon the arrangement of her towy hair, and there was something like a blush of conscious satisfaction when she handed me back my looking glass and remarked ironically, "O no, I guess not—no, sir."

I begged her to accept the comb and glass, which she did with maidenly joy.

This unusual toilet had stimulated with self-respect Susan's every fiber, and as she sprung back across the brook and approached her mother's campfire, I could not fail to admire the magnificent turn of her shoulders and the powerful, queenly poise of her head. Her full, grand form and heavy strength reminded me of the statues of Ceres; yet there was withal a very unpleasant suggestion of fighting trim, a sort of prize-ring manner of swinging the arms and hitching of the shoulders.

It required my Pike County friends but ten minutes to swallow their pork and begin the labors of the day.

Susan, after a second appeal from her mother, ran over to the corral and let out the family capital, who streamed with exultant grunt through the forest, darkening the fair green meadow gardens and happily passing out of sight.

When I had breakfasted I joined Mr. Newty in his trip to the corral, where we stood together for hours, during which I had mastered the story of his years since, in 1850, he left his old home in Pike of Missouri.

It was one of those histories common enough through this wide West, yet never failing to startle me with its horrible lesson of social disintegration, of human retrogression.

That brave spirit of Westward Ho! which has been the pillar of fire and cloud leading on the weary march of progress over stretches of desert, lining the way with graves of strong men; of newborn lives; of sad, patient mothers, whose pathetic longing for the new home died with them; of the thousand old and young

whose last agony came to them as they marched with eyes straining after the sunken sun, and whose shallow barrows scarcely lift
over the drifting dust of the desert; that restless spirit which has
dared to uproot the old and plant the new, kindling the grand
energy of California, laying foundations for a state to be, is admirable, is poetic, is to fill an immortal page in the story of America;
but when, instead of wresting from new lands something better
than the old can give, it degenerates into mere weak-minded rest-
lessness, killing the power of growth, the ideal of home, the
faculty of repose, it results in that race of perpetual emigrants who
roam as dreary waifs over the West, losing possessions, love of life,
love of God, slowly dragging from valley to valley till they fall
by the wayside, happy if some chance stranger performs for them
the last rites—often less fortunate, as blanched bones and fluttering
rags upon too many hillsides plainly tell.

The Newtys were of this dreary brotherhood. In 1850, with a
small family of that authentic strain of highbred swine for which
Pike County is widely known, as Mr. Newty avers, they bade
Missouri and their snug farm good-by, and, having packed their
household goods into a wagon drawn by two spotted oxen, set out
with the baby Susan for Oregon, where they came after a year's
march, tired and cursed with a permanent discontent. There they
had taken up a rancho, a quarter section of public domain, which
at the end of two years was "improved" to the extent of the "neat-
est little worm fence this side of Pike," a barn, and a smokehouse.
"In another year," said my friend, "I'd have dug for a house, but
we tuck ager and the second baby died." One day there came a
man who "let on that he knowed" land in California much fairer
and more worthy tillage than Oregon's best; so the poor Newtys
harnessed up the wagon and turned their backs upon a home
nearly ready for comfortable life, and swept south with pigs and
plunder. Through all the years this story had repeated itself; new
homes got to the verge of completion, more babies born, more
graves made, more pigs, which replenished as only the Pike County
variety may, till it seemed to me the mere multiplication of them
must reach a sufficient dead weight to anchor the family; but this
was dispelled when Newty remarked: "These yer hogs is awkward about moving, and I've pretty much made my mind to put
'em all into bacon this fall, and sell out and start for Montana."

Poor fellow! At Montana he will probably find a man from Texas who in half an hour will persuade him that happiness lies there.

As we walked back to their camp, and when Dame Newty hove in sight, my friend ventured to say, "Don't you mind the old woman and her coons. She's from Arkansas. She used to say no man could have Susan who couldn't show coonskins enough of his own killing to make a bedquilt, but she's over that mostly." In spite of this assurance my heart fell a trifle when, the first moment of our return, she turned to her husband and asked, "Do you mind what a dead-open-and-shut on coons our little Johnny was when he was ten years old?" I secretly wondered if the dead-open-and-shut had anything to do with his untimely demise at eleven, but kept silence.

Regarding her as a sad product of the disease of chronic emigration, her hard thin nature, all angles and stings, became to me one of the most depressing and pathetic spectacles, and the more when her fever-and-ague boy, a mass of bilious lymph, came and sat by her, looking up with great haggard eyes as if pleading for something, he knew not what, but which I plainly saw only death could bestow.

Noon brought the hour of my departure. Susan and her father talked apart a moment; then the old man said the two would ride along with me for a few miles, as he had to go in that direction to look for new hog-feed.

I dispatched my two men with the pack horse, directing them to follow the trail, then saddled my Kaweah and waited for the Newtys. The old man saddled a shaggy little mountain pony for himself, and for Susan strapped a sheepskin upon the back of a young and fiery mustang colt.

While they were getting ready, I made my horse fast to a stake and stepped over to bid good-by to Mrs. Newty. I said to her in tones of deference, "I have come to bid you good-by, madam, and when I get back this way I hope you will be kind enough to tell me one or two really first-rate coon stories. I am quite ignorant of that animal, having been raised in countries where they are extremely rare, and I would like to know more of what seems to be to you a creature of such interest." The wet, gray eyes relaxed, as I fancied, a trifle of their asperity; a faint kindle seemed to light them for an instant as she asked, "You never see coons catch frogs in a spring branch?"

"No, madam," I answered.

"Well, I wonder! Well, take care of yourself, and when you come back this way stop along with us, and we'll kill a yearlin', and I'll tell you about a coon that used to live under grandfather's barn." She actually offered me her hand, which I grasped and shook in a friendly manner, chilled to the very bone with its damp coldness.

Mr. Newty mounted, and asked me if I was ready. Susan stood holding her prancing mustang. To put that girl on her horse after the ordinary plan would have required the strength of Samson, or the use of a stepladder, neither of which I possessed; so I waited for events to develop themselves. The girl stepped to the left side of her horse, twisted one hand in the mane, laying the other upon his haunches, and, crouching for a jump, sailed through the air, alighting upon the sheepskin. The horse reared, and Susan, twisting herself around, came right side up with her knee upon the skeepskin, shouting, as she did so, "I guess you don't get me off, sir!" I jumped upon Kaweah, and our two horses sprang forward together, Susan waving her hand to her father and crying, "Come along after, old man!" and to her mother, "Take care of yourself!" which is the Pike County for *Au revoir!* Her mustang tugged at the bit and bounded wildly into the air. We reached a stream bank at full gallop, the horses clearing it at a bound, sweeping on over the green floor and under the magnificent shadow of the forest. Newty, following at a humble trot, slopped through the creek, and when I last looked he had nearly reached the edge of the wood.

I could but admire the unconscious excellence of Susan's riding, her firm, immovable seat, and the perfect coolness with which she held the fiery horse. This quite absorbed me for five minutes, when she at last broke the silence by the laconic inquiry, "Does yourn buck?" To which I added the reply that he had only occasionally been guilty of that indiscretion. She then informed me that the first time she had mounted the colt he had "nearly bucked her to pieces; he had jumped and jounced till she was plum tuckered out" before he had given up. Gradually reining the horses down and inducing them to walk, we rode side by side through the most magnificent forest of the Sierras, and I determined to probe Susan to see whether there were not, even in the most latent condition, some germs of the appreciation of nature. I looked from base to summit of the magnificent shafts, at the green plumes which traced themselves against the sky, the exquisite fall of purple shadows and golden light upon trunks, at the labyrinth of glowing flowers, at the sparkling whiteness of the mountain brook, and up to the clear matchless blue that vaulted over us, then turned to Susan's plain, honest face, and gradually introduced the subject of trees. Ideas of lumber and utilitarian notions of fence rails were uppermost in her mind; but I briefly penetrated what proved to be only a superficial stratum of the materialistic, and asked her point-blank if she did not admire their stately symmetry. A strange, new light gleamed in her eye as I described to her the growth and distribution of forests, and the marvelous change in their character and aspects as they approached the tropics. The palm and the pine, as I worked them up to her, really filled her with delight, and prompted numerous interested and intelligent queries, showing that she thoroughly comprehended my drift.

In the pleasant hour of our chat I learned a new lesson of the presence of undeveloped seed in the human mind.

Mr. Newty at last came alongside and remarked that he must stop about here. "But," he added, "Susan will go on with you about half a mile, and come back and join me here after I have taken a look at the feed." As he rode out into the forest a little way he called me to him, and I was a little puzzled at what seemed to be the first traces of embarrassment I had seen in his manner.

"You'll take care of yourself, now, won't you?" he asked. I tried to convince him that I would.

A slight pause.

"You'll take care of yourself, won't you?"

He might rely on it, I was going to say.

He added, "Thet—thet—thet man what gets Susan *has half the hogs!*"

Then, turning promptly away, he spurred the pony, and his words as he rode into the forest were, "Take good care of yourself!"

Susan and I rode on for half a mile, until we reached the brow of a long descent, which she gave me to understand was her limit.

We shook hands and I bade her good-by, and as I trotted off these words fell sweetly upon my ear, "Say, you'll take good care of yourself, won't you, say?"

I took pains not to overtake my camp men, wishing to be alone; and as I rode for hour after hour the picture of this family stood before me in all its deformity of outline, all its poverty of detail, all its darkness of future, and I believe I thought of it too gravely to enjoy as I might the subtle light of comedy which plays about these hard, repulsive figures.

In conversation I had caught the clew of a better past. Newty's father was a New Englander, and he spoke of him as a man of intelligence and, as I should judge, of some education. Mrs. Newty's father had been an Arkansas judge, not perhaps the most enlightened of men, but still very far in advance of herself. The conspicuous retrogression seemed to me an example of the most hopeless phase of human life. If, as I suppose, we may all sooner or later give in our adhesion to the Darwinian view of development, does not the same law which permits such splendid scope for the better open up to us also possible gulfs of degradation, and are not these chronic emigrants whose broken-down wagons and weary faces greet you along the dusty highways of the far West melancholy examples of beings who have forever lost the conservatism of home and the power of improvement?

William Alexander Percy

A Note on Racial Relations

William A. Percy (1885-1942) was a native of Greenville, Mississippi, the son of the Mississippi Senator Le Roy Percy, who with his son successfully conducted a fight against the Ku Klux Klan in 1922. Percy was graduated from the Harvard Law School in 1908,

but devoted most of his time to pursuits other than the law, in-
cluding the management of the three thousand acres of the Percy
plantation. The New Republic *said of him that, regardless of where*
you stood, "you have rarely heard his side stated with so much
wisdom, gentleness, and wit."

A superabundance of sympathy has always been expended on
the Negro, neither undeservedly nor helpfully, but no sympathy
whatever, so far as I am aware, has ever been expended on the
white man living among Negroes. Yet he, too, is worthy not only
of sympathy but of pity, and for many reasons. To live habitually
as a superior among inferiors, be the superiority intellectual or
economic, is a temptation to dishonesty and hubris, inevitably
deteriorating. To live among a people whom, because of their
needs, one must in common decency protect and defend is a sore
burden in a world where one's own troubles are about all any life
can shoulder. To live in the pretense that whites and blacks share
a single, identical culture and way of life is not only hypocritical
but illusory and obfuscating. And, last, to live among a people
deceptively but deeply alien and unknowable guarantees heart-
aches, unjust expectations, undeserved condemnations. Yet such
living is the fate of the white man in the South. He deserves all
the sympathy and patience he doesn't get. Poor as his results have
been, they are better than any wise realist could have anticipated.

It is true in the South that whites and blacks live side by side,
exchange affection liberally, and believe they have an innate and
miraculous understanding of one another. But the sober fact is we
understand one another not at all. Just about the time our proxim-
ity appears most harmonious something happens—a crime of violence, perhaps a case of voodooism—and to our astonishment we
sense a barrier between. To make it more bewildering the barrier
is of glass; you can't see it, you only strike it.

The incomprehension is wider than the usual distance between
practitioners of the security and of the survival virtues. Apparently
there is something peculiarly Negroid in the Negro's attitude toward, and aptitude for, crimes of violence. He seems to have resisted, except on the surface, our ethics and to have rejected our
standards. Murder, thieving, lying, violence—I sometimes suspect
the Negro doesn't regard these as crimes or sins, or even as regret-

table occurrences. He commits them casually, with no apparent feeling of guilt. White men similarly delinquent become soiled or embittered or brutalized. Negroes are as charming after as before a crime. Committing criminal acts, they seem never to be criminals.

The gentle, devoted creature who is your baby's nurse can carve her boy-friend from ear to ear at midnight and by seven A.M. will be changing the baby's diaper while she sings "Hear the Lambs a-calling," or indulges in a brand of baby-talk obviously regarded as highly communicative and extremely amusing. All white families expend a large amount of time, money, and emotion in preventing the criminals they employ from receiving their legal deserts. They feel that the murderers and thieves in their service are not evil and have not been made more unfit for society by their delinquencies.

Prosecuting attorneys, judges, and police officers are eternally at their wits' end trying to deal justly with crimes committed by simple and affectionate people whose criminal acts do not seem to convert them into criminal characters. To punish them as you would a white man appears not only unjust but immoral. Consequently, for a stabbing or a shooting a white man will be charged with assault with intent to kill (a felony), but a Negro with simple assault (a misdemeanor). Those convicted and sentenced to a few weeks in the city jail are often turned loose at night, so they may enjoy the pleasures of domesticity. The injunction to return next morning in time for breakfast is always obeyed.

I asked a learned gentleman from Yale, who was psychoanalyzing the whole Negro population of a neighboring town in three months, for some explanation of the Negro's propensity to crimes of violence. The oracle spoke: "I should say, tentatively you understand, that the frustrated hatred of the Negro for the white man, because of the frustration, is transferred to his own kind for fulfillment." It sounded like Uncle George's "They bite in the mouth."

I submitted the problem to Ford: "Ford, why do colored folks fight, shoot, stab, and kill one another so much?"

Ford giggled: "Well, s'pose a woman comes home and finds her man in bed with another woman—she's sho goin' to slap him in the face with the lamp, ain't she?"

This seemed to me only an argument for rural electrification, so I urged Ford to proceed.

"Well, s'pose some nigger crooks you in a crap game—you sho ain't goin' to let him get away with that and with your thin dime too, is you?"

I demurred and Ford went further:

"To tell the truth, most scrappin' and cuttin' and sech comes from checkin'."

"What in the world is checking?"

"Well, a bunch of boys starts off jest talkin', then they starts kiddin', jest for fun, you know, and then they starts checkin'. That's kiddin' what's rough. Everybody gets kinder riled and big-gety. Then some fool nigger puts you in the dozen."

Ford stopped as if the problem had been completely elucidated.

"What's putting you in the dozen?"

"That's sho nuff bad talk."

"Like what?"

"Well," said Ford, modest and hesitant, "that's talkin' about your mommer."

"What do they say?"

Ford was scandalized by the request.

"I couldn't tell you that, Mr. Will, it wouldn't be nice."

Explaining that my inquiry was solely in the interest of science, Ford divulged sheepishly:

"Somebody says: 'Well, your mommer hists her tail like a alley cat.' Then the shootin' begins."

It would require a fat volume to record all the crimes which were committed on my plantation during the nine years I managed it—the thieving of corn and gasoline, of gear and supplies, of hay and merchandise, the making and selling of whisky, the drunkenness and gambling, the adultery and bigamy, the cuttings, lambastings, and shootings. That volume I shall never write, but I can't help believing that some short mention of a few of the casual incidents which within that same period have befallen the transitory dark members of my own ménage might help the earnest outlander to understand, if not to alter, the moral climate in which the well-meaning, puzzled, exasperated Southern white man, day in and day out, pursues his foggy way in his dealings with the Southern Negro.

The last time I saw Mims I asked him how he and his wife were getting along. He poked out his mouth: "Pretty good, pretty good, I reckon. Cose, I always goes up the front steps whistlin'."

I praised his cheerfulness.

"That ain't it, Mr. Will. I want to give anybody what's in the house and don't belong there time to git out the back way. You know I never did like no rookus."

And then there was Nick's contretemps which came near being serious. He gravely told me about it. Nick had dignity, besides a certain astuteness.

"I knew that woman was married and her husband was servin' time up in Leavenworth. I told her when he got out he could have her back. So we was runnin' the café, doin' very good, and I was treatin' her right. We slept there too, in a little room, and kept the café open all night. It was hard work, but we'd kept at it four years and was doin' good. Well, here last week, in walks that husband of hers from Leavenworth. Cose, it was all right 'cause I had told her it would be all right. They went on to bed and I kept on workin'. I was tired and she couldn't help me none that night. 'Bout four o'clock out they come from the bedroom. I didn't fire but two shots, Mr. Will, but I got 'em both."

Nick paused reflectively and gave me a quick intimate glance. "I forgot to say, cose he made a motion-like in his bosom before I shot."

Nick had destroyed the evidence and in court bore down hard on that "motion-like." When the charge against him had been dismissed he thanked me for a message I'd sent him, but said he hadn't needed no lawyer. He hadn't. That astuteness of his coupled with the excellence of his aim made one unnecessary.

Ernest was a truly devoted creature and loved Mother, but when after ten years in our service I discovered his thefts, he merely observed: "Well, to tell you the truth, Mr. Will, I just love money too much."

Of course drunkenness and running off with automobiles and smashing them up cannot be assigned to the category of crimes. When, however, Lige (the gardener) at high noon on Sunday, against my vigorous instructions, in a Dionysiac frenzy, drove my new car to the top of the levee and turned somersaults down the other side, I was unduly fretted. I lay in bed next morning preparing a speech designed to annihilate him, but while I was putting on the last scarifying touches, Lige glided in with a folded trunk strap, came to the bedside, and presented it to me. "Whup me," was his sole remark, and mine was about as brief: "Get out! Get out!" We have never referred to automobiles since.

Jim was different. He was the most efficient and intelligent servant I ever had in the house; besides he had book-learning and read the Bible assiduously. When I first saw him he was being borne into my office with a cracked skull and trembling as if with palsy. He wanted me to sue the sheriff. He had been in jail on a charge which he convinced me had been trumped up and, while there, had been struck over the head, accidentally or maliciously, with a billet of wood by the jailer. Thoroughly indignant, I procured a doctor and filed suit against the sheriff. The sheriff was furious, stormed, threatened, and became my bitter enemy. I recovered a few hundred dollars for Jim and, considering it inadequate, gave it to him without deducting a fee. But the whole sheriff's office was so venomously hostile to me and to the Negro that I feared he might be attacked and hid him for three weeks on the plantation. Then, to keep him near me for safety, I gave him a job as house-boy and a room on the yard.

Within a few months Jim had stolen all the personal trinkets on the premises, everything from German field glasses to rings and studs. The colored population was familiar with the whole story. Jim is now a dapper and popular preacher in good standing.

Thinking over these incidents, so close to me and so usual, I wonder and fear. Is the inner life of the Negro utterly different from ours? Has he never accepted our standard of ethics? I remember too those fragments of another world on which I have stumbled, hints of a traditional lore alien to us and unfathomable by us.

I remember the sick Negro in the clinic at Leland, which I visited on an inspection trip during the flood. The doctors explained to me their dilemma: the Negro said he had been hoodooed by a witch-doctor and was going to die on the following Friday. Physically he was perfectly sound, they had made every kind of examination and test—but he was fading away before their eyes. I suggested getting the witch-doctor and forcing him to remove the spell. He had disappeared into the flood. I looked at the Negro.

He was quiet, lying on his cot and gazing at the ceiling. I spoke to him. He heard and understood, but was not interested. His eyes were smoldering with terror. On Friday he died.

I asked Jim if he believed in hoodoo. He said, of course not, but he knew of a curious thing that had happened a little while before just three blocks down Percy Street. The sister of a friend of his was low sick; she got thinner and thinner, till you could see her bones. The white doctor couldn't do nothing, so her brother got up the money and sent to New Orleans for the big hoodoo doctor. He came to her bedside, leaned over her, said some strange words, and announced she had swallowed a frog. The frog jumped out of her mouth. The hoodoo doctor went away and the girl began to recover. She gained flesh and strength, then once more she went into a decline and became nothing but skin and bones and eyes. The hoodoo doctor returned. He leaned over her and said: "You've swallowed a cooter. I can't do nothing 'bout cooters." In a few days she was dead.

The county prosecuting attorney (incidentally he had been the Cyclops of the Klan) asked me what to do in a pending criminal case. A woman had cut her husband to shreds with a long knife the Negroes call a crab-apple switch. He was recovering. She acknowledged the occurrence, but pleaded in defense that he had placed a spell on her by means of a cunjer-bag. The bag, still in his possession, contained a piece of her red flannel drawers and a hank of her hair. Its effect was to rob her of connubial allure—in her words, "it stole her nature." She pleaded justification and I thought clearly she was justified. After many consultations with the distracted justice of the peace, on our recommendation the charge against her was dismissed. In the crowded court-room we expected an emotional scene of gratitude. Instead, the woman burst into tears. She lamented that it didn't make no difference to her if she was out of jail, seeing as how she didn't have her nature back. This seemed reasonable and we asked what we could do about it. We were advised that if we could git that cunjer-bag, she could sew the piece of red flannel "back where it come from" and all would be well. We told the husband he'd be immediately chucked into jail if he didn't fetch that bag instanter. He disappeared, while we waited in the court-room. In an incredibly short time he was

back with it. The judge solemnly presented the bag to the woman.
Everybody was happy. The couple left arm in arm, showing signs
of resurgent nature.

How is it possible for the white man to communicate with
people of this sort, people whom imagination kills and fantasy
makes impotent, who thieve like children and murder ungrudg-
ingly as small boys fight?

Appreciating as I do the Negro's excellences—his charm, his
humor, his patience, his exquisite sensibilities, his kindness to his
own poor, his devotion and sweetness to all children, black and
white, his poetry of feeling and expression, his unique tactual medieval faith, his songs more filled with humility and heart-break
than Schubert's or Brahms's—I want with all my heart to help
him. But helping him is well-nigh impossible because of one tragic
characteristic. No Negro trusts unreservedly any white man—that
is understandable enough, though exceedingly unfortunate—but,
still more unfortunate, no Negro trusts unreservedly any Negro.
That too is understandable, because his leaders betray him, either
from their childish ambition to appear "big shots" or from their
willingness to exploit his simplicity. So the Negro has cut himself
off from any leadership, and leadership is desperately needed by
him. He turns not to the rare but magnificent leaders of his own
race, but to his country preachers, uneducated, immoral, and ava-
ricious. Trusting no one, without moral stamina, without discipline,
without standards, the Negro gropes blindly through an alien white
man's world, intricate in the extreme, and gleaming with attractive
shoddiness.

The whole atmosphere of America is such as to mislead and
endanger the Negro. The sickening adulation paid to Negro ath-
letes and artists, not because of their great abilities but because
they are Negroes; rumors of what the Negro does in Paris, in Mos-
cow, in the Northern cities; the promises and bribes of demagogic
politicians interested not in his welfare but in his vote; the Negro
press's hatred of the white man, its demand for social equality, its
bitterness, its untrustworthiness—all these combine to create about
the young Southern Negro an atmosphere as dangerous as it is fe-
brile and unwholesome. The work of white sentimentalists is
equally perilous. When personal relations with the Negro are too
familiar, they are misinterpreted by him. He reasons, plausibly, that

if you are willing to dine with him, you are willing and probably anxious to sleep with him. With the genius of the poor for misinterpreting the motives of the rich, added to the Negro's own special genius for suspicion and mistrust, it should require little except common sense to deduce what the efforts of white sentimentalists may lead to. The noblest of them, such as Mrs. Roosevelt, accomplish their insidious evil quite unsuspectingly and with the highest motives. It will never occur to them that the results, however pitiful or savage, will have been of their making.

It is said that race relations in the South are improving because lynching has declined to the vanishing-point and outburst of violence against the Negro are almost unknown. It should be noted, however, that the improvement, if improvement there is, is due solely to the white man. It should be further noted that the Negro is losing his most valuable weapon of defense—his good manners. When a Negro now speaks of a "man" he means a Negro; when he speaks of a "fellow" he means a white man; when he speaks of a "lady" he means a Negress; when he speaks of a "woman" he means a white woman. Such manners are not only bad, they are not safe, and the frame of mind that breeds them is not safe. Covert insolence is not safe for anybody, anywhere, at any time.

The Negro, not having assimilated the white man's ethics, giving only lip service to the white man's morality, must for his own peace and security accept whole-heartedly the white man's mores and taboos. In the South the one sacred taboo, assumed to be Southern, but actually and universally Anglo-Saxon, is the untouchability of white women by Negro men. It is academic to argue the wisdom or justice of this taboo. Wise or unwise, just or unjust, it is the cornerstone of friendly relations, of interracial peace. In the past it has been not the eleventh but the first commandment. Even to question it means the shattering of race relations into hideous and bloody ruin. But I fear it is coming to be questioned.

It is not difficult to reason why the young Negro is beginning to question this taboo their forefathers accepted so whole-heartedly and unthinkingly. Every black buck in the South today has gone or will go to Chicago, where it is not only possible but inexpensive to sleep with a white whore. Likewise, there are Negro bell-boys in Southern hotels frequented by white whores. But there is a further and more humiliating reason. In former generations, when the taboo was unquestioned, Southern women felt a corresponding obligation so to conduct themselves that any breach of the taboo was unthinkable. Those were the times when Southern white women were either ladies or loose. Today white women drink in public places, become drunk in public places, and public places are filled with scandalized and grossly human Negro waiters. Cars at night park on the sides of roads, and Negroes, like everyone else, deduce what the couple inside is doing. Whenever there's a moral failure on the part of the Southern white, there's a corresponding moral failure on the part of the Southern Negro.

Influenced by bitter half-castes, the young Negro argues that there is no justice in the white man's woman being untouchable to the Negro man, while the Negro woman is not untouchable to the white man. On the surface this seems an unanswerable argument, but it is not even sincere. The whites make outcasts of their white women who have violated the taboo, sometimes punishing them as grossly as they punish the offending Negro. Never are they accepted into even the lowest stratum of white society. But when a Negro girl sleeps with a white man, not only is she not ostracized by the Negroes, she becomes an object of increased allure to Negro youths. Unconsciously and pitifully they pay tribute to the white man by finding desirable his cast-off baggage. The Negro's resentment toward the practice springs from jealousy and from his imitation of the white man's fury when his own women are touched. Though they are sincerely bitter, theirs is only a pseudo-indignation. The Negroes themselves could stop the practice, if they truly resented it, by treating their offending girls as the white man treats his. The Negro's incapacity for moral indignation is one of his most terrifying characteristics. His moral flabbiness is his charm and his undoing.

It is not pleasant to make these bald and bitter statements. I make them because they are true and because I am afraid for the Negro. Only the truth can help him, and that can help him little unless he helps himself.

I have received visits from so many people whose sole reason for wishing to see me was their interest in the Negro problem that I am forced to conclude I am regarded in some quarters as an authority on the problem or as a typical Southerner who happens to be articulate. I am certainly no authority, and I doubt that I am entirely typical. I claim only to be one of that vast number of men of good will who try, with indifferent success, to see wisely and to act justly. As such, I would say to the Negro: before demanding to be a white man socially and politically, learn to be a white man morally and intellectually—and to the white man: the black man is our brother, a younger brother, not adult, not disciplined, but tragic, pitiful, and lovable; act as his brother and be patient.

Sherwood Anderson

The Egg

Sherwood Anderson (1876-1941) left a career in business to become an author. The stories on which his reputation will probably depend were collected in Winesburg, Ohio *(1919),* The Triumph of the Egg *(1921), and* Horses and Men *(1923). He tried his hand less successfully at novels.*

My father was, I am sure, intended by nature to be a cheerful, kindly man. Until he was thirty-four years old he worked as a farmhand for a man named Thomas Butterworth whose place lay near the town of Bidwell, Ohio. He had then a horse of his own, and on Saturday evenings drove into town to spend a few hours in social intercourse with other farmhands. In town he drank several glasses of beer and stood about in Ben Head's saloon—crowded on Saturday evenings with visiting farmhands. Songs were sung and glasses thumped on the bar. At ten o'clock father drove home along a lonely country road, made his horse comfortable for the night, and himself went to bed, quite happy in his position in life. He had at that time no notion of trying to rise in the world.

It was in the spring of his thirty-fifth year that father married my mother, then a country school-teacher, and in the following spring I came wriggling and crying into the world. Something hap-

From *The Triumph of the Egg.* Copyright 1920 by Eleanor Anderson. Reprinted by permission of Harold Ober Associates.

pened to the two people. They became ambitious. The American passion for getting up in the world took possession of them.

It may have been that mother was responsible. Being a school-teacher she had no doubt read books and magazines. She had, I presume, read of how Garfield, Lincoln, and other Americans rose from poverty to fame and greatness, and as I lay beside her—in the days of her lying-in—she may have dreamed that I would some day rule men and cities. At any rate she induced father to give up his place as a farmhand, sell his horse, and embark on an independent enterprise of his own. She was a tall silent woman with a long nose and troubled gray eyes. For herself she wanted nothing. For father and myself she was incurably ambitious.

The first venture into which the two people went turned out badly. They rented ten acres of poor stony land on Grigg's Road, eight miles from Bidwell, and launched into chicken-raising. I grew into boyhood on the place and got my first impressions of life there. From the beginning they were impressions of disaster, and if, in my turn, I am a gloomy man inclined to see the darker side of life, I attribute it to the fact that what should have been for me the happy joyous days of childhood were spent on a chicken farm.

One unversed in such matters can have no notion of the many and tragic things that can happen to a chicken. It is born out of an egg, lives for a few weeks as a tiny fluffy thing such as you will see pictured on Easter cards, then becomes hideously naked, eats quantities of corn and meal bought by the sweat of your father's brow, gets diseases called pip, cholera, and other names, stands looking with stupid eyes at the sun, becomes sick and dies. A few hens and now and then a rooster, intended to serve God's mysterious ends, struggle through to maturity. The hens lay eggs out of which come other chickens and the dreadful cycle is thus made complete. It is all unbelievably complex. Most philosophers must have been raised on chicken farms. One hopes for so much from a chicken and is so dreadfully disillusioned. Small chickens, just setting out on the journey of life, look so bright and alert and they are in fact so dreadfully stupid. They are so much like people they mix one up in one's judgments of life. If disease does not kill them, they wait until your expectations are thoroughly aroused and then walk under the wheels of a wagon—to go squashed and dead back to their maker. Vermin infest their youth, and fortunes must be spent for curative powders. In later life I have seen how a literature has been built up on the subject of fortunes to be made out of the raising of chickens. It is intended to be read by the gods who have just eaten of the tree of the knowledge of good and evil. It is a hopeful literature and declares that much may be done by simple ambitious people who own a few hens. Do not be led astray by it. It was not written for you. Go hunt for gold on the frozen hills of Alaska, put your faith in the honesty of a politician, believe if you will that the world is daily growing better and that good will triumph over evil, but do not read and believe the literature that is written concerning the hen. It was not written for you.

I, however, digress. My tale does not primarily concern itself with the hen. If correctly told it will center on the egg. For ten years my father and mother struggled to make our chicken farm pay and then they gave up that struggle and began another. They moved into the town of Bidwell, Ohio, and embarked in the restaurant business. After ten years of worry with incubators that did not hatch, and with tiny—and in their own way lovely—balls of fluff that passed on into semi-naked pullethood and from that into dead henhood, we threw all aside and, packing our belongings on a wagon, drove down Grigg's Road toward Bidwell, a tiny caravan of hope looking for a new place from which to start on our upward journey through life.

We must have been a sad-looking lot, not, I fancy, unlike refugees fleeing from a battlefield. Mother and I walked in the road. The wagon that contained our goods had been borrowed for the day from Mr. Albert Griggs, a neighbor. Out of its sides stuck the legs of cheap chairs, and at the back of the pile of beds, tables, and boxes filled with kitchen utensils was a crate of live chickens, and on top of that the baby carriage in which I had been wheeled about in my infancy. Why we stuck to the baby carriage I don't know. It was unlikely other children would be born and the wheels were broken. People who have few possessions cling tightly to those they have. That is one of the facts that make life so discouraging.

Father rode on top of the wagon. He was then a bald-headed man of forty-five, a little fat, and from long association with mother and the chickens he had become habitually silent and discouraged. All during our ten years on the chicken farm he had worked as a laborer on neighboring farms and most of the money

he had earned had been spent for remedies to cure chicken diseases, on Wilmer's White Wonder Cholera Cure or Professor Bid-
low's Egg Producer or some other preparations that mother
found advertised in the poultry papers. There were two little
patches of hair on father's head just above his ears. I remember that
as a child I used to sit looking at him when he had gone to sleep
in a chair before the stove on Sunday afternoons in the winter.
I had at that time already begun to read books and have notions
of my own, and the bald path that led over the top of his head
was, I fancied, something like a broad road, such a road as Caesar
might have made on which to lead his legions out of Rome and
into the wonders of an unknown world. The tufts of hair that grew
above father's ears were, I thought, like forests. I fell into a half-
sleeping, half-waking state and dreamed I was a tiny thing going
along the road into a far beautiful place where there were no
chicken farms and where life was a happy eggless affair.

One might write a book concerning our flight from the
chicken farm into town. Mother and I walked the entire eight
miles—she to be sure that nothing fell from the wagon and I to see
the wonders of the world. On the seat of the wagon beside father
was his greatest treasure. I will tell you of that.

On a chicken farm, where hundreds and even thousands of
chickens come out of eggs, surprising things sometimes happen.
Grotesques are born out of eggs as out of people. The accident
does not often occur—perhaps once in a thousand births. A chicken
is, you see, born that has four legs, two pair of wings, two heads, or
what not. The things do not live. They go quickly back to the
hand of their maker that has for a moment trembled. The fact that
the poor little things could not live was one of the tragedies of
life to father. He had some sort of notion that if he could but bring
into henhood or roosterhood a five-legged hen or a two-headed
rooster his fortune would be made. He dreamed of taking the
wonder about to county fairs and of growing rich by exhibiting it
to other farmhands.

At any rate, he saved all the little monstrous things that had
been born on our chicken farm. They were preserved in alcohol
and put each in its own glass bottle. These he had carefully put
into a box, and on our journey into town it was carried on the
wagon seat beside him. He drove the horses with one hand and

with the other clung to the box. When we got to our destination, the box was taken down at once and the bottles removed. All during our days as keepers of a restaurant in the town of Bidwell, Ohio, the grotesques in their little glass bottles sat on a shelf back of the counter. Mother sometimes protested, but father was a rock on the subject of his treasure. The grotesques were, he declared, valuable. People, he said, liked to look at strange and wonderful things.

Did I say that we embarked in the restaurant business in the town of Bidwell, Ohio? I exaggerated a little. The town itself lay at the foot of a low hill and on the shore of a small river. The railroad did not run through the town and the station was a mile away to the north at a place called Pickleville. There had been a cider mill and pickle factory at the station, but before the time of our coming they had both gone out of business. In the morning and in the evening busses came down to the station along a road called Turner's Pike from the hotel on the main street of Bidwell. Our going to the out-of-the-way place to embark in the restaurant business was mother's idea. She talked of it for a year and then one day went off and rented an empty store building opposite the railroad station. It was her idea that the restaurant would be profitable. Traveling men, she said, would be always waiting around to take trains out of town and town people would come to the station to await incoming trains. They would come to the restaurant to buy pieces of pie and drink coffee. Now that I am older I know that she had another motive in going. She was ambitious for me. She wanted me to rise in the world, to get into a town school and become a man of the towns.

At Pickleville father and mother worked hard, as they always had done. At first there was the necessity of putting our place into shape to be a restaurant. That took a month. Father built a shelf on which he put tins of vegetables. He painted a sign on which he put his name in large red letters. Below his name was the sharp command—"EAT HERE"—that was so seldom obeyed. A showcase was bought and filled with cigars and tobacco. Mother scrubbed the floor and the walls of the room. I went to school in the town and was glad to be away from the farm and from the presence of the discouraged, sad-looking chickens. Still I was not very joyous. In the evening I walked home from school along Turner's Pike and remembered the children I had seen playing in the town school yard. A troop of little girls had gone hopping about and singing. I tried that. Down along the frozen road I went hopping solemnly on one leg. "Hippity Hop To The Barber Shop," I sang shrilly. Then I stopped and looked doubtfully about. I was afraid of being seen in my gay mood. It must have seemed to me that I was doing a thing that should not be done by one who, like myself, had been raised on a chicken farm where death was a daily visitor.

Mother decided that our restaurant should remain open at night. At ten in the evening a passenger train went north past our door followed by a local freight. The freight crew had switching to do in Pickleville, and when the work was done they came to our restaurant for hot coffee and food. Sometimes one of them ordered a fried egg. In the morning at four they returned northbound and again visited us. A little trade began to grow up. Mother slept at night and during the day tended the restaurant and fed our boarders while father slept. He slept in the same bed mother had occupied during the night and I went off to the town of Bidwell and to school. During the long nights, while mother and I slept, father cooked meats that were to go into sandwiches for the lunch baskets of our boarders. Then an idea in regard to getting up in the world came into his head. The American spirit took hold of him. He also became ambitious.

In the long nights when there was little to do, father had time to think. That was his undoing. He decided that he had in the past been an unsuccessful man because he had not been cheerful enough and that in the future he would adopt a cheerful outlook on life. In the early morning he came upstairs and got into bed with mother. She woke and the two talked. From my bed in the corner I listened.

It was father's idea that both he and mother should try to entertain the people who came to eat at our restaurant. I cannot now remember his words, but he gave the impression of one about to become in some obscure way a kind of public entertainer. When people, particularly young people from the town of Bidwell, came into our place, as on very rare occasions they did, bright entertaining conversation was to be made. From father's words I gathered that something of the jolly innkeeper effect was to be sought. Mother must have been doubtful from the first, but she said nothing discouraging. It was father's notion that a passion for the company of himself and mother would spring up in the breasts of the younger people of the town of Bidwell. In the evening bright happy groups would come singing down Turner's Pike. They would troop shouting with joy and laughter into our place. There would be song and festivity. I do not mean to give the impression that father spoke so elaborately of the matter. He was, as I have said, an uncommunicative man. "They want some place to go. I tell you they want some place to go," he said over and over. That was as far as he got. My own imagination has filled in the blanks.

For two or three weeks this notion of father's invaded our house. We did not talk much, but in our daily lives tried earnestly to make smiles take the place of glum looks. Mother smiled at the boarders and I, catching the infection, smiled at our cat. Father became a little feverish in his anxiety to please. There was, no doubt, lurking somewhere in him, a touch of the spirit of the showman. He did not waste much of his ammunition on the railroad men he served at night, but seemed to be waiting for a young man or woman from Bidwell to come in to show what he could do. On the counter in the restaurant there was a wire basket kept always filled with eggs, and it must have been before his eyes when the idea of being entertaining was born in his brain. There was something pre-natal about the way eggs kept themselves connected with the development of his idea. At any rate, an egg ruined his new impulse in life. Late one night I was awakened by a roar of anger coming from father's throat. Both mother and I sat upright in our beds. With trembling hands she lighted a lamp that stood on a table by her head. Downstairs the front door of our restaurant went shut with a bang and in a few minutes father tramped up the stairs. He held an egg in his hand and his hand trembled as though he were having a chill. There was a half-insane light in his eyes. As he stood glaring at us I was sure he intended throwing the egg at either mother or me. Then he laid it gently on the table beside the lamp and dropped on his knees beside mother's bed. He began to cry like a boy, and I, carried away by his grief, cried with him. The two of us filled the little upstairs room with our wailing voices. It is ridiculous, but of the picture we made I can remember only the fact that mother's hand continually stroked the bald path that ran across the top of his head. I have forgotten what mother said to him and how she induced him to tell her of what had happened downstairs. His explanation also has gone out of my mind. I remember only my own grief and fright and the shiny path over father's head glowing in the lamplight as he knelt by the bed.

As to what happened downstairs. For some unexplainable reason I know the story as well as though I had been a witness to my father's discomfiture. One in time gets to know many unexplainable things. On that evening young Joe Kane, son of a merchant of Bidwell, came to Pickleville to meet his father, who was expected on the ten-o'clock evening train from the South. The train was three hours late and Joe came into our place to loaf about and to wait for its arrival. The local freight train came in and the freight crew were fed. Joe was left alone in the restaurant with father.

From the moment he came into our place the Bidwell young man must have been puzzled by my father's actions. It was his notion that father was angry at him for hanging around. He noticed that the restaurant-keeper was apparently disturbed by his presence and he thought of going out. However, it began to rain and he did not fancy the long walk to town and back. He bought a five-cent cigar and ordered a cup of coffee. He had a newspaper in his pocket and took it out and began to read. "I'm waiting for the evening train. It's late," he said apologetically.

For a long time father, whom Joe Kane had never seen before, remained silently gazing at his visitor. He was no doubt suffering from an attack of stage fright. As so often happens in life he had thought so much and so often of the situation that now confronted him that he was somewhat nervous in its presence.

For one thing, he did not know what to do with his hands. He thrust one of them nervously over the counter and shook hands with Joe Kane. "How-de-do," he said. Joe Kane put his newspaper down and stared at him. Father's eyes lighted on the basket of eggs that sat on the counter and he began to talk. "Well," he began hesitatingly, "well, you have heard of Christopher Columbus, eh?" He seemed to be angry. "That Christopher Columbus was a cheat," he declared emphatically. "He talked of making an egg stand on its end. He talked, he did, and then he went and broke the end of the egg."

My father seemed to his visitor to be beside himself at the duplicity of Christopher Columbus. He muttered and swore. He

declared it was wrong to teach children that Christopher Columbus
was a great man when, after all, he cheated at the critical moment.
He had declared he would make an egg stand on end and then,
when his bluff had been called, he had done a trick. Still grumbling
at Columbus, father took an egg from the basket on the counter
and began to walk up and down. He rolled the egg between the
palms of his hands. He smiled genially. He began to mumble words
regarding the effect to be produced on an egg by the electricity
that comes out of the human body. He declared that, without
breaking its shell and by virtue of rolling it back and forth in his
hands, he could stand the egg on its end. He explained that the
warmth of his hands and the gentle rolling movement he gave the
egg created a new center of gravity, and Joe Kane was mildly interested. "I have handled thousands of eggs," father said. "No one
knows more about eggs than I do."

He stood the egg on the counter and it fell on its side. He tried
the trick again and again, each time rolling the egg between the
palms of his hands and saying the words regarding the wonders of
electricity and the laws of gravity. When after a half-hour's effort
he did succeed in making the egg stand for a moment, he looked up
to find that his visitor was no longer watching. By the time he had
succeeded in calling Joe Kane's attention to the success of his effort,
the egg had again rolled over and lay on its side.

Afire with the showman's passion and at the same time a good
deal disconcerted by the failure of his first effort, father now took
the bottles containing the poultry monstrosities down from their
place on the shelf and began to show them to his visitor. "How
would you like to have seven legs and two heads like this fellow?"
he asked, exhibiting the most remarkable of his treasures. A cheerful smile played over his face. He reached over the counter and
tried to slap Joe Kane on the shoulder as he had seen men do in
Ben Head's saloon when he was a young farmhand and drove to
town on Saturday evenings. His visitor was made a little ill by the
sight of the body of the terribly deformed bird floating in the alcohol in the bottle and got up to go. Coming from behind the
counter, father took hold of the young man's arm and led him back
to his seat. He grew a little angry and for a moment had to turn his
face away and force himself to smile. Then he put the bottles back
on the shelf. In an outburst of generosity he fairly compelled Joe

Kane to have a fresh cup of coffee and another cigar at his expense. Then he took a pan and filling it with vinegar, taken from a jug that sat beneath the counter, he declared himself about to do a new trick. "I will heat this egg in this pan of vinegar," he said. "Then I will put it through the neck of a bottle without breaking the shell. When the egg is inside the bottle it will resume its normal shape and the shell will become hard again. Then I will give the bottle with the egg in it to you. You can take it about with you wherever you go. People will want to know how you got the egg in the bottle. Don't tell them. Keep them guessing. That is the way to have fun with this trick."

Father grinned and winked at his visitor. Joe Kane decided that the man who confronted him was mildly insane but harmless. He drank the cup of coffee that had been given him and began to read his paper again. When the egg had been heated in vinegar, father carried it on a spoon to the counter and going into a back room got an empty bottle. He was angry because his visitor did not watch him as he began to do his trick, but nevertheless went cheerfully to work. For a long time he struggled, trying to get the egg to go through the neck of the bottle. He put the pan of vinegar back on the stove, intending to reheat the egg, then picked it up and burned his fingers. After a second bath in the hot vinegar, the shell of the egg had been softened a little, but not enough for his purpose. He worked and worked and a spirit of desperate determination took possession of him. When he thought that at last the trick was about to be consummated, the delayed train came in at the station and Joe Kane started to go nonchalantly out at the door. Father made a last desperate effort to conquer the egg and make it do the thing that would establish his reputation as one who knew how to entertain guests who came into his restaurant. He worried the egg. He attempted to be somewhat rough with it. He swore and the sweat stood out on his forehead. The egg broke under his hand. When the contents spurted over his clothes, Joe Kane, who had stopped at the door, turned and laughed.

A roar of anger rose from my father's throat. He danced and shouted a string of inarticulate words. Grabbing another egg from the basket on the counter, he threw it, just missing the head of the young man as he dodged through the door and escaped.

Father came upstairs to mother and me with an egg in his

hand. I do not know what he intended to do. I imagine he had some idea of destroying it, of destroying all eggs, and that he intended to let mother and me see him begin. When, however, he got into the presence of mother, something happened to him. He laid the egg gently on the table and dropped on his knees by the bed as I have already explained. He later decided to close the restaurant for the night and to come upstairs and get into bed. When he did so, he blew out the light and after much muttered conversation both he and mother went to sleep. I suppose I went to sleep also, but my sleep was troubled. I awoke at dawn and for a long time looked at the egg that lay on the table. I wondered why eggs had to be and why from the egg came the hen who again laid the egg. The question got into my blood. It has stayed there, I imagine, because I am the son of my father. At any rate, the problem remains unsolved in my mind. And that, I conclude, is but another evidence of the complete and final triumph of the egg—at least as far as my family is concerned.

Oliver La Farge

American Splinter

Oliver La Farge (1901-   ) is an anthropologist, ethnologist, archaeologist, and novelist. As author and editor, he has constantly advocated the cause of the American Indian. His Laughing Boy, *a novel of life among the Navahos, won the Pulitzer Prize for fiction in 1930. The essay that follows is autobiographical. La Farge's family is an old one in America; he is a descendant of both Benjamin Franklin and Oliver Hazard Perry.*

People brought up as I was have had the changing world practically slapped in their faces. To this they have responded in different ways. Some feel it to be a good thing and are changing with it, some are making a virtue of necessity. A sizeable part of the class

This selection from *Raw Material* by Oliver La Farge is reprinted by permission of and arrangement with Houghton Mifflin Company, the authorized publishers.

to which I am supposed to belong is either fighting with all its might to stop the change—or at least to nullify its effects upon them—or is combining that effort in an odd way with an ostrich denial that such a thing is happening.

My kind, in my time, grew up to order, security and privilege of a degree which it is difficult for most Americans to grasp. Their world-view, ethics, and code of manners, all their mechanisms, were aimed at the perpetuation of that security. Now it is more than threatened, it is in the course of being destroyed. This is an old situation, recurring over and over again in the world's history, it is a situation which arouses unexpected viciousness in those whose way of life is threatened. The drab, deep emotions behind Chamberlain's Munich and the suicide of France, the exceptional bitterness both in serious talk and in jest, the violence of feeling levelled against President Roosevelt, have sprung from it in our time.

I was born to this security and I no longer have it. I find it curious now to look back and see what that lost world was like.

It was a world and it is still trying to be one. Some years ago there were published two maps, one showing a Bostonian's, one a New Yorker's view of America, amusing distortions of the surface and proportions of the country, the Atlantic Seaboard huge, the rest dwindled away, the centre of the country vaguely filled in with items of misinformation. They were entertaining maps and they were quite correct.

As far as America was concerned, we recognized a narrow zone running along the coast from a short distance north of Boston to the Mason and Dixon line. Within this zone was civilization, people who mattered (and an unfortunate intrusion of low persons of Irish, Italian, and other alien descents), this was what we meant when we said "everybody," or "America," or "the country." Across the Mason and Dixon line there was another tribe in Virginia which we recognized, and which also mattered, but with which one could not have close relations since it was almost impossible to persuade a Virginian that anyone from north of him could be a gentleman. On the California coast around San Francisco there was a sort of colony of our kind, and one had connections and knew people in Saint Louis, really quite a civilized place and not nearly as middle-western as one would think.

The rest of the country was what a Frenchman would have called "the provinces." It was strange, often ludicrous, and of no importance. We had absolutely no conception whatsoever of its scale, let alone its population. In one section there was a rather glamorous folk called "Southerners," genteel and faded. There was a lot of thinly populated desert country where cowboys and Indians roved. There were exotic sections worth visiting for play or sport. Then there was the Middle West, producer of objectionable things such as Babbit, Prohibition, and the La Follettes. People from the Middle West behaved stupidly when they went to Europe and made the French and English think we lacked culture. But they were not America, we were America.

In fact, of course, our numbers were infinitesimal, but we did not know that. We were so few that we were no more than a splinter of America. But included in our ranks, either by birth or by an established system of wise incorporation, were those who controlled the flow of money; that power added to our advantages of education and general distribution of wealth and our network of mutual help enabled us to make trouble away out of proportion to our numbers. We thought we were the country, we were in fact a splinter of it, but the splinter was firmly imbedded in America's thumb.

I find it hard now to believe what our view of America was. I remember that when I was an undergraduate, not only boys my age but our elders seriously stated, over and over again, that "the country" did not want prohibition, it had been put over upon us by the Middle West. That by this they meant that an overwhelming majority of the American people had voted in favour of Prohibition, did not occur to them. Somehow all those citizens did not really count, they might swing election after election, but they were not "the country." We were.

It was an Englishman who first forced me to look my own concepts in the face. I had been several times to Arizona, I knew the look and breadth of the land, but I had not allowed that to penetrate my insularity. He was seeking knowledge of America, and various of us, his friends, invited him to come and sample this or that part of it. I wanted him to see the Indian country of the Southwest, a picturesque appendage to the nation of my conception. Others urged him to Bar Harbor and Charleston. He chose to take a job on the Kansas City *Star*, at which we all protested in horror.

"I don't understand you," he told me. "Almost every day I hear you and your friends damning the Middle West. It supported the Bull Moose Party, and you're worried now about La Follette's campaign. You say it hung Prohibition on you and won't let you get rid of it. It has produced the Farm Bloc and the Progressive Bloc, it controls your foreign policy. And yet all of you say it doesn't count and that there's no point in studying it. It seems to me it's the most important part of America and you'd all do well to go and take a look at it."

He was quite right, but no such idea had occurred to me until then.

Part of this attitude was wishful thinking. One did not want to admit that the group which once did control the Union had lost most of its power. If one's own ancestors did not include senators, cabinet officers, governors, and so forth, at least these were sprinkled liberally among one's acquaintances. Also fairly common was descent from men who had taken an important part in freeing and founding the Union. Those had been the good days, when the country wasn't full of foreigners and politics were clean and genteel. In our own time, we clung to individual resurgences—Theodore Roosevelt (distressingly radical, but still a gentleman in politics), Henry Cabot Lodge. Andrew Jackson had started a regrettable revolt of the masses which continued with ever-increasing strength, and it was comforting to dismiss these masses by pointing to their ignorance, provincialism, and naïveté, as if by so doing one could talk away the living facts of history.

The strength of this class lay, and lies, in its control of money. A person like myself, neither rich nor affiliated with a financial family, did not formulate this thought. But the great men of our kind were financiers, and they, realists to the core, knew that their power was stabler and more enduring than ever-shifting political power. In the long run money could outlast and wear down any popular movement, with a concession here and there.

That was the strength, or perhaps better, that was the trustworthy weapon which the strength wielded. Perhaps the strength in itself lay in an interlocking directorate just as important as the actual directorates of corporations which have been described so much. This was an interlock of friendships, loyalties, affections, relationships, a responsibility to one's kind which bound the whole group together, and out of which in turn the individual received the sense of security and order which would make him a loyal fighter for his kind.

To a young man growing up this created a situation which no one would find it easy to relinquish of his own free will. My family was not rich. My parents made severe sacrifices to put us through college, and even so we were hard up. In fact, we thought of ourselves as poor. This conception of poverty was not reached by contemplating the average per capita national income. It was a poverty which made a real effort to win scholarships, which regarded "Final Club" dues as a necessary expense, which would not think of wearing a suit unless it had been made in England or bought at Brooks Brothers'. There was nothing to be afraid of in our lack of spare cash, merely an irritating disadvantage in entertaining girls, a mild amount of foregoing some of the fun the boys around us enjoyed. If anyone had suggested to me as an undergraduate that I consider my financial situation in terms of the average national income, I should have rejected the idea. In terms of my class I was poor, and no one could tell me differently.

Poor—but safe. There was an interlock of thousands of people, commanding infinite resources, to watch over me. When people of my kind were arrested, they didn't get the third degree. One was accustomed to courtesy everywhere, to ready credit, one was "placed." Hardly recognizing the existence of habitable land outside of our narrow, coastal province, one didn't have to give much thought to what might happen if one moved to Podunk not to visit but to live. In Europe, of course, one went armed with introductions and letters of credit, and was confident of adequate attention from consulates and embassies. If needed, there was almost no one to whom one could not have access.

So, too, being reared in New York, I not only took for granted my inherited acquaintance with a network of wealth and influence, but also the reception ready for me, through numerous relatives and parents' friends, in Philadelphia, and the always somewhat cooler but still definite acceptance awaiting me in Boston.

Here was a snug world full of friendliness, of real affections, and privilege. In that world one foresaw a clear course, which can be typified by the fact that, during the First World War, we completely took it for granted that if we got into the army it would be as officers—almost everyone we knew had a commission. The way was made straight for our kind.

In college it was time for me to think pretty seriously about my career. In my sophomore year I realized, definitely and for all time, that more than anything else in this world I loved writing, that a writer, pure and simple, was what I wanted to be. I was already started in anthropology. This new realization involved important decisions.

From my father I had acquired a distaste for people who fooled with the arts. Any art was a serious career which must support itself. I knew, too, the struggle my father and mother were making to send us through college. Unproven in writing, it was clear that I could not ask them to support me while I went through what would probably be the long process of learning my craft and developing it into a source of income. It did not, of course, occur to me that on graduating, or even before, I might simply go forth and live in real, not relative, poverty. It wasn't that I thought of this and lacked the courage to carry it out, I didn't think of it.

In order to stop being a burden to my parents as soon as possible, I must continue as a scientist with the expectation that shortly I could win scholarships and other aids. Writing I must pursue in my spare time until the day when I had sold enough to enable me to tell myself, my father, the world, that in fact I was a writer and could make a go of it.

All of this was realistic enough, the plan of a young man who expects to make his own living, a schedule of double work to which I stuck for eight long, discouraging years. But in this planning and the initial will to endure a period of drudgery there entered another element—the complete assurance that in time, by one means or another, drudgery would lighten and straitened circumstances be replaced by relative prosperity. The network of connections assured a young man of some kind of position with good prospects of advancement. Men who got into trouble or who failed badly were the subject of a good deal of consultation and headshaking, but niches were found for them. Granted a reasonable amount of intelligence and industry one could be perfectly certain

of a decent job of some sort, a gentleman's job. In due course
there would be marriage to a girl of one's own kind and place. She
might bring money with her, she would surely bring additional
connections and aids. One would continue all through life to have
plenty of use for a tuxedo and evening clothes, one would belong
to a club or two, and one could look forward in time to seeing his
son graduate from his own college, a member of the same Final
Club as his father. Rich or poor, there would always be certain
amenities, the gap between one member of the group and another
would never become so great as to cut off social relations, there
was, in short, the certainty that one would continue always in the
general type of life into which one had been born.

The last war and its aftereffects struck a terrible blow at this
group security. Events since then have continued hacking at its
very roots. That is what has had the endowed classes all over the
world so desperately up in arms. The wolf who has just made his
pile and intends to hang onto it is one thing, nothing he feels can
compare in intensity to the emotions of the men and women who
have never known anything but security, who feel that security is
theirs by right, and see it all going by the board. It is not just a
matter of the crude feeling of safety; attached to it are a thousand
graces of life, a certain kind of education for their children, riches
of the mind and spirit that come with the possession of leisure and
some means, the well-being of friends and relatives, the powerful
feelings attached to an ancestral home, to a bit of countryside in
which one grew up, to institutions, customs, manners. The cry that
Mr. Roosevelt has betrayed his class is not an idiotic wail referring
to the loss of certain extra profits, it is the expression of a genuine
dismay and indignation at one born within the group, endowed
with all its blessings, who has helped to undermine the entire structure. It refers to everything from the pleasure of owning many
books to the children's future.

Not being a literary historian I cannot carry out an accurate
comparison between the writings of those who were always secure,
in the sense I have described, and of those who had to make their
own way. Conning the matter in my mind, the odds seem heavily
in favour of the latter. I have a feeling that one can see in some
genuine talents of the protected group, such as Owen Wister, the
recurrent, harmful effects of being too free, too far removed from

need. If I have as much money and position as I need anyhow, it is not important to me, that is, not important in any real sense of the word, that my book sell more than moderately, although I should appreciate the gratification of wide sales. If in addition I am quite sure of my position in my own group and feel that mankind outside that group is less important, I am relatively impervious to the opinions of those who know and judge me only by my works. So Henry James can wander off into England and preciousness, so Wister, who is nonetheless the best writer on the West we have yet produced, can intrude an irritating set of stuffy reflections into the mastery of *The Virginian* and can perpetrate *Lady Baltimore* with entire serenity.

A snug world. If you are brought up entirely within it you are as innocent of its actual scale as you would be of the real meaning of "mountain" had you never seen anything but the hill behind your house. In this I had a little luck. My parents were not perfect conformists. My misery at school gave me a little cynicism, a touch of detachment, largely vitiated by my emotional craving to align myself with the pattern which had rejected me. The habit of unpopularity and the offensive behaviour which arises from a roaring inferiority complex stayed with me at college. Success for my kind at Harvard depended more than anything else upon social honours, election to the Institute and to a Final Club. In my sophomore year I was elected to nothing. This God-sent year of disgrace enabled me to form strong friendships outside of my predestined group. When I did make the clubs I had not become emancipated, but a few ideas were rattling round inside my head. I was at least conscious of the mathematical fact that all the Final Clubs between them comprised not over a hundred men out of the eight hundred in my class, and that that was definitely not a majority. I knew and loved certain splendid men whom the clubs would not accept.

When I left Harvard for New Orleans there were no signs that I would learn to participate in the real America. I held to the habit of mind of the secure and privileged. I had begun to perceive dimly that forty-eight states actually meant forty-eight states full of human beings possessed of an equal right to say how the country should be run; there were some leaks in the dyke through which new thinking might come, that was all. With many good intentions towards my fellow men, and desires for social reform, I was nonetheless a little conservative, responding to the instinct which shies away from any threat to the enfolding structure.

Russell Lynes

The Upper Bohemians

Russell Lynes (1910-   ) is one of the senior editors of Harper's Magazine. *He is a shrewd and witty observer of the classes in American society. The essay that follows was originally published in* Harper's Magazine *in 1953, and, in a slightly revised form, it appears in Mr. Lynes's book,* A Surfeit of Honey *(1957).*

I

In a twilight zone in our society, neither below the aristocracy nor above the middle class, lives a somewhat ornamental and by no means an inconsequential group of Upper Bohemians. They are a reasonably constant element in a social structure that has some of the qualities of a feather bed. In the center of the bed lies the great body politic, and when this body rolls over slightly, as it does from time to time, our society takes on a new shape. No matter how conscientious may be our efforts to be classless, the leveling off process when it pushes down a social tuft here pushes one up over there.

For a nation that prides itself on the democratic premise that one man is as good as another, we produce a remarkable number of aristocrats and a remarkable variety of aristocracies. Unlike the upper classes of Europe which maintain some kind of permanent if uneasy tenure even when their fortunes are impaired, our upper classes constitute a highly fluid aristocracy with its feet in quicksand and its head in storm clouds. Today's aristocracy is more than likely to be tomorrow's middle class, and our middle class is constantly tossing up new and somewhat astonished aristocrats. When, for example, we lopped off the heads of the old moneyed aristocracy by taxes, we produced an expense-account aristocracy to take

Reprinted from *Harper's Magazine*, February, 1953, by permission of the author. Copyright by Russell Lynes, 1953.

its place; when we more or less laughed out of countenance the old aristocracy of breeding, we nurtured a new one of industrial tycoons. Just now we are beginning to see the rise of an entertainment and communications aristocracy which embraces not only the Goldwyns and the Skourases, the Sarnoffs and Luces, the Bentons and Bowleses but also the cream of the talent that serves them in their movies, television, radio, publications and advertising empires.

The Upper Bohemians regard this ebb and flow of aristocratic tides with detached amusement because they consider themselves to be genuinely unconcerned with the social ladder. I should like to venture briefly into their twilight zone and look at their habitat and their mores. I do not believe that they have been defined before, and it is my hope that this preliminary invasion of their privacy may tempt some qualified social scientist, who is endeavoring to make the quixotic structure of our society seem reasonable, to find a handy pigeonhole for some of my best friends—who least like to be pigeonholed.

In Bohemian society it is the convention to look upon all conventions, all codes of behavior, and all rules of taste as matters never to be taken for granted. Conventions by their very nature are regarded with suspicion, for on the surface they seem to have been devised only to obscure and make palatable man's basic inhumanity to man. It is the convention of Bohemianism to say, "To hell with all that; we live by the rules of our own morality."

Traditionally the Bohemian is a romanticist with his eyes raised to the higher truths of art and nature, a walking protest against social sham and all sorts of rules of behavior. He is a man in search of the truth who finds it in the cold north light of a studio garret. There he makes love and poetry and song and worries about his soul; he does not fret about tomorrow or yesterday or about wealth or position or any of the cushions of life that we now group under the unromantic heading of Security. This is the "*Vie de Bohème*" or simon-pure kind of Bohemianism of song and story, of the old Left Bank and the old Greenwich Village, of Murger and berets and beards.

It is a far cry from the Upper Bohemianism of today, though some of the romanticism remains, some of the soul-searching, some of the mannerisms of social revolt, or at least of social eccentricity.

The Upper Bohemians look down on the new aristocracies, or perhaps they look sideways at them. In either case they couldn't exist without them.

But let me explain, if I can, who they are and what place they occupy in our social panoply and what their function is. Perhaps I can best do this by introducing you to a few of them at the risk of your already knowing them as well as I do or better.

Mr. and Mrs. U. B. happen to live in New York though you might as easily meet them in Cincinnati or Chicago or Los Angeles; you are apt to find more than a handful of their like in smaller cities or towns. Their house is a remodeled brownstone, possibly somewhat modernized on the outside but still largely indistinguishable from the other houses in the block. If you were to peer through the living-room window, you would notice that they indulge in rather definite and slightly odd colors on the walls, have rather more than the usual number of books, some drawings and probably a painting or two—one an abstraction and one a somewhat unconventional landscape—and possibly a mobile. Their house is not in a currently fashionable part of town; it is not close to Park Avenue, for instance, but neither is it in an unfashionable district, nor a socially improper one. They live, one might say, not quite on the fringe but, rather, on the verge. The twilight of residence between the fashionable and the worthy is their natural habitat out of conviction. They do not want to be classified.

Mr. U. B. is a publisher, though he might as easily be a lawyer, or writer, or an architect, or an editor, or, but less likely, a business man. If he is in business, the chances are that he is in advertising or some other form of communications, though there are a few Upper Bohemians in any big business, free spirits who are models of buttoned-down-collar conformity on the job but quite independent of their business associates and deportment from five o'clock on. In his professional life Mr. U. B. usually moves in and out of the arts or near them, but in any case he calls them by their pet names and is alive to their latest alarums and excursions. He is aware of what exhibitions are on 57th Street, what plays are current and imminent, and he has definite convictions about which ones he will bother to see and which he will eschew. The same might be said of his attitude toward current

books, motion pictures, and ballet. He is culturally hep, but he is
not a cultural hepcat. Many things interest him but few things
"send" him. He is a sophisticated patron of the arts, so sophisticated that for the most part he lets other people gamble on them.
His discriminating taste in paintings and books and furniture has
nothing, he is convinced, to do with fashion; it has only to do
with permanent quality. He is not likely to be a collector in any
orderly or elaborate way; that sort of thing he leaves to the aristocrats who collect under the guidance of a dealer and who have, he
believes, no taste of their own. He is merely an acquirer of
miscellaneous items of artistic or literary interest. For this reason
his house is customarily furnished with a chef's salad of a few
modern pieces and a good many old, "amusing" ones—nineteenth-
century Gothic, for example—and just plain comfortable and un-
classifiable and well-made upholstered pieces that by no standards
of taste are "objectionable." Mr. U. B. wouldn't be caught dead
reading *House and Garden* or *House Beautiful*. He is not in the
least worried about his taste or concerned with being told what
is chic. He might, on the other hand, subscribe to an architectural
magazine because he is interested in changes in style. He makes a
sharp distinction between fashion and style. Anyone can follow
fashion, he believes; only a man of taste can distinguish style.

His wife, Mrs. U. B., shares this attitude, as is evidenced most
clearly by her manner of dress. She isn't above peeking into *Vogue*
or *Harper's Bazaar* though it is usually to complain about what she
finds there. She dresses in her own style, which is likely to be a
slightly eccentric version of what other women are wearing and
may even be a "thing" she has picked off the rack at Klein's or
Ohrbach's and endowed with her own touch. Her costume jewelry is "Victorian heirloom" or extravagantly fake in order that it
may make no pretense of looking like real jewelry. Ideally she
would like a piece of brass cut into a mobile by Alexander Calder,
big and bold and defiant, but short of that, a chunk of Mexican silver or even small jadeite rocks or something that looks like an old
bedspring will suffice. But whatever it may be, it is not a cheap
copy of something expensive. Expensive conventional jewels, like
expensive furs, are, she believes, a mere matter of publishing one's
bank balance on one's person. That is for the socially pretentious
or the socially insecure, not for her. Furthermore she discards gar-

ments that merely have what she derisively calls a "well bred" or a "ladies' club" look. She owns a hat ("In case I need it for a funeral or something . . ."), but never wears it if she can help it, which she usually can.

Her husband's dress is not eccentric, but it is casual. The tweed jacket and slacks as a costume for office wear were almost surely introduced not by sportsmen, who are strong adherents to the conventional costume for the proper occasion, but by Upper Bohemians who put comfort and casualness before routine propriety. The Upper Bohemian would not, however, wear the loud be-palmed and be-flowered sport shirt with its abbreviated tails hanging outside his slacks; his country play clothes are more likely than not to be the true countryman's work clothes. Not long ago I saw on a railroad platform in rural Connecticut what I consider the quintessence of Upper Bohemian male attire—army shoes, a red-and-black checked woolen shirt, and dungarees. From the wearer's watch pocket hung a Victorian gold chain dangling a Phi Beta Kappa key.

From their outward appearance you will see that Mr. and Mrs. U. B. are more confident and more free-and-easy about their taste than are the members of the various aristocracies who depend on decorators to give consistency and style to their homes (or rely on accepted conventions) and couturiers to embellish their person. But how do they live? What goes on in these somewhat eccentric houses and in these unconventional clothes?

2

Let us look first at some of the more superficial aspects of Upper Bohemian life before we attempt to see what lies beneath the casual surface. The surface, first of all, is casual; life in the Upper Bohemian household is studiedly informal. It might almost be said that an Upper Bohemian will always sit on the floor in preference to a chair in any room where a group is gathered, no matter how many chairs there may be. He also prefers his dinner on a card table in the living-room to sitting at a dining-room table conventionally accoutered. His attitude toward servants (though he would be unlikely to refer to anyone as a servant, lest the word sound patronizing) is cozy rather than pretentious. He doesn't care a fig about maids in black dresses and white aprons; that is merely

sham for sham's sake. He would always rather have a rough and
ready type who is "an instinctive cook" than a trained maid who
understands the art of waiting on table. He wants his meals when
he wants them, and he has a special intolerance of anyone whose
life is dictated by what he calls "a tyranny of servants." In his
mind the only justification for service is to make life more relaxed,
not more formal, though if he happens to be well off (which he
not infrequently is) his parties may be well staffed and rather
quietly elegant.

This relaxed attitude toward convention is typical of the
Upper Bohemian and basic to an understanding of his behavior.
But there is in his mind always a good reason for unconventional-
ity, for he is not sloppy in his manners. He merely thinks of manners of all sorts as an expression of good will, not of good training.
He treats his friends in a somewhat offhand and casual way which
he expects them to accept as a sign of affection. He assumes that
they are perceptive of his moods and do not need to be treated like
strangers or children; they should know that if he disliked them
he would be elaborately polite to them. Only rarely, only when
provoked, and only to a member of one of the aristocracies, would
he be elaborately rude.

If he is a true Upper Bohemian and a serious one, he scarcely
dares to let down the bars that separate him from the conservatism
of the new aristocracies or from what he would call the "middle-
class moralities." His horror of the philistinism of Main Street is
exceeded only by his amusement at the cultural pretensions of
Park Avenue and Beverly Hills and Westchester. He looks upon
all culture but his own, all other standards of behavior, and all
other measures of success with tolerant suspicion.

Other people are likely to underestimate the importance of
the Upper Bohemians, the Upper Bohemians are likely to over-
estimate themselves. Their number is not legion, and yet there are
more of them than one might suspect from a superficial look at
one's own community or one's friends. I have suggested that they
are most likely to be found in fairly sizable and large cities but
you will find them also wherever there is an academic community,
such as for example, Princeton, New Jersey, which is within difficult but possible commuting distance of a metropolis. Some of
the Upper Bohemians in such a community are directly connected

with the university, but many others have moved there because they like the pleasant breeze of intellectualism that blows off such an academic reservoir. They enjoy the opportunity to number among their friends those whose profession requires them to think in large and abstract terms about the arts or about the state of the world, and they like to mingle with others who put, often perforce, the satisfactions of the mind and spirit ahead of those of social status. While there is social status within a university (indeed, there may be no other society save the Army so rigidly classified), the scholar is to the world outside the university a classless man, and so the Upper Bohemians find him congenial.

You are unlikely to find the Upper Bohemian in the suburbs which closely surround big cities; if he is a suburbanite (a name he would abhor) he lives in the more inaccessible and peripheral suburbs, so that he and his wife can enjoy the freedom of the country without fear of being observed over the back fence by neighbors. They want to sunbathe stark naked if they feel like it. You will not, however, find them in a remote suburb in which there are no others of their own kind. Upper Bohemians are no less gregarious than most people, though they are strong in their protestations of independence and confident of their ability to keep themselves entertained.

They are not joiners and are likely to shun country clubs, ladies' clubs, civic organizations, and all other forms of what they consider artificially contrived social media. It doesn't occur to them that the fact that they run in droves, that any party they may go to is likely to consist of the same dozen or so couples making the same kinds of conversation (art, politics, music, books) over the same kind of drinks (martinis, bourbon, wine and soda) is very like the country-club pattern without the country club.

Wherever an Upper Bohemian may travel in this country or abroad he will, if he sticks to the sizable cities, always land with his own kind. There is a sort of unacknowledged and unofficial grapevine by which he travels, and if he goes from New York to Denver or San Francisco, for instance, he finds himself with letters of introduction to a business-man-poet or a physician who paints and he will soon be taken to the bosom of the local Upper Bohemia. Furthermore he will discover that nearly everyone he meets knows a friend of his or a friend of a friend. This same grapevine will lead him to his own kind in London, Paris, and Rome; he can go anywhere without ever leaving Upper Bohemia more than a day's journey ahead or behind.

The Upper Bohemian might be willing to concede that he is something of an intellectual snob. He does, after all, set more store by intellectual pursuits than does any other class except the professional academics and the artists. If he lives geographically in a sort of social no man's land, he also lives in a sort of intellectual neutral zone. He thinks of himself as a bridge between the bright light of intellectualism and the artificially illuminated world of affairs. His conversation bears this out. Unlike most people's conversation which proceeds from the general to the specific, from "How's business?" to the price of gaskets, his is apt to go from the specific to the general. A casual remark about a tomato is likely to end in a heated discussion of the comparative values of organic gardening, or a reference to a Buick to a speculative argument about the state of American industrial design. The Upper Bohemian likes to see things in the large and to savor their implications.

The same might be said of his attitude toward his children. Children are problems before they are people, and as a parent he is full of theories about the rounded development of the complete personality. For this reason he inclines toward progressive schools and away from traditional institutions.

He encourages his children to call him and his wife and their friends by their first names, and to engage in adult conversations which as often as not mystify and benumb them. This is part and parcel of his theory that every child is a little adult whose mind should be stretched and whose interests should parallel his parents'. This forced growth and over-insistence on intellectual interests in some cases breeds hardened little Philistines and in other cases monstrous little prodigies; it also breeds its fair share of average children.

The Upper Bohemian attitude toward sex may be summarized as open-minded. He is not a defender of promiscuity, but he maintains such a tolerant attitude toward other people's behavior that he often finds it exceedingly difficult to make clear-cut decisions for himself. When an Upper Bohemian talks about his doctor, it is a safe guess that he is as likely to be talking about his psychiatrist as about his physician, but his readiness to seek psychiatric advice is probably sound. Because the Upper Bohemians recognize the uses of psychiatry, I doubt very much if the incidence of mental breakdown among them is as high as it is among the aristocracies or the middle classes, who think of psychiatrists as witch doctors.

There may, however, be a quite different reason for this stability. The Upper Bohemian is essentially secure in his social position. He is more likely to be interested in keeping even with "the people" than up with the Joneses.

3

To understand this we must retrace our steps for a moment and consider the origins of the Upper Bohemian. What is it that endows him with this sense of security that makes it possible for him to stand apart and look at other strata of society, to consider their mores, and to fashion a style of living and a code of belief out of his distrust for theirs? Let's see where he came from and how he has got where he is.

The Upper Bohemians do not lend themselves to statistical analysis (at least they do not lend themselves to *me* for this purpose), but they come mainly from two socially secure segments of society. It would be my guess that the largest number are the sons and daughters of the professional classes, the offspring of the law and medicine, of academics and clergymen. They have been brought up in an atmosphere in which the achievements of the mind have been put ahead of the achievements of the bank balance —if not actually, then at least conversationally and by precept. It is well, in this connection, to remember that there is always in the back of the mind of the professional man the comforting thought that if he is not a financial success he can without losing face be an "interesting intellectual"; no one holds it against an intellectual that he hasn't made money; on the contrary, it is unfashionable for him to do so. When, however, a professional man makes a great deal of money, as writers and architects occasionally do and lawyers do far more often, he is likely to regard this bonanza as something over and beyond his real satisfactions in life and not essential to them. In this respect he is obviously quite distinct from the business man who, when he has accumulated his wealth, then looks around at the cultural ornaments of life and decides in which ones he would like to indulge. So it is out of professional families that I believe the largest number of today's Upper Bohemians have come. They have been brought up to mistrust the kind of life in which money and the ostentation that it can buy are all-important. During the past ten or fifteen years the status of the intellectual in America has risen considerably in the social scale, as I have pointed out in another essay,[1] so that today's progeny of yesterday's intellectuals have a newly built-in social position. In order to maintain this status and not let it become confused with other and to them less distinguished social groups, they have formed their own . . . though they would be the last ones to recognize how neatly stratified they have become.

Also into the Upper Bohemian group have migrated the intellectually inclined sons and daughters of the rich who are embarrassed about Father's lack of what they would call "any real culture." They come from a socially secure group well versed in the gentle amenities of decorous behavior and well able to give their children all of what are known as "the advantages." These scions of wealth and manners are refugees to Upper Bohemia from the upper classes, seeking sanctuary from aristocratic stuffiness.

The third main reservoir of recruits for Upper Bohemia is more difficult to define because it has no single character and no clear edges. It might be called the Pool of the Arts, for it is fed by streams from all the social classes. Into it flows a steady trickle of moderately to considerably successful, intellectually respectable, and socially perceptive writers, artists, academics, and architects, along with a few actors. Many of them are "bright young things," extremely clever, extremely ambitious, and already at a tender age self-made. Acceptability in Upper Bohemian circles is to them the achievement of a social ambition. To them Upper Bohemia is a desirable sort of aristocracy to which to belong, and of all the Upper Bohemians they are the most conscientiously and cautiously Bohemian.

[1] "Highbrow, Lowbrow, Middlebrow," *Harper's Magazine*, February, 1949. If you are familiar with these categories, you will have recognized that Upper Bohemia is peopled entirely by Highbrows and Upper Middlebrows.

4

It cannot be denied that the Upper Bohemian serves a useful purpose in our cultural and civic life. Since he believes that his interests are not identified with those of any special social or economic class he serves as a minor social, political, and cultural balance wheel. He is a believer in social progress but, as he is not a faddist, he is suspicious and scornful of dogma; sometimes his beliefs and his suspicions cancel each other out and leave him inert. This is not to say, however, that he is a middle-of-the-roader; he is far more likely to be on one side of the road on some questions and on the other side on others. In general, however, you will find that the Upper Bohemian inclines to take the side of the labor aristocracy against the business aristocracy, inclines to the Freudian interpretation of behavior, and the Keynesian interpretation of economics, and a free-thought interpretation of religion. He goes overboard about none of these. His deepest belief is in personal and intellectual freedom. He is not a theorist, though he enjoys theory, any more than he is a realist (as the business man uses that word) though he is a respecter of the realities.

Where the arts are concerned he keeps what he dearly hopes is an open mind. He believes in freedom of expression and he resents the recent political incursions into arguments about the arts. He will argue violently on one side or the other of such a question as whether the main current in painting today is abstractionist, but the question is of far less moment to him than whether or not there seems to be vitality in the arts in general. He deplores the commercialism of television, and settles this problem for himself either by not having a set or by using one with fastidious discrimination. He considers the movies an art form and his attitude toward them, as toward other arts, stresses the honest, as he calls it, against the pretentious.

Not all of his behavior in relation either to the arts or to the world around him is aloof. He likes to mix with the other classes, to partake in causes in which he believes, even to do menial jobs in a political campaign (part of his pride is in making it quite clear that he doesn't think he is better than other people . . . just different), so long as he can escape into his own comfortable

Bohemianism when he is through with his job. He does not really want to be one of the boys any more than Lady Bountiful wants to be one of the girls, but while he is with them he wants to be identified as one with the people though not quite one of them. One of the characteristics of Bohemianism has always been its questionable respectability in the eyes of the community. It is looked on by all classes of society as something not quite real—by the poor as an affectation of poverty by people who could be better off if they wanted to be, by the middle classes as darn fools and dreamers who are free and easy in their morals and have no fear of God or the Treasury Department, and by the Upper Classes as quaint. But the real strength of the Bohemians and their vital function, both of which are out of all proportion to their numbers, have been rooted in their eagerness to flaunt convention for the purpose, sometimes sincere and sometimes affected, of fostering new ideas and bringing about the destruction of sham and flummery.

In this the Upper Bohemian believes, and if he is caught in a kind of sham and flummery that is all his own, it is unlikely that it would bother him, because, remember, he is not only a social introvert but an observer and in some ways a self-appointed policeman of the social scene. He is not above casting a critical eye upon himself, though when he does he is inclined to be pleased with what he sees. Whether his tribe is on the increase or the decrease at this moment is difficult to tell, though recent events tend to indicate that middle-class morality rather than intellectual independence and agility is generally on the rise. The pressures for conformity, by the same token, are strong, and the tide is running against the free-wheeling individual who declines to accept this as the greatest of all possible societies. Dr. Pangloss rides again.

On the other hand, there has never been a Bohemianism so essentially respectable as this one. To its fold may flock more and more men and women who wish to identify themselves with the side of revolt against what they consider to be the false standards of the new aristocracies and the dreary conventionality of the middle classes. There is always a reservoir of eager spirits who wish to enjoy the titivation of flaunting convention, and who at the same time never want to stray far from the warmth of a secure social hearth. There are always those who believe that they

can take convention or leave it. Those who leave it with a flourish
are true Bohemians. It is those who manage both to take it *and*
leave it who are the true Upper Bohemians.

Frederick Lewis Allen

Horatio Alger, Jr.

*Frederick Lewis Allen (1890-1954) taught as an assistant in English
at Harvard University for two years after his graduation in 1912.
He then began his career as an editor, serving as assistant editor of*
The Atlantic Monthly, *managing editor of* The Century Magazine,
editor of Harper's Magazine, *and vice-president of Harper &
Brothers. His reputation as an author rests on his informal histories
of American life in the twentieth century, the best known of which
is still the first,* Only Yesterday (1931), *a chronicle of the so-called
Jazz Age.*

If you relish paradoxes, consider the career of Horatio Alger,
Jr. He made his fame writing books in which boys rose "from rags
to riches"—yet he himself did not begin life in rags and did not die
rich. The boys in his books got ahead by outwitting thieves and
sharpers—yet he himself, a mild and generous little man who gave
freely of his earnings to newsboys and bootblacks on the New
York streets (the sort of boys who were his favorite heroes), was
an easy mark for impostors. His books were, and are, generally
regarded by the critical as trash—yet their sales mounted into the
millions, he was one of the most popular of all American authors,
if not of all authors of all time; and there can be little doubt that
he had a far-reaching influence upon the economic and social
thought of America—an influence all the greater, perhaps, because
it was innocently and naïvely and undogmatically exerted.

Alger wrote always about boys who were on their own,
making their way for themselves, usually in the big city. His own

From *The Saturday Review of Literature,* September 17, 1938. Reprinted
by permission of *The Saturday Review* and of the executors of the estate
of Frederick Lewis Allen.

boyhood was quite different. It was highly protected and regimented. He was born in 1832 in Revere, Massachusetts, a town which has become one of the northern suburbs of Boston; Horatio Alger, senior, his father, a Unitarian minister, was a bleak, God-fearing man who fought the sins of the flesh and wanted to rear up young Horatio to join him in the spiritual leadership of America. Young Horatio was kept away from all playmates who might prove naughty influences; was put through such a strict course of study that by the time he was eight years old he could explain the Revolutionary War, add fractions in his head, and write the synopsis of a sermon; and became such a little prig that the neighbors' children called him Holy Horatio. When he was fourteen he was sent away to school and learned for the first time the joys of natural play and of mischief; but even after he reached Harvard his primness remained. He fell in love with Patience Stires of Cambridge when he was nineteen, and wanted to marry her, but gave her up—to his lasting regret—when his father told him that marriage would prevent him from continuing his preparation for the church. And later he left a boarding-house at college because, seeing his landlady scantily dressed in the doorway of her room, he resolved to "move to where there is greater respect for decency." Yet, earnest puritan though young Alger was, he did not want to follow his father into the ministry. He wanted to write.

After he left Harvard College he went through a long period of false starts and indecision and frustration. He tried to write but failed miserably. He completed a long theological course but hated it. He went to Paris, tasted the Bohemian life, tasted briefly also the delights of the flesh (because, as he wrote in his diary, genius had prerogatives and he would have prerogatives too), but went through agonies of shame over his affair with Elise Monselet— and produced in Paris nothing of any literary moment. He returned to America and became a minister at Brewster, Massachusetts. But still he was so obsessed by his literary ambition that he would sketch out plots on the margins of his sermons; and in 1866 —when the Civil War had ended and he was thirty-four years old—he gave up the church once and for all and went to New York to write boys' books.

There he remained most of the rest of his life. He never married; there was a period when he was pathetically in love with a married woman, but even then he did not apparently hope to win her from her husband, though he so adored her that when she tired of him he went into a mental breakdown. One of his closest attachments was to a Chinese boy whom he befriended and fathered for three years, until the boy was tragically killed in a street accident. Another close attachment was to Charles O'Connor, who ran the Newsboys' Lodging House in New York. It was at this Lodging House that he spent most of his time, for he was devoted to the ragged boys who frequented it, and found in them a constant gold-mine of the sort of literary material that he could use. And year by year he turned out Horatio Alger books in profusion—always wanting to write important books for adults, always dreaming of the novel (to be called "Tomorrow") that he would some day produce, but always unable to make a go of anything but the boys' stories which flowed from his pen in a torrent.

The truth seems to be that Horatio Alger never fully grew up to adult life, that he shunned its passions and battles and hard realities. Always, deep down in his heart, he wanted a boy's life—not a boy dominated by a stern father and dressed up in neat and proper clothes, but rather a boy free from parental supervision, free to soil and rumple his clothes, free to make a living for himself and test his budding self-reliance. Alger wanted also to be a man of letters, but could not achieve this ambition because his mind, while clear and logical, was childishly naïve, unimaginative, and bewildered by the complexities of mature life. After his books had become widely known, and people began to turn to him as an authority on slum conditions in New York, he was asked to serve on charitable and civic committees, but though he was happy to be treated as a person of importance he usually sat silent at board meetings; either he was too self-distrustful to speak or the problems discussed there took him beyond his depth.

Once, to be sure, he briefly plunged into city affairs with ardor and courage. Having learned how the Italian *padrones* in New York kept little Italian immigrant boys in virtual slavery, lived on their earnings, and thrashed them cruelly, Alger not only wrote a book exposing the *padrone* system (*Phil the Fiddler*), but conducted a campaign of public protest, made speech after speech, and was instrumental in ending the abuse, though more than once he was beaten up by irate *padrones* or their hired thugs. But most of the time, what Alger most enjoyed was to shun adult society and play with the Lodging House boys: to go dashing off with them to fires, to beat the drum in their children's band, to ride on the open horse-cars, to go to Barnum's Museum, to work at organizing a children's theater. One excited entry in his diary, about an especially splendid fire, ended with the triumphant words, "Rode back on engine." As he made money with his books he would spend it on the boys—giving them presents, setting up a bootblack in business, helping a newsboy's mother with the rent payments. He died in 1899, at the age of sixty-seven—still a nice boy, hardworking, generous, friendly, innocent of heart.

It was this perpetual youth's singular fortune to have just that simplicity, that elementary directness of approach to fiction-writing, which would make his books a joy to immature minds. From the moment when William T. Adams, the author of the "Oliver Optic" books, encouraged him, in 1865, to write *Ragged Dick*, the way was clear for him. *Ragged Dick* was followed by over a hundred other volumes—exactly how many, it would take an indefatigable bibliographer to discover. (Herbert R. Mayes, writing Alger's biography, ran the total up to 119, and later found that he had left out several.) Some of the titles, such as *Bound to Rise, Luck and Pluck, Sink or Swim, Do and Dare, Strive and Succeed,* will evoke nostalgic memories in many an older reader today. And almost all of the books were essentially the same—variations upon an invariable theme.

The standard Horatio Alger hero was a fatherless boy of fifteen or thereabouts who had to earn his way, usually in New York City. Sometimes he had to help support a widowed mother with his boot-blacking or peddling; sometimes his parentage was unknown and he lived with an aged and eccentric miser, or with a strange hermit who claimed to be his uncle. It might even be that his father was living, but was having trouble with the mortgage on the old farm. Always, however, the boy had to stand on his own feet and face the practical problem of getting on.

This problem was set before the reader in exact financial detail. On the very first page of *Do and Dare*, for example, it was disclosed that the young hero's mother, as postmistress at Wayneboro, had made during the preceding year just $398.50. Whenever "our hero" had to deal with a mortgage, the reader was told the precise amount, the rate of interest, and all other details. When our hero took a job, the reader could figure for himself exactly how much progress he was making by getting $5 a week in wages at the jewelry store and another $5 a week tutoring Mrs. Mason's son in Latin. Our hero was always a good boy, honest, abstemious (in fact, sometimes unduly disposed to preach to drinkers and smokers), prudent, well-mannered (except perhaps for the preaching), and frugal. The excitement of each book lay in his progress toward wealth.

Always there were villains who stood in his way—crooks who would rob him of his earnings, sharpers who would prey upon his supposed innocence. His battles with these villains furnished plenty of melodrama. They tried to sell him worthless gold watches on railroad trains, held him up as he was buggy-driving home with his employer's funds, kidnapped him and held him prisoner in a New York hide-out, chloroformed him in a Philadelphia hotel room, slugged him in a Chicago alley-tenement. But always he overcame them—with the aid of their invariable cowardice. (There must be many men now living who remember the shock of outraged surprise with which they discovered that the village bully did not, as in Alger books, invariably run whimpering away at the first show of manly opposition, but sometimes packed a nasty right.) The end of the book—or series of books, for often several volumes were devoted to the varied adventures of a single boy—found our hero well on his way toward wealth: a fortune which might reach to more than a hundred thousand dollars, which, to the average boy reader of the seventies and eighties, was an astronomical sum.

The Alger style was incredibly simple, matter-of-fact, and unoriginal. Whenever Alger turned aside from plain literal fact for a bit of analysis or description, he became a fountain-head of eighth-grade clichés. Nothing whatever was left to the reader's imagination. The dialogue, though it had little relation to the confusing way in which people speak in real life, had at least the merit of transparency. When young Rufus wanted to take Miss Manning and his little sister Rosie out for an evening's diversion, for instance, there would be no beating about the bush:

"Miss Manning," he said, "have you any engagement this evening?"

"It is hardly necessary to ask, Rufus," she replied; "my company is not in very great demand."

"You have heard of the Japanese jugglers at the Academy of Music?"

"Yes; Mrs. Florence was speaking of them this morning. She and her husband went last evening."

"And we are going this evening. Wouldn't you like to go, Rosie?"

"Ever so much, Rufie. Will you take me?"

"Yes, I have got tickets; see here"; and Rufus drew out the three tickets which he had purchased in the morning.

"Thank you, Rufus," said Miss Manning. "I shall like very much to go. It is long since I went to any place of amusement. How much did the tickets cost?"

"A dollar and a half apiece."

"Isn't that rather extravagant?"

"It would be if we went every week; but now and then we can afford it."

The reader, you will see, always knew just where he was. No frills, no literary antics; always the story moved with elementary clarity.

Nor did any subtleties of character-drawing prevent one from determining immediately who were the good characters and who were the bad ones. They were labeled plainly. When Andy Grant, the poor farmer's son, met Conrad Carter, the rich squire's son, and said to him, "That's a new bicycle, isn't it?" Conrad replied,

"Yes; I got tired of the old one. This is a very expensive one. Wouldn't you like to own a bicycle?"

"Yes."

"Of course, you never will."

From that moment on, the reader could feel sure that Conrad would never say a decent word or do a decent thing; that Andy would outdistance Conrad in the boat race and Conrad would whine excuses for his defeat; that Conrad would try to burn up Andy's boat and burn his own by mistake; and that when Andy's hard work in New York at last enabled him to pay off Squire Carter's mortgage on the Grant Farm, Conrad would go into a dreadful rage, as all thwarted villains do. Similarly, the good characters were always definitely noble and uttered splendid sentiments. And always virtue triumphed. Thus the reading of an Alger story was like watching a football game in which you knew the names and numbers of all the players, and the home team made all the touchdowns.

Any writer who in thirty-three years turned out well over a hundred such books and whose memory (especially as he got on in life) was often faulty, must have been expected to make mistakes. Alger made them. Frequently he got his characters mixed, to the dismay of his publishers, who had to rearrange the names. But he had talent for improvisation. When his hero was to be taken out for a ride on the savage horse Bucephalus—which the villain hoped would run away and kill him—it would suddenly be divulged that the boy had been taking riding lessons the preceding year and had won a reputation as a rider of surpassing skill. Nothing had been said in preceding pages about this course of instruction, but Alger didn't bother to go back and insert a reference on page 45; the accomplishment was sprung upon the delighted reader, Bucephalus was mastered, and the story roared right ahead, to the triumph of the young Jehu and the downfall of the villain.

When one considers that the period in which these books were the delight of millions of American boys was that very period when the economic expansion of the United States was going on full tilt, to the accompaniment of every sort of financial knavery and speculative excess; and when one realizes that to most of these millions of young readers the Alger books provided their first intelligible picture of economic life and the making of an individual fortune, one looks again, with an analytical eye, to see how the Alger hero's fortune was achieved. And one notes, not without amusement, that the boy never got rich from the direct fruits of his industrious labor. How could he, starting in at $5 a week, even with rapid increases in pay? No; he got his hands on capital.

Sometimes this capital was inherited: the supposed orphan, ragged though he was, proved to be the son of a man whose supposedly worthless mining stock was good for $100,000. Sometimes the capital was a gift: rich Mr. Vanderpool was so impressed with the boy's pluck that he made over to him the $50,000 that the boy had helped him to save from the robbers. Or the boy was out in Tacoma, buying lots as a real-estate agent (on his boss's inside information that the Northern Pacific was to be extended to the

Coast), and in a Tacoma hotel he befriended an invalid gentleman, who out of gratitude gave him a part interest in some lots
that promptly soared in value and put him on Easy Street. The
method varied; but when the time came for our hero to get into
the money, it was a transaction in capital which won the day for
him.

Yet always he was so good, and husbanded so prudently the
$175 in his savings account (though he was generous, too, to the
poor washer-woman and to the other bootblacks), that to the
casual reader the lesson of these stories was not that hard work
brings in but a pittance, or that the way to succeed is to stand in
with the men who have the capital, but something quite different.
The lesson was that capital comes as a reward from heaven to him
who labors mightily and uses his head all the time. Work, save, be
a good boy, shun the fleshpots, and presently the mining stock will
fall into your lap and all will be well.

Possibly this explains something about the Gilded Age—when
Americans worked furiously, and opened up the West, and accomplished wonders in invention and manufacturing; when the
average American of moderate means was hard-headed, diligent,
and on the whole fairly scrupulous; but when the ethical level of
the big operations in capital was often well-nigh barbaric. Once
capital began to fall into a man's lap, he did not inquire unduly
whence it came. He had labored meritoriously; merit was always
rewarded—was it not?—and now his reward was at hand; obviously it must come from heaven. One remembers Rockefeller
saying, "God gave me my money," and one knows that other men
of millions felt as he did. Who knows but that to some of them—
and to some of their successors in more recent times—this conviction grew, in part at least, out of early lessons in economics from
Andy Grant's Pluck or *Tom the Bootblack*—lessons learned when
the man of millions had been a farm boy reading in the shade of
the barn, or a grocer's clerk hiding under the counter the latest
enthralling volume in the "Brave and Bold" series?

The total sale of the Alger books will probably never be
known, for he had numerous publishers, many of the publishing
firms were short-lived, and the books went through many editions
—in cloth at $1 or $1.25, in paper at 40 or 25 or 10 cents. But one
can get at least a clue from the fact that M. A. Donahue & Com-

pany of Chicago, who did not begin publishing them till after Alger's death, estimate their own total, very roughly, at close to ten million copies; and that Street & Smith's estimated total, likewise very roughly computed, would be above two million. The John C. Winston Co. estimate their total sales at five million. Probably it is safe to guess that the grand total must have been well beyond twenty million copies, and may have been far greater. One seldom sees an Alger book nowadays; when the Children's Aid Society questioned seven thousand boys in 1932 (on the hundredth anniversary of Alger's birth), it found that less than twenty per cent of them had ever heard of Alger, only fourteen per cent of them had ever read an Alger book, and not a single boy owned one. But during the Alger heyday, from about 1870 to about the time of the World War, the results of any such inquiry would have been far different. Parents who were people of cultivation generally frowned on the books as rubbish of a low intellectual order; some parents frowned on them as likely to tempt boys to run away from home (a charge that so distressed Alger that he inserted in many of his later volumes an explicit warning that boys in happy homes had better stay there); but other parents welcomed them as valuable incentives to thrift and ambition. And boys of all ages and conditions ate them up.

As they read, they must have dreamed of success—which included wealth, of course, and power, and the thrill of being on the way up, of being prominent, being envied—and also, presumably, a chance to marry happily, and live in a fine house, and enjoy the good things of this earth. What would they have thought, one wonders, had they been able to see, through those dreams of theirs, the man Alger himself—scribbling away in his room in the bare, dour-looking building of the Newsboys' Home in a dingy part of downtown New York; leaving his labors to play with the little newsboys and bootblacks, and perhaps to take a group of them to the circus; a man disappointed in the defeat of his real literary ambitions, disappointed in love, awkward in the society of mature men and women, and apparently almost unaware, as he went innocently and obscurely about the city, that his influence was reaching into millions of families and helping to determine the trend and tradition of American business life?

Peter F. Drucker

Henry Ford: Success and Failure

Peter Drucker (1909-   ) was born in Vienna but has spent most of his life in England and the United States. He teaches economics at Bennington College and undertakes research projects for American corporations.

I

Henry Ford's hold on America's imagination—indeed on the imagination of the world's masses—was not due to his fabulous financial success. And it can only partly be explained by the overwhelming impact of the automobile on our way of life. For Henry Ford was less the symbol and embodiment of new wealth and of the automobile age than the symbol and embodiment of our new industrial mass-production civilization.

He perfectly represented its success in technology and economics; he also perfectly represented its political failure so far, its failure to build an industrial order, an industrial society. The central problem of our age is defined in the contrast between the functional grandeur of the River Rouge plant, with its spotless mechanical perfection, and the formlessness and tension of the social jungle that is Detroit. And the two together comprise Henry Ford's legacy.

Both his success and his failure can be traced to his being thoroughly representative of that most native and most dominant of all American traditions, the one which in Populism found its major political expression. Indeed, Henry Ford was both the last Populist and perhaps the greatest one. He owed all his basic convictions to Bryan: pacifism, isolationism, hatred of monopoly and of "Wall Street" and of "international bankers," firm belief in a sinister international conspiracy, and so forth. He also made true the great

From *Harper's Magazine*, July, 1947. Copyright by Harper & Brothers, 1947. Reprinted by permission of the publishers and the author.

dream of the political crusaders of 1896: that industrial production might be made to serve the common man. This dream had obsessed the American people since Brook Farm and Robert Owen's New Lanark, half a century before Bryan.

The Populists had believed that a Jeffersonian millennium would result automatically from eliminating "monopoly" and the "money power" and the "satanic mills" of crude industrialism—as these terms were understood in the nineteenth century. Ford fulfilled the dream. He succeeded without benefit of monopoly, he defied the big bankers, he gave his factories a clean and airy efficiency which would have delighted nineteenth-century reformers. But in fulfilling the dream he dispelled it. And in the place of the old enemies which he vanquished we have today, in the industrial system which Ford did so much to develop, new problems to face: the long-term depression, and the political and social problems of industrial citizenship in the big plant. Henry Ford's solution of the industrial problems with which the nineteenth century had wrestled unsuccessfully constituted his success, his achievement. His inability to solve the problems of the new industrial system, his inability to see even that there were such problems, was the measure of his final and tragic failure.

It may seem paradoxical to interpret Henry Ford's importance in terms of a concept—especially a political concept such as Populism. He himself had nothing but contempt for concepts and ideas, and prided himself on being neither a theoretician nor a politician but a "practical man." And the main criticism which has been leveled against him and against everything he stood for—the criticism embodied in, for instance, Charlie Chaplin's "Modern Times"—has been that he made mechanical perfection an end in itself. But even his contribution to technology was not really a technical but a conceptual one—superb production man and engineer though he was. For he invented nothing, no new technique, no new machine, not even a new gadget. What he supplied was *the idea of mass production itself*—organization of man, machines, and materials into one productive whole.

In economics too Ford discovered no new facts; the data showing the effect of volume production on costs had all been collected and analyzed. But Ford was the first manufacturer to understand that these data disproved the traditional theory that

restricted production and a high profit margin—that is, monopoly
—provided the most profitable form of industrial production. He
demonstrated that one could raise wages, cut prices, produce in
tremendous volume, and still make millions.

Above all Ford himself regarded his technical and economic
achievements primarily as means to a social end. He had a definite
political and social philosophy to which he adhered to the point of
doctrinaire absurdity. Concern with the social effects of his actions determined every one of his steps and decisions throughout
his entire life. It underlay the break with his early partners who
wanted to produce a luxury car for the rich rather than follow
Ford's harebrained idea of a cheap utility car for the masses. It
motivated the radical wage policy of the early Ford who in 1914
fixed his minimum wage at the then utopian figure of $5.00 a
day for unskilled labor. It showed in Ford's lifelong militant pacifism, of which the tragicomic Peace Ship episode of 1915-16 was
only one manifestation. It showed in his isolationism, in his hos-
tility to Wall Street, and in the raucous pamphleteering of the
Dearborn *Independent* in the twenties. This social philosophy
explains the millions he poured into "chemurgy" or into utopian
village communities of self-sufficient, sturdy, yeoman farmers. It
was responsible for his belief in decentralization, and for his nostalgic attempt to recreate the atmosphere of an earlier and simpler
America in a museum community—right next door to the River
Rouge plant.

It might almost be said that Henry Ford's life work, despite
these moves of his, brought about the opposite kind of world from
the one he hoped for and believed in. Thus Ford, the pacifist, built
up one of the world's greatest armament plants and helped to
make possible the mechanized warfare of our age. Ford, the isola-
tionist, more than any other man has made it impossible for this
country to stay out of international politics and international wars:
for he made this country the most powerful industrial nation on
earth. Ford, the agrarian decentralist, left as his life's work the
River Rouge plant, the most highly centralized and most completely mechanized concentration of industrial power in the world.
The enemy of finance-capital and bank credit, he made installment
buying a national habit. An orthodox Jeffersonian, he has come
to stand for the extreme application of the assembly-line principle,

with its subordination of the individual to the machine. And the very workers at the Ford Motor Company whose mass production was to give economic security and full industrial citizenship to all, are today organized in the most class-conscious union in America —and in a Communist-dominated local at that.

Yet it would be wrong to argue from the failure of Ford's social ideas that they never were anything but "eccentric hobbies," as the obituaries rather condescendingly called them. The tragic irony with which his every move turned against him in the end does not alter the fact that his was the first, and so far the only, systematic attempt to solve the social and political problems of an industrial civilization. There is also little doubt that Ford himself believed—certainly until 1941 when the Ford workers voted for the CIO, and perhaps even afterward—that he had actually found the answer for which the American people had been searching for almost a century: the realization of the Jeffersonian society of independent equals through industrial technology and economic abundance.

Nor was he alone in this appraisal of the meaning of his work. It was shared by the American people as a whole in the years immediately following the first World War—witness Wilson's urging in 1918 that Ford run for the Senate, and the powerful "Ford for President" boom of 1923. The view was also held abroad, especially in the Europe of the early twenties and in Lenin's Russia —perhaps even more generally there than here. Indeed, it was the performance of Henry Ford's America which in 1918 and 1919 gave substance to Wilson's promise of the millennium of peace, democracy, and abundance, and which established America's moral and political authority in those years. And the Ford spell remained potent long after Wilson's promise had faded under the cold light of the international realities of the nineteen-twenties.

The postwar world of today is at least as much under the spell of Franklin D. Roosevelt's name as an earlier generation was under that of Wilson. But Henry Ford today no longer symbolizes an America that has successfully solved the basic social problems of an industrial world. He stands instead for the lack of a solution. And that surely accounts in large measure for the difference between 1919 and 1947 in the acceptance and the effectiveness of America's moral and economic leadership.

2

Henry Ford took the conveyor belt and the assembly line from the meat-packing industry where they had been in general use as early as 1880. The interchangeability of precision-made parts was an even older principle; it went back to the rifle plant which Eli Whitney built in Bridgeport for the War of 1812. The idea of breaking down a skilled job into the constituent elementary motions, so that it could be performed by unskilled men working in series, had been thoroughly explored—by Taylor among others—and had been widely used in American industry twenty years before Ford came on the scene, as for example by Singer Sewing Machine and National Cash Register. Yet we associate all these principles with Henry Ford, and rightly so. For each of them had been employed only as an auxiliary to the traditional manufacturing process. It was Ford who first combined them and evolved out of them consciously and deliberately a new concept of industrial production, a new technology. It is this new concept of mass production which in scarcely more than one generation has given us a new industrial civilization.

To Ford the importance of this new principle lay in its impact upon society—as the means for producing an abundance of cheap goods with the minimum of human effort and toil. Mass production itself, however, he considered as something purely technical, as simply a new method of organizing *mechanical* forces. Ford disciples, heirs, and imitators, the engineers and production men who today run our big industries, are certainly as convinced as their master that mass production is a mechanical technique; many use it as if it were a mere gadget. And Charlie Chaplin took the same view when, in "Modern Times," he caricatured our modern industrial civilization.

But if mass production were indeed only a technique, and primarily mechanical—if it were different in degree but not in kind from pulley, lever, or wheel—it could be applied only to mechanical tasks similar to the ones for which it was first developed. But long before the recent war, mass-production principles were used for such jobs as the sorting and filling of orders in a mail-order house or the diagnosis of patients in the Mayo Clinic. Henry Luce even used it successfully to organize writers—traditionally regarded as extreme individualists—for the mass production of inter-changeable "formula-writing." And during the war we applied mass-production principles to thousands of new products and processes and to such problems as the selection and training of men in the armed services. In all these uses the mechanisms of the assembly line are purely subordinate if indeed applied at all. In other words, mass production is not, fundamentally, a mechanical principle but *a principle of social organization*. It does not co-ordinate machines or the flow of parts; it organizes men and their work.

Ford's importance lies precisely in the fact that his principle of mass production substitutes the co-ordination of human beings for the co-ordination of inanimate parts and of mechanical forces on which industry was originally based. When we talk of the Indus-trial Revolution, we think at once of Watt's steam engine. It is true that there was a lot more to the Industrial Revolution than new machines; but the steam engine is a good symbol for it because the essence of early industry was the new organization of mechanical forces. Mass production is based, however, on the organization of human beings and of human work—something radically different from anything that was developed in the early days of industry. Indeed it has brought about a new Industrial Revolution. The as-sembly line is a symbol for a new principle of social organization, a new relationship between men who work together in a common task, if not for a common purpose.

On what basis does this mass-production principle organize men? What kind of society does it either assume or create? It as-sumes or creates a society in which things are produced by the co-operation of individuals, not by a single individual. By himself the individual in modern mass-production industry is completely unproductive and ineffectual. But the organized group pro-duces more, better, and more effectively than any individual or any number of individuals working by themselves ever could. In this society the whole—the organized group—is clearly not only more than, but different from, the sum of its parts.

Proof of this is what happens when a man loses his place in the organized group, or his access to the productive organism; when, in other words, he becomes unemployed. Under modern mass-production conditions, the man who has lost his job is not just out of luck economically; in fact, in a rich country such as ours, the direct economic consequences of unemployment can be minimized almost to the vanishing point. But he is incapable of producing anything, of being effective in society; in short, he is incapable of being a citizen, he is cast out. For he derives his productiveness, his function in the community, his citizenship—at least his effective rather than purely formal citizenship—from his position in the group effort, in the team, in the productive organism.

It is this social effect of unemployment, incidentally, rather than the economic effect, that makes it the major catastrophe it is. That unemployment endangers people's standards of living is, of course, bad enough; but that it endangers their citizenship and self-respect is its real threat and explains our panicky fear of the "next depression."

In the society of the modern mass-production plant everyone derives his effectiveness from his position in an organized group effort. From this follow some important consequences. One is that such a society needs a government, a direction, a management responsible to no one special-interest group, to no one individual but to the over-all purpose, the over-all maintenance and strengthening of the whole without which no individual, no special-interest group could be effective. It also follows that in such a society there must be rank: a difference of authority and prestige based on the differentiation of functions. But at the same time, in such a society no one individual is less important or more important than another. For while no one individual is irreplaceable—only the organized relationship between individuals is irreplaceable and essential— every single operation, every single function is equally necessary; the whole order would collapse, the entire productive machine would come to a stop, were one to take out one function, one job —just as the whole chain becomes useless if one takes out one link. That is why, in such a society, there should be simultaneously an inequality of subordination and command based on the differentiation of functions, and a basic equality based on membership and citizenship.

This is by no means a new type of social organization; on the contrary, it is a very old one. It was described in the old Roman fable retold in Shakespeare's "Coriolanus" which likened society to the human body, none of whose organs—neither feet, nor hands, nor heart, nor stomach—could exist or work by itself, while yet the body could not properly work without any of them. It was expressed in the medieval metaphors of the order of the spheres and of the chain of being. And even as a practical way of organizing men for economic production, the mass-production principle is not new. Indeed, the first thorough applications of mass production and the assembly line were not in the Ford plant in Detroit, but hundreds of years earlier and thousands of miles away, in the workshops of the medieval stone masons who built the great cathedrals. In short, mass-production society, of which the assembly line is the symbol, is a hierarchical one.

This shows clearly when we analyze what popularly passes for a clear expression of the essence of mass production: the saying that it replaces skilled by unskilled labor. That is pure nonsense, if taken literally. Of course, in mass production manual skill is eliminated by breaking up each operation into the component simple operations, with each worker performing only one unskilled operation or a series of such. But this presupposes a fantastic skill in analyzing and breaking up the operation. The skill that is taken out of the manual operation has to be put back again further up the line, in the form of much greater knowledge, much more careful planning for the job; for there is such a thing as a law of the preservation of skill. And in addition mass production needs a new skill: that of organizing and leading the human team. Actually "unskilled" mass production needs proportionately more and more highly skilled men than "skilled" production. The skills themselves have changed from those of the craftsman to those of engineer, draftsman, and foreman; but the number of trained and skilled men in American industry has been growing twice as fast since 1910 as that of unskilled and semi-skilled men.

Above all, the co-operation and co-ordination which are needed to make possible the elimination of manual skill presuppose an extraordinarily high level of social skill and social understanding, of experience in working together. The difficulties that our war plants had with new labor showed that very graphically. And contrary to popular belief, it is no more difficult to export the old methods of industrial production to a new industrial country, even though those methods require considerable manual skill on the part of the worker, than it is to export mass-production techniques where no manual but a great deal of social skill is required.

What we mean when we say that mass production is based on unskilled labor is simply that the individual becomes effective and productive only through his contribution to the whole, and not if viewed separately. While no individual does the job, each one is necessary to get the job done. And the job, the end-product of co-operative effort, is more skilled than anything the most skilled person could have produced by himself. As in every hierarchical society, there is no answer in the mass-production plant to the question who does the job; but there is also no answer to the question who does not do the job. For everybody has a part in it.

There are a good many industries today which do not use the mass-production principle. Among them are some of the most efficient ones, for instance, the modern cotton mills (in which one worker may manage a great many looms) and a good many of our chemical industries (in which one worker may perform a number of different functions). Nevertheless, the mass-production industries are representative of our American industry as a whole because they express in the purest form the essence of industrial production, *i.e.*, a principle of social organization. The real Industrial Revolution of our day—the one which Henry Ford led and symbolized—was not a technological one, was not based on this or that machine, this or that technique, but on the hierarchical co-ordination of human efforts which mass production realizes in its purest form.

3

It is understandable that Henry Ford's disciples and imitators failed to see the political and social implications of mass production until they were confronted by them in the form of an aggressive union movement—and very often not even then. For most of these men were really only concerned with technical problems, and really believed in mechanical efficiency as an end in itself. But Henry Ford's own blindness cannot be so simply explained as due to a lack of social or political concern—not even as due to a lack of social or political imagination. The real explanation is that Ford was concerned exclusively with the solution of the *social and political problems of the pre-Ford, the pre-mass-production in-*

dustrial civilization. And because his answers really did solve these problems, or at least the more important of them, it never entered his mind to subject this answer of his in turn to a social and political analysis. His gaze was firmly fixed on the industrial reality of his own youth, the industrial reality against which Populism had revolted in vain. He never even saw what he himself had called into being. As a high official of his own company once said: "What Mr. Ford really sees when he looks at River Rouge is the machine shop in which he started in 1879."

Though Henry Ford may never have heard of Brook Farm, of Robert Owen's New Lanark, or of any of the many other utopian communities that had dotted the Midwest not so many years before his birth in 1863, they were his intellectual ancestors. He took up where they had left off; and he succeeded where they had failed. Colonel McCormick's Chicago *Tribune* called him an "anarchist" in the red-hunting days of 1919 when the term meant more or less what "Communist" would mean today in the same paper. But in spite of the obvious absurdity of the charge, the jury awarded Ford only six cents in damages when he sued for libel; for he was undeniably a radical. He turned into a stand-patter after 1932, when his life's work had shown itself a failure in its inability to produce the stable and happy society of which he had dreamed. But the Henry Ford of the earlier Model T days was an iconoclast attacking in the name of morality and science the established order of J. P. Morgan and of Mark Hanna's Republican party.

The Utopias of the 1830's and 1840's were in themselves the reaction to a failure: the abortive attempt during Jackson's administration to bring back to America the lost innocence of the Jeffersonian society of self-sufficient independent farmers. The Utopians no longer hoped to be able to do away with the modern division of labor or even with industry. On the contrary, they promised to obtain for mankind the full benefits of industrial productivity, but without its having to pay the price of subjecting itself to the "money power" or to "monopoly," or of having to work in the "satanic mills" of Blake's great and bitter poem. These were to be eliminated by a blend of pious sentiment, community regulations, and social science.

Of all the Utopians only the Mormons survived—and they

only by flight from the land of the Gentiles. But though they failed, Brook Farm, New Zion, New Lanark, and all the other attempts at the American industrial Jerusalem left a very deep imprint on the consciousness of the American people. Neither Fourier, whose ideas fathered Brook Farm, nor Robert Owen was an American. Yet it is possible, indeed probable, that the mixture of earnest, semireligious sentiment and trust in a "scientific" principle which is so typical of the American "reformer" or "radical" has its roots in much older and deeper layers in our history than the Utopias. But it is certain that the Utopias determined the specific form which American radicalism was to take for a whole century. They provided the targets, the battle cries, and the weapons for Populism, for Wilson's New Freedom, and even for much of the early New Deal (such as the "scientific" gold magic of 1933). They fathered Henry George, Bellamy, and the antitrust laws. They molded the beliefs and the hopes of America's inland empire in the Midwest. But they remained a futile gesture of revolt until Henry Ford came along.

Today we know that in depression and unemployment we have as serious an economic problem as "monopoly" and the "money power" ever were. We see very clearly that mass production creates as many new social and political questions as it answers. Today we realize that as a *final* solution to the problems of an industrial civilization Henry Ford's solution is a failure.

But Ford's mass production was not aimed at these new dangers but at the traditional devils of American radicalism. And these it actually did exorcise. Ford succeeded in showing that industrial production can be production *for* the masses—instead of production for the benefit of monopolist or banker. Indeed, he showed that the most profitable production is production for the masses. He proved that industrial production could give the workers increasing purchasing power to buy industrial products and to live on a middle-class standard; that was the meaning of his revolutionary $5.00-a-day minimum wage.

Finally—and to him most importantly—he proved that, properly analyzed and handled, industrial production would free the workers from arduous toil. Under modern mass-production conditions, the worker is confined to one routine operation requiring neither skill nor brawn nor mental effort. This fact would not have appeared to Henry Ford as a fatal defect but as a supreme achievement; for it meant that—in contrast to the tradition of the "satanic mills"—the worker's skill, intelligence, and strength would be fully available for his community life as an independent Jeffersonian citizen outside of the plant and after working hours.

At Brook Farm, too, the "real life" was supposed to come in the "communion of the spirits" in the evening after the day's work had been done; but the day's work took so much time and effort that the "real life" could be lived only by neglecting the work. Mass production cuts both time and energy required for the day's work so as to give the worker plenty of scope for this "real life." No wonder that Ford—the Ford of 1919—thought he had built the "New Jerusalem" on a permanent foundation of steel, concrete, and four-lane highways.

4

It was Ford's personal tragedy to live long enough to see his Utopia crumble. He was forced to abandon his basic economic principle—the principle of the cheapest possible production of the most utilitarian commodity. First he scrapped the Model T. That was in 1927. Then, five years later, he abandoned the Model A and adopted the annual model change which substitutes the appeal of prestige and fashion for the appeal of cheapness and utility. When he did this he became just another automobile manufacturer. Even so his share in the market dropped from nearly half in 1925 to less than twenty per cent in 1940. Even more decisively proven was his failure to give the worker industrial citizenship; in 1941 the Ford workers voted to join the CIO almost three to one.

Up to the hour when the results were announced, the old man is said to have firmly believed that "his" workers would never vote for a union. All along he had fought off realization of his defeat by pretending to himself that his downfall was being caused by sinister conspiracies rather than by faults in the structure of the community which he had built. This tendency to look for personal devils —itself a legacy from the Utopians—had shown itself quite early in the tirades of the Dearborn *Independent* against international bankers, Wall Street, and the Jews during the nineteen-twenties. It became the basis on which he fought the unions all through the thirties. It also probably explains why Harry Bennett, starting as the plant's chief cop, rose to be the most powerful single individual in the Ford organization of the thirties, and the only one who really seemed to enjoy the old man's confidence. But the union victory—followed shortly by the unionization of the foremen—must have hit Henry Ford as a repudiation of all he had thought he had achieved, and had achieved primarily for the workers. The last years of the old man must have been very bitter ones indeed.

The lesson of Ford's ultimate failure is that we cannot hope to solve the problems of the mass-production society by technological devices or by changing the economics of distribution. These were the two approaches on which all nineteenth-century thought had relied, whether orthodox or rebel. Henry Ford went as far along these lines as it is possible to go.

For the time being, the political results of Ford's achievement were extraordinary. It took the wind out of the sails of the socialist critique of capitalist society. In this country it brought about the change from the fiery political action of Eugene Debs to the politically impotent moralism of Norman Thomas; in continental Europe it converted social democracy from a millennial fighting creed into a respectable but timid bureaucracy. Even more telling was the reaction of Communist Russia to Ford. In the twenties the Russians had to add to the messianic hopes of Karl Marx the promise of achieving eventually in a socialist society what Ford had already achieved in a capitalist one: a chance for the worker to drive to the plant in his own car and to work in collar and tie, and without getting calluses on his hands. And until 1929—as every meeting of the Third International affirmed—the Communists were completely convinced that Ford's America had actually solved the basic problems of capitalism and had restored it to ascendancy all the world over. Not until the great depression were the Communist leaders able to revitalize their creed, by making it appear to do what it cannot do: to solve, by the sheer force of the police state, the new, the post-Ford problems of industrial society as they appeared after 1929.

As we in America confront these problems, the economic ones will not be the most difficult. Indeed the chief economic problem of our time—the prevention of depressions—should be solvable by basically mechanical means: by adapting our employment, fiscal, and budgeting practices to the time-span of industrial production

—that is, to the business cycle. Much more baffling, and more basic, is the political and social problem with which twentieth-century industrialism confronts us: the problem of developing order and citizenship within the plant, of building a free, self-governing industrial society.

The fact that Henry Ford, after his superb success, failed so signally—that there is today such a grim contrast between his social utopia and our social reality—emphasizes the magnitude of the political task before us. But however treacherous the social jungle of our present mass-production society, however great the danger that it will fester into civil war and tyranny, the twentieth-century evils which Henry Ford left to us may well be less formidable than the nineteenth-century evils which he vanquished.

II

Leonard Sidney Woolf

Chronicle and History

Leonard Woolf (1880-   ) is an English author and editor. He was the founder of the Hogarth Press in association with his wife, the novelist Virginia Woolf. During the 1920's he was literary editor of The Nation; *since 1951 he has been the editor of* The Political Quarterly.

Mankind in the mass has often been compared, cynically or otherwise, to insects. To the historian proper the image of an ant-heap is almost inevitable. When he looks back into the past, he sees no great men or famous names, but myriads of minute and nameless human insects, hurrying this way and that, making wars and laws, building and destroying cities and civilizations. The swarm ebbs and flows over the earth and through the centuries, the groups converging and coalescing or breaking up and scattering. The story of this ant-heap, of its impersonal groups and communities and of their ebb and flow upon the earth, is history.

History may be a bare record of mankind in groups or communities. The historian takes a section of the ant-heap at a certain time or period, examines its records and documents, and tells us what was happening at the moment inside it. "They" were wearing togas or trousers, building Nineveh or burning Rome, making a king into a god or cutting his head off. The works of these recorders are often called chronicles, and it is frequently said that early historians should rightly be called chroniclers. But the point of view of the chronicler still exists, even when history has become highly developed and sophisticated. He is impersonal and undiscriminating in the sense that he rarely has a theory or is concerned with cause and effect. The scope of his vision into the past is lim-

Reprinted from *After the Deluge* by permission of The Hogarth Press, Ltd.

ited to a particular moment of time, for he is the natural historian of the human insect, and what interests him is the bare fact that the insect was doing a particular thing at a particular time. In consequence the resemblance between the activities of the human race and those of an ant-heap is nowhere more striking than in the pages of chroniclers. There is the same hurrying and scurrying of hordes of little creatures, each terribly intent upon its own particular piece of business, which at the same time in some mysterious way is obviously part of the communal business. And that business in the unanalyzed and isolated narrative of the chronicle seems to be made up of a number of blind, irrational, and inexplicable impulses. Read, for instance, in such a book as the *History of Persia* by Sir Percy Sykes, which is essentially a chronicle, the narrative of what is known about those "early civilizations" of Assyrians, Elamites, Babylonians, who built and burned their cities and slaughtered one another for many centuries in and around Mesopotamia. If we were not hypnotized by the tradition and dogma that there is some meaning and purpose in human history, it would be impossible to read that bare story without the same kind of shrinking or disgust as is caused by the spectacle of a mass of flies and other insects swarming over a dead body. Or take a long leap forward with the imagination, from this chronicle of what we are pleased to call primitive civilizations or uncivilized peoples, to our own times: imagine the history of the years 1914 to 1918 told in the style of a chronicle. The chronicler, with little or no comment or explanation, without searching for causes or troubling about effects, would relate the bald story of what the human race, divided into the groups called European nations, was doing between September 1914 and November 1918. Such a narrative might be extremely interesting and illuminating, but, if it were read by anyone who did not know that European man was highly civilized and rational, with a divine spark in his breast or brain (sometimes called a soul), with his eyes turned heavenwards and his feet steadily mounting the ladder of evolution, he would only see a strange spectacle of millions of little creatures engaged in destroying one another (when not burrowing in the earth); of other swarms frantically beating their ploughshares into shells; of lesser swarms, in the safe background and over the heads of the fighters, perpetually screaming abuse and noble words of defiance at one another; while here and there some little creatures, raised somewhat above their fellows, shake their fists at one another and explain in unintelligible language the causes of the commotion and their determination never to allow it to end.

It is possible that the chronicler is the only really scientific and philosophical historian, that there is no more to be said about the human insect than such facts as these: that in the year 2218 B.C. upon a plain in the land of Shinar it was trying to build out of bricks and slime a tower which might reach to heaven; that 1700 or 1800 years later around the Aegean Sea it was fighting, producing the plays of Sophocles and Aeschylus, and at nights upon Greek mountains by the light of torches, clothed in deer-skins and carrying ivy-wreathed wands, it tore in pieces goats and other animals and danced wildly to the sound of flutes and cymbals; that in A.D. 33 it crucified the Son of God; that 1500 years later it slaughtered in Germany and Holland 100,000 persons because they not only demanded the right to fish and hunt, but believed that adults and not infants should be baptized; and that in 1914 it slaughtered millions of persons in an effort to decide whether the world should be ruled by the German Emperor or by democracy. It may indeed be that there is nothing more to be recorded of the human race than bare facts such as these, and that history, unperverted by human arrogance, should be an almost infinite series of such facts. If so, the chronicler is a far profounder historian than philosophers like Signor Croce would ever be capable of imagining.

The philosophy of history which underlies the chronicle is so pessimistic and so humiliating that in this age of science and proud idealism we cannot accept it without a struggle. The historian introduces two theories, which are alien to the chronicler and his outlook, in order at least to make the story of human communities compatible with human dignity. These are the theories of progress and regression and of cause and effect. As I propose to accept them as a working hypothesis in this book, it is necessary to explain in what sense they are to be accepted.

History differs from chronicle, when besides recording a mere series of facts or events, it traces or implies in its record of them a movement and direction. And the movement is that of the life of the human animal as it is lived in communities, while the direction is conceived as either up or down, forward or backward. History is, in fact, either consciously or implicitly directed and inspired by the idea of "civilization." It no longer conceives the communal past of the human race as consisting of an infinite number of isolated events, acts, and activities, all of them equally significant and important, but as a continuous "life" in whose procession a series of events only acquires historical significance in so far as it indicates progress or regression. To the chronicler the fact that slime was used instead of mortar to build the tower of Babel is just as important, and therefore as worthy of record, as the object of the architecture; the historian may be able to read in the slime some evidence as to the level which material civilization had reached in the land of Shinar, but the fact which he will seize upon as infinitely more relevant is the communal object of the builders, for it is that which really throws light upon their "cultural development," their civilization.

Carl Lotus Becker

Everyman His Own Historian

Carl Becker (1873-1945) became a professor of history at Cornell University in 1917 and taught there until his death. The essay that follows was a presidential address delivered before the American Historical Association.

Once upon a time, long long ago, I learned how to reduce a fraction to its lowest terms. Whether I could still perform that operation is uncertain; but the discipline involved in early training had its uses, since it taught me that in order to understand the essential nature of anything it is well to strip it of all superficial and irrelevant accretions—in short, to reduce it to its lowest terms. That operation I now venture, with some apprehension and all due apologies, to perform on the subject of history.

I ought first of all to explain that when I use the term history

Reprinted from *The American Historical Review*, January, 1932, by permission of *The American Historical Review* and Appleton-Century-Crofts, Inc.

I mean knowledge of history. No doubt throughout all past time there actually occurred a series of events which, whether we know what it was or not, constitutes history in some ultimate sense. Nevertheless, much the greater part of these events we can know nothing about, not even that they occurred; many of them we can know only imperfectly; and even the few events that we think we know for sure we can never be absolutely certain of, since we can never revive them, never observe or test them directly. The event itself once occurred, but as an actual event it has disappeared; so that in dealing with it the only objective reality we can observe or test is some material trace which the event has left—usually a written document. With these traces of vanished events, these documents, we must be content since they are all we have; from them we infer what the event was, we affirm that it is a fact that the event was so and so. We do not say "Lincoln is assassinated"; we say "it is a fact that Lincoln was assassinated." The event *was,* but is no longer; it is only the affirmed fact about the event that *is,* that persists, and will persist until we discover that our affirmation is wrong or inadequate. Let us then admit that there are two histories: the actual series of events that once occurred; and the ideal series that we affirm and hold in memory. The first is absolute and unchanged —it was what it was whatever we do or say about it; the second is relative, always changing in response to the increase or refinement of knowledge. The two series correspond more or less; it is our aim to make the correspondence as exact as possible; but the actual series of events exists for us only in terms of the ideal series which we affirm and hold in memory. This is why I am forced to identify history with knowledge of history. For all practical purposes history is, for us and for the time being, what we know it to be.

It is history in this sense that I wish to reduce to its lowest terms. In order to do that I need a very simple definition. I once read that "History is the knowledge of events that have occurred in the past." That is a simple definition, but not simple enough. It contains three words that require examination. The first is knowledge. Knowledge is a formidable word. I always think of knowledge as something that is stored up in the *Encyclopaedia Britannica* or the *Summa Theologica;* something difficult to acquire, something at all events that I have not. Resenting a definition that denies me the title of historian, I therefore ask what is most essential to knowledge. Well, memory, I should think (and I mean memory in the broad sense, the memory of events inferred as well as the memory of events observed); other things are necessary too, but memory is fundamental: without memory no knowledge. So our definition becomes, "History is the memory of events that have occurred in the past." But events—the word carries an implication of something grand, like the taking of the Bastille or the Spanish-American War. An occurrence need not be spectacular to be an event. If I drive a motor car down the crooked streets of Ithaca, that is an event—something done; if the traffic cop bawls me out, that is an event—something said; if I have evil thoughts of him for so doing, that is an event—something thought. In truth anything done, said, or thought is an event, important or not as may turn out. But since we do not ordinarily speak without thinking, at least in some rudimentary way, and since the psychologists tell us that we cannot think without speaking, or at least not without having anticipatory vibrations in the larynx, we may well combine thought events and speech events under one term; and so our definition becomes, "History is the memory of things said and done in the past." But the past—the word is both misleading and unnecessary: misleading, because the past, used in connection with history, seems to imply the distant past, as if history ceased before we were born; unnecessary, because after all everything said or done is already in the past as soon as it is said or done. Therefore I will omit that word, and our definition becomes, "History is the memory of things said and done." This is a definition that reduces history to its lowest terms, and yet includes everything that is essential to understanding what it really is.

If the essence of history is the memory of things said and done, then it is obvious that every normal person, Mr. Everyman, knows some history. Of course we do what we can to conceal this invidious truth. Assuming a professional manner, we say that so and so knows no history, when we mean no more than that he failed to pass the examinations set for a higher degree; and simple-minded persons, undergraduates and others, taken in by academic classifications of knowledge, think they know no history because they have never taken a course in history in college, or have never read Gibbon's *Decline and Fall of the Roman Empire.* No doubt the academic convention has its uses, but it is one of the superficial accretions that must be stripped off if we would understand history reduced to its lowest terms. Mr. Everyman, as well as you and I, remembers things said and done, and must do so at every waking moment. Suppose Mr. Everyman to have awakened this morning unable to remember anything said or done. He would be a lost soul indeed. This has happened, this sudden loss of all historical knowledge. But normally it does not happen. Normally the memory of Mr. Everyman, when he awakens in the morning, reaches out into the country of the past and of distant places and instantaneously recreates his little world of endeavor, pulls together as it were things said and done in his yesterdays, and coördinates them with his present perceptions and with things to be said and done in his tomorrows. Without this historical knowledge, this memory of things said and done, his today would be aimless and his tomorrow without significance.

Since we are concerned with history in its lowest terms, we will suppose that Mr. Everyman is not a professor of history, but just an ordinary citizen without excess knowledge. Not having a lecture to prepare, his memory of things said and done, when he awakened this morning, presumably did not drag into consciousness any events connected with the Liman von Sanders mission or the Pseudo-Isidorian Decretals; it presumably dragged into consciousness an image of things said and done yesterday in the office, the highly significant fact that General Motors has dropped three points, a conference arranged for ten o'clock in the morning, a promise to play nine holes at four-thirty in the afternoon, and other historical events of similar import. Mr. Everyman knows more history than this, but at the moment of awakening this is sufficient: memory of things said and done, history functioning, at seven-thirty in the morning, in its very lowest terms, has effectively oriented Mr. Everyman in his little world of endeavor.

Yet not quite effectively after all perhaps; for unaided memory is notoriously fickle; and it may happen that Mr. Everyman, as he drinks his coffee, is uneasily aware of something said or done that he fails now to recall. A common enough occurrence, as we all know to our sorrow—this remembering, not the historical event, but only that there was an event which we ought to remember but can not. This is Mr. Everyman's difficulty, a bit of history lies dead and inert in the sources, unable to do any work for Mr. Everyman because his memory refuses to bring it alive in consciousness. What then does Mr. Everyman do? He does what any historian would do: he does a bit of historical research in the sources. From his little Private Record Office (I mean his vest pocket) he takes a book in MS., volume XXXV, it may be, and turns to page 23, and there he reads: "December 29, pay Smith's coal bill, 20 tons, $1017.20." Instantaneously a series of historical events comes to life in Mr. Everyman's mind. He has an image of himself ordering twenty tons of coal from Smith last summer, of Smith's wagons driving up to his house, and of the precious coal sliding dustily through the cellar window. Historical events, these are, not so important as the forging of the Isidorian Decretals, but still important to Mr. Everyman: historical events which he was not present to observe, but which, by an artificial extension of memory, he can form a clear picture of, because he has done a little original research in the manuscripts preserved in his Private Record Office.

The picture Mr. Everyman forms of Smith's wagons delivering the coal at his house is a picture of things said and done in the past. But it does not stand alone, it is not a pure antiquarian image to be enjoyed for its own sake; on the contrary, it is associated with a picture of things to be said and done in the future; so that throughout the day Mr. Everyman intermittently holds in mind, together with a picture of Smith's coal wagons, a picture of himself going at four o'clock in the afternoon to Smith's office in order to pay his bill. At four o'clock Mr. Everyman is accordingly at Smith's office. "I wish to pay that coal bill," he says. Smith looks dubious and disappointed, takes down a ledger (or a filing case), does a bit of original research in his Private Record Office, and announces: "You don't owe me any money, Mr. Everyman. You ordered the coal here all right, but I didn't have the kind you wanted, and so turned the order over to Brown. It was Brown delivered your coal: he's the man you owe." Whereupon Mr. Everyman goes to Brown's office; and Brown takes down a ledger, does a bit of original research in his Private Record Office, which happily confirms the researches of Smith; and Mr. Everyman pays his bill, and in the evening, after returning from the Country

Club, makes a further search in another collection of documents, where, sure enough, he finds a bill from Brown, properly drawn, for twenty tons of stove coal, $1017.20. The research is now completed. Since his mind rests satisfied, Mr. Everyman has found the explanation of the series of events that concerned him.

Mr. Everyman would be astonished to learn that he is an historian, yet it is obvious, isn't it, that he has performed all the essential operations involved in historical research. Needing or wanting to do something (which happened to be, not to deliver a lecture or write a book, but to pay a bill; and this is what misleads him and us as to what he is really doing), the first step was to recall things said and done. Unaided memory proving inadequate, a further step was essential—the examination of certain documents in order to discover the necessary but as yet unknown facts. Unhappily the documents were found to give conflicting reports, so that a critical comparison of the texts had to be instituted in order to eliminate error. All this having been satisfactorily accomplished, Mr. Everyman is ready for the final operation—the formation in his mind, by an artificial extension of memory, of a picture, a definitive picture let us hope, of a selected series of historical events—of himself ordering coal from Smith, of Smith turning the order over to Brown, and of Brown delivering the coal at his house. In the light of this picture Mr. Everyman could, and did, pay his bill. If Mr. Everyman had undertaken these researches in order to write a book instead of to pay a bill, no one would think of denying that he was an historian.

I have tried to reduce history to its lowest terms, first by defining it as the memory of things said and done, second by showing concretely how the memory of things said and done is essential to the performance of the simplest acts of daily life. I wish now to note the more general implications of Mr. Everyman's activities. In the realm of affairs Mr. Everyman has been paying his coal bill; in the realm of consciousness he has been doing that fundamental thing which enables man alone to have, properly speaking, a history: he has been reënforcing and enriching his immediate perceptions to the end that he may live in a world of semblance more spacious and satisfying than is to be found within the narrow confines of the fleeting present moment.

We are apt to think of the past as dead, the future as nonexist-

ent, the present alone as real; and prematurely wise or disillusioned counselors have urged us to burn always with "a hard,
gemlike flame" in order to give "the highest quality to the moments as they pass, and simply for those moments' sake." This no
doubt is what the glow-worm does; but I think that man, who
alone is properly aware that the present moment passes, can for that
very reason make no good use of the present moment simply for its
own sake. Strictly speaking, the present doesn't exist for us, or is
at best no more than an infinitesimal point in time, gone before we
can note it as present. Nevertheless, we must have a present; and
so we create one by robbing the past, by holding on to the most
recent events and pretending that they all belong to our immediate
perceptions. If, for example, I raise my arm, the total event is a
series of occurrences of which the first are past before the last have
taken place; and yet you perceive it as a single movement executed
in one present instant. This telescoping of successive events into a
single instant philosophers call the "specious present." Doubtless
they would assign rather narrow limits to the specious present; but
I will willfully make a free use of it, and say that we can extend
the specious present as much as we like. In common speech we do
so: we speak of the "present hour," the "present year," the "present
generation." Perhaps all living creatures have a specious present;
but man has this superiority, as Pascal says, that he is aware of himself and the universe, can as it were hold himself at arm's length
and with some measure of objectivity watch himself and his fellows functioning in the world during a brief span of allotted years.
Of all the creatures, man alone has a specious present that may be
deliberately and purposefully enlarged and diversified and enriched.

The extent to which the specious present may thus be enlarged and enriched will depend upon knowledge, the artificial
extension of memory, the memory of things said and done in the
past and distant places. But not upon knowledge alone; rather upon
knowledge directed by purpose. The specious present is an unstable pattern of thought, incessantly changing in response to our
immediate perceptions and the purposes that arise therefrom. At
any given moment each one of us (professional historian no less
than Mr. Everyman) weaves into this unstable pattern such
actual or artificial memories as may be necessary to orient us in our

little world of endeavor. But to be oriented in our little world of
endeavor we must be prepared for what is coming to us (the payment of a coal bill, the delivery of a presidential address, the establishment of a League of Nations, or whatever); and to be prepared
for what is coming to us it is necessary, not only to recall certain
past events, but to anticipate (note I do not say predict) the future.
Thus from the specious present, which always includes more or
less of the past, the future refuses to be excluded; and the more of
the past we drag into the specious present, the more an hypotheti-
cal, patterned future is likely to crowd into it also. Which comes
first, which is cause and which effect, whether our memories construct a pattern of past events at the behest of our desires and
hopes, or whether our desires and hopes spring from a pattern of
past events imposed upon us by experience and knowledge, I shall
not attempt to say. What I suspect is that memory of past and anticipation of future events work together, go hand in hand as it
were in a friendly way, without disputing over priority and leadership.

At all events they go together, so that in a very real sense it
is impossible to divorce history from life: Mr. Everyman cannot
do what he needs or desires to do without recalling past events; he
cannot recall past events without in some subtle fashion relating
them to needs or desires to do. This is the natural function of history, of history reduced to its lowest terms, of history conceived as
the memory of things said and done: memory of things said and
done (whether in our immediate yesterdays or in the long past of
mankind), running hand in hand with the anticipation of things to
be said and done, enables us, each to the extent of his knowledge
and imagination, to be intelligent, to push back the narrow confines
of the fleeting present moment so that what we are doing may be
judged in the light of what we have done and what we hope to do.
In this sense all *living* history, as Croce says, is contemporaneous:
in so far as we think the past (and otherwise the past, however
fully related in documents, is nothing to us) it becomes an integral
and living part of our present world of semblance.

It must then be obvious that living history, the ideal series of
events that we affirm and hold in memory, since it is so intimately
associated with what we are doing and with what we hope to do,
cannot be precisely the same for all at any given time, or the same

for one generation as for another. History in this sense cannot be reduced to a verifiable set of statistics or formulated in terms of universally valid mathematical formulas. It is rather an imaginative creation, a personal possession which each one of us, Mr. Everyman, fashions out of his individual experience, adapts to his practical or emotional needs, and adorns as well as may be to suit his esthetic tastes. In thus creating his own history, there are, nevertheless, limits which Mr. Everyman may not overstep without incurring penalties. The limits are set by his fellows. If Mr. Everyman lived quite alone in an unconditioned world, he would be free to affirm and hold in memory any ideal series of events that struck his fancy, and thus create a world of semblance quite in accord with the heart's desire. Unfortunately, Mr. Everyman has to live in a world of Browns and Smiths; a sad experience, which has taught him the expediency of recalling certain events with much exactness. In all the immediately practical affairs of life Mr. Everyman is a good historian, as expert, in conducting the researches necessary for paying his coal bill, as need be. His expertness comes partly from long practice, but chiefly from the circumstance that his researches are prescribed and guided by very definite and practical objects which concern him intimately. The problem of what documents to consult, what facts to select, troubles Mr. Everyman not at all. Since he is not writing a book on "Some Aspects of the Coal Industry Objectively Considered," it does not occur to him to collect all the facts and let them speak for themselves. Wishing merely to pay his coal bill, he selects only such facts as may be relevant; and not wishing to pay it twice, he is sufficiently aware, without ever having read Bernheim's *Lehrbuch*, that the relevant facts must be clearly established by the testimony of independent witnesses not self-deceived. He does not know, or need to know, that his personal interest in the performance is a disturbing bias which will prevent him from learning the whole truth or arriving at ultimate causes. Mr. Everyman does not wish to learn the whole truth or to arrive at ultimate causes. He wishes to pay his coal bill. That is to say, he wishes to adjust himself to a practical situation, and on that low pragmatic level he is a good historian precisely because he is not disinterested: he will solve his problems, if he does solve them, by virtue of his intelligence and not by virtue of his indifference.

Nevertheless, Mr. Everyman does not live by bread alone; and on all proper occasions his memory of things said and done, easily enlarging his specious present beyond the narrow circle of daily affairs, will, must inevitably, in mere compensation for the intol-' erable dullness and vexation of the fleeting present moment, fashion for him a more spacious world than that of the immediately practical. He can readily recall the days of his youth, the places he has lived in, the ventures he has made, the adventures he has had—all the crowded events of a lifetime; and beyond and around this central pattern of personally experienced events, there will be embroidered a more dimly seen pattern of artificial memories, memories of things reputed to have been said and done in past times which he has not known, in distant places which he has not seen. This outer pattern of remembered events that encloses and completes the central pattern of his personal experience, Mr. Everyman has woven, he could not tell you how, out of the most diverse threads of information, picked up in the most casual way, from the most unrelated sources—from things learned at home and in school, from knowledge gained in business or profession, from newspapers glanced at, from books (yes, even history books) read or heard of, from remembered scraps of newsreels or educational films of *ex cathedra* utterances of presidents and kings, from fifteen-minute discourses on the history of civilization broadcast by the courtesy (it may be) of Pepsodent, the Bulova Watch Company, or the Shepard Stores in Boston. Daily and hourly, from a thousand unnoted sources, there is lodged in Mr. Everyman's mind a mass of unrelated and related information and misinformation, of impressions and images, out of which he somehow manages, undeliberately for the most part, to fashion a history, a patterned picture of remembered things said and done in past times and distant places. It is not possible, it is not essential, that this picture should be complete or completely true: it is essential that it should be useful to Mr. Everyman; and that it may be useful to him he will hold in memory, of all the things he might hold in memory, those things only which can be related with some reasonable degree of relevance and harmony to his idea of himself and of what he is doing in the world and what he hopes to do.

In constructing this more remote and far-flung pattern of remembered things, Mr. Everyman works with something of the freedom of a creative artist; the history which he imaginatively recreates as an artificial extension of his personal experience will inevitably be an engaging blend of fact and fancy, a mythical adaptation of that which actually happened. In part it will be true, in part false; as a whole perhaps neither true nor false, but only the most convenient form of error. Not that Mr. Everyman wishes or intends to deceive himself or others. Mr. Everyman has a wholesome respect for cold, hard facts, never suspecting how malleable they are, how easy it is to coax and cajole them; but he necessarily takes the facts as they come to him, and is enamored of those that seem best suited to his interests or promise most in the way of emotional satisfaction. The exact truth of remembered events he has in any case no time, and no need, to curiously question or meticulously verify. No doubt he can, if he be an American, call up an image of the signing of the Declaration of Independence in 1776 as readily as he can call up an image of Smith's coal wagons creaking up the hill last summer. He suspects the one image no more than the other; but the signing of the Declaration, touching not his practical interests, calls for no careful historical research on his part. He may perhaps, without knowing why, affirm and hold in memory that the Declaration was signed by the members of the Continental Congress on the fourth of July. It is a vivid and sufficient image which Mr. Everyman may hold to the end of his days without incurring penalties. Neither Brown nor Smith has any interest in setting him right; nor will any court ever send him a summons for failing to recall that the Declaration, "being engrossed and compared at the table, was signed by the members" on the second of August. As an actual event, the signing of the Declaration was what it was; as a remembered event it will be, for Mr. Everyman, what Mr. Everyman contrives to make it: will have for him significance and magic, much or little or none at all, as it fits well or ill into his little world of interests and aspirations and emotional comforts.

What then of us, historians by profession? What have we to do with Mr. Everyman, or he with us? More, I venture to believe, than we are apt to think. For each of us is Mr. Everyman too. Each of us is subject to the limitations of time and place; and for each of us, no less than for the Browns and Smiths of the world, the pattern of remembered things said and done will be woven, safeguard the process how we may, at the behest of circumstance and purpose.

True it is that although each of us is Mr. Everyman, each is something more than his own historian. Mr. Everyman, being but an informal historian, is under no bond to remember what is irrelevant to his personal affairs. But we are historians by profession. Our profession, less intimately bound up with the practical activities, is to be directly concerned with the ideal series of events that is only of casual or occasional import to others; it is our business in life to be ever preoccupied with that far-flung pattern of artificial memories that encloses and completes the central pattern of individual experience. We are Mr. Everybody's historian as well as our own, since our histories serve the double purpose, which written histories have always served, of keeping alive the recollection of memorable men and events. We are thus of that ancient and honorable company of wise men of the tribe, of bards and story-tellers and minstrels, of soothsayers and priests, to whom in successive ages has been entrusted the keeping of the useful myths. Let not the harmless, necessary word "myth" put us out of countenance. In the history of history a myth is a once valid but now discarded version of the human story, as our now valid versions will in due course be relegated to the category of discarded myths. With our predecessors, the bards and story-tellers and priests, we have therefore this in common: that it is our function, as it was theirs, not to create, but to preserve and perpetuate the social tradition; to harmonize, as well as ignorance and prejudice permit, the actual and the remembered series of events; to enlarge and enrich the specious present common to us all to the end that "society" (the tribe, the nation, or all mankind) may judge of what it is doing in the light of what it has done and what it hopes to do.

History as the artificial extension of the social memory (and I willingly concede that there are other appropriate ways of apprehending human experience) is an art of long standing, necessarily so since it springs instinctively from the impulse to enlarge the range of immediate experience; and however camouflaged by the disfiguring jargon of science, it is still in essence what it has always been. History in this sense is story, in aim always a true story; a story that employs all the devices of literary art (statement and generalization, narration and description, comparison and comment and analogy) to present the succession of events in the life of man, and from the succession of events thus presented to derive a satisfactory meaning. The history written by historians, like the history informally fashioned by Mr. Everyman, is thus a convenient blend of truth and fancy, of what we commonly distinguish as "fact" and "interpretation." In primitive times, when tradition is orally transmitted, bards and story-tellers frankly embroider or improvise the facts to heighten the dramatic import of the story. With the use of written records, history, gradually differentiated from fiction, is understood as the story of events that actually occurred; and with the increase and refinement of knowledge the historian recognizes that his first duty is to be sure of his facts, let their meaning be what it may. Nevertheless, in every age history is taken to be a story of actual events from which a significant meaning may be derived; and in every age the illusion is that the present version is valid because the related facts are true, whereas former versions are invalid because based upon inaccurate or inadequate facts.

Never was this conviction more impressively displayed than in our own time—that age of erudition in which we live, or from which we are perhaps just emerging. Finding the course of history littered with the *débris* of exploded philosophies, the historians of the last century, unwilling to be forever duped, turned away (as they fondly hoped) from "interpretation" to the rigorous examination of the factual event, just as it occurred. Perfecting the technique of investigation, they laboriously collected and edited the sources of information, and with incredible persistence and ingenuity ran illusive error to earth, letting the significance of the Middle Ages wait until it was certainly known "whether Charles the Fat was at Ingelheim or Lustnau on July 1, 887," shedding their "life-blood," in many a hard fought battle, "for the sublime truths of Sac and Soc." I have no quarrel with this so great concern with hoti's business. One of the first duties of man is not to be duped, to be aware of his world; and to derive the significance of human experience from events that never occurred is surely an enterprise of doubtful value. To establish the facts is always in order, and is indeed the first duty of the historian; but to suppose that the facts, once established in all their fullness, will "speak for themselves" is an illusion. It was perhaps peculiarly the illusion of those historians of the last century who found some special magic in the word "scientific." The scientific historian, it seems, was one who set forth the facts without injecting any extraneous meaning into them. He was the objective man whom Nietzsche described—"a mirror: accustomed to prostration before something that wants to be known, . . . he waits until something comes, and then expands himself sensitively, so that even the light footsteps and gliding past of spiritual things may not be lost in his surface and film." "It is not I who speak, but history which speaks through me," was Fustel's reproof to applauding students. "If a certain philosophy emerges from this scientific history, it must be permitted to emerge naturally, of its own accord, all but independently of the will of the historian." Thus the scientific historian deliberately renounced philosophy only to submit to it without being aware. His philosophy was just this, that by not taking thought a cubit would be added to his stature. With no other preconception than the will to know, the historian would reflect in his surface and film the "order of events throughout past times in all places"; so that, in the fullness of time, when innumerable patient expert scholars, by "exhausting the sources," should have reflected without refracting the truth of all the facts, the definitive and impregnable meaning of human experience would emerge of its own accord to enlighten and emancipate mankind. Hoping to find something without looking for it, expecting to obtain final answers to life's riddle by resolutely refusing to ask questions—it was surely the most romantic species of realism yet invented, the oddest attempt ever made to get something for nothing!

That mood is passing. The fullness of time is not yet, overmuch learning proves a weariness to the flesh, and a younger generation that knows not Von Ranke is eager to believe that Fustel's counsel, if one of perfection, is equally one of futility. Even the most disinterested historian has at least one preconception, which is the fixed idea that he has none. The facts of history are already set forth, implicitly, in the sources; and the historian who could restate without reshaping them would, by submerging and suffocating the mind in diffuse existence, accomplish the superfluous task of depriving human experience of all significance. Left to themselves, the facts do not speak; left to themselves they do not exist, not really, since for all practical purposes there is no fact until someone affirms it. The least the historian can do with any historical fact is to select and affirm it. To select and affirm even the simplest complex of facts is to give them a certain place in a certain pattern of ideas, and this alone is sufficient to give them a special meaning. However "hard" or "cold" they may be, historical facts are after all not material substances which, like bricks or scantlings, possess definite shape and clear, persistent outline. To set forth historical facts is not comparable to dumping a barrow of bricks. A brick retains its form and pressure wherever placed; but the form and substance of historical facts, having a negotiable existence only in literary discourse, vary with the words employed to convey them. Since history is not part of the external material world, but an imaginative reconstruction of vanished events, its form and substance are inseparable: in the realm of literary discourse substance, being an idea, *is* form; and form, conveying the idea, *is* substance. It is thus not the undiscriminated fact, but the perceiving mind of the historian that speaks: the special meaning which the facts are made to convey emerges from the substance-form which the historian employs to re-create imaginatively a series of events not present to perception.

In constructing this substance-form of vanished events, the historian, like Mr. Everyman, like the bards and story-tellers of an earlier time, will be conditioned by the specious present in which alone he can be aware of his world. Being neither omniscient nor omnipresent, the historian is not the same person always and everywhere; and for him, as for Mr. Everyman, the form and significance of remembered events, like the extension and velocity of physical objects, will vary with the time and place of the observer. After fifty years we can clearly see that it was not history which spoke through Fustel, but Fustel who spoke through history. We see less clearly perhaps that the voice of Fustel was the voice, amplified and freed from static as one may say, of Mr. Everyman; what the admiring students applauded on that famous occasion was neither history nor Fustel, but a deftly colored pattern of selected events which Fustel fashioned, all the more skillfully for not being aware of doing so, in the service of Mr. Everyman's emotional needs—the emotional satisfaction, so essential to

Frenchmen at that time, of perceiving that French institutions were not of German origin. And so it must always be. Played upon by all the diverse, unnoted influences of his own time, the historian will elicit history out of documents by the same principle, however more consciously and expertly applied, that Mr. Everyman employs to breed legends out of remembered episodes and oral tradition.

Berate him as we will for not reading our books, Mr. Everyman is stronger than we are, and sooner or later we must adapt our knowledge to his necessities. Otherwise he will leave us to our own devices, leave us it may be to cultivate a species of dry professional arrogance growing out of the thin soil of antiquarian research. Such research, valuable not in itself but for some ulterior purpose, will be of little import except in so far as it is transmuted into common knowledge. The history that lies inert in unread books does no work in the world. The history that does work in the world, the history that influences the course of history, is living history, that pattern of remembered events, whether true or false, that enlarges and enriches the collective specious present, the specious present of Mr. Everyman. It is for this reason that the history of history is a record of the "new history" that in every age rises to confound and supplant the old. It should be a relief to us to renounce omniscience, to recognize that every generation, our own included, will, must inevitably, understand the past and anticipate the future in the light of its own restricted experience, must inevitably play on the dead whatever tricks it finds necessary for its own peace of mind. The appropriate trick for any age is not a malicious invention designed to take anyone in, but an unconscious and necessary effort on the part of "society" to understand what it is doing in the light of what it has done and what it hopes to do. We, historians by profession, share in this necessary effort. But we do not impose our version of the human story on Mr. Everyman; in the end it is rather Mr. Everyman who imposes his version on us—compelling us, in an age of political revolution, to see that history is past politics, in an age of social stress and conflict to search for the economic interpretation. If we remain too long recalcitrant Mr. Everyman will ignore us, shelving our recondite works behind glass doors rarely opened. Our proper function is not to repeat the past but to make use of it, to correct and rationalize for common use Mr. Everyman's mythological adaptation of what actually happened. We are surely under bond to be as honest and as intelligent as human frailty permits; but the secret of our success in the long run is in conforming to the temper of Mr. Everyman, which we seem to guide only because we are so sure, eventually, to follow it.

Neither the value nor the dignity of history need suffer by regarding it as a foreshortened and incomplete representation of the reality that once was, an unstable pattern of remembered things redesigned and newly colored to suit the convenience of those who make use of it. Nor need our labors be the less highly prized because our task is limited, our contributions of incidental and temporary significance. History is an indispensable even though not the highest form of intellectual endeavor, since it makes, as Santayana says, a gift of "great interests . . . to the heart. A barbarian is not less subject to the past than is the civic man who knows what the past is and means to be loyal to it; but the barbarian, for want of a transpersonal memory, crawls among superstitions which he cannot understand or revoke and among people whom he may hate or love, but whom he can never think of raising to a higher plane, to the level of a purer happiness. The whole dignity of human endeavor is thus bound up with historic issues, and as conscience needs to be controlled by experience if it is to become rational, so personal experience itself needs to be enlarged ideally if the failures and successes it reports are to touch impersonal interests."

I do not present this view of history as one that is stable and must prevail. Whatever validity it may claim, it is certain, on its own premises, to be supplanted; for its premises, imposed upon us by the climate of opinion in which we live and think, predispose us to regard all things, and all principles of things, as no more than "inconstant modes or fashions," as but the "concurrence, renewed from moment to moment, of forces parting sooner or later on their way." It is the limitation of the genetic approach to human experience that it must be content to transform problems since it can never solve them. However accurately we may determine the "facts" of history, the facts themselves and our interpretations of them, and our interpretation of our own interpretations, will be seen in a different perspective or a less vivid light as mankind moves into the unknown future. Regarded historically, as a process of becoming, man and his world can obviously be understood only tentatively, since it is by definition something still in the making, something as yet unfinished. Unfortunately for the "permanent contribution" and the universally valid philosophy, time passes; time, the enemy of man as the Greeks thought; tomorrow and tomorrow and tomorrow creeps in this petty pace, and all our yesterdays diminish and grow dim: so that, in the lengthening perspective of the centuries, even the most striking events (the Declaration of Independence, the French Revolution, the Great War itself; like the Diet of Worms before them, like the signing of the Magna Carta and the coronation of Charlemagne and the crossing of the Rubicon and the battle of Marathon) must inevitably, for posterity, fade away into pale replicas of the original picture, for each succeeding generation losing, as they recede into a more distant past, some significance that once was noted in them, some quality of enchantment that once was theirs.

Herbert Joseph Muller

The Roman Empire and the United States

Herbert Muller (1905-   ), now Professor of English at Indiana University, was educated at Cornell University. He has taught at Cornell and at Purdue University, and served in the Department of State and with the War Production Board.

From the melancholy spectacle of the decline and fall of Rome, the skeptical Gibbon was able to derive comfort by reflecting on the manifest superiority of his own enlightened age, and by drawing "the pleasing conclusion that every age of the world has increased and still increases the real wealth, the happiness, the knowledge, and perhaps the virtue, of the human race." Today we are no longer so complacent, at least about the in-

From *The Uses of the Past* by Herbert Muller. Copyright 1952 by Oxford University Press, Inc. Reprinted by permission.

crease in happiness and virtue. The fashion now is to dwell on the deadly analogies between the Roman world and our own, in the suspicion that history may repeat itself after all. We have reason to feel that we too may have lost control of our destiny. We know the "schism in the soul" that Toynbee analyzes in disintegrating societies—the common symptoms of abandon and truancy, drift and promiscuity, vulgarity and barbarism. ("Bongo, bongo," ran the popular song; then "Enjoy yourself, it's later than you think.") We are now prone, indeed, to overlook the essential differences between our civilization and the Roman, which have become much more conspicuous since Gibbon wrote. Yet we might well begin with the analogies. We always have to deal with the invariable basic problems of rulers and ruled, haves and havenots, and to struggle with the invariable enemies, selfishness and greed. More specifically, we have retraced the Roman adventure of brutal conquest and exploitation, followed by ideal aspirations to a universal commonwealth. If the barbarian hordes that finally overran Rome have dwindled to a negligible power, the West has been breeding its own barbarians, of a type still more dangerous. I assume that no thoughtful person believes we shall escape the fate of Rome because the Huns have technically disappeared from history.

Gibbon wrote that the fall of Rome was "the natural and inevitable effect of immoderate greatness." Spengler and Toynbee specifically regard empire itself as a historic sign of decadence, instead of the vigorous growth it appears to be. It breeds the disease of gigantism as well as militarism—a swaggering in size and quantity and material power, which corrupts artistic, intellectual, political, and moral standards alike. It gives rise to the great world-city and the city masses. "There is a new sort of nomad," wrote Spengler, "cohering unstably in fluid masses: the parasitical city-dweller, traditionless, utterly matter-of-fact, without religion, clever, unfruitful . . ." The man on the street is in fact likely to be a shallower and shoddier type than the simple peasant, lacking piety, lacking a genuine folk culture. In ancient Rome he demanded only bread and circuses; he hardly noticed the fall of Rome because the games went on. In America today he glances at the headlines and then turns to the sports page and the comics.

Another consequence of Roman imperialism was the rise of

the businessman and the rule of money. Although the growing materialism was cloaked by the traditional contempt of trade, as today it is cloaked by the conventions of Christian service, it corroded the old traditions and cheapened the tone of the national life. The rising bourgeoisie had the limitations typical of their class. At worst, their notion of grandeur was the vulgar ostentation satirized by Juvenal and Petronius; at best, their civic ideals were exemplified by the beloved Antoninus Pius, who was a kind of benign Coolidge. To the administration of the empire they contributed some practical ability but little vision or statesmanship. The plainest analogy is the complacency of the bourgeoisie, rooted in their material well-being, their civic pride, their superficial culture, and their economic ignorance. The voice of Rome under the Antonines, just before the deluge, sounds much like the voice of Victorian England.

It is America, however, that offers the happy hunting ground for the analogist. America too has risen, without conscious plan, to a position of world leadership; and while some of its senators want to pull back and escape the responsibilities of this role, others call for an aggressive leadership that to Europeans looks like Roman imperialism. As the inheritor of a great culture, it stands to Europe much as Rome did to Greece. The Americans too are a practical people who have distinguished themselves by their material contributions, notably their engineering feats; they glory in their roads, bridges, and dams, and in their plumbing. They have the same ambivalent attitude toward Europeans as the Romans had toward the Greeks, now humbly admiring their superior culture, now scorning them as corrupt and effete. They are prone to the same narrow, short view of the useful, the same distrust of theory and "brain trusts." Their common sense is as cloudy a sense as the theories they live by.

Hence Americans were as unprepared for the economic and political problems that resulted from their rapid expansion. Both nations entered a feverish get-rich-quick era, marked by prodigies of exploitation and orgies of speculation. On the morning after, both woke up to chronic unemployment, inflation, the cycle of boom and crash, and bitter class war. Rome tried to solve its problems by *ad hoc* "new deal" measures, which outraged wealthy conservatives but brought only temporary or superficial relief to the poor. (Among the experiments outlined in Haskell's *The New Deal in Ancient Rome* were debt moratoriums, farm-labor acts, resettlement administrations, the ever-normal granary, work relief, and public subsidies or doles.) The outcome was the dictatorship of Augustus, which some Americans saw coming under Franklin D. Roosevelt. Now America faces the further problem that beset the Roman Republic, the necessity of adapting its democratic institutions to its new responsibilities as a world power. Its problem is complicated by reverence for a Constitution designed for a much simpler society, and specifically by the elaborate system of checks and balances that it inherited from Rome. It has a deep-rooted fear of strong government. But the chief bogey of its conservatives remains the kind of prophecy that Macaulay made a century ago. Once there was no longer a frontier to absorb the discontented and unemployed, he wrote, America would be rent by class war and its prosperity destroyed by demagogues bent on despoiling the rich; whereupon either some Caesar or Napoleon would seize the reins of government or the republic would be laid waste by its own barbarians.

So it might be. But now we need to pause in this popular hunt of analogies, and return to the obvious. There is literally a world of difference between America and ancient Rome—politically, economically, socially, culturally. Western civilization as a whole is still more different, sprawling over whole continents, impinging on all other societies, involving the entire world in its destiny; by comparison the mighty Roman Empire was a piddling local affair. Never before has there been a civilization so vast and dynamic, with such immense powers and incalculable possibilities. Never again will there be such a civilization, one might add, given an atomic war; but this possibility only emphasizes the profound differences in our situation. Such differences are not necessarily in our favor and by no means guarantee our success. The point is merely that they must be taken into account before we draw any final lessons from the failure of Rome. They make nonsense of all neat patterns got by analogy, and more especially of the efforts of Spengler and Toynbee to locate the exact position of our civilization on the downcurve of their historic cycles. We cannot even count on the time that Toynbee gives us when he calculates that Western Christendom has experienced only one-and-a-half of the standard three-and-a-half beats he makes out in the rhythm of disintegrating societies.

Briefly, the major differences may be traced to the growth of democracy, science, and technology. These achievements Toynbee dismisses as "an almost meaningless repetition of something that the Greeks and Romans did before us and did supremely well." In fact, they are strictly, profoundly unique. Rome experienced nothing like the political, scientific, and industrial revolutions that have created the modern world, and that are still revolutionizing it. Even in its periods of anarchy the Roman world was not a revolutionary world. Even in times of peace the modern world is.

The Industrial Revolution alone has brought the most radical changes in human life since the Urban Revolution with which civilization began. Like all other societies, Rome ultimately rested on the manual labor of slaves or serfs. However immoderate its greatness, it was spared the problem of managing an immense machine civilization. Likewise its subject peoples were spared the profound disruption that the impact of Western civilization has caused in other societies today; Roman rule brought a change in masters but relatively little economic, cultural, or social change in the Eastern provinces. By the same token, however, the Roman Empire had nothing like our material resources. Its famed wealth and power were negligible in comparison—the imperial revenues were a mere fraction of the annual income of United States Steel, or the annual budget of the city of New York. Lacking the basic idea of systematically applied knowledge, the Romans had no real command of their physical environment; and as their material resources were depleted by extravagance, plague, war, and exhaustion of mine and soil, they were helpless. They could only turn to magic and prayer. (Thus the medical science developed so brilliantly by the Greeks was swamped by superstition as the empire was devastated by plagues; it was lost to Europe for a thousand years.) A major symptom of their impotence was a sharp decline in population, which further weakened the empire; whereas another unparalleled consequence of the Industrial Revolution has been an enormous increase in population, which has continued even through the unparalleled slaughter of the world wars.

This immense population is utterly dependent upon science and industry. Its masses, however, are by no means so slavish or inert as the masses of the Roman Empire. Spengler's "megalopolis" is now productive, not parasitic, and there is no longer a great gulf between it and the country. If the city masses are rootless and formless, they are nevertheless energetic and busy; they earn their bread and enjoy their circuses in their leisure. When they go on relief or demand social security, conservatives are like to fear for their character, pointing out how the Roman masses were demoralized by hereditary doles and free grain; yet what the modern worker is demanding first of all is the opportunity to work.[1] Hence there is some reason for optimism even in the "spiritual barrenness" that Toynbee notes in the proletariat today. Since spirituality in his analysis is a portent of worldly doom, our perverse failure to exhibit some of the appropriate symptoms of disintegration (such as a resurgence of asceticism and the sense of sin) leads him to venture the "cynical conclusion" that our case has not yet reached the advanced stage; but at least he grants that the schism in the soul of the workers seems to have been repaired. Unlike the Roman masses who took to Oriental gods, they have not lost faith in their society.

One reason for this obstinate faith is that common men now enjoy political rights, or at least the illusion of political power. Nietzsche and Spengler pictured the rise of democracy and socialism as a typical mark of a society in decay, signifying the dominance of the herd-values of the mass-man; but on the face of it this is an astonishing misreading of history. Until recent centuries the masses have had no real political power in any civilization except the Greco-Roman, and there democracy was steadily on the decline after the fall of Athens. The Roman Republic was essentially a timocracy, which in diplomacy and in conquest supported local oligarchies everywhere. The Roman Empire granted a kind of equality before the law, but it granted the masses no rights what-

---

[1] It is worth recalling that the millions of WPA workers who were pictured leaning on their shovels, reveling in the taxpayers' money, flocked back to the factories as soon as war production offered jobs again. Their character proved to be as sturdy as that of the businessmen who had rushed to Washington for help early in the depression, when relief to workers was still stigmatized as a "dole"; and businessmen are notable for a peculiarly stalwart character, which enables them to enjoy without loss of self-reliance the benefits of tariffs, franchises, and even outright government subsidies.

ever in the making of the law. As for the socialism of its last phase, with the regimentation that now serves as a horrid example for Chambers of Commerce, this was a far cry from an experiment in the "welfare state." It was neither demanded by the common man nor designed for his benefit; it was designed to aid the imperial government, and merely sealed his slavery to the State. In short, never before our own time has virtually the entire population of large nations been a genuine citizenry, with a voice in selecting its rulers and deciding its destiny.

With the rise of democracy has come an unprecedented humanitarianism, in the name of the dignity and worth of the individual. It is often sentimental and unenlightened, seldom a match for prejudice or the profit motive. It makes more hideous such contradictions as the unprecedented horrors of modern war—the barbarism that we cannot afford to regard as a mere "reversion," or incidental relic of our primitive ancestry. Still the humanitarianism is a real force, which has brought real changes. The Roman ideal of *humanitas* was an intellectual concept that involved little concern for the individual; under the formal ideals of classicism, the individual was merely an example of some formal "type." Good Romans were seldom disturbed by the wretchedness of the masses and saw no particular evil in gladiatorial games, judicial torture, slavery, or war. In the democracies today there are still plenty of social evils, but they are commonly regarded as evils that should be remedied. The barbarism of our times is at least called by that name.

Most important, however, is the active faith on which democracy is based—the faith in reason, freedom, individualism, with its stress on "opportunity" and the active effort to improve life. The Romans clung to an essentially passive ideal, relying on discipline rather than initiative, encouraging patient endurance rather than wilful endeavor. Their characteristic wisdom was the wisdom of Epictetus: "Seek not that the things which happen to you should happen as you wish, but wish the things that happen to be as they are, and you will find tranquility." This is always a genuine kind of wisdom, and may be the best kind for life in the atomic age; it is no longer necessary to emphasize the dangers of Western wishfulness and wilfulness. Here, at any rate, is the basic difference between the Roman world and ours, the ultimate source of all the specific economic, political, and cultural differences. Rome had no faith in progress, expecting the future to be merely a recurrence; it sought to keep things as they were, and when things went wrong it looked backward, to a Utopian past. We keep looking forward, much less hopefully than we used to, but still with a vivid sense of possibilities, of things that could or should be done. Rome suffered from a lack of energy and enterprise, a stagnation; its decline was a creeping paralysis. We suffer from an excess of energy, or misguided enterprise; and we are likely to end with a bang.

In this perspective, the apparent analogies between the Roman world and our own may take on a quite different aspect. Thus the skepticism and irreligion of the educated class, which Spengler and many others view as a symptom of disease, is not the same old story. In Rome such skepticism was apt to be unhealthy because it was primarily negative, reflecting only a loss of faith. Today it is often as unhealthy or even more so, springing from a deeper confusion or a stronger aversion; it is more apt to produce a cynical indifference than a stoical resignation. Yet it commonly springs from a positive faith in reason and science. Many men are critical of the traditional absolutes because of this faith; they insist on the principle of uncertainty implied in the method of science, and in the ideals of freedom and the open society. Modern skepticism has therefore produced much creative criticism, as in Rome it did not. Modern irreligion has generally been an optimistic religion of humanity. Both have been a positive moral force.

For such reasons the ancient faiths may also have a vitality that traditionalism obscures. The genius of Christianity has been more enterprising, resourceful, and versatile than the orthodox make it out to be. It has known a Protestant Reformation—something of which Roman piety was wholly incapable. Today millions of churchgoers recall this piety as they go through their routine rituals, recite ancient Creeds that they do not really believe or even understand; yet many leaders of Christianity are striving to readapt it to the needs of a revolutionary world. Similarly with the arts. Whereas Roman art suffered from a sterile classicism, modern art suffers from a feverish confusion, intensified by the romantic tradition of individualism, self-expression, and free imagination; the obvious trouble with it is not lifeless formality but strain and excess. I should not predict what will come out of all this experimentation. The point is simply that something rich may come out of it—it is a live growth, however deformed.

Again, the social enterprise of modern democracy has always been more extensive and energetic than champions of private enterprise seem to realize. In pointing to the obvious evils of Roman bureaucracy, and the failure of the final experiment in state socialism, they forget that until this experiment the imperial policy was more consistently laissez faire than that of capitalistic America in its nineteenth-century heyday. The Roman government did not restrict free enterprise by patent laws, hamper free trade by tariffs, or interfere in business by giving franchises or subsidies to a favored few. Neither did it enter the postal business or provide socialized education through public schools. Certainly its mismanagement of its economic resources was not due to a rage for "planning"—it was due rather to lack of any plan. The Romans were more consistent than conservatives today in their obedience to Nature or Necessity, even though they had not consciously formulated the Laws of Competition and of Supply and Demand. For modern capitalism has never really respected these sacrosanct laws that it has written into its bill of rights. It has always tended to evade them by seeking monopoly; it has always got more or less government protection against them. And if conservatives have stubbornly resisted every measure to extend similar protection to workers and consumers, they have steadily lost ground, and by now take for granted a great deal of social legislation that horrified their fathers. When the national economy is threatened by a rugged individualist like John L. Lewis, who still believes in free private enterprise, they are the first to demand that the government should do something about it. In spite of themselves, they are committed to the Western faith in active intelligence— the faith that man can make his own laws, control his society, and determine his future.

Hence the experience of the Roman Empire is hardly a guide in our experiment of a democratically planned society. It does suggest, however, that the experiment is worth trying. It supports John Stuart Mill's argument that a benevolent autocracy is inferior to self-government, and in the long run even more harmful than a vicious autocracy, because more enervating. Self-government makes for a vigorous, self-reliant people; whereas a people deprived of political life loses energy, becomes mentally passive, at length becomes helpless—as helpless as the Romans proved to be after the reign of Marcus Aurelius.

But Mill also raised the final issue, of the objects of democratic energy and enterprise, the goods sought by free men; and here the testimony of Rome is less clear. In one sense the Roman masses had the last word: their mentality, based on religion, in time dominated their masters. To Toynbee this was a triumph of transcendence, the victory of Christ over Caesar. Worldlier historians have dwelt rather on its immediate meaning, which was the death of a civilization. Rostovtzeff summarizes the whole story of the decline of the Roman Empire as "the gradual absorption of the educated classes by the masses and the consequent simplification of all the functions of political, social, economic, and intellectual life, which we call the barbarization of the ancient world." The lesson of Rome, he believes, is that a civilization cannot endure if it rests on a small class, not on the masses; but then he points out that the masses debase a civilization. He concludes with a question: "Is not every civilization bound to decay as soon as it begins to penetrate the masses?"

It is an open question. The creative achievements of civilization to date have been primarily the work of an elite, and the greatest achievements will always be due immediately to the gifted few. Ideally, democracy would mean not merely a general rise in the culture of the masses but an elite that is freely recruited, that may be enlarged and constantly invigorated by special talents from the ranks. Actually, democracy has indeed enlisted vast reserves of energy and talent, but it has also meant a lowering of standards of excellence, a blurring of the all-important distinction between common and uncommon men. It has produced the half-educated man—a type relatively rare in other societies—who is apt to have less respect for learning and culture than the uneducated man. And with industrialism has come a universal vulgarization. An immense machinery is now geared to the tastes and desires of common men, which are an offense by the standards of all civilizations before ours. It produces the appalling confusion of values reflected in radio programs, on which a breathless announcement of impending world catastrophe is preceded by a jingle in praise of some eyewash and followed by a popular comic.

Let us spell out the worst about this notorious mass-man and his mass-culture. He has a meager idea of the abundant life, confusing quantity with quality, size with greatness, comfort with culture, gadgetry with genius. He has as little appreciation of pure science as of the fine arts, and as little capacity for the discipline that both require; although he may stand in awe of them his real veneration goes to the engineers and inventors, the manufacturers of True Romances and Tin Pan Alley airs. He is frequently illiberal, suspicious of "radical" ideas, scornful of "visionary" ideals, hostile to "aliens"; in America he has developed a remarkable vocabulary of contempt that manages to embrace most of mankind—the nigger, the mick, the chink, the wop, the kike, et cetera. He is the chief foe of the individualism he boasts of, a patron of standard brands in tastes and opinions as in material possessions, with a morbid fear of being thought queer or different from the Joneses; individuality to him is "personality," which may be acquired in six easy lessons or his money back, is then turned on to win friends and influence people, and is confirmed by the possession of "personalized" objects, which are distinguished only by having his initials on them. In short, he appears to be a spoiled child, fundamentally ungrateful to the scientists, political philosophers, social reformers, and religious idealists who have given him his unprecedented opportunities. He is therefore the natural prey of advertisers, politicians, millionaire publishers, and would-be dictators.

Yet he is much more than this, else he would never have got where he has. The "mass-man" is also a bogey—a monstrous abstraction that conceals the infinite varieties of common men, in interest, ability, character, and aspiration. It conceals all the degrees in culture, the frequent lustiness of the low-brow, the earnestness of the middle-brow. In particular it conceals the idealism that underlies the obvious materialism. This expresses itself in such commonplace sentiments as that every man ought to have a fair chance—a very novel commonplace, in the light of history. In times of crisis it has enabled such loyalty, fortitude, and unpretentious heroism as won the Battle for Britain. At all times it inspires an enthusiasm for vast co-operative enterprises, kindles the energy and imagination that have made the kingdom of common men the most adventurous in history. "An idealist working on matter" Santayana has called the American; and his fine enthusiasm might be touched to finer issues. Meanwhile it is again an inhuman spirituality that cannot see idealism in the effort to eliminate the poverty and wretchedness once accepted as the will of God, and to enable all men to enjoy the material well-being once enjoyed only by a privileged few—by aristocrats who could afford to exalt noneconomic interests and values because they took for granted their wealth and luxury, and seldom had to earn it.

Rostovtzeff's question remains open for the simple reason that common men are having their first real change in history, and have not had it long. It is hardly surprising if they still fall short of their opportunities and their responsibilities—as throughout history their masters consistently did. In judging this new adventure, accordingly, we must at least face squarely the historic alternatives. Many critics of democratic culture are not candid. They yearn for all the advantages of an aristocratic society without being willing to commit themselves to the moral and intellectual responsibilities of arguing for an aristocratic government, shouldering the human cost. Even T. S. Eliot, who frankly condemns the ideal of equality of opportunity and maintains that a hereditary privileged class is essential to culture, is vague or irresponsible at the critical points of his argument. He arbitrarily dismisses the "myth" of the mute, inglorious Milton, ignoring the plain reasons for believing that a great deal of potential talent or even genius went to waste among the illiterate masses of the past. He merely asserts that his privileged elite will have special responsibilities, ignoring the historic fact that they usually evaded these responsibilities, and suggesting no safeguards against the historic abuses of privilege. He declares very simply that "no sane person can be consumed with bitterness at not having had more exalted ancestors," ignoring the very good reasons for bitterness that millions of poor devils have had. Possibly Eliot's kind of culture does require a hereditary aristocracy; but given the historic record, I should say that a more reasonable ideal is culture and education for all, within their capacities, even if democracy is not the best soil for the very choicest flowers of the human spirit.

As for Rome, at any rate, the masses cannot be held responsible for its fall. If they "absorbed" the educated classes, the fault lay with these privileged classes, who had failed to educate or uplift them, failed to maintain either the material prosperity or the spiritual health of the nation. Rome illustrates the maxim that societies die at the top. As it rose to greatness it rehearsed the old story of the selfishness and short-sightedness of the elite. The aristocratic families who ran the senatorial machine proved utterly incapable of the statesmanship that the rising empire called for. They turned on their liberal members, such as the Gracchi, with the kind of fury that was inspired by "that man" Roosevelt; they rejected the compromises that might have preserved the privileges they jealously clung to; and so they perversely brought on the military dictatorship that destroyed their power. The bourgeois class that replaced them was less suicidal, if only because it had less political power, but ultimately it proved as incapable of enlightened leadership. Nor was it enlightened by Roman intellectuals. If the cultivated class was well-intentioned, it proved wanting in creative intelligence and imagination.

For the Romans, we may then speak the last word in charity, and even in awe. They had nothing like our material and intellectual resources; the wonder is not that their empire fell but that it endured so long and so grandly. For us, the last word is a challenge to the educated, privileged classes. The problem today is not merely a matter of improving the minds and tastes of common men. It is also a question of whether the elite can provide better political, intellectual, and spiritual leadership than it has in all previous societies. For if the creative achievements of civilization have been due primarily to the elite, so too have the failures of civilization. "No civilized minority," observed Leonard Woolf, "has yet been found willing to make the necessary sacrifices."

Philip Guedalla

Charleston, S. C., 1861

*Philip Guedalla (1889-1944) was graduated with a First in Modern
History from Oxford University in 1912 and received the degree
of Master of Arts in the following year. He became a barrister at
the Inner Temple in London, but after ten years he retired from the
legal profession to devote his time to writing. His knowledge of the
history of the nineteenth century was as conspicuous as is his particular vision of the past.*

A low outline lay off the shore. Beyond the city spires and
warehouses, beyond the watching houses on the Battery where all
Charleston strolled on cool evenings it lay like a dismasted ship
across the harbour mouth. Inland the little balconies behind their
blinds surveyed the shaded alleys of the town, and tall, pillared
porches beneath the empty grace of a white pediment withdrew
with dignity behind the rusted tracery of iron gates to dream of
a lost age among the flowers or to look bravely out across the
water, as the Ashley River crept past Charleston to the sea. The
spring tides set the palmetto swamps whispering up-river; and
shrouded trees along the country roads were veiled in a dim fog
of hanging moss or shadowed an unlikely blaze of flowers,
where a gentle angle of the river elbowed an incomparable garden. The bright flowers burned in the Carolina spring; gray moss
hung dimly from the live-oaks; and at Charleston, where the
hours struck slowly from St. Philip's and St. Michael's, the unpleasant outline of the fort hung midway between sea and sky.

It hung there shadowing their world, an angular reminder, as
the Stars and Stripes ran up each morning on Fort Sumter's flag-
staff, that the United States continued to exist, whatever Southern
eloquence might say; and all the lightnings of that fatal gift
played round the uneasy question. It was an awkward problem,

since there were other forts in Charleston Harbour and they flew another flag. For South Carolina in solemn session at St. Andrew's Hall upon the velvet chairs sacred at other times to Charleston chaperons had seceded from the Union. Their reasons were a shade obscure. A growing feeling that the South was challenged in its age-long mastery of the United States disturbed them. It was unthinkable that regions which had provided Presidents and ministers in such profusion should be outnumbered in the nation. Their sons had been its leaders for so long; the Senate was their private forum and West Point their training school; they officered its army, made its laws, and commanded its ships. Their self-esteem was pardonable, since the country was beyond a doubt their United States. But would it always be? That was the disturbing question; and an uncomfortable feeling stole through the South that the United States were not so safe as they had been for Southern elements. The Union grew less congenial, as its balance was disturbed by immigration and the thrust of its new populations towards the West. Industrial expansion in the North imposed new fiscal policies, in which the needs of Southern cotton-growers were not the sole consideration. For the United States were changing fast; and it was highly doubtful to the Southern mind how long the country would continue to be their United States.

Besides, an irritating tendency of Northern thought and speech had dared to question the sole basis of the South's existence. They were a community of cotton-growers living by slave labour; and the noisy challenge of the North was too threatening to be ignored, since slavery was the foundation of their economics, and the whole life of the South hung by a thread of cotton. The Northern challenge was anything but academic, as it took the form of Abolitionist corroborees, at which philanthropists of either sex, discarding all restraints of courtesy or fact, lashed one another into paroxysms of denunciation that left the South, never deficient in repartee, under the dangerous impression that a fair proportion of its fellow-citizens were "hot as the hellish passions of their own black hearts, foul as streams from the sewers of Pandemonium." This duel of abuse, unpromising for the prospects of national harmony, passed from the platform into politics; and a long struggle opened on the thorny topics of escaping slaves, State jurisdiction, and the future of slavery in the new Territories, culminating in the demented heroism of John Brown's half-witted foray at Harper's Ferry.

But the gravest consequence of the protracted controversy was a growing sense of isolation in the South. Its apologists were conscientiously instructed that "the rest of Christendom stands united against us, and are almost unanimous in pronouncing a verdict of condemnation"; its bread-winners believed that they were bound to live by means of which their fellow-countrymen could not approve; and, human perversity being what it was, the Southern mind sought compensation for this disparagement in a vast expansion of Southern self-esteem. For if they had been proud before, they were ten times prouder now. Always romantic, the Southern mind had long been subject to illusions as to the aristocratic nature of its origins and way of life. Watering a tenacious Cavalier tradition with a minimum of Cavalier blood, it was always prone to see a belle in every woman and a gallant gentleman in every man. An allied hallucination implied that the ownership of land was in some occult way a patent of nobility; and this, once predicated, entitled land-owners to condemn the base commercial classes of the North in favour of *independent* South Carolina *country gentlemen,* the nearest to *noblemen* of any possible class in America." Their reading served to add fuel to this fire, since it was said that they absorbed vast quantities of fiction from the chivalrous pen of Walter Scott, imported to the South in car-load lots; and gentlemen in pleasant houses on the Ashley River began to see themselves as belted knights who might be called upon at any moment to defend the Holy Sepulchre against the paynim hosts.

Few moods are more unfriendly to clear thinking than a crusading temper; and as the South grew more self-conscious, it was fortified by the last absurdity of all, race-theory. For, exasperated by Yankee self-righteousness and the facile caricature of *Uncle Tom's Cabin,* it was not content to tell the North that its "priesthood prostitutes itself to a level with the blackguard, and enters the field of secular politics, in the spirit of a beer-house bully," adding without unnecessary chivalry that Northern womanhood, "deserting their nurseries, stroll over the country as politico-moral reformers, delivering lewd lectures upon the beauties of free-love or spiritualism, or writing yellow-back literature, so degraded in taste, so prurient in passion, so false in fact, so wretched in execution, and so vitiating to the morals of mothers in the land, as almost to force them to bring up daughters without virtue and sons without bravery." But Southern vanity found a more convincing explanation of its fatal disagreement with the North, since it began to be convinced that "the Cavaliers, Jacobites, and Huguenots, who settled the South, naturally hate, condemn, and despise the Puritans who settled the North. The former are master races; the latter a slave race, descendants of the Saxon serfs." Pursuing their researches, Southern genealogists detected a monopoly of Norman blood among themselves; and where Norman blood was present, it was pardonable to expect a Norman Conquest, which might take the form either of regenerated United States or of "a vast, opulent, happy and glorious slave-holding Republic throughout tropical America." Such were the unhealthy dreams engendered in the South by Northern disapproval and an unpleasant sense of isolation.

These tendencies were deepened and accelerated by the Presidential election of 1860, which emphasised the shrinkage of their influence by sending Lincoln to the White House. The South was horrified; and the wild diagnosis of a Richmond journal informed thoughtful Virginians that "with Lincoln comes something worse than slang, rowdyism, brutality, and all moral filth; something worse than the rag and tag of Western grog-shops and Yankee factories. . . . With all those comes the daring and reckless leader of Abolitionists." Before that prospect the last thread of Southern self-restraint snapped, and South Carolina seceded from the Union. Its life had always been a little isolated, and now the isolation was past bearing. So the Palmetto flag was substituded for the Stars and Stripes; and up-country gentlemen came riding into town, prepared for knightly deeds. They drilled with gusto, though most Southerners believed that there would be no fighting. For Southern honour had been satisfied by secession; and if Southern honour had been satisfied, there was no more to be said. The North was far away, and Northern honour was less susceptible. Indeed, it had already survived a shot fired upon its flag by eager Southerners, as a Federal supply ship came steaming into Charleston Harbour with stores for the little garrison. But it was always possible that the North might entertain a preference for the continuance of the United States, though the Palmetto flag waved gaily over Charleston; and the unpleasant outline of Fort Sumter, vaguely seen across three miles of water, hung midway between sea and sky.

It shadowed Charleston; and it shadowed Washington as well, since the national situation was full of explosive possibilities so long as an isolated harbour fort was held by Union troops, while the surrounding forces marched behind the flag of a seceding State. The Northern mind was anything but clear as to the immediate problem. But few governments are so long-suffering as to submit indefinitely to armed rebellion within their territories; and whatever resolutions might be passed by the representatives of South Carolina, there could not be the slightest doubt that until recently they had formed part of the United States. That was an essential point in Northern eyes, as Northern loyalty was growing capable of something larger than allegiance to a single State. To traders with interests in a dozen States the Union was something more than a constitutional formality, since it created the territorial unit within which they were at liberty to operate. It was impossible for Northerners to trade with the expanding West without developing a national conception of the Union transcending their municipal attachment to the State in which they lived. Commerce, in fine, enlarged their loyalties and, finding them New Yorkers, made them Americans. Besides, a fair proportion of their population had escaped from Europe with the simple objective of a fresh start in a new country and without local predilections on the subject of States, however admirable, with whose names they were largely unfamiliar; and to recent immigrants the United States meant infinitely more than any of their components.

Upon this background of Union sentiment bewildered gentlemen at Washington surveyed the awkward problem of the South in the winter days of 1861, as six more States followed the perilous example of South Carolina and Southern delegates trooped into the State House at Montgomery, Alabama, to make solemn speeches beneath its curving galleries and vote a new constitution for the Confederate States of America. Mr. Jefferson Davis walked across from the first White House of the Confederacy for his Inaugural beneath the grave, approving eyes of Southern gentlemen. His eyes were grave as well; for when the telegram had

come announcing that he was to be their President, he could
hardly bring himself to tell his wife, and Mrs. Davis, when she saw
the look that clouded his lean handsomeness, felt sure the telegram
contained bad news. They cheered him as he spoke, since hardly
one of them saw war as the inevitable end of their proceedings.
The Southern *pundonor* demanded their secession, and it was
widely assumed that they would be allowed to go in peace.
This hopeful view prevailed among the delegates at Montgomery, and it was significant that the post offices of the new Confederacy were ordered to conform peacefully to official routine
by accounting to Washington until the June half-year of 1861. But
Mr. Davis was less cheerful; and beyond the cheers he "saw
troubles and thorns innumerable. We are without machinery,
without means, and are threatened by a powerful opposition." And
as he spoke from the tall steps between the great fluted pillars of
that Southern portico, he looked down the long avenue between
the balconies and shaded porches of comfortable Alabama houses
and the endless vista that led straight to Gettysburg, the "Bloody
Angle," and the long agony in the winter trenches before Peters-
burg.

What was to happen next? Bewildered Washington, faced
with an exodus of Southerners, balanced uneasily between the two
alternatives of coercion and acquiescence. As the first meant civil
war and heroics were less fashionable north of the Mason and
Dixon Line, there was a considerable tendency to play for time,
murmuring wistfully to the seceded States, "Wayward Sisters, de-
part in peace." But time might prove to be an awkward ally, so
long as the unpleasant riddle of Fort Sumter was unsolved. Nobody seemed to know the answer; and it was anything but simple
to devise a satisfactory finale for the piece which had marooned
Major Anderson and eighty-four fellow-creatures in the Union
service upon an island in a neighbourhood by which the Union
had been vociferously repudiated. Charleston's notion of a happy
ending was an interlude of Southern chivalry, in which the garrison was given free access to food supplies while gallant planters
toiled beside their slaves at the revetments of the new Southern
batteries, followed by a spirited *dénouement* enabling everyone to
display gallantry and ending with the Palmetto waving unchallenged over South Carolina. Washington's requirements were less

spirited, if something could be worked out that was reasonably dignified and did not involve an inadmissible surrender. There was no desire to turn the fortress guns on Charleston in a wild effort to recall it to its late allegiance. Even the Abolitionists inclined to leave the South in a disgraceful solitude, and the most vocal of them doubted whether the Union had any "right to a soldier in Fort Sumter." No government, however, can desert subordinates; and since withdrawal would be tantamount to an admission that the Confederacy was sovereign in South Carolina, Lincoln and his colleagues resolved that the embarrassed fort must be revictualled. A flotilla of supply ships loaded stores at the Brooklyn Navy Yard and sailed for the South.

But the decision hardly lay with Washington, where Secretary Seward aired his evident superiority to the new President. For a ring of Southern guns, controlled by the Confederacy, was trained upon the lonely fort from every angle of the harbour; and the decisive word in the imbroglio must be spoken at Montgomery. Scarcely more inclined than Washington to precipitate a civil war, the South found it less easy to avoid heroic attitudes. Mr. Davis in his White House on the Alabama River was no more belligerent than Mr. Lincoln in his other White House on the Potomac. But strong language and the use of arms came more easily in Southern latitudes; and there was something to be said for a decisive action which might stimulate Virginia, still hanging in the wind, to march with the Confederacy. So an official telegram from Montgomery ordered the dashing Beauregard, in command at Charleston, to reduce the fort if it would not surrender. Anderson refused, adding the welcome information that if he were let alone, he would be starved out in three days. Southern punctilio required the date and hour of his evacuation; but when he gave both with a further undertaking that his guns would not be used in the interval unless fresh supplies or orders came from his government, his answer was found insufficient and he was duly warned that the shore batteries would open fire. Nothing more unreal could be imagined than the situation of Fort Sumter, where three days of starvation, if Anderson could be believed, would solve the problem. But Southern etiquette, enamoured of the duel, imposed a meaningless exchange; and if it was to be avoided, Beauregard was unhappy in his choice of intermediaries, since at least one of them was spoiling for a fight which would "put Virginia in the Southern Confederacy in less than an hour by Shrewsbury clock." (The language of Falstaff was not inappropriate on those martial lips.) The cartel was carried to the reluctant Anderson; and Charleston waited for the duel to begin at dawn. The little pillared houses waited in the night; still gardens by the silent river, where tall trees stood listening in their long draperies of smoky moss, lay waiting for the dawn, whilst all the watchers on the waterfront strained through the darkness and the lonely fort, hull-down across the harbour-mouth, hung midway between the night sky and the black waters of the bay.

It hung there as the darkness turned to dawn; and as the fort hung between night and day, the United States—mile after mile across the continent from silent beaches in New England to the last promontory that looked down on the Pacific—hung midway between peace and war. Fourscore years of growth had made them the most hopeful fact in the world of 1861, where the Emperor Napoleon III aired his slightly reminiscent splendors, Czar Alexander II his good intentions, and Lord Palmerston his firm conviction that the not too recent past was good enough for him, as well as for the subjects of Queen Victoria. It was, to some extent, a retrospective age in which men took their last glance at the receding outlines of the eighteenth century. Some took it, like Lord Palmerston, with unconcealed regret, while more progressive figures like Garibaldi or Cavour drew inspiration from those principles of nationality and secularism which were the last bequest of the departed century. Dedicated to the proposition that all men were created equal (and no less eighteenth-century in their initial inspiration), the United States had seemed to point to a more modern future in which trade would rule the peaceful scene and states vie only in prosperity. Trade, indeed, was not confined to the United States; but elsewhere it conducted itself a shade apologetically beneath the borrowed grandeur of a Second Empire title or discreetly ranged in its appointed place in the Victorian hierarchy, halfway between the upper levels of the landed gentry or the cathedral close and the last indignity of manual work. Beyond the Atlantic it was more unashamed. Society was simpler, and there were less categories to embarrass the pursuit of happiness. Achievement was the only test in a new country, success the sole

nobility; and even government, preserved elsewhere as a hereditary mystery, was there a simple exercise by the people of the
people's right. Small wonder that a fair proportion of the world
looked enviously at the United States, at the vast opportunity and
the consoling featurelessness of the social scene. Repellent to ro-
mantics—did not Disraeli titter that American society was like
"the best society in Manchester"?—it was a standing inspiration to
Radicals with its hopeful indication of a future in which a man
could call his soul (and a fair amount of property) his own.
That was the commonplace sublimity of the American experiment, which had dedicated half a continent to peaceful work;
and on that spring night in 1861 the whole experiment hung midway between peace and war.

This interruption of its ordered growth seemed so uncalled
for. Faced with the cruel fact, subsequent attempts to rationalise
the haphazard course of events have represented the conflict
between North and South as irrepressible. For there is always a
temptation to assign ineluctable causes to chance happenings, since
history is infinitely more impressive when it is inevitable. One cannot draw lessons from pure accidents. Besides, it would be too bitter to attribute all the misery that followed to an unhappy chance.
Yet there was no compelling reason in economics or sociology for
the war between the States, and the tragic outcome was almost
completely lacking in Marxian inevitability. The North had no
quarrel with the South for mastery of a disputed country, since
the true lines of the United States ran east and west across the
continent. Their duel, if there had ever been one, ended when the
South was outflanked by the march of time, the westward march
that sent the wagons creaking overland across the Plains; and as
the tide of population set westward towards California and the
steel ribbon of the railroads crept behind the advancing fringe,
the South was relegated past recall to a secondary place in the
United States. That was a process of history which could not be
revised by force of arms; and the unhappy outcome of the war
did little more than emphasise it.

Yet there was one incalculable consequence that outweighed
all the suffering, since the ensuing agony ensured for all time the
unchallenged unity of the United States. That was a fact of
deep significance for America and later, as their influence began

to radiate, for the world beyond the ocean. For the cruel price exacted from the wartime generation purchased the continuance of that immense community. Its unity could not be challenged now without sacrilege; and so long as its growing millions lived and worked in peace from the Great Lakes to the Rio Grande, something more precious to mankind than comfort was preserved, since government of the people, by the people, for the people, could not perish from the earth.

A tragic generation paid the price in four years of gunfire and fratricide; and what a price it was. It paid it marching through the midsummer dust along the unshaded roads that ended in the little wooded hills along the Bull Run where Beauregard sent the startled Federals streaming back to Washington in the first flurry of the war, or beside the Rappahannock flowing tidily between its ridges whilst Lee parried the Northern thrust at Fredericksburg, or under the wide skies that looked down on the sloping fields in front of Richmond where the South turned to bay behind its shallow breastworks, scooped in the thirsty, sandy soil along the vast, untidy water-line of the Chickahominy. It paid where the small rounded hills of Tennessee climb steeply to the Ridge, the straight-backed Pyrenean Ridge above the gleaming levels of a river of blue steel that runs beneath the cliffs at Chattanooga, and beside the great angle of the river where Vicksburg peers across the broad and gleaming shield of the Mississippi and the tall shoulder of the river-fortress stands in a sort of tangled Devonshire, a moist green country of amazing verdure and tall trees growing out of their own reflections in still swamps that echoed with the dull discharges of Grant's batteries until the fortress guns fell silent and the Northern gunboats could run clear from Memphis to New Orleans and an incomparable tongue at Washington announced that "the Father of Waters goes again unvexed to the sea." It paid in heat and cold, by night and day, for four bitter years as the slow struggle swayed across the country and the South writhed in an unyielding grip. The red earth of Georgia saw them go by, as the Northern thrust went deeper into the South and Sherman, a little wild-eyed, told them grimly to prepare the people for his coming; and the black waters of the Yorktown peninsula, that invite the noiseless onset of canoes between the silent pinepoles, reflected their marching columns. The open country beyond Gettysburg, where men spent their lives with reckless prodigality, had felt the furthest ripple of the Southern wave; and later as the angry tide receded, it drew slowly nearer to the green hollows and bare uplands of the last Southern stronghold, where Richmond watched from its brown escarpments and the news, the last unbelievable news, came to Mr. Davis in his pew at St. Paul's, and Lee trailed westward towards Lynchburg under the wide skies, watched by the friendly slopes of the Blue Ridge through which Jackson had so often slipped out of the Valley to startle Washington or to scare unsuspecting Federals by a sudden apparition on their unguarded flank. But now there was no Jackson, and no Stuart to go riding round the Northern rear and cut the telegraphs; only a road winding before him past the little Court House and down the slope towards the Appomattox. Grant came towards him up the road, and the two men walked together to a house. Finding no table there, they strolled up a brick path into another small dwelling-house that stood a little back from the highway. So the two soldiers sat talking; and all round them the easy slopes lay under the clear April light. The woods were full of halted men, and on the distant sky the Blue Ridge looked down in pity at the South's surrender.

But that was still four years away, as Charleston waited for the dawn and the black muzzles of the Southern guns tilted towards the silent fort. Grant was a dusty salesman somewhere in the West, and Sherman had come north from the superintendent's desk of an academy in Louisiana, and Lee in a dim room at Arlington was facing the harsh syllogism of his conflicting duties as a Virginian and a commissioned officer of the United States. Even the President was still a shadowy, almost an unknown figure with a distressing tendency to damp excited callers with homely answers in a Western drawl that struck them sometimes as a little clownish. For the incomparable voice at Washington had not yet found the full compass of its utterance that still hangs on the air with the clear purity of a struck bell, from its deep note of consecration in a new birth of freedom to the dying fall of his last purpose to proceed with malice toward none, with charity for all, with firmness in the right, as God gives us to see the right. . . . That was still hidden in the night, as the sky began to pale behind Fort Sumter. A gun thudded; a shell whined across a mile of water; and the war began. It was about half-past four in the morning of April 12, 1861.

Henry Adams

President Grant

Henry Adams (1838-1918) was the great-grandson of one president and the grandson of another. He was extraordinarily well placed to observe the American scene and might well have participated actively in American political life, had he not been out of sympathy with what he felt to be the prevailing spirit of post-Civil War America.

At least four-fifths of the American people—Adams among the rest—had united in the election of General Grant to the Presidency, and probably had been more or less affected in their choice by the parallel they felt between Grant and Washington. Nothing could be more obvious. Grant represented order. He was a great soldier, and the soldier always represented order. He might be as partisan as he pleased, but a general who had organized and commanded half a million or a million men in the field, must know how to administer. Even Washington, who was, in education and experience, a mere cave-dweller, had known how to organize a government, and had found Jeffersons and Hamiltons to organize his departments. The task of bringing the Government back to regular practices, and of restoring moral and mechanical order to administration, was not very difficult; it was ready to do it itself, with a little encouragement. No doubt the confusion, especially in the old slave States and in the currency, was considerable, but the general disposition was good, and every one had echoed the famous phrase: "Let us have peace."

This selection from *The Education of Henry Adams* by Henry Adams is reprinted by permission of and arrangement with Houghton Mifflin Company, the authorized publishers.

Adams was young and easily deceived, in spite of his diplomatic adventures, but even at twice his age he could not see that this reliance on Grant was unreasonable. Had Grant been a Congressman one would have been on one's guard, for one knew the type. One never expected from a Congressman more than good intentions and public spirit. Newspaper-men as a rule had no great respect for the lower House; Senators had less; and Cabinet officers had none at all. Indeed, one day when Adams was pleading with a Cabinet officer for patience and tact in dealing with Representatives, the Secretary impatiently broke out: "You can't use tact with a Congressman! A Congressman is a hog! You must take a stick and hit him on the snout!" Adams knew far too little, compared with the Secretary, to contradict him, though he thought the phrase somewhat harsh even as applied to the average Congressman of 1869—he saw little or nothing of later ones—but he knew a shorter way of silencing criticism. He had but to ask: "If a Congressman is a hog, what is a Senator?" This innocent question, put in a candid spirit, petrified any executive officer that ever sat a week in his office. Even Adams admitted that Senators passed belief. The comic side of their egotism partly disguised its extravagance, but faction had gone so far under Andrew Johnson that at times the whole Senate seemed to catch hysterics of nervous bucking without apparent reason. Great leaders, like Sumner and Conkling, could not be burlesqued; they were more grotesque than ridicule could make them; even Grant, who rarely sparkled in epigram, became witty on their account; but their egotism and factiousness were no laughing matter. They did permanent and terrible mischief, as Garfield and Blaine, and even McKinley and John Hay, were to feel. The most troublesome task of a reform President was that of bringing the Senate back to decency.

Therefore no one, and Henry Adams less than most, felt hope that any President chosen from the ranks of politics or politicians would raise the character of government; and by instinct if not by reason, all the world united on Grant. The Senate understood what the world expected, and waited in silence for a struggle with Grant more serious than that with Andrew Johnson. Newspaper-men were alive with eagerness to support the President against the Senate. The newspaper-man is, more than most men, a double personality; and his person feels best satisfied in its double instincts when writing in one sense and thinking in another. All newspaper-men, whatever they wrote, felt alike about the Senate. Adams floated with the stream. He was eager to join in the fight which he foresaw as sooner or later inevitable. He meant to support the executive in attacking the Senate and taking away its two-thirds vote and power of confirmation, nor did he much care how it should be done, for he thought it safer to effect the revolution in 1870 than to wait till 1920.

With this thought in mind, he went to the Capitol to hear the names announced which should reveal the carefully guarded secret of Grant's Cabinet. To the end of his life, he wondered at the suddenness of the revolution which actually, within five minutes, changed his intended future into an absurdity so laughable as to make him ashamed of it. He was to hear a long list of Cabinet announcements not much weaker or more futile than that of Grant, and none of them made him blush, while Grant's nominations had the singular effect of making the hearer ashamed, not so much of Grant, as of himself. He had made another total misconception of life—another inconceivable false start. Yet, unlikely as it seemed, he had missed his motive narrowly, and his intention had been more than sound, for the Senators made no secret of saying with senatorial frankness that Grant's nominations betrayed his intent as plainly as they betrayed his incompetence. A great soldier might be a baby politician.

Adams left the Capitol, much in the same misty mental condition that he recalled as marking his railway journey to London on May 13, 1861; he felt in himself what Gladstone bewailed so sadly, "the incapacity of viewing things all round." He knew, without absolutely saying it, that Grant had cut short the life which Adams had laid out for himself in the future. After such a miscarriage, no thought of effectual reform could revive for at least one generation, and he had no fancy for ineffectual politics. What course could he sail next? He had tried so many, and society had barred them all! For the moment, he saw no hope but in following the stream on which he had launched himself. The new Cabinet, as individuals, were not hostile. Subsequently Grant made changes in the list which were mostly welcome to a Bostonian—or should have been—although fatal to Adams. The name of Hamilton Fish, as Secretary of State, suggested extreme conservatism and probable deference to Sumner. The name of George S. Boutwell, as Secretary of the Treasury, suggested only a somewhat lugubrious joke; Mr. Boutwell could be described only as the opposite of Mr. McCulloch, and meant inertia; or, in plain words, total extinction for any one resembling Henry Adams. On the other hand, the name of Jacob D. Cox, as Secretary of the Interior, suggested help and comfort; while that of Judge Hoar, as Attorney-General, promised friendship. On the whole, the personal outlook, merely for literary purposes, seemed fairly cheerful, and the political outlook, though hazy, still depended on Grant himself. No one doubted that Grant's intention had been one of reform; that his aim had been to place his administration above politics; and until he should actually drive his supporters away, one might hope to support him. One's little lantern must therefore be turned on Grant. One seemed to know him so well, and really knew so little.

By chance it happened that Adam Badeau took the lower suite of rooms at Dohna's, and, as it was convenient to have one table, the two men dined together and became intimate. Badeau was exceedingly social, though not in appearance imposing. He was stout; his face was red, and his habits were regularly irregular; but he was very intelligent, a good newspaper-man, and an excellent military historian. His life of Grant was no ordinary book. Unlike most newspaper-men, he was a friendly critic of Grant, as suited an officer who had been on the General's staff. As a rule, the newspaper correspondents in Washington were unfriendly, and the lobby sceptical. From that side one heard tales that made one's hair stand on end, and the old West Point army officers were no more flattering. All described him as vicious, narrow, dull, and vindictive. Badeau, who had come to Washington for a consulate which was slow to reach him, resorted more or less to whiskey for encouragement, and became irritable, besides being loquacious. He talked much about Grant, and showed a certain artistic feeling for analysis of character, as a true literary critic would naturally do. Loyal to Grant, and still more so to Mrs. Grant, who acted as his patroness, he said nothing, even when far gone, that was offensive about either, but he held that no one except himself and Rawlins understood the General. To him, Grant appeared as an intermittent energy, immensely powerful when awake, but passive and plastic in repose. He said that neither he nor the rest of the staff knew why Grant succeeded; they believed in him because of his success. For stretches of time, his mind seemed torpid. Rawlins and the others would systematically talk their ideas into it, for weeks, not directly, but by discussion among themselves, in his presence. In the end, he would announce the idea as his own, without seeming conscious of the discussion; and would give the orders to carry it out with all the energy that belonged to his nature. They could never measure his character or be sure when he would act. They could never follow a mental process in his thought. They were not sure that he did think.

In all this, Adams took deep interest, for although he was not, like Badeau, waiting for Mrs. Grant's power of suggestion to act on the General's mind in order to germinate in a consulate or a legation, his portrait gallery of great men was becoming large, and it amused him to add an authentic likeness of the greatest general the world had seen since Napoleon. Badeau's analysis was rather delicate; infinitely superior to that of Sam Ward or Charles Nordhoff.

Badeau took Adams to the White House one evening and introduced him to the President and Mrs. Grant. First and last, he saw a dozen Presidents at the White House, and the most famous were by no means the most agreeable, but he found Grant the most curious object of study among them all. About no one did opinions differ so widely. Adams had no opinion, or occasion to make one. A single word with Grant satisfied him that, for his own good, the fewer words he risked, the better. Thus far in life he had met with but one man of the same intellectual or unintellectual type—Garibaldi. Of the two, Garibaldi seemed to him a trifle the more intellectual, but, in both, the intellect counted for nothing; only the energy counted. The type was pre-intellectual, archaic, and would have seemed so even to the cave-dwellers. Adam, according to legend, was such a man.

In time one came to recognize the type in other men, with differences and variations, as normal; men whose energies were the greater, the less they wasted on thought; men who sprang from the soil to power; apt to be distrustful of themselves and of others; shy; jealous; sometimes vindictive; more or less dull in outward appearance; always needing stimulants; but for whom action was the highest stimulant—the instinct of fight. Such men were forces of nature, energies of the prime, like the *Pteraspis*, but they made short work of scholars. They had commanded thousands of such and saw no more in them than in others. The fact was certain; it crushed argument and intellect at once.

Adams did not feel Grant as a hostile force; like Badeau he saw only an uncertain one. When in action he was superb and safe to follow; only when torpid he was dangerous. To deal with him one must stand near, like Rawlins, and practice more or less sympathetic habits. Simple-minded beyond the experience of Wall Street or State Street, he resorted, like most men of the same intellectual calibre, to commonplaces when at a loss for expression: "Let us have peace!" or, "The best way to treat a bad law is to execute it"; or a score of such reversible sentences generally to be gauged by their sententiousness; but sometimes he made one doubt his good faith; as when he seriously remarked to a particularly bright young woman that Venice would be a fine city if it were drained. In Mark Twain, this suggestion would have taken rank among his best witticisms; in Grant it was a measure of simplicity not singular. Robert E. Lee betrayed the same intellectual commonplace, in a Virginian form, not to the same degree, but quite distinctly enough for one who knew the American. What worried Adams was not the commonplace; it was, as usual, his own education. Grant fretted and irritated him, like the *Terebratula*, as a defiance of first principles. He had no right to exist. He should have been extinct for ages. The idea that, as society grew older, it grew one-sided, upset evolution, and made of education a fraud. That, two thousand years after Alexander the Great and Julius Caesar, a man like Grant should be called—and should actually and truly be—the highest product of the most advanced evolution, made evolution ludicrous. One must be as commonplace as Grant's own commonplaces to maintain such an absurdity. The progress of evolution from President Washington to President Grant, was alone evidence enough to upset Darwin.

Vernon Louis Parrington

General Grant

Vernon L. Parrington (1871-1929), late Professor of English at the University of Washington, is best known as the author of Main Currents in American Thought, which won the Pulitzer Prize in History in 1928. He includes Grant with Jay Cooke as "authentic folk-heroes of the Gilded Age, fashioned out of the commonest stuff and realizing such greatness as multitudes of Americans were then dreaming of."

Greatest of all the heroes of the age was the victor of Appomattox. His fame was in all men's mouths, and his reputation was substantial enough to withstand the attacks of enemies and the gross shortcomings of his own character. It was not for any singular or remarkable qualities of mind or personality that General Grant was taken to the heart of his generation, but rather because he was so completely a product of the times, so strikingly an embodiment of its virtues and weaknesses. In his spectacular career were the sharp contrasts that appealed to a plebeian people wanting in fine and discriminating standards of appraisal. He had come up from the people, and the marks of his origins—the slovenly manners and uncritical force of frontier folk-ways—were stamped on him as indelibly as they were stamped on his fellow soldiers who proclaimed his greatness. To a later generation he seems an odd and unaccountable figure for the high rôle of national hero; yet he was as native and homespun as Lincoln, like him sprung from the common stock and learning his lessons from harsh experience, a figure blown to huge dimensions by the passions of civil war. A generation that discovered something praiseworthy in the "smartness" of Jim Fisk, in the burly acquisitiveness of Commodore Vanderbilt, or in the clever humbuggery of Barnum the

Showman, certainly would judge with no very critical eyes the claims to greatness of a grim leader of armies who succeeded where so many before had failed.

General Grant was no conventional military hero. It was not the gold stars on his epaulets that dazzled his generation. The people of the North had seen too many gold stars rise and set on the military horizon, they had been stricken too sorely by the bitter struggle, to be caught by military popinjays. They had gone through the fire and any hero of theirs must himself have passed through the fire. It was something veracious in the man, something solid and unyielding in the soldier, something plain as an old shoe in the field marshal of bloody battles, that caught the imagination of the North and made Grant a hero—this together with a certain gift of pungent phrase, befitting the leader of democratic hosts, that served to spread his fame amongst the common people. Vicksburg did much for his reputation, but the demand for "unconditional surrender," sent to a Confederate leader, did far more. The words fixed his character in the popular mind. Here at last was a fighting man who instead of planning how to fall back, as other generals did, thought only of going ahead; so the popular judgment shut its eyes to his dull plebeian character and set a wreath on his brows. It rested there somewhat grotesquely. In spite of a deep unconscious integrity and a stubborn will that drove him forward along whatever path his feet were set on, he was the least imposing of military heroes. Short, stooped, lumpish in mind and body, unintellectual and unimaginative, devoid of ideas and with no tongue to express the incoherent emotions that surged dully in his heart, he was a commonplace fellow that no gold braid could set off. He hated war and disliked soldiering; yet accepting life with a stolid fatalism he fought his bloody way to ultimate victory.

Graduated from West Point after four sterile years of drill, quite uneducated and unread even in his profession, he served for a time at different army posts, went through the Mexican War —which he looked upon as a stupid imperialistic debauch—as quartermaster without gaining distinction, and eventually, oppressed by the eventless routine of garrison life, he fell into the habit of solitary drinking and was dismissed from the service. Misfortune that it seemed, it was his making. Only as a volunteer could he have risen so quickly to high command; as a captain or major in the regular army he would have been detailed as drill-master to the raw troops and have had no chance. Nevertheless hard times came with his dismissal. Indolent by nature and inclined to drift, he was as incompetent a man in practical affairs as one could find in a frontier township. But with a wife and children to support he must turn his hand to something; so he tried his luck at farming, selling real estate, and various odd jobs, yet all the time growing poorer and seedier, till the war came and picking him up flung him to mountain heights of popularity and reputation. Thereafter till his death he was accounted the greatest American of his generation. No accumulating evidence of his well-meaning but witless incapacity in civic and political affairs could pluck from his brows the wreath that had been thrust upon him.

In his spectacular career Grant was an embodiment of the dreams of all the Beriah Sellerses of the Gilded Age. He was a materialistic hero of a materialistic generation. He was dazzled by wealth and power, and after years of bitter poverty he sat down in the lap of luxury with huge content. He took what the gods sent, and if houses and fast horses and wines and cigars were showered upon him, he accepted them as a child would accept gifts from a fairy godmother. He had had enough of skimping meanness; with his generation he wanted to slough off the drabness of the frontier; he wanted the good things of life that had so long been denied him, and he was not scrupulous about looking a gift horse in the mouth. He sought out the company of rich men. He was never happier than when enjoying the luxury of Jay Cooke's mansion in Philadelphia or riding with A. T. Stewart in Central Park. As he grew fat and stodgy the vulgar side of his plebeian nature was thrown into sharper relief. He accepted gifts with both hands, and he seems never to have suspected the price that would be exacted of the President for the presents to the General. He never realized how great a bill was sent to the American people for the wine he drank or the cigars he smoked with his wealthy hosts; yet if the wine had been molten gold and the cigars platinum they would have been far cheaper. In return for a few boxes of choice Havanas, Jay Cooke laid his hands on millions of western lands for the Northern Pacific Railway. It was the way of the Gilded Age, and Grant was only doing what all his friends and associates were doing. If he accepted a fifty-thousand-dollar house in Philadelphia, his comrade General Sherman accepted a hundred-thousand-dollar house at Washington. Such gifts were not bribes; they were open and aboveboard; it was the free and easy way of the times. What the age was careless about is the fact that it is hard to refuse a reasonable request from one's fairy godmother, and what the General never understood is that if one is President such a godmother is certain to be a very dangerous member of the family.

There was far too much of that sort of thing all about him for Grant to serve as President with credit to himself or profit to the country. Honest himself, he was the source of more dishonesty in others than any other American President. His eight years in the White House marked the lowest depths—in domestic affairs at least—to which any American administration has fallen. They were little better than a national disgrace. All the festering evils of post-war times came to a head and pock-marked the body politic from head to foot. Scandal and corruption whispered all about him; the hands of his closest advisers were dirty; yet he stubbornly refused to hear the whispers or see the dirt. In judging men and policies he was no more than a child. He could never distinguish between an honest man and a rascal. He was loyal to his friends, and open-handedness he regarded as a mark of friendship. In the end it turned out that like the thieves of Jerico his blatant followers despoiled him of pretty nearly everything.

In what must pass for his political views Grant was as naïvely uninformed as a Wyoming cowboy. Utterly wanting in knowledge of political principles, he was a fit leader for the organized mob that called itself the Republican party, whose chief objective was the raiding of the treasure-box of which it was the responsible guardian. He had been nominally a Democrat, and the first vote he cast for President he cast for Buchanan. After Lincoln's death he turned naturally to President Johnson and was one of his supporters till the wily Radical group got his ear and carried him over to the rival camp. They wanted his reputation to hide under, and they took possession of it with no great credit to the General's reputation. Thereafter he was a Republican of the Whig wing. It was where he belonged. He was swayed politically by his emotional reactions, and it was natural for him to drift into the opulent camp of money and power. His frontier democracy sloughed away, and with his generation he went over easily to a buccaneer capitalism. No social conscience obtruded itself to give him trouble. His millionaire friends were Whig Republicans, and with his respect for rich men, his admiration for material success, he found himself in congenial company amongst the Whig group. About the only political policy he ever interested himself in was the policy of a protective tariff, and his Whig associates took care that his interest did not wane. Yet so completely did the naïve General reflect the spirit of the Gilded Age that his noisy followers, conspiring to confuse in the public mind southern reconstruction and capitalistic expansion, and hiding a precious set of rascals in the folds of the bloody flag, came near to making him President for a third term. The General was bitterly disappointed at their failure, and the General's wife, who liked to live in the White House, was even more disappointed. To millions of Americans Grant was an authentic hero, to Mark Twain he was a very great man, and to Jay Cooke he was a pawn to be used in the noble strategy of fortune-seeking. What a comedy it all seems now—yet one that leaves an unpleasant taste in the mouth.

Yet to dismiss the stolid General thus is scarcely to do justice to the substantial core of the man. There remains the work written in pain during his last days, the two volumes of *Memoirs* that in their plain directness—as uninspired, says a late biographer, as "a bale of hay"—laid bare his honest simplicity and rugged meagerness. No blackguard and no charlatan could have written such pages. If General Grant was not the great man so many thought, he was a native growth from American soil, endowed like his age with a dogged will and a plodding energy, and he gave his country what he had. Though the branches of the tree were ungainly and offered too hospitable shelter to unseemly birds of the night, the gnarly trunk was sound at the heart.

Thomas Beer

The Bulletheaded General

Thomas Beer (1889-1940), essayist and novelist, graduated from Yale in 1911, in law from Columbia in 1917, and for a time was a member of his father's law firm, from which he retired to devote himself to writing. Perhaps his most characteristic book is The Mauve Decade, *an urbane interpretation of American life in the latter part of the nineteenth century. This essay is from an early section of Beer's life of Mark Hanna, a conspicuous American political figure and a friend and associate of Thomas Beer's father.*

A society of the positively neurotic waited to welcome Ulysses Grant in Washington. Many of these sufferers were soldiers who had served under the taciturn general; others had taken malaria under McClellan in the Virginia swamps. For years their nerves were kept at a certain palpitating pitch, and now they drank and gamed to keep up the tension of nights in camp along the Potomac. They alarmed ladies at dinner by twitchings and bursts of tearfulness over nothing. "Shell shock" had not been invented then, and the ladies did not imagine that a recurrent sense of the inane, war's least comfortable acquirement, was disturbing some giant in broadcloth between the baked shad and the roast duck. One member of Congress always left the House when Gettysburg was mentioned; another could not sleep in a dark room. Nothing seemed amiss with the whiskered men in loose velvet jackets who wore a tea rose in imitation of the Duc de Morny and swallowed champagne before luncheon in Willard's Hotel or drank six of the famous brandy cocktails at the Saint Nicholas in New York on their way to the stock exchange. Their grandsons, after 1919, were just as gay companions, with the whole vocabulary of the neurologist ready to explain their malady. It was the pay-day of a vast military exploit. Only, at the end of the sixties, men were not supposed to have nerves, and there was no talk about neuroses.

Anything for a thrill, though! They turned to ferocious amusements of finance and legislation, and roared in Congress when James Blaine told Roscoe Conkling that he was a dunghill, a singed cat, a whining puppy and some other things. Their taste in oratory had been formed by the sickening, rhythmic vituperations that preceded the war, and their logic had not been increased by fifty months of subjection to mere command. It did not bruise their sense of proportion to hear Abraham Lincoln and the "dead of a thousand fields" summoned up against a bill to deflate the currency, and they did not mind—it was exciting!—if an orator asked God to strike dead the Postmaster General who hadn't given someone's pet orderly an office in Iowa. They must be amused. Our historians primly tell us that "they joined in the mad scramble for worldly success." Perhaps historians may yet discover that success is just a form of amusement, mostly sacred to those who have not brains enough to attain it.

But as for the smart men whose interest in the war had been the costly shipping of soldiers and mail or the sale of munitions, and damn the quality, to the bewildered government, they were now in smoothest function as a medium between the American and his country, ready to explain its possibilities. They had money and machinery at their disposal and useful examples for their argument. The star of Empire, they said, glittered in the West. It was already a traditional saying; expansion was an old catchword. In the fifties there had been little difficulties about grants of land in the territories, but the Homestead Act and the donations to the railroads had countered that precedent. Hotels and boardinghouses in Washington now jammed with people eager to have the government run a railway across their acres, or appropriate ten millions to build a governmental school on their mountain, or widen their river. The popular mind had grown used to the government's benevolences, and smart men would surely not discourage this state of things. The expansionist mania, really, was washing back upon itself; the individual neurosis of the pioneer, his profound belief in future wealth, now mingled with the other neuroses in the East and made the smart man happy.

Huge tracts of Western land passed into the keeping of gentlemen who had rooms and pretty ladies at the disposal of excited Westerners wanting something done at Washington. Everybody was opening the country up. It was a pastime. The pioneers came eastward with charts of their possessions, and the smart battalion at the Saint Nicholas and the Willard entertained them suitably with promises and champagne, a drink popular among Englishmen and Americans because its gaseous nature recalls the ginger beer or soda water of infantile revelries. Confidence in the government was the note of the smart battalion's discourse to the returning pioneer; all that had been done for the Union Pacific and the Northern Pacific could be done again, and ought to be done. Now, as to expenses. . . . There was a deal of whispering about a man in Washington, who. . . . Soon every Western settlement had its sour loungers, aware of the best bars and hotels in New York and the capital, but bitter forever against the East. They had gone to meet the sunrise and came home shrivelled. They knew all about the damned capitalists of the Saint Nicholas bar, at least. Some of the capitalists locked away deeds to thousands of Western acres and waited for the country's movement to manure this unearned increment. While waiting they roundly applauded the Honorable Roscoe Conkling when he passionately argued, before Federal courts, that the Fourteenth Amendment of the Constitution forbade a mere state to regulate rates of railroads passing through its territories. Mr. Conkling could prove by sheer force of oratory that states should not regulate anything. The less regulation you had, the better. Was not the country being opened up? Even Mr. James Blaine agreed that the country was being opened up. It went on being opened up until the panic of 1873 halted the practice.

This society, not at all unlike the society surrounding another President from Ohio fifty-two years later, welcomed Ulysses Grant in 1869. Amusement-hunters, power-seekers, and orators swarmed on the guileless, tired soldier. He was no fool, but his weariness was clear even to the young daughter of William Lloyd Garrison when she saw him at Washington in 1866. That he became the subject of a game is common history, and the game was safe until such time as his stubborn temper roused and his suspicion leaped at his plausible friends. But he was tired and he wanted to be entertained; he had been poor all his days and he had a simple reverence for wealth. Rich people who could dine him in gilded private parlors on steamboats, where colored windows projected sheen on rattling silver and cut-glass goblets, circled the President, with various intentions. Handsome Congressmen who understood a horse, and Ben Butler, who understood the plebeian mind, rose and fell in his favor for eight years. He might buck out of their grooming hands and veto a bill to increase the inconvertible cur-

rency; he might sign a bill setting a date for the resumption of payments in real money of the government's debts. He might listen
to reformers and establish a commission for the improvement of
the Civil Service. He would decide three times to withdraw the
soldiers from the racked South and let a conquered people disen-
tangle itself from its miseries by its own will. But, for six days in
the week, the smart men had him dazzled. He was tired.

Failure and war had eaten out of this man any essential will;
he had been nothing for years, a drudge in a crude community,
and then he had been exhausted by an incredible tension of command. "Let us have peace," was not just a political expression, but
a personal and immediate prayer. He wanted no more trouble. It
was easier to take advice from his friends, and it was soothing to
have such pretty things given to him, horses and bonds and jeweled
pins. Let the Senators and Congressmen make the appointments to
the Civil Service; if the Cabinet made trouble, get another cabinet.
Let him have peace!

His presidency will provide gossip for a dozen more biogra-
phies. The society about him can be dissected into a hundred layers of scandal. His failures were notorious from the first month
of his vacillating reign. But, beyond the orators and the journalists,
this general had a special audience, and it saw him not unjustly.
He was Grant. He was not the President or the military commander to this legion, but a man. Historians cannot be taught to
remember steadily the force of the human aspect on a people. You
can pick Grant's effect from any volume of the *Photographic History of the Civil War*. . . . See, here is a circular bench under
dusty pines. A group of officers and correspondents gabble in the
sunlight. Orderlies and messengers are dimmer upon tall horses
beneath the boughs. And here, somehow lonely on the bench, is a
hard, lounging body, a plain hat drawn over a bearded face, a
cigar, and a pair of dirty boots. This is Grant, familiar to the men
watching him as Bill or Ed or Jason waiting outside the smithy at
home for a colt to be shod. Everything since dug up by destructive analysts in the case of Grant was a commonplace of his camp.
His men knew that he had hauled wood for a living in Missouri,
but that did not disturb them. If his staff pumped ideas into him,
what of it? A man ought to listen to his friends. He was supposed
to drink two quarts of whisky a day. His men were not concerned.
He was no figure to be increased by religious lights, and verbal

gestures were not expected of him. He was no Liberator. He was their neighbor. He had only to pause beside a cot in the hospital below Vicksburg, saying, "I bet that hurts," to a lad with a smashed arm, in order to have the fealty of a whole county in Iowa. So criticism of the President was immaterial to this grand army. They might curse him for a fool and even vote the Democratic ticket, but he was still Grant.

He gained by an unspoken contrast with his background of noisy creatures on paper stilts. The word "great" flooded the press; great orators, great editors, great railroads, great thieves, and great strumpets were on every page of the newspapers. Mark Twain became a great humorist, as he once said, between two lectures. The rapidity of creation stunned, and the presidential sphinx, who had really done something, seemed larger in this smear of shams. And there was nothing else to look at, now. The giants vanished or waned as querulous freaks. Thaddeus Stevens died. Wendell Phillips had gone crazy over fads, such as female suffrage and prohibition. Sumner was lost in his obsessions, wanting the English flag washed off the American continent, quarreling tiresomely with Grant over the annexation of Santo Domingo or bully-ragging the President to get the fantastic item of two billion dollars for "indirect damages" inserted among the *Alabama* claims. Ben Butler wallowed between the parties, grossly impudent and jolly. Roscoe Conkling leaned on a mantelshelf of yellow marble, now and then adjusting the famous curls on his advertised brow, and aspirants for his favor waited a gesture of Kate Chase's round fan before approaching the chief of the spoilsmen with some request or a new slander of James Blaine. This is the chart of the Gilded Age, a fierce assumption of greatness in a circumfluent weariness. Everyone was tired and wanted to be entertained.

Thus the first bulletheaded general becomes an emblem of his nation in that time. He was himself a victim in the comedy of the expansionist mania; his merits, which were solid as the merits of many men, had been diluted, expanded in all directions; the force so excellent in the drilling of a raw regiment exploded vainly. He did small things very well, as President, and wanted to do large things. But he strayed among his projects, as the expanding nation strayed, and his result was a network of incomplete roads towards a proper government, and the demolition of any respect for its rulers that survived in the United States.

III

Tobias Dantzig

Fingerprints

Tobias Dantzig (1884-   ), born in Russia in 1884, came to the United States in 1910. After receiving his Ph.D. in mathematics from Indiana University in 1916, he taught at Indiana, at Columbia, and at the University of Maryland, where he is now professor emeritus. His book, Number, *from which this essay is taken, is written for the "cultured non-mathematician."*

> Ten cycles of the moon the Roman year comprised:
> This number then was held in high esteem,
> Because, perhaps, on fingers we are wont to count,
> Or that a woman in twice five months brings forth,
> Or else that numbers wax till ten they reach
> And then from one begin their rhythm anew.
>
> OVID, Fasti, III

I

Man, even in the lower stages of development, possesses a faculty which, for want of a better name, I shall call *Number Sense*. This faculty permits him to recognize that something has changed in a small collection when, without his direct knowledge, an object has been removed from or added to the collection.

Number sense should not be confused with counting, which is probably of a much later vintage, and involves, as we shall see, a rather intricate mental process. Counting, so far as we know, is an attribute exclusively human, whereas some brute species seem to possess a rudimentary number sense akin to our own. At least, such is the opinion of competent observers of animal behavior, and the theory is supported by a weighty mass of evidence.

This selection is from Tobias Dantzig: *Number: The Language of Science*, 1st ed. Copyright, 1930, by The Macmillan Company and used with their permission.

Many birds, for instance, possess such a number sense. If a nest contains four eggs one can safely be taken, but when two are removed the bird generally deserts. In some unaccountable way the bird can distinguish two from three. But this faculty is by no means confined to birds. In fact the most striking instance we know is that of the insect called the "solitary wasp." The mother wasp lays her eggs in individual cells and provides each egg with a number of live caterpillars on which the young feed when hatched. Now, the number of victims is remarkably constant for a given species of wasp: some species provide 5, others 12, others again as high as 24 caterpillars per cell. But most remarkable is the case of the *Genus Eumenus*, a variety in which the male is much smaller than the female. In some mysterious way the mother knows whether the egg will produce a male or a female grub and apportions the quantity of food accordingly; she does not change the species or size of the prey, but if the egg is male she supplies it with five victims, if female with ten.

The regularity in the action of the wasp and the fact that this action is connected with a fundamental function in the life of the insect make this last case less convincing than the one which follows. Here the action of the bird seems to border on the conscious:

A squire was determined to shoot a crow which made its nest in the watch-tower of his estate. Repeatedly he had tried to surprise the bird, but in vain: at the approach of man the crow would leave its nest. From a distant tree it would watchfully wait until the man had left the tower and then return to its nest. One day the squire hit upon a ruse: two men entered the tower, one remained within, the other came out and went on. But the bird was not deceived: it kept away until the man within came out. The experiment was repeated on the succeeding days with two, three, then four men, yet without success. Finally, five men were sent: as before, all entered the tower, and one remained while the other four came out and went away. Here the crow lost count. Unable to distinguish between four and five it promptly returned to its nest.

2

Two arguments may be raised against such evidence. The first is that the species possessing such a number sense are exceedingly few, that no such faculty has been found among mammals, and that even the monkeys seem to lack it. The second argument is that in all known cases the number sense of animals is so limited in scope as to be ignored.

Now the first point is well taken. It is indeed a remarkable fact that the faculty of perceiving number, in one form or another, seems to be confined to some insects and birds and to men. Observation and experiments on dogs, horses and other domestic animals have failed to reveal any number sense.

As to the second argument, it is of little value, because the scope of the human number sense is also quite limited. In every practical case where civilized man is called upon to discern number, he is consciously or unconsciously aiding his direct number sense with such artifices as symmetric pattern reading, mental grouping or counting. *Counting* especially has become such an integral part of our mental equipment that psychological tests on our number perception are fraught with great difficulties. Nevertheless some progress has been made; carefully conducted experiments lead to the inevitable conclusion that the direct *visual* number sense of the average civilized man rarely extends beyond four, and that the *tactile* sense is still more limited in scope.

Anthropological studies on primitive peoples corroborate these results to a remarkable degree. They reveal that those savages *who have not reached the stage of finger counting* are almost completely deprived of all perception of number. Such is the case among numerous tribes in Australia, the South Sea Islands, South America, and Africa. Curr, who has made an extensive study of primitive Australia, holds that but few of the natives are able to discern four, and that no Australian in his wild state can perceive seven. The Bushmen of South Africa have no number-words beyond *one*, *two* and *many*, and these words are so inarticulate that it may be doubted whether the natives attach a clear meaning to them.

We have no reasons to believe and many reasons to doubt that our own remote ancestors were better equipped, since practically all European languages bear traces of such early limitations. The English *thrice*, just like the Latin *ter*, has the double meaning: three times, and many. There is a plausible connection between the

Latin *tres*, three, and *trans*, beyond; the same can be said regarding the French *très*, very, and *trois*, three.

The genesis of number is hidden behind the impenetrable veil of countless prehistoric ages. Has the concept been born of experience, or has experience merely served to render explicit what was already latent in the primitive mind? Here is a fascinating subject for metaphysical speculation, but for this very reason beyond the scope of this study.

If we are to judge of the development of our own remote ancestors by the mental state of contemporary tribes we cannot escape the conclusion that the beginnings were extremely modest. A rudimentary number sense, not greater in scope than that possessed by birds, was the nucleus from which the number concept grew. And there is little doubt that, left to this direct number perception, man would have advanced no further in the art of reckoning than the birds did. But through a series of remarkable circumstances man has learned to aid his exceedingly limited perception of number by an artifice which was destined to exert a tremendous influence on his future life. This artifice is counting, and it is to *counting* that we owe the extraordinary progress which we have made in expressing our universe in terms of number.

3

There are primitive languages which have words for every color of the rainbow but have no word for color; there are others which have all number words but no word for number. The same is true of other conceptions. The English language is very rich in native expressions for particular types of collections: *flock, herd, set, lot* and *bunch* apply to special cases; yet the words *collection* and *aggregate* are of foreign extraction.

The concrete preceded the abstract. "It must have required many ages to discover," says Bertrand Russell, "that a brace of pheasants and a couple of days were both instances of the number two." To this day we have quite a few ways of expressing the idea *two*: pair, couple, set, team, twin, brace, etc., etc.

A striking example of this extreme concreteness of the early number concept is the Thimshian language of a British Columbia tribe. There we find seven distinct sets of number words: one for flat objects and animals; one for round objects and time; one for counting men; one for long objects and trees; one for canoes; one for measures; one for counting when no definite object is referred to. The last is probably a later development; the others must be relics of the earliest days when the tribesmen had not yet learned to count.

It is counting that consolidated the concrete and therefore heterogeneous notion of plurality, so characteristic of primitive man, into the *homogeneous abstract number concept*, which made mathematics possible.

4

Yet, strange though it may seem, it is possible to arrive at a logical, clear-cut number concept without bringing in the artifices of counting.

We enter a hall. Before us are two collections: the seats of the auditorium, and the audience. *Without counting* we can ascertain whether the two collections are equal and, if not equal, which is the greater. For if every seat is taken and no man is standing, *we know without counting* that the two collections are equal. If every seat is taken and some in the audience are standing, *we know without counting* that there are more people than seats.

We derive this knowledge through a process which dominates all mathematics and which has received the name of *one-to-one correspondence*. It consists in assigning to every object of one collection an object of the other, the process being continued until one of the collections, or both, are exhausted.

The number technique of many primitive peoples is confined to just such a matching or tallying. They keep the record of their herds and armies by means of notches cut in a tree or pebbles gathered in a pile. That our own ancestors were adept in such methods is evidenced by the etymology of the words *tally* and *calculate*, of which the first comes from the Latin *talea*, cutting, and the second from the Latin *calculus*, pebble.

It would seem at first that the process of correspondence gives only a means for comparing two collections, but is incapable of creating number in the absolute sense of the word. Yet the transition from relative number to absolute is not difficult. It is necessary only to create *model collections,* each typifying a possible collection. Estimating any given collection is then reduced to the selection among the available models of one which can be matched with the given collection member by member.

Primitive man finds such models in his immediate environment: the wings of a bird may symbolize the number two, cloverleaves three, the legs of an animal four, the fingers on his own hand five. Evidence of this origin of number words can be found in many a primitive language. Of course, once the *number-word* has been created and adopted, it becomes as good a model as the object it originally represented. The necessity of discriminating between the name of the borrowed object and the number symbol itself would naturally tend to bring about a change in sound, until in the course of time the very connection between the two is lost to memory. As man learns to rely more and more on his language, the sounds supersede the images for which they stood, and the originally concrete models take the abstract form of number-words. Memory and habit lend concreteness to these abstract forms, and so mere words become measures of plurality.

5

The concept I just described is called *cardinal* number. The cardinal number rests on the principle of correspondence: it implies *no counting.* To create a counting process it is not enough to have a motley array of models, comprehensive though this latter may be. We must devise a number *system:* our set of models must be arranged in an ordered sequence, a sequence which progresses in the sense of growing magnitude, the *natural sequence:* one, two, three. . . . Once this system is created, *counting a collection* means assigning to every member a term in the natural sequence in *ordered succession* until the collection is exhausted. The term of the natural sequence assigned to the *last* member of the collection is called the *ordinal number* of the collection.

The ordinal system may take the concrete form of a rosary, but this, of course, is not essential. The *ordinal* system acquires existence when the first few number-words have been committed to memory in their *ordered succession,* and a phonetic scheme has been devised to pass from any larger number to its *successor.*

We have learned to pass with such facility from cardinal to ordinal number that the two aspects appear to us as one. To determine the plurality of a collection, i.e., its cardinal number, we do not bother any more to find a model collection with which we can match it—we *count* it. And to the fact that we have learned to identify the two aspects of number is due our progress in mathematics. For whereas in practice we are really interested in the cardinal number, this latter is incapable of creating an arithmetic. The operations of arithmetic are based on the tacit assumption that *we can always pass from any number to its successor,* and this is the essence of the ordinal concept.

And so matching by itself is incapable of creating an art of reckoning. Without our ability to arrange things in ordered succession little progress could have been made. Correspondence and succession, the two principles which permeate all mathematics—nay, all realms of exact thought—are woven into the very fabric of our number system.

6

It is natural to inquire at this point whether this subtle distinction between cardinal and ordinal number had any part in the early history of the number concept. One is tempted to surmise that the cardinal number, based on matching only, preceded the ordinal number, which requires both matching and ordering. Yet the most careful investigations into primitive culture and philology fail to reveal any such precedence. Whenever any number technique exists at all, both aspects of number are found.

But, also, wherever a counting technique, worthy of the name, exists at all, *finger counting* has been found to either precede it or accompany it. And in his fingers man possesses a device which permits him to pass imperceptibly from cardinal to ordinal number. Should he want to indicate that a certain collection contains four objects he will raise or turn down four fingers *simultaneously;* should he want to count the same collection he will raise or turn down these fingers *in succession.* In the first case he is using his fingers as a cardinal model, in the second as an ordinal system. Unmistakable traces of this origin of counting are found in practically every primitive language. In most of these tongues the number "five" is expressed by "hand," the number "ten" by "two hands," or sometimes by "man." Furthermore, in many primitive languages the number-words up to four are identical with the names given to the four fingers.

The more civilized languages underwent a process of attrition which obliterated the original meaning of the words. Yet here too "fingerprints" are not lacking. Compare the Sanskrit *pantcha*, five, with the related Persian *pentcha*, hand; the Russian "piat," five, with "piast," the outstretched hand.

It is to his *articulate ten fingers* that man owes his success in calculation. It is these fingers which have taught him to count and thus extend the scope of number indefinitely. Without this device the number technique of man could not have advanced far beyond the rudimentary number sense. And it is reasonable to conjecture that without our fingers the development of number, and consequently that of the exact sciences, to which we owe our material and intellectual progress, would have been hopelessly dwarfed.

7

And yet, except that our children still learn to count on their fingers and that we ourselves sometimes resort to it as a gesture of emphasis, finger counting is a lost art among modern civilized people. The advent of writing, simplified numeration, and universal schooling have rendered the art obsolete and superfluous. Under the circumstances it is only natural for us to underestimate the rôle that finger counting has played in the history of reckoning. Only a few hundred years ago finger counting was such a widespread custom in Western Europe that no manual of arithmetic was complete unless it gave full instructions in the method. . . .

The art of using his fingers in counting and in performing the simple operations of arithmetic was then one of the accomplishments of an educated man. The greatest ingenuity was displayed in devising rules for adding and multiplying numbers on one's fingers. Thus, to this day, the peasant of central France (Auvergne) uses a curious method for multiplying numbers above 5. If he wishes to multiply 9×8, he bends down 4 fingers on his left hand (4 being the excess of 9 over 5), and 3 fingers on his right hand $(8 - 5 = 3)$. Then the number of the bent-down fingers gives him the tens of the result $(4 + 3 = 7)$, while the product of the unbent fingers gives him the units $(1 \times 2 = 2)$.

Artifices of the same nature have been observed in widely separated places, such as Bessarabia, Serbia and Syria. Their striking similarity and the fact that these countries were all at one time parts of the great Roman Empire lead one to suspect the Roman origin of these devices. Yet, it may be maintained with equal plausibility that these methods evolved independently, similar conditions bringing about similar results.

Even today the greater portion of humanity is counting on fingers: to primitive man, we must remember, this is the only means of performing the simple calculations of his daily life.

8

How old is our number language? It is impossible to indicate the exact period in which number words originated, yet there is unmistakable evidence that it preceded written history by many thousands of years. One fact we have mentioned already: all traces of the original meaning of the number words in European languages, with the possible exception of *five*, are lost. And this is the more remarkable, since, as a rule, number words possess an extraordinary stability. While time has wrought radical changes in all other aspects we find that the number vocabulary has been practically unaffected. In fact this stability is utilized by philologists to trace kinships between apparently remote language groups. . . .

Why is it then that in spite of this stability no trace of the original meaning is found? A plausible conjecture is that while number words have remained unchanged since the days when they originated, the names of the concrete objects from which the number words were borrowed have undergone a complete metamorphosis.

9

As to the structure of the number language, philological researches disclose an almost universal uniformity. Everywhere the ten fingers of man have left their permanent imprint.

Indeed, there is no mistaking the influence of our ten fingers on the "selection" of the base of our number system. In all Indo-European languages, as well as Semitic, Mongolian, and most primitive languages, the base of numeration is ten, i.e., there are independent number words up to ten, beyond which some compounding principle is used until 100 is reached. All these languages have independent words for 100 and 1000, and some languages for even higher decimal units. There are apparent exceptions, such as the English *eleven* and *twelve*, or the German *elf* and *zwölf*, but these have been traced to *ein-lif* and *zwo-lif; lif* being old German for *ten*.

It is true that in addition to the decimal system, two other bases are reasonably widespread, but their character confirms to a remarkable degree the *anthropomorphic* nature of our counting scheme. These two other systems are the quinary, base 5, and the vigesimal, base 20.

In the *quinary* system there are independent number words up to *five*, and the compounding begins thereafter. It evidently originated among people who had the habit of counting on one hand. But why should man confine himself to one hand? A plausible explanation is that primitive man rarely goes about unarmed. If he wants to count, he tucks his weapon under his arm, the left arm as a rule, and counts on his left hand, using his right hand as check-off. This may explain why the left hand is almost universally used by right-handed people for counting.

Many languages still bear the traces of a quinary system, and it is reasonable to believe that some decimal systems passed through the quinary stage. Some philologists claim that even the Indo-European number languages are of a quinary origin. They point to the Greek word *pempazein*, to count by fives, and also to the unquestionably quinary character of the Roman numerals. However, there is no other evidence of this sort, and it is much more probable that our group of languages passed through a preliminary *vigesimal stage.*

This latter probably originated among the primitive tribes who counted on their toes as well as on their fingers. A most striking example of such a system is that used by the Maya Indians of Central America. Of the same general character was the system of the ancient Aztecs. The day of the Aztecs was divided into 20 hours; a division of the army contained 8000 soldiers ($8000 = 20 \times 20 \times 20$).

While pure vigesimal systems are rare, there are numerous languages where the decimal and the vigesimal systems have

merged. We have the English *score, two-score,* and *three-score;*
the French *vingt* (20) and *quatre-vingt* (4×20). The old French
used this form still more frequently; a hospital in Paris originally
built for 300 blind veterans bears the quaint name of *Quinze-
Vingt* (Fifteen-score); the name *Onze-Vingt* (Eleven-score) was
given to a corps of police-sergeants comprising 220 men.

10

There exists among the most primitive tribes of Australia
and Africa a system of numeration which has neither 5, 10, nor
20 for base. It is a *binary* system, i.e., of base two. These savages
have not yet reached finger counting. They have independent
numbers for one and two, and composite numbers up to six. Beyond six everything is denoted by "heap."

Curr, whom we have already quoted in connection with the
Australian tribes, claims that most of these count by pairs. So
strong, indeed, is this habit of the native that he will rarely notice
that two pins have been removed from a row of seven; he will,
however, become immediately aware if one pin is missing. His
sense of *parity* is stronger than his number sense.

Curiously enough, this most primitive of bases had an eminent advocate in relatively recent times in no less a person than
Leibnitz. A binary numeration requires but two symbols, 0 and 1,
by means of which all other numbers are expressed, as shown in
the following table:

Decimal	1	2	3	4	5	6	7	8
Binary	1	10	11	100	101	110	111	1000

Decimal	9	10	11	12	13	14	15	16
Binary	1001	1010	1011	1100	1101	1110	1111	10000

The advantages of the *base two* are economy of symbols and
tremendous simplicity in operations. It must be remembered that
every system requires that tables of addition and multiplication
be committed to memory. For the binary system these reduce to
$1+1=10$ and $1 \times 1=1$; whereas for the decimal, each table has 100
entries. Yet this advantage is more than offset by lack of com-
pactness: thus the decimal number $4096=2^{12}$ would be expressed
in the binary system by 1,000,000,000,000.

It is the mystic elegance of the binary system that made Leibnitz exclaim: *Omnibus ex nihil ducendis sufficit unum.* (One suffices to derive all out of nothing.) Says Laplace:

Leibnitz saw in his binary arithmetic the image of Creation. . . . He imagined that Unity represented God, and Zero the void; that the Supreme Being drew all beings from the void, just as unity and zero express all numbers in his system of numeration. This conception was so pleasing to Leibnitz that he communicated it to the Jesuit, Grimaldi, president of the Chinese tribunal for mathematics, in the hope that this emblem of creation would convert the Emperor of China, who was very fond of the sciences. I mention this merely to show how the prejudices of childhood may cloud the vision even of the greatest men!

II

It is interesting to speculate what turn the history of culture would have taken if instead of flexible fingers man had had just two "inarticulate" stumps. If any system of numeration could at all have developed under such circumstances, it would have probably been of the binary type.

That mankind adopted the decimal system is a *physiological accident.* Those who see the hand of Providence in everything will have to admit that Providence is a poor mathematician. For outside its physiological merit the decimal base has little to commend itself. Almost any other base, with the possible exception of *nine,* would have done as well and probably better.

Indeed, if the choice of a base were left to a group of experts, we should probably witness a conflict between the practical man, who would insist on a base with the greatest number of divisors, such as *twelve,* and the mathematician, who would want a prime number, such as *seven* or *eleven,* for a base. As a matter of fact, late in the eighteenth century the great naturalist Buffon proposed that the duodecimal system (base 12) be universally adopted. He pointed to the fact that 12 has 4 divisors, while 10 has only two, and maintained that throughout the ages this inadequacy of our decimal system had been so keenly felt that, in spite of ten being the universal base, most measures had 12 secondary units.

On the other hand the great mathematician Lagrange claimed that a prime base is far more advantageous. He pointed to the fact that with a prime base every systematic fraction would be irreducible and would therefore represent the number in a unique

way. In our present numeration, for instance, the decimal fraction
.36 stands really for many fractions: 36/100, 18/50, and 9/25 . . .
Such an ambiguity would be considerably lessened if a prime base,
such as eleven, were adopted.

But whether the enlightened group to whom we would en-
trust the selection of the base decided on a prime or a composite
base, we may rest assured that the number *ten* would not even be
considered, for it is neither prime nor has it a sufficient number of
divisors.

In our own age, when calculating devices have largely supplanted mental arithmetic, nobody would take either proposal
seriously. The advantages gained are so slight, and the tradition of
counting by tens so firm, that the challenge seems ridiculous.

From the standpoint of the history of culture a change of base,
even if practicable, would be highly undesirable. As long as man
counts by tens, his ten fingers will remind him of the human
origin of this most important phase of his mental life. So may the
decimal system stand as a living monument to the proposition:

Man is the measure of all things.

Sir James George Frazer

The Magic Spring

*Sir James Frazer (1854-1941), born in Glasgow, Scotland, a Fellow
of Trinity College, Cambridge, was the author of the best-known
work on anthropology and folklore,* The Golden Bough, *the first
volume of which appeared in 1890 and the twelfth and last in 1915.*

The general explanation which we have been led to adopt of
. . . many [ancient] ceremonies is that they are, or were in
their origin, magical rites intended to insure the revival of nature
in spring. The means by which they were supposed to effect this
end were imitation and sympathy. Led astray by his ignorance of

the true causes of things, primitive man believed that in order to produce the great phenomena of nature on which his life depended, he had only to imitate them, and that immediately, by a secret sympathy or mystic influence, the little drama which he acted in forest glade or mountain dell, on desert plain or windswept shore, would be taken up and repeated by mightier actors on a vaster stage. He fancied that by masquerading in leaves and flowers he helped the bare earth to clothe herself with verdure, and that by playing the death and burial of winter he drove that gloomy season away, and made smooth the path for the footsteps of returning spring. If we find it hard to throw ourselves even in fancy into a mental condition in which such things seem possible, we can more easily picture to ourselves the anxiety which the savage, when he first began to lift his thoughts above the satisfaction of his merely animal wants and to meditate on the causes of things, may have felt as to the continued operation of what we now call the laws of nature. To us, familiar as we are with the conception of the uniformity and regularity with which the great cosmic phenomena succeed each other, there seems little ground for apprehension that the causes which produce these effects will cease to operate, at least within the near future. But this confidence in the stability of nature is bred only by the experience which comes of wide observation and long tradition; and the savage, with his narrow sphere of observation and his short-lived tradition, lacks the very elements of that experience which alone could set his mind at rest in face of the ever-changing and often menacing aspects of nature. No wonder, therefore, that he is thrown into a panic by an eclipse and thinks that the sun or the moon would surely perish if he did not raise a clamor and shoot his puny shafts into the air to defend the luminaries from the monster who threatens to devour them. No wonder he is terrified when in the darkness of night a streak of sky is suddenly illumined by the flash of the meteor, or the whole expanse of the celestial arch glows with the fitful light of the northern streamers. Even phenomena which recur at fixed and uniform intervals may be viewed by him with apprehension before he has come to recognize the orderliness of their recurrence. The speed or slowness of his recognition of such periodic or cyclic changes in nature will depend largely on the length of the particular cycle. The cycle, for example, of day and night is everywhere, except in the polar regions, so short and hence so frequent that men probably soon ceased to discompose themselves seriously as to the chance of its failing to recur, though the ancient Egyptians, as we have seen, daily wrought enchantments to bring back to the east in the morning the fiery orb which had sunk at evening in the crimson west. But it was far otherwise with the annual cycle of the seasons. To any man a year is a considerable period, seeing that the number of our years is but few at best. To the primitive savage, with his short memory and imperfect means of marking the flight of time, a year may well have been so long that he failed to recognize it as a cycle at all, and watched the changing aspects of earth and heaven with a perpetual wonder, alternately delighted and alarmed, elated and cast down, according as the vicissitudes of light and heat, of plant and animal life, ministered to his comfort or threatened his existence. In autumn when the withered leaves were whirled about the forest by the nipping blast and he looked up at the bare boughs, could he feel sure that they would ever be green again? As day by day the sun sank lower and lower in the sky, could he be certain that the luminary would ever retrace his heavenly road? Even the waning moon, whose pale sickle rose thinner and thinner every night over the rim of the eastern horizon, may have excited in his mind a fear lest, when it had wholly vanished, there should be moons no more.

These and a thousand such misgivings may have thronged the fancy and troubled the peace of the man who first began to reflect on the mysteries of the world he lived in, and to take thought for a more distant future than the morrow. It was natural, therefore, that with such thoughts and fears he should have done all that in him lay to bring back the faded blossom to the bough, to swing the low sun of winter up to his old place in the summer sky, and to restore its orbed fullness to the silver lamp of the waning moon. We may smile at his vain endeavors if we please, but it was only by making a long series of experiments, of which some were almost inevitably doomed to failure, that man learned from experience the futility of some of his attempted methods and the fruitfulness of others. After all, magical ceremonies are nothing but experiments which have failed and which continue to be repeated merely because, for reasons which have already been indicated, the operator is unaware of their failure. With the advance of knowledge these ceremonies either cease to be performed altogether or are kept up from force of habit long after the intention with which they were instituted has been forgotten. Thus fallen from their high estate, no longer regarded as solemn rites on the punctual performance of which the welfare and even the life of the community depend, they sink gradually to the level of simple pageants, mummeries, and pastimes, till in the final stage of degeneration they are wholly abandoned by older people and, from having once been the most serious occupation of the sage, become at last the idle sport of children. It is in this final stage of decay that most of the old magical rites of our European forefathers linger on at the present day, and even from this their last retreat they are fast being swept away by the rising tide of those multitudinous forces, moral, intellectual, and social, which are bearing mankind onward to a new and unknown goal. We may feel some natural regret at the disappearance of quaint customs and picturesque ceremonies, which have preserved to an age often deemed dull and prosaic something of the flavor and freshness of the olden time, some breath of the springtime of the world; yet our regret will be lessened when we remember that these pretty pageants, these now innocent diversions, had their origin in ignorance and superstitition; that if they are a record of human endeavor, they are also a monument of fruitless ingenuity, of wasted labor, and of blighted hopes; and that for all their gay trappings—their flowers, their ribbons, and their music—they partake far more of tragedy than of farce.

The interpretation which, following in the footsteps of W. Mannhardt, I have attempted to give of these ceremonies has been not a little confirmed by the discovery, made since this book was first written, that the natives of Central Australia regularly practice magical ceremonies for the purpose of awakening the dormant energies of nature at the approach of what may be called the Australian spring. Nowhere, apparently, are the alternations of the seasons more sudden and the contrasts between them more striking than in the deserts of central Australia, where at the end of a long period of drought the sandy and stony wilderness, over which the silence and desolation of death appear to brood, is suddenly, after a few days of torrential rain, transformed into a landscape smiling with verdure and peopled with teeming multitudes of insects and lizards, of frogs and birds. The marvelous change which passes over the face of nature at such times has been compared even by European observers to the effect of magic; no wonder, then, that the savage should regard it as such in very deed. Now it is just when there is promise of the approach of a good season that the natives of central Australia are wont especially to perform those magical ceremonies of which the avowed intention is to multiply the plants and animals they use as food. These ceremonies, therefore, present a close analogy to the spring customs of our European peasantry, not only in the time of their celebration, but also in their aim; for we can hardly doubt that in instituting rites designed to assist the revival of plant life in spring our primitive forefathers were moved, not by any sentimental wish to smell at early violets or pluck the rathe primrose or watch yellow daffodils dancing in the breeze, but by the very practical consideration, certainly not formulated in abstract terms, that the life of man is inextricably bound up with that of plants and that if they were to perish he could not survive. And as the faith of the Australian savage in the efficacy of his magic rites is confirmed by observing that their performance is invariably followed, sooner or later, by that increase of vegetable and animal life which it is their object to produce, so, we may suppose, it was with European savages in the olden time. The sight of the fresh green in brake and thicket, of vernal flowers blowing on mossy banks, of swallows arriving from the south, and of the sun mounting daily higher in the sky, would be welcomed by them as so many visible signs that their enchantments were indeed taking effect, and would inspire them with a cheerful confidence that all was well with a world which they could thus mold to suit their wishes. Only in autumn days, as summer slowly faded, would their confidence again be dashed by doubts and misgivings at symptoms of decay, which told how vain were all their efforts to stave off forever the approach of winter and of death.

Margaret Bryant and Janet Aiken

The Origin of Grammar

Margaret Bryant (1900-   ), Professor of English at Brooklyn College, has written extensively on language and folklore. Janet Aiken (1892-   ) is best known for the liberal position which she has maintained on matters of English grammar.

In any language the structure of grammar tends to grow simpler with the passage of time. It may reasonably be conjectured that we look back at what may be compared to one side of a hill or mountain of complication, and that there must be another side, hidden from our eyes, which includes the stages of grammatical development which occurred while the systems were acquiring complication. Obviously speech cannot have burst complete into being; and it may be profitable to include in our study some conjectures concerning the primary stages of grammar.

Earlier theorists, more naïve than we, were sure there was such a thing as a first word, and they even theorized concerning what part of speech that first word must have been. Was the noun first? Did primitive man learn to point to a tree, a mammoth, a flint, and give to each that particular grunt which was the great-great-grandfather of our word? Now and again one sees references to nouns as "the oldest words," or "the earliest forms of language." How much credence may we place in such phrases?

Similar superlatives are applied to the verb, and it is easy to recognize the usefulness of the verb to primitive man in giving commands, transmitting messages, and generally showing action. Is the verb, then, the oldest word? The term itself, deriving from *verbum,* which means *word,* seems to indicate it.

Few if any linguists have favored the adjective as the earliest sort of word, and yet it may be that it does not lack all claim to that distinction. One can visualize a primitive message bearer gasping out the primitive equivalent of "sick," or "dead." A primitive mother might easily say *Sh-h-h*, or its equivalent, meaning *quiet*, to her baby. And if the tender emotions brought words to man as they brought the mating calls to birds, there must have been very early equivalents for *beautiful* or *dear*.

The interjection was designated by many nineteenth-century linguists as the earliest word. When hurt, even animals emit distinctive cries corresponding semantically to the human *Ow*. Indeed, an entire explanation or theory of language origins has been built on the notion that interjections were the heralds of speech. These independent utterances of no particular grammatical type are still viewed by many as the oldest words.

But today linguists refuse to dwell long on the relative claims to priority of the various parts of speech. The controversy is shelved as not worth fighting over. In the nature of things, it is held, we cannot know what word was first said by man; there is neither television nor telaudition to the past. It is a waste of time to give thought to a matter which must remain in the sphere of what has been called "lunar politics." For is not the genesis of human speech as insoluble a puzzle as that old game of squaring the circle?

It may be possible at least to throw some light upon this question by holding to a psychological view of it and by pointing out as a necessary preliminary to its consideration that language was and is a natural by-product of voice, occurring inevitably and independently as soon as mental development has attained a certain degree or standard.

In the older theories of the origin of language it was a well-nigh universal error to attempt to account for the origin of sound, or of meaningful sound. Since language was thought of as having been created out of nothing, theories were built up to explain what required no explanation. It is entirely true that the old theories of speech origin are vulnerable, but this is because they are all based on a false assumption—the assumption that sounds, even communications, are peculiar to human language.

Everything human has grown out of something earlier, and language is no exception. It grew out of the multiplicity of primitive cries and calls such as are made today by monkeys, birds, cats, dogs, and many other animals. It is entirely probable that this development occurred at the same time or at different times independently in various parts of the earth: it may even be that it has occurred within very recent times. Prehistoric man found himself at the dawn of human language with an animal language already fully developed. From this point on, his speech progress is to be explained by principles of psychology rather than of history or science.

But just what is the difference between animal language and human language? At what point does a significant cry such as the animals make become a human word or sentence? All of us have had experience with the "language" of animals, and we know that it implies a certain degree of reasoning power on the part of the animal using it. What is it then that differentiates such language from human speech?

The key to the solution may be found in the idea of context. Birds, cats, dogs, and monkeys—all the animals capable of emitting significant cries—make these cries in context, that is, in the particular situation which naturally gives rise to them. When a dog growls defiance it is because he means it. His playful growl is a different "sentence," reserved for a different occasion. He cannot talk about growling, cannot tell his master the story of a situation where growling was called for—cannot lift growling out of its context in his mind.

This is not, of course, to imply that dogs lack memory. Given a repetition of the occasion for growls, or even a part repetition of it, the growl may result. But this is still a growl in context. Canine noises out of context, such as the "speaking" which is rewarded by a bit of food, are the result of human training.

In the same way a hen may give a danger signal to her chicks if she sees or fancies approaching danger. It is incredible that such a signal could be given out of context or that on the roost at night the hen should talk over the various perils of the day. In a way it shows a greater honesty on the part of hens, and of the animal world generally, this inability to tell anything but the actual fact about danger. It distinguishes man as the only animal capable of lying; for that is how speaking out of context may at times be regarded.

Human speech alone enables the speaker to talk about his experiences without actually living them, to discuss hunger when well fed and rest when fatigued. And it was at the precise moment when cries came to be used out of context that they became, not cries, but human speech. The word *meow* (as contrasted to the feline cry *meow*) is a word, just because it is not a response to a physical or mental stimulus, but an idea capable of use under any circumstances. The difference between word and cry is not one of genesis, of meaning, or of usefulness; it is a difference of motive, of outlook, of circumstance.

Thus language in the human sense is seen to be conditioned on memory and imagination, the ability to make a topic of conversation out of what one says. The origin of language is subjective rather than objective and denotes a psychological change in the use of meaningful cries. And it is important to remember that at the moment when this subjective change occurred primitive man found himself already supplied with a limited "wordhoard," or stock of cries, which by their new use became language.

Slowly at first, and then perhaps more rapidly, this new use of cries stimulated an increase in the number and complexity of language elements. Speech was found to be a toy as well as a tool, a delightful game as well as a protection and a weapon. This multiplying of speech-cries, of course, served still further to differentiate them from animal cries, which as everyone knows are sharply limited in number, the animal's "vocabulary" seldom or never including more than a dozen items. It is the manner in which speech-cries developed which constitutes the history of primitive grammar.

Consider once again the warning cluck of the hen to her chicks. It may be interpreted variously as a noun, *danger*, as a verb, *beware*, as an adjective, *unsafe*, as an interjection, *scat*, as a preposition, *off*. We cannot read into it a part-of-speech classification; in fact, it is no one part of speech as opposed to any other.

Is it not apparent that this significant cry of the hen has no more to do with English syntax and word-analysis than with Chinese? Completely formulated, perhaps what the hen is saying is, "Danger is approaching, my children, and you had better make yourselves as scarce as you can, as soon as possible." All those twenty words are implicit in the single note. The squawk of the hen is obviously the great-great-grandmother of the sentence, not of the word. In itself it is precisely what we call a nonsentence in modern English.

But here again we encounter the fallacy almost universal among linguists, the fallacy of the sentence. A sentence is, or it is not, a group of words complete with subject and predicate, expressing a thought. If it is, then language is not made up exclusively of sentences, since the nonsentence, a complete thought lacking formal subject and predicate, is extremely common in speech, and to a less degree in writing. It is the nonsentence rather than the sentence which is the primitive unit of grammar, and it is the nonsentence rather than the word which explains the character of the earliest language.

What we may call "pre-language" consisted of meaningful cries used exclusively in context to express emotions, messages, commands, and other necessities of communication. Eventually such cries came to be used apart from the particular situation which might evoke them. People began to "talk over" their experiences, as well as to experience them; and with this "talking over" language and grammar were simultaneously born. The nonsentence is nearer to this primitive type of communication just because it is a conglomerate similar to and less analyzable grammatically than the sentence. Gradually, over long ages of human progress, the word emerged, through the breaking up into parts of this primitive nonsentence. As the word appeared, the parts of nonsentences became free as separate units suitable for recombining, and such recombinations paved the way for the gradual development of the formally complete sentence containing subject and predicate.

These primitive "pre-sentences" came to be broken up, and in the *Ursprache* which ancestored our own English they came regularly or normally to follow the subject-verb pattern. In Chinese, Eskimo, and many other languages, while they broke into parts, they never adopted the sentence pattern. Besides subject and predicate, the Indo-European languages developed more minute subdivisions, which attained great complexity in such languages as Greek and German; in English many such subdivisions have been sloughed off as unnecessary and trammeling.

Thus the progress of language is from significant cries to the pre-sentence or complete communication in unanalyzable form; from this to the word as a separable part of the communication unit; and from this differently in various language families to their distinctive syntactical elements and patterns. It is mirrored in our word *word*, which may apply to a message of any extent and is often used (for example, in the Bible) to mean communication. The first words were words only in this large sense. They were sentence words such as the animals now use, but used by primitive man imaginatively, lyingly, out of their proper occasion and context.

But in pointing out the subjective character of the beginning of grammar and its dependence upon the nonsentence, we are only setting off on the long march from primitiveness to complexity, around the corner, and back toward simplicity. Our next task must be to trace the later development of grammar so that we may understand why it looks as it does today.

We may notice, then, that the primitive cries out of which grammar was to develop were entirely independent of one another, as much so as are today the various items in the cat's "vocabulary." The earliest grammar of all would have consisted merely of an inventory (if primitive man ever bothered to make one) of sound complexes, each as different from the other as a whistle from a sob. No synthesis was possible because there were no elements common to all the nonsentence cries which made up this earliest vocabulary.

Even today it is noticeable that nonsentences are far less analyzable grammatically than are sentences, and this may be one of the reasons why they are almost entirely disregarded in books of grammar. It is the nonsentence which retains most clearly the character of primitive speech, just as the so-called irregular verb is older than the regular verb. And it is certain that long before there existed anything which could be called a verb, man had his little stock or hoard of nonsentences, each one grammatically a law to itself.

Grammar began to develop as more nonsentences began to be added to this initial stock. These new items were, no doubt, often as distinct from all the rest as these had been from one another. But as time progressed, and more items were added to the language stock, it became impracticable to find new sound combinations, even if it was desirable. Synthesis began to come into being.

No doubt primitive ears were not sensitive to such small differentiations in sound as exist, for example, between the words *fern* and *farm*, and the aim in adding new speech-cries was undoubtedly clarity, intelligibility, and differentiation from anything already in the inventory. Perhaps a modern analogy to the progression of primitive utterances may be found in the choice of names for new telephone exchanges. Such names must be very distinctly different from the old, as Susquehanna and Butterfield and Endicott differ from Worth and John and Main. New non-sentences must be easily distinguishable to primitive ears from the old ones, and this necessitated a wide range of speech sounds and clear differentiation of sound combinations.[1]

New speech-cries might be made up out of nothing, but if modern word making is any criterion, it does not seem likely that this occurred often, since it almost never happens in modern speech that a new word is made up out of whole cloth. It seems probable that even at the very start existing speech-cries were modified or combined in the making of new cries. No doubt much innovation took place as well, but it must have been very early that nonsentence combinations were developed. If, for example, there was a grunt accompanied perhaps by a pointing to indicate what we call *he*, then this grunt might from early times have been combined with other sounds indicating *danger* or *love* or *discomfort*.

Many speech-cries no doubt were originated which never came to general use; but out of babbling, whining, cooing, growling, grunting, and so forth, there must have emerged the regular combinations which we may call syntactical.

With this combining of speech-cries we have the beginning of grammar; previous additions to the stock of speech-cries were in the nature of vocabulary. Such combining had later to be differentiated into inflexions and syntax, but the latter term better de-

---

[1] In Aiken, *Why English Sounds Change*, it is shown how the range of speech sounds has narrowed even within historic times. It can scarcely be doubted that primitive speech, like animal language, was drawn from a wider vocal area than is civilized speech.

scribes this primitive juxtaposing of nonsentence cries. Many speech-cries were no doubt combined in whole or in part to express new ideas or idea-combinations, and it is these new speech patterns which we may call syntactical.

No doubt much grammar was originated by children, and much from play, as well as from the sterner preoccupations of life. The fascination of language juggling must have been early felt, and one new combining led rapidly to another, so that the linguistic stock expanded at a comparatively quick rate because of the pleasures of out-of-context use.

It is important to emphasize that inflexions were in all probability a later development than syntax. As many writers on the subject have pointed out, the pronouns still show themselves clearly embedded in verbal and other affixes in such languages as Latin and Hebrew, and Hebrew also shows prepositional and conjunctional affixes, which may well point to the manner in which case may have originated in the Indo-European group of tongues. Inflexion is a younger process than syntax and one which we may reasonably suppose grew out of it.

If this is the fact, then the earliest inflexion, like the earliest speech-cry itself, was an independent communication. It was not an inflexion in the modern sense, that is, a sound or syllable added to a certain "part of speech" with complete or fair regularity. It was merely a tag or modification in a single word, somewhat of the nature of a compounding, but susceptible of extension to other words after the fashion of an inflexion.

On this basis it is easy to understand how inflexions should have grown up so luxuriantly in the early stages of grammar. Every word was a potential inflexion. It had only to prove itself useful in combination with numerous words, not necessarily all of a single kind, and it was likely to become more and more closely embedded in these words, until finally it lost its separate existence.

Modern English illustrates the process (which of course is recurrent and not confined to primitive languages) in the adverbial termination *ly*, used in *readily, easily, frankly, silently*, and hosts of other English words. Even so recently as the Anglo-Saxon period this *ly* was *līce*, meaning *like*. The compounded adverb is still found, particularly in Irish dialect: *He walked soft-like*. In most uses the word has become a suffix of a semi-inflexional character.

It was inevitable, likewise, that inflexions should be partial rather than complete in their applicability, since several different words might be used for a given idea, such as *many* or *past*, and such words might compound readily with only a few other terms. There is nothing peculiar in the fact that we find primitive languages with a plethora of declensions, conjugations, and other such categories. Even in Modern English, which has dropped most of its inflexional forms, we still have two ways (*more* and *er*, *most* and *est*) of forming the comparative and the superlative; and plurals are formed in several different ways.

Synthesis is a power relatively lacking in early stages of mental and social development. In many departments of grammar in many languages synthesis has failed to appear, even down to present times. Anyone could construct an English more synthesized than the one we speak. It is entirely consistent with what we know of the mentality of man in the various stages of his development to conclude that he would at first see grammatical relationships one by one rather than in categories. It was only very slowly and gradually that such grammatical categories could have developed, if indeed they ever developed at all.

In the beginning of grammar every word must have formed a category by itself, and it may be that in the Chinese language we have an example of a speech which never abandoned this primitive heterogeneity. Scholars are divided on the question whether Chinese ever went through an inflexional or a syntactical stage; but it is evident that so far as its grammar goes the language is today in a state similar to that which must have obtained in primitive speech.

In Chinese, as is well known, every word consists of a single syllable, and there are no such things as inflexions. Inflexional relationships are indicated, if at all, by separate words. There are no parts of speech; words shift around freely from function to function just as they are increasingly doing in the English language. Intelligibility is attained by sentence order and context. A distinction is made between "full" and "empty" words, the latter being what are known as "structural" words, such as prepositions, conjunctions, articles, and so forth. This absence of inflexions by no means hinders the Chinese from expressing complicated meanings with complete clarity, and it is entirely possible that the inflexionless state of Chinese has existed since the origin of that language.

In the western dialects, as well as in many eastern tongues, categories of person, gender, case, tense, mood, and the rest appeared. In the manner just described these categories multiplied themselves; but no sooner had great diversity appeared than certain categories began to merge and simplify.

To recur to the figure of a mountain used at the beginning of this chapter, we had in the early stages of grammar a steeply ascending curve of grammatical complication. The peak came at the point where the tendency to simplify overtook the tendency to multiply complications, and language began to descend to the state well represented by Modern English, where grammatical complications of form are tending to disappear.

Thus grammar in the shape of inflexions tends to be simple only at the birth and at the complete maturity of a language. In the field of syntax, on the other hand, grammar develops by juxtaposition of elements into a more or less fixed word order, out of which, in the Indo-European and Semitic languages, the sentence as we know it has developed.

The chief syntactical necessity in any language is to achieve a word pattern or group of patterns which will convey meanings with clarity. In Chinese nothing like the English sentence has developed, and the order of sentence elements is extremely fluid. In the Semitic- and Indo-European-language families we have roughly parallel developments into a fixed word order to which the term *sentence* may be applied.[2]

It is worth noting that all these developments into and out of grammatical forms are impelled by a variety of forces, most of them having little or nothing to do with logic. We can understand these forces as they apply to Modern English, and we may conjecture that they were similar at earlier stages of linguistic experience. In this fashion can grammatical origins be analyzed.

[2] This order differs in the Hebrew in that it is ordinarily verb-subject-complement, instead of subject-verb-complement as in English.

Gilbert Keith Chesterton

Science and the Savages

G. K. Chesterton (1874-1936) was a prolific and provocative author who almost succeeded in making G.K.C. as famous a set of initials as G.B.S.

A permanent disadvantage of the study of folklore and kindred subjects is that the man of science can hardly be in the nature of things very frequently a man of the world. He is a student of nature; he is scarcely ever a student of human nature. And even where this difficulty is overcome, and he is in some sense a student of human nature, this is only a very faint beginning of the painful progress towards being human. For the study of primitive race and religion stands apart in one important respect from all, or nearly all, the ordinary scientific studies. A man can understand astronomy only by being an astronomer; he can understand entomology only by being an entomologist (or, perhaps, an insect); but he can understand a great deal of anthropology merely by being a man. He is himself the animal which he studies. Hence arises the fact which strikes the eye everywhere in the records of ethnology and folklore—the fact that the same frigid and detached spirit which leads to success in the study of astronomy or botany leads to disaster in the study of mythology or human origins. It is necessary to cease to be a man in order to do justice to a microbe; it is not necessary to cease to be a man in order to do justice to men. That same suppression of sympathies, that same waving away of intuitions or guesswork which make a man preternaturally clever in dealing with the stomach of a spider, will make him preternaturally stupid in dealing with the heart of man. He is making himself inhuman in order to understand humanity. An ignorance of the other world is boasted by many men of science; but in this matter their defect arises, not from ignorance of the other world, but from ignorance of this world. For the secrets about which anthropologists concern themselves can be best learnt, not from books or voyages, but from the ordinary commerce of man with man. The secret of why some savage tribe worships monkeys or the moon is not to be found even by travelling among those savages and taking down their answers in a notebook, although the cleverest man may pursue this course. The answer to the riddle is in England; it is in London; nay, it is in his own heart. When a man has discovered why men in Bond Street wear black hats he will at the same moment have discovered why men in Timbuctoo wear red feathers. The mystery in the heart of some savage war-dance should not be studied in books of scientific travel; it should be studied at a subscription ball. If a man desires to find out the origins of religions, let him not go to the Sandwich Islands; let him go to church. If a man wishes to know the origin of human society, to know what society, philosophically speaking, really is, let him not go into the British Museum; let him go into society.

This total misunderstanding of the real nature of ceremonial gives rise to the most awkward and dehumanized versions of the conduct of men in rude lands or ages. The man of science, not realizing that ceremonial is essentially a thing which is done without a reason, has to find a reason for every sort of ceremonial, and, as might be supposed, the reason is generally a very absurd one— absurd because it originates not in the simple mind of the barbarian, but in the sophisticated mind of the professor. The learned man will say, for instance, "The natives of Mumbojumbo Land believe that the dead man can eat, and will require food upon his journey to the other world. This is attested by the fact that they place food in the grave, and that any family not complying with this rite is the object of the anger of the priests and the tribe." To anyone acquainted with humanity this way of talking is topsy-turvy. It is like saying, "The English in the twentieth century believed that a dead man could smell. This is attested by the fact that they always covered his grave with lilies, violets, or other flowers. Some priestly and tribal terrors were evidently attached to the neglect of this action, as we have records of several old ladies who were very much disturbed in mind because their wreaths had not arrived in time for the funeral." It may be of course that savages put food with a dead man because they think that a dead man can eat, or weapons with a dead man because they think that a dead man can fight. But personally I do not believe that they think anything of the kind. I believe they put food or weapons on the dead for the same reason that we put flowers, because it is an exceedingly natural and obvious thing to do. We do not understand, it is true, the emotion which makes us think it obvious and natural; but that is because, like all the important emotions of human existence, it is essential irrational. We do not understand the savage for the same reason that the savage does not understand himself. And the savage does not understand himself for the same reason that we do not understand ourselves either.

The obvious truth is that the moment any matter has passed through the human mind it is finally and for ever spoilt for all purposes of science. It has become a thing incurably mysterious and infinite; his mortal has put on immortality. Even what we call our material desires are spiritual, because they are human. Science can analyse a pork-chop, and say how much of it is phosphorus and how much is protein; but science cannot analyse any man's wish for a pork-chop, and say how much of it is hunger, how much custom, how much nervous fancy, how much a haunting love of the beautiful. The man's desire for the pork-chop remains literally as mystical and ethereal as his desire for heaven. All attempts, therefore, at a science of any human things, at a science of history, a science of folklore, a science of sociology, are by their nature not merely hopeless, but crazy. You can no more be certain in economic history that a man's desire for money was merely a desire for money than you can be certain in hagiology that a saint's desire for God was merely a desire for God. And this kind of vagueness in the primary phenomena of the study is an absolutely final blow to anything in the nature of a science. Men can construct a science with very few instruments, or with very plain instruments; but no one on earth could construct a science with unreliable instruments. A man might work out the whole of mathematics with a handful of pebbles, but not with a handful of clay which was always falling apart into new fragments, and falling together into new combinations. A man might measure heaven and earth with a reed, but not with a growing reed.

As one of the enormous follies of folklore, let us take the case of the transmigration of stories, and the alleged unity of their source. Story after story the scientific mythologists have cut out of its place in history, and pinned side by side with similar stories in their museum of fables. The process is industrious, it is fascinating, and the whole of it rests on one of the plainest fallacies in the world. That a story has been told all over the place at some time or other not only does not prove that it really never happened; it does not even faintly indicate or make slightly more probable that it never happened. That a large number of fishermen have falsely asserted that they have caught a pike two feet long does not in the least affect the question of whether anyone ever really did so. That numberless journalists announce a Franco-German war merely for money is no evidence one way or the other upon the dark question of whether such a war ever occurred. Doubtless in a few hundred years the innumerable Franco-German wars that did not happen will have cleared the scientific mind of any belief in the legendary war of '70 which did. But that will be because, if folklore students remain at all, their nature will be unchanged; and their services to folklore will be still as they are at present, greater than they know. For in truth these men do something far more godlike than studying legends; they create them.

There are two kinds of stories which the scientists say cannot be true, because everybody tells them. The first class consists of the stories which are told everywhere, because they are somewhat odd or clever; there is nothing in the world to prevent their having happened to somebody as an adventure any more than there is anything to prevent their having occurred, as they certainly did occur, to somebody as an idea. But they are not likely to have happened to many people. The second class of their "myths" consist of the stories that are told everywhere for the simple reason that they happen everywhere. Of the first class, for instance, we might take such an example as the story of William Tell, now generally ranked among legends upon the sole ground that it is found in the tales of other peoples. Now, it is obvious that this was told everywhere because whether true or fictitious it is what is called "a good story"; it is odd, exciting, and it has a climax. But to suggest that some such eccentric incident can never have happened in the whole history of archery, or that it did not happen to any particular person of whom it is told, is stark impudence. The idea of shooting at a mark attached to some valuable or beloved person is an idea doubtless that might easily have occurred to any inventive poet. But it is also an idea that might easily occur to any boastful archer. It might be one of the fantastic caprices of some story-teller. It might equally well be one of the fantastic caprices of some tyrant. It might occur first in real life and afterwards occur in legends. Or it might just as well occur first in legends and afterwards occur in real life. If no apple has ever been shot off a boy's head from the beginning of the world, it may be done tomorrow morning, and by somebody who has never heard of William Tell.

This type of tale, indeed, may be pretty fairly paralleled with the ordinary anecdote terminating in a repartee or an Irish bull. Such a retort as the famous "Je ne vois pas la necessité" [1] we have all seen attributed to Talleyrand, to Voltaire, to Henri Quatre, to an anonymous judge, and so on. But this variety does not in any way make it more likely that the thing was never said at all. It is highly likely that it was really said by somebody unknown. It is highly likely that it was really said by Talleyrand. In any case, it is not any more difficult to believe that the *mot* might have occurred to a man in conversation than to a man writing memoirs. It might have occurred to any of the men I have mentioned. But there is this point of distinction about it, that it is not likely to have occurred to all of them. And this is where the first class of so-called myth differs from the second to which I have previously referred. For there is a second class of incident found to be common to the stories of five or six heroes, say to Sigurd, to Hercules, to Rustem, to the Cid, and so on. And the peculiarity of this myth is that not only is it highly reasonable to imagine that it really happened to one hero, but it is highly reasonable to imagine that it really happened to all of them. Such a story, for instance, is that of a great man having his strength swayed or thwarted by the mysterious weakness of a woman. The anecdotal story, the story of William Tell, is, as I have said, popular because it is peculiar. But this kind of story, the story of Samson and Delilah, of Arthur

---

[1] "I do not see the necessity"—the reputed answer given to one who said by way of defence that he had to live somehow.

and Guinevere, is obviously popular because it is not peculiar. It is popular as good, quiet fiction is popular, because it tells the truth about people. If the ruin of Samson by a woman, and the ruin of Hercules by a woman, have a common legendary origin, it is gratifying to know that we can also explain, as a fable, the ruin of Nelson by a woman and the ruin of Parnell by a woman. And, indeed, I have no doubt whatever that, some centuries hence, the students of folklore will refuse altogether to believe that Elizabeth Barrett eloped with Robert Browning, and will prove their point up to the hilt by the unquestionable fact that the whole fiction of the period was full of such elopements from end to end.

Possibly the most pathetic of all the delusions of the modern students of primitive belief is the notion they have about the thing they call anthropomorphism. They believe that primitive men attributed phenomena to a god in human form in order to explain them, because his mind in its sullen limitation could not reach any further than his own clownish existence. The thunder was called the voice of a man, the lightning the eyes of a man, because by this explanation they were made more reasonable and comfortable. The final cure for all this kind of philosophy is to walk down a lane at night. Anyone who does so will discover very quickly that men pictured something semi-human at the back of all things, not because such a thought was natural, but because it was supernatural; not because it made things more comprehensible, but because it made them a hundred times more incomprehensible and mysterious. For a man walking down a lane at night can see the conspicuous fact that as long as nature keeps to her own course, she has no power with us at all. As long as a tree is a tree, it is a top-heavy monster with a hundred arms, a thousand tongues, and only one leg. But so long as a tree is a tree, it does not frighten us at all. It begins to be something alien, to be something strange, only when it looks like ourselves. When a tree really looks like a man our knees knock under us. And when the whole universe looks like a man we fall on our faces.

Rebecca West

Savtat

*Rebecca West is the pseudonym of Cicily Fairfield (1892-   ).
The essay that follows is taken from Miss West's account of a
journey through Yugoslavia in 1937. It is dedicated "to my friends
all dead or enslaved." Dubrovnik is on the Adriatic Sea.*

The road runs along the coast between rocky banks dripping
with the golden hair of broom. The hillside above and below us
was astonishing in its fertility, although even here the rain was
diluting the spring to a quarter of its proper strength. There was
everywhere the sweet-smelling scrub, and thickets of oleander,
and the grey-blue swords of aloes; and on the lower slopes were
olive terraces and lines of cypresses, spurting up with a vitality
strange to see in what is black and not green. Oaks there were—
the name Dubrovnik means a grove of oaks; and where there were
some square yards of level ground there were thick-trunked patri-
archal planes, with branches enough to cover an army of concu-
bines. The sea looked poverty-stricken, because, being here without islands, it had no share in this feast served up by the rising sap.
There was presented a vision of facility, of effortless growth as
the way to salvation. This coast, in ancient times, was a centre of
the cult of Pan.

There were, however, other interesting residents of a supernatural character. Somewhere up in the mountains on this road is
the cave in which Cadmus and his wife suffered their metamorphosis. They were so distressed by the misfortunes of their children, who were persecuted by Hera, that they begged the gods to
turn them into snakes. Ovid made a lovely verse of it. When Cadmus had suffered the change

> . . . . ille suae lambebat coniugis ora
> inque sinus caros, veluti cognosceret, ibat

et dabat amplexus adsuetaque colla petebat.
quisquis adest (aderant comites), terrentur; at illa
lubrica permulcet cristati colla draconis,
et subito duo sunt iunctoque volumine serpunt,
donec in adpositi nemoris subiere latebras,
nunc quoque nec fugiunt hominem nec vulnere laedunt
quidque prius fuerint, placidi meminere dracones.[1]

It is an apt symbol of the numbness that comes on the broken-
hearted. They become wise; they find comfort in old companionship; but they lose the old human anatomy, the sensations no
longer follow the paths of the nerves, the muscles no longer offer
their multifold reaction to the behests of the brain, there is no
longer a stout fortress of bones, there is nothing but a long, slid-
ing, writhing sorrow. But what happened to Cadmus was perhaps
partly contrived by the presiding deity of the coast, for he was
the arch-enemy of Pan, since he invented letters. He made hu-
mankind eat of the tree of knowledge; he made joy and sorrow
dangerous because he furnished the means of commemorating
them, that is to say of analysing them, of being appalled by them.

That was not an end of the strange events on the coast. We
learn from St. Jerome's life of St. Hilarion that when (in the
fourth century) the holy man went to Epidaurus, which was a
town founded by the Greeks not far from here, he found the whole
district terrorized by a monster living in a cave near by, who
could draw peasants and shepherds to his lair by his breath. It
was certainly Cadmus; literature has always found readers. St.
Hilarion went to the mouth of the cave and made the sign of the
cross and bade the dragon come forth. It obeyed and followed the
saint as meekly as might be back to Epidaurus: all literature
worth naming is an expression of the desire to be saved. There the
saint said to the townspeople, "Build a pyre"; and when they had
done that, he said to the dragon, "Lie down on that pyre." It
obeyed. The townspeople set the pyre alight, and it lay quietly till

---

[1] "He licked his wife's face, and crept into her dear familiar breasts,
enfolded her and sought the throat he knew so well. All who were there
—for they had friends with them—shuddered with horror. But she
stroked the sleek neck of the crested reptile, and all at once there were
two snakes there with intertwining coils, which after a little while glided
away into the woods near by. Now, as when they were human, they
neither fear men nor wound them and are gentle creatures, who still
remember what they were."

it was burned to ashes. Without doubt it was Cadmus, it was literature. It knew that it was not a dragon, it was a phoenix and would rise restored and young from its ashes; it knew that pagan literature was dying and Christian literature was being born.

Since then Epidaurus has changed its name twice. It was destroyed by the barbarians in the seventh century and its population fled ten miles further north and founded Dubrovnik, or Ragusa. But after a time some stragglers returned to the ruins of the sacked city and built another of a simpler sort, which came to be known as Ragusa Vecchia. Now it is called Savtat, which is said to be a Slavonic version of the word "*civitas*." We stopped there and found that the story about St. Hilarion and the dragon was perfectly true. It cannot be doubted. The town lies on a double-humped dromedary of a peninsula, and the road can be seen where the dragon trotted along behind the saint, looking as mild as milk but sustained by its inner knowledge that not only was it to be reborn from the flames, but that those who kindled them were to know something about death on their own account. It was aware that when we visited the scene fifteen hundred years later we should be able to see in our mind's eye the tall villas which it passed on the way to its martyrdom, and the elegant and serious people who held their torches to the pyre; and it knew why. It knew that one day the sailors and crofters would come to live among the ruins of the town and would delve among the burnt and shattered villas and take what they would of sculptures and bas-reliefs to build up their cottage walls, where they can be seen today, flowers in the buttonhole of poverty. It knew that the peasants' spades would one day attack a part of the peninsula which, in the Greek town, had been the jewellers' quarter; and that afterwards intaglios on the hungry breasts and rough fingers of people who had never known what it was to satisfy necessity, would evoke a dead world of elegant and serious ladies and gentlemen, otherwise sunk without trace. "Lie down," St. Hilarion was obliged to say to the dragon, "lie down, and stop laughing."

Yet even that was not the last event to happen here as it does nowhere else. Two seafaring families of this place became rich and famous shipowners, and just after the war a woman who had been born into the one and had married into the other conceived the desire that Mestrovitch should build a mausoleum for herself, her father, her mother, and her brother. She held long discussions with the sculptor, and then she and her father and her brother all died suddenly, for no very probable medical reason; and the mother had only time to make the final arrangements for the execution of the plan before she joined them. There is something splendid and Slav about this. They had resolved to provoke an analysis of death by their own deaths, and hastened to carry out their resolution.

Mestrovitch made the mausoleum in the form of a Chapel of Our Lady of the Angels, standing among the cypresses in the cemetery on one of the two summits of the peninsula. It is characteristic of him in the uncertainty with which it gropes after forms: there are some terrible errors, such as four boy musician angels who recall the horrid Japaneseries of Aubrey Beardsley. There is no getting over the troublesome facts that the Turkish occupation sterilized South Slav art for five hundred years, and that when it struggled back to creativeness it found itself separated by Philistine Austria from all the artistic achievements that the rest of Europe had been making in the meantime. But there are moments in the Chapel which exquisitely illustrate the theory, the only theory that renders the death of the individual not a source of intolerable grief: the theory that the goodness of God stretches under human destiny like the net below trapeze artists at the circus. The preservation offered is not of a sort that humanity would dare to offer; a father would be lynched if he should do so badly for his son. Yet to die, and to know a meaning in death, is a better destiny than to be saved from dying. This discussion Mestrovitch carries on not by literary suggestion, but as a sculptor should, by use of form.

But this coast belongs to Pan. In this mausoleum Cadmus goes too far, he delves into matters which the natural man would forget and ignore, and he is punished. The sexton in charge of this cemetery, whose work it is to show visitors the tomb, is a cheerful soul who has taken up mortuary interests as if they were football or racing. He has himself tried his hand at sculpture, and his carvings are all excruciating parodies of Mestrovitch, criticisms which none of his enemies have ever surpassed in venom; and, as every artist knows, there are tortures which a dragon dreads far more than the pyre.

IV

William James

Reverie, Inference, and Reasoning

William James (1842-1910) was an American philosopher and the older brother of the novelist Henry James. He began his career as an instructor in physiology at Harvard University, gradually became interested in the then relatively new subject of psychology, and moved finally into philosophy, where he was largely responsible for the development of the doctrines of pragmatism. George Santayana, his colleague at Harvard, thought that his "best achievement" was The Principles of Psychology *(1890), from which the following selection is taken.*

I

We talk of man being the rational animal; and the traditional intellectualist philosophy has always made a great point of treating the brutes as wholly irrational creatures. Nevertheless, it is by no means easy to decide just what is meant by reason, or how the peculiar thinking process called reasoning differs from other thought sequences which may lead to similar results.

Much of our thinking consists of trains of images suggested one by another, of a sort of spontaneous reverie of which it seems likely enough that the higher brutes should be capable. This sort of thinking leads nevertheless to rational conclusions, both practical and theoretical. The links between the terms are either "contiguity" or "similarity," and with a mixture of both these things we can hardly be very incoherent. As a rule, in this sort of irresponsible thinking, the terms which fall to be coupled together are empirical concretes, not abstractions. A sunset may call up the vessel's deck from which I saw one last summer, the companions of my voyage, my arrival into port, etc.; or it may make me think

From *The Principles of Psychology*, Vol. II. By permission of Henry Holt and Company, Inc.

of solar myths, of Hercules' and Hector's funeral pyres, of Homer and whether he could write, of the Greek alphabet, etc. If habitual contiguities predominate, we have a prosaic mind; if rare contiguities, or similarities, have free play, we call the person fanciful, poetic, or witty. But the thought, as a rule, is of matters taken in their entirety. Having been thinking of one, we find later that we are thinking of another, to which we have been lifted along, we hardly know how. If an abstract quality figures in the procession, it arrests our attention but for a moment and fades into something else and is never very abstract. Thus, in thinking of the sun myths, we may have a gleam of admiration at the gracefulness of the primitive human mind or a moment of disgust at the narrowness of modern interpreters. But, in the main, we think less of qualities than of whole things, real or possible, just as we may experience them.

The upshot of it may be that we are reminded of some practical duty; we write a letter to a friend abroad, or we take down the lexicon and study our Greek lesson. Our thought is rational and leads to a rational act, but it can hardly be called reasoning in a strict sense of the term.

There are other shorter flights of thought, single couplings of terms which suggest each other by association, which approach more to what would commonly be classed as acts of reasoning proper. Those are where a present sign suggests an unseen, distant, or future reality. Where the sign and what it suggests are both concretes which have been coupled together on previous occasions, the inference is common to both brutes and men, being really nothing more than association by contiguity. A and B, dinner bell and dinner, have been experienced in immediate succession. Hence A no sooner falls upon the sense than B is anticipated, and steps are taken to meet it. The whole education of our domestic beasts, all the cunning added by age and experience to wild ones, and the greater part of our human knowingness consists in the ability to make a mass of inferences of this simplest sort. Our "perceptions" or recognitions of what objects are before us are inferences of this kind. We feel a patch of color, and we say "a distant house"; a whiff of odor crosses us, and we say "a skunk"; a faint sound is heard, and we call it "a railroad train." Examples are needless, for such inferences of sensations not presented form the staple and tissue of our perceptive life, . . . illusory or veracious. They have been called *unconscious inferences*. Certainly we are commonly unconscious that we are inferring at all. The sign and the signified melt into what seems to us the object of a single pulse of thought. . . .

2

There are two great points in reasoning: First, an extracted character is taken as equivalent to the entire datum from which it comes; and second, the character thus taken suggests a certain consequence more obviously than it was suggested by the total datum as it originally came. . . .

1. Suppose I say, when offered a piece of cloth, "I won't buy that; it looks as if it would fade," meaning merely that something about it suggests the idea of fading to my mind—my judgment, though possibly correct, is not reasoned, but purely empirical; but if I can say that into the color there enters a certain dye which I know to be chemically unstable and that *therefore* the color will fade, my judgment is reasoned. The notion of the dye which is one of the parts of the cloth is the connecting link between the latter and the notion of fading. So, again, an uneducated man will expect from past experience to see a piece of ice melt if placed near the fire, and the tip of his finger look coarse if he views it through a convex glass. In neither of these cases could the result be anticipated without full previous acquaintance with the entire phenomenon. It is not a result of reasoning.

But a man who should conceive heat as a mode of motion, and liquefaction as identical with increased motion of molecules; who should know that curved surfaces bend light rays in special ways and that the apparent size of anything is connected with the amount of the "bend" of its light rays as they enter the eye—such a man would make the right inferences for all these objects, even though he had never in his life had any concrete experience of them; and he would do this because the ideas which we have above supposed him to possess would mediate in his mind between the phenomena he starts with and the conclusions he draws. But these ideas or reasons for his conclusions are all mere extracted portions or circumstances singled out from the mass of characters which make up the entire phenomena. The motions which form heat, the bending of the light waves, are, it is true, excessively recondite ingredients. . . . But each and all agree in this, that they bear a *more evident relation* to the conclusion than did the immediate data in their full totality.

The difficulty is, in each case, to extract from the immediate data that particular ingredient which shall have this very evident relation to the conclusion. Every phenomenon or so-called "fact" has an infinity of aspects or properties, as we have seen, amongst which the fool, or man with little sagacity, will inevitably go astray. But no matter for this point now. The first thing is to have seen that every possible case of reasoning involves the extraction of a particular partial aspect of the phenomena thought about, and that whilst empirical thought simply associates phenomena in their entirety, reasoned thought couples them by the conscious use of this extract.

2. And now to prove the second point: Why are the couplings, consequences, and implications of extracts more evident and obvious than those of entire phenomena? For two reasons. First, the extracted characters are more general than the concretes, and the connections they may have are, therefore, more familiar to us, having been more often met in our experience. Think of heat as motion, and whatever is true of motion will be true of heat; but we have had a hundred experiences of motion for every one of heat. Think of the rays passing through this lens as bending toward the perpendicular, and you substitute for the comparatively unfamiliar lens the very familiar notion of a particular change in direction of a line, of which notion every day brings us countless examples.

The other reason why the relations of the extracted characters are so evident is that their properties are so *few* compared with the properties of the whole from which we derived them. In every concrete total the characters and their consequences are so inexhaustibly numerous that we may lose our way among them before noticing the particular consequence it behooves us to draw. But if we are lucky enough to single out the proper character, we take in, as it were, by a single glance all its possible consequences. Thus the character of scraping the sill has very few suggestions, prominent among which is the suggestion that the scraping will cease if we raise the door; whilst the entire refractory door suggests an enormous number of notions to the mind.

Take another example. I am sitting in a railroad car, waiting for the train to start. It is winter, and the stove fills the car with pungent smoke. The brakeman enters, and my neighbor asks him to "stop that stove smoking." He replies that it will stop entirely as soon as the car begins to move.

"Why so?" asks the passenger.

"It *always* does," replies the brakeman.

It is evident from this "always" that the connection between car moving and smoke stopping was a purely empirical one in the brakeman's mind, bred of habit. But if the passenger had been an acute reasoner, he, with no experience of what the stove always did, might have anticipated the brakeman's reply and spared his own question. Had he singled out, of all the numerous points involved in a stove's not smoking, the one special point of smoke pouring freely out of the stovepipe's mouth, he would, probably, owing to the few associations of that idea, have been immediately reminded of the law that a fluid passes more rapidly out of a pipe's mouth if another fluid be at the same time streaming over that mouth; and then the rapid draught of air over the stovepipe's mouth, which is one of the points involved in the car's motion, would immediately have occurred to him.

Thus a couple of extracted characters, with a couple of their few and obvious connections, would have formed the reasoned link in the passenger's mind between the phenomena, smoke stopping and car moving, which were only linked as wholes in the brakeman's mind. Such examples may seem trivial, but they contain the essence of the most refined and transcendental theorizing. The reason why physics grows more deductive the more the fundamental properties it assumes are of a mathematical sort, such as molecular mass or wave length, is that the immediate consequences of these notions are so few that we can survey them all at once and promptly pick out those which concern us.

3

To reason, then, we must be able to extract characters—not any characters, but the right characters for our conclusion. If we extract the wrong character, it will not lead to that conclusion. Here, then, is the difficulty: *How are characters extracted, and why does it require the advent of a genius in many cases before the fitting character is brought to light?* Why cannot anybody reason as well as anybody else? Why does it need a Newton to notice the law of the squares, a Darwin to notice the survival of the fittest? To answer such questions we must begin a new research and see how our insight into the facts naturally grows.

All our knowledge at first is vague. When we say that a thing is vague, we mean that it has no subdivisions *ab intra* nor precise limitations *ab extra*, but still all the forms of thought may apply to it. It may have unity, reality, externality, extent, and what not —*thinghood*, in a word, but thinghood only as a whole. In this vague way, probably, does the room appear to the babe who first begins to be conscious of it as something other than his moving nurse. It has no subdivisions in his mind, unless, perhaps, the window is able to attract his separate notice. In this vague way, certainly, does every entirely new experience appear to the adult. A library, a museum, a machine shop, are mere confused wholes to the uninstructed, but the machinist, the antiquary, and the bookworm perhaps hardly notice the whole at all, so eager are they to pounce upon the details. Familiarity has in them bred discrimination. Such vague terms as "grass," "mold," and "meat" do not exist for the botanist or the anatomist. They know too much about grasses, molds, and muscles. A certain person said to Charles Kingsley, who was showing him the dissection of a caterpillar, with its exquisite viscera, "Why, I thought it was nothing but skin and squash!" A layman present at a shipwreck, a battle, or a fire is helpless. Discrimination has been so little awakened in him by experience that his consciousness leaves no single point of the complex situation accented and standing out for him to begin to act upon. But the sailor, the fireman, and the general know directly at what corner to take up the business. They "see into the situation"—that is, they analyze it—with their first glance. It is full of delicately differenced ingredients which their education has little by little brought to their consciousness, but of which the novice gains no clear idea. . . .

We dissociate the elements of originally vague totals by attending to them or noticing them alternately, of course. But what determines which element we shall attend to first? There are two immediate and obvious answers: first, our practical or instinctive interests, and second, our aesthetic interests. The dog singles out of any situation its smells, and the horse its sounds, because they may reveal facts of practical moment and are instinctively exciting to these several creatures. The infant notices the candle flame or the window, and ignores the rest of the room, because those objects give him a vivid pleasure. So the country boy dissociates the blackberry, the chestnut, and the wintergreen, from the vague mass of other shrubs and tress, for their practical uses, and the savage is delighted with the beads, the bits of looking glass brought by an exploring vessel, and gives no heed to the features of the vessel itself, which is too much beyond his sphere. These aesthetic and practical interests, then, are the weightiest factors in making particular ingredients stand out in high relief. What they lay their accent on, that we notice; but what they are in themselves we cannot say. We must content ourselves here with simply accepting them as irreducible ultimate factors in determining the way our knowledge grows.

Now a creature which has few instinctive impulses or interests, practical or aesthetic, will dissociate few characters and will at best have limited reasoning powers, whilst one whose interests are very varied will reason much better. Man, by his immensely varied instincts, practical wants, and aesthetic feelings, to which every sense contributes, would, by dint of these alone, be sure to dissociate vastly more characters than any other animal; and accordingly we find the lowest savages reason incomparably better than the highest brutes. . . .

4

But now, since nature never makes a jump, it is evident that we should find the lowest men occupying in this respect an intermediate position between the brutes and the highest men. And so we do. Beyond the analogies which their own minds suggest by breaking up the literal sequence of their experience, there is a whole world of analogies which they can appreciate when imparted to them by their betters, but which they could never excogitate alone. This answers the question why Darwin and Newton had to be waited for so long. The flash of similarity between an apple and the moon, between the rivalry for food in nature and the rivalry for man's selection, was too recondite to have occurred to any but exceptional minds. *Genius, then,* as has already been said, *is identical with the possession of similar association to an extreme degree.* Professor Bain says: "This I count the leading fact of genius. I consider it quite impossible to afford any explanation of intellectual originality except on the supposition of unusual energy on this point." Alike in the arts, in literature, in practical affairs, and in science, association by similarity is the prime condition of success.

But as, according to our view, there are two stages in reasoned thought, one where similarity merely *operates* to call up cognate thoughts, and another further stage where the bond of identity between the cognate thoughts is *noticed,* so *minds of genius may be divided into two main sorts, those who notice the bond and those who merely obey it.* The first are the abstract reasoners, properly so called, the men of science and philosophers—the analysts, in a word; the latter are the poets, the critics—the artists, in a word, the men of intuitions. These judge rightly, classify cases, characterize them by the most striking analogic epithets, but go no further. At first sight it might seem that the analytic mind represented simply a higher intellectual stage and that the intuitive mind represented an arrested stage of intellectual development, but the difference is not so simple as this. Professor Bain has said that a man's advance to the scientific stage (the stage of noticing and abstracting the bond of similarity) may often be due to an *absence* of certain emotional sensibilities. The sense of color, he says, may no less determine a mind away from science than it determines it toward painting. There must be a penury in one's interest in the details of particular forms in order to permit the forces of the intellect to be concentrated on what is common to many forms. In other words, supposing a mind fertile in the suggestion of analogies, but at the same time keenly interested in the particulars of each suggested image, that mind would be far less apt to single out the particular character which called up the analogy than one whose interests were less generally lively. A certain richness of the aesthetic nature may, therefore, easily keep one in the intuitive stage. All the poets are examples of this. Take Homer:

Ulysses, too, spied round the house to see if any man were still alive and hiding, trying to get away from gloomy death. He found them all fallen in the blood and dirt, and in such number as the fish which the fishermen to the low shore, out of the foaming sea, drag with their meshy nets. These all, sick for the ocean water, are strewn around the sands, while the blazing sun takes their life from them. So there the suitors lay strewn round on one another.

Or again:

And as when a Maeonian or a Carian woman stains ivory with purple to be a checkpiece for horses, and it is kept in the chamber, and many horsemen have prayed to bear it off; but it is kept a treasure for a king, both a trapping for his horse and a glory to the driver—in such wise were thy stout thighs, Menelaos, and legs and fair ankles stained with blood.

A man in whom all the accidents of an analogy rise up as vividly as this may be excused for not attending to the ground of the analogy. But he need not on that account be deemed intellectually the inferior of a man of drier mind, in whom the ground is not as liable to be eclipsed by the general splendor. Rarely are both sorts of intellect, the splendid and the analytic, found in conjunction. Plato among philosophers, and M. Taine, who cannot quote a child's saying without describing the *voix chantante, étonnée, heureuse* in which it is uttered, are only exceptions whose strangeness proves the rule.

An often-quoted writer has said that Shakespeare possessed more *intellectual power* than anyone else who ever lived. If by this he meant the power to pass from given premises to right or congruous conclusions, it is no doubt true. The abrupt transitions in Shakespeare's thought astonish the reader by their unexpectedness no less than they delight him by their fitness. Why, for instance, does the death of Othello so stir the spectator's blood and leave him with a sense of reconcilement? Shakespeare himself could very likely not say why, for his invention, though rational, was not ratiocinative. Wishing the curtain to fall upon a reinstated Othello, that speech about the turbaned Turk suddenly simply flashed across him as the right end of all that went before. The dry critic who comes after can, however, point out the subtle bonds of identity that guided Shakespeare's pen through that speech to the death of the Moor. Othello is sunk in ignominy, lapsed from his height at the beginning of the play. What better way to rescue him at last from this abasement than to make him for an instant identify himself in memory with the old Othello of better days and then execute justice on his present disowned body, as he used then to smite all enemies of the state? But Shakespeare, whose mind supplied these means, could probably not have told why they were so effective.

But though this is true, and though it would be absurd in an absolute way to say that a given analytic mind was superior to any intuitional one, yet it is none the less true that the former *represents* the higher stage. Men, taken historically, reason by analogy long before they have learned to reason by abstract characters. Association by similarity and true reasoning may have identical results. If a philosopher wishes to prove to you why you should do a certain thing, he may do so by using abstract considerations exclusively; a savage will prove the same by reminding you of a similar case in which you notoriously do as he now proposes, and this with no ability to state the *point* in which the cases are similar. In all primitive literature, in all savage oratory, we find persuasion carried on exclusively by parables and similes, and travelers in savage countries readily adopt the native custom. Take, for example, Dr. Livingstone's argument with the Negro conjurer. The missionary was trying to dissuade the savage from his fetichistic ways of invoking rain.

"You see," he said, "that, after all your operations, sometimes it rains and sometimes it does not, exactly as when you have not operated at all."

"But," replied the sorcerer, "it is just the same with you doctors; you give your remedies, and sometimes the patient gets well and sometimes he dies, just the same as when you do nothing at all."

To that the pious missionary replied: "The doctor does his duty, after which God performs the cure if it pleases Him."

"Well," rejoined the savage, "it is just so with me. I do what is necessary to procure rain, after which God sends it or withholds it according to His pleasure."

This is the stage in which proverbial philosophy reigns supreme. "An empty sack can't stand straight" will stand for the reason why a man with debts may lose his honesty, and "a bird in the hand is worth two in the bush" will serve to back up one's exhortations to prudence. Or we answer the question: "Why is snow white?" by saying: "For the same reason that soapsuds or whipped eggs are white"—in other words, instead of giving the *reason* for a fact, we give another *example* of the same fact. This offering a similar instance instead of a reason has often been criticized as one of the forms of logical depravity in men. But manifestly it is not a perverse act of thought, but only an incomplete one. Furnishing parallel cases is the necessary first step toward abstracting the reason imbedded in them all.

As it is with reasons, so it is with words. The first words are probably always names of entire things and entire actions, of extensive coherent groups. A new experience in the primitive man can only be talked about by him in terms of the old experiences which have received names. It reminds him of certain ones from among them, but the *points* in which it agrees with them are neither named nor dissociated. Pure similarity must work before the abstraction can work which is based upon it. The first adjectives will therefore probably be total nouns embodying the striking character. The primeval man will say, not "the bread is hard" but "the bread is stone"; not "the face is round," but "the face is moon"; not "the fruit is sweet," but "the fruit is sugar cane." The first words are thus neither particular nor general, but *vaguely* concrete; just as we speak of an "oval" face, a "velvet" skin, or an "iron" will, without meaning to connote any other attributes of the adjective-noun than those in which it *does* resemble the noun it is used to qualify. After a while certain of these adjectively-used nouns come only to signify the particular quality for whose sake they are most often used; the *entire thing* which they originally meant receives another name, and they become true abstract and general terms. "Oval," for example, with us suggests *only* shape. The first abstract qualities thus formed are, no doubt, qualities of one and the same sense found in different objects—as big, sweet; next analogies between different senses, as sharp (of taste), high (of sound), etc.; then analogies of motor combinations or form of relation, as simple, confused, difficult, reciprocal, relative, spontaneous, etc. The extreme degree of subtlety in analogy is reached in such cases as when we say certain English art critics' writing reminds us of a close room in which pastilles have been burning or that the mind of certain Frenchmen is like old Roquefort cheese. Here language utterly fails to hit upon the basis of resemblance.

Over immense departments of our thought we are still all of us, in the savage state. Similarity operates in us, but abstraction has not taken place. We know what the present case is like, we know what it reminds us of, we have an intuition of the right course to take, if it be a practical matter. But analytic thought has made no tracks, and we cannot justify ourselves to others. In ethical, psychological, and aesthetic matters, to give a clear reason for one's judgment is universally recognized as a mark of rare genius. The helplessness of uneducated persons to account for their likes and dislikes is often ludicrous. Ask the first Irish girl why she likes this country better or worse than her home, and see how much she can tell you. But if you ask your most educated friend why he prefers Titian to Paul Veronese, you will hardly get more of a reply; and you will probably get absolutely none if you inquire why Beethoven reminds him of Michelangelo or how it comes that a bare figure with unduly flexed joints, by the latter, can so suggest the moral tragedy of life. His thought obeys a *nexus*, but cannot name it. And so it is with all those judgments of *experts*, which even though unmotived are so valuable. Saturated with experience of a particular class of materials, an expert intuitively feels whether a newly reported fact is probable or not, whether a proposed hypothesis is worthless or the reverse. He instinctively knows that, in a novel case, this and not that will be the promising course of action. The well-known story of the old judge advising the new one never to give reasons for his decisions—"The decisions will probably be right, the reasons will surely be wrong"— illustrates this. The doctor will feel that the patient is doomed, the dentist will have a premonition that the tooth will break, though neither can articulate a reason for his foreboding. The reason lies imbedded, but not yet laid bare, in all the countless previous cases dimly suggested by the actual one, all calling up the same conclusion, which the adept thus finds himself swept on to, he knows not how or why.

Bertrand Russell

Individual and Social Knowledge

Bertrand Russell (1872-   ) is one of the best-known contemporary philosophers. His range of interest is wide; he writes lucidly, and has in mind as his audience the general educated public. In 1950 he was awarded the Nobel Prize for literature. The essay that follows is the opening chapter of his book on Human Knowledge *(1948) in which he raises a question that is constantly perplexing in many areas of discourse.*

Scientific knowledge aims at being wholly impersonal, and tries to state what has been discovered by the collective intellect of mankind. In this chapter I shall consider how far it succeeds in this aim, and what elements of individual knowledge have to be sacrificed in order to achieve the measure of success that is possible.

The community knows both more and less than the individual: it knows, in its collective capacity, all the contents of the encyclopedia and all the contributions to the proceedings of learned bodies, but it does not know the warm and intimate things that make up the color and texture of an individual life. When a man says, "I can never convey the horror I felt on seeing Buchenwald" or "No words can express my joy at seeing the sea again after years in a prison camp," he is saying something which is strictly and precisely true: he possesses, through his experience, knowledge not possessed by those whose experience has been different, and not completely capable of verbal expression. If he is a superb literary artist, he may create in sensitive readers a state of mind not wholly unlike his own, but if he tries scientific methods the stream of his experience will be lost and dissipated in a dusty desert.

Language, our sole means of communicating *scientific* knowledge, is essentially social in its origin and in its main functions. It is true that if a mathematician were wrecked on a desert island with a notebook and a pencil, he would, in all likelihood, seek to make his solitude endurable by calculations using the language of mathematics; it is true also that a man may keep a diary which he intends to conceal from all eyes but his own. On a more every-day plane, most of us use words in solitary thinking. Nevertheless, the chief purpose of language is communication, and to serve this purpose it must be public, not a private dialect invented by the speaker. It follows that what is most personal in each individual's experience tends to evaporate during the process of translation into language. What is more, the very publicity of language is in large part a delusion. A given form of words will usually be interpreted by competent hearers in such a way as to be true for all of them or false for all of them, but in spite of this it will not have the same meaning for all of them. Differences which do not affect the truth or falsehood of a statement are usually of little practical importance and are therefore ignored, with the result that we all believe our private world to be much more like the public world than it really is.

This is easily proved by considering the process of learning to understand language. There are two ways of getting to know what a word means: one is by a definition in terms of other words, which is called *verbal* definition; the other is by frequently hearing the word when the object which it denotes is present, which is called *ostensive* definition. It is obvious that ostensive definition is alone possible in the beginning, since verbal definition presupposes a knowledge of the words used in the *definiens*. You can learn by a verbal definition that a pentagon is a plane figure with five sides, but a child does not learn in this way the meaning of everyday words such as "rain," "sun," "dinner," or "bed." These are taught by using the appropriate word emphatically while the child is noticing the object concerned. Consequently the meaning that the child comes to attach to the word is a product of his personal experience, and varies according to his circumstances and his sensorium. A child who frequently experiences a mild drizzle will attach a different idea to the word "rain" from that formed by a child who has only experienced tropical torrents. A short-sighted and a long-sighted child will connect different images with the word "bed."

It is true that education tries to depersonalize language, and with a certain measure of success. "Rain" is no longer the familiar phenomenon, but "drops of water falling from clouds toward the earth," and "water" is no longer what makes you wet, but H_2O. As for hydrogen and oxygen, they have verbal definitions which have to be learned by heart; whether you understand them does not matter. And so, as your instruction proceeds, the world of words becomes more and more separated from the world of the senses; you acquire the art of using words correctly, as you might acquire the art of playing the fiddle; in the end you become such a virtuoso in the manipulation of phrases that you need hardly ever remember that words have meanings. You have then become completely a public character, and even your inmost thoughts are suitable for the encyclopedia. But you can no longer hope to be a poet, and if you try to be a lover you will find your depersonalized language not very successful in generating the desired emotions. You have sacrificed expression to communication, and what you can communicate turns out to be abstract and dry.

It is an important fact that the nearer we come to the complete abstractness of logic, the less is the unavoidable difference between different people in the meaning attached to a word. I see no reason why there should be any difference at all between two suitably educated persons in the idea conveyed to them by the word "3481." The words "or" and "not" are capable of having exactly the same meaning for two different logicians. Pure mathematics, throughout, works with concepts which are capable of being completely public and impersonal. The reason is that they derive nothing from the senses, and that the senses are the source of privacy. The body is a sensitive recording instrument, constantly transmitting messages from the outside world; the messages reaching one body are never quite the same as those reaching another, though practical and social exigencies have taught us ways of disregarding the differences between the percepts of neighboring persons. In constructing physics we have emphasized the spatio-temporal aspect of our perceptions, which is the aspect that is most abstract and most nearly akin to logic and mathematics. This we have done in the pursuit of publicity, in order to communicate what is communicable and to cover up the rest in a dark mantle of oblivion.

Space and time, however, as human beings know them, are not
in reality so impersonal as science pretends. Theologians conceive
God as viewing both space and time from without, impartially,
and with a uniform awareness of the whole; science tries to imitate
this impartiality with some apparent success, but the success is
in part illusory. Human beings differ from the theologians' God
in the fact that their space and time have a *here* and *now*. What is
here and now is vivid; what is remote has a gradually increasing
dimness. All our knowledge of events radiates from a space-time
center, which is the little region that we are occupying at the moment. "Here" is a vague term: in astronomical cosmology the
Milky Way may count as "here"; in the study of the Milky Way
"here" is the solar system; in the study of the solar system "here"
is the earth; in geography it is the town or district in which
we live; in physiological studies of sensation it is the brain as opposed to the rest of the body. Larger "heres" always contain
smaller ones as parts; all "heres" contain the brain of the speaker,
or part of it. Similar considerations apply to "now."

Science professes to eliminate "here" and "now." When some
event occurs on the earth's surface, we give its position in the
space-time manifold by assigning latitude, longitude, and date. We
have developed a technique which insures that all accurate observers with accurate instruments will arrive at the same estimate of
latitude, longitude, and date. Consequently there is no longer anything personal in these estimates, in so far as we are content with
numerical statements of which the meaning is not too closely investigated. Having arbitrarily decided that the longitude of Greenwich and the latitude of the equator are to be zero, other latitudes
and longitudes follow. But what is "Greenwich"? This is hardly
the sort of term that ought to occur in an impartial survey of the
universe, and its definition is not mathematical. The best way to
define "Greenwich" is to take a man to it and say, "Here is Greenwich." If someone else has already determined the latitude and
longitude of the place where you are, "Greenwich" can be defined
by its latitude and longitude relative to that place; it is, for example, so many degrees east and so many degrees north of New
York. But this does not get rid of "here," which is now New York
instead of Greenwich.

Moreover it is absurd to *define* either Greenwich or New

York by its latitude and longitude. Greenwich is an actual place, inhabited by actual people, and containing buildings which antedate its longitudinal pre-eminence. You can, of course, describe Greenwich, but there always might be another town with the same characteristics. If you want to be *sure* that your description applies to no other place, the only way is to mention its relation to some other place—for instance, by saying that it is so many miles down the Thames from London Bridge. But then you will have to define "London Bridge." Sooner or later you are faced with the necessity of defining some place as "here," and this is an egocentric definition, since the place in question is not "here" for everybody. There may be a way of escape from this conclusion; at a later stage, we will resume the question. But there is no obvious or easy way of escape, and until one is found all determinations of latitude and longitude are infected with the subjectivity of "here." This means that although different people assign the same latitude and longitude to a place, they do not, in ultimate analysis, attach the same meaning to the figures at which they arrive.

The common world in which we believe ourselves to live is a construction, partly scientific, partly pre-scientific. We perceive tables as circular or rectangular, in spite of the fact that a painter, to reproduce their appearance, has to paint ellipses or non-rectangular quadrilaterals. We see a person as of about the same size whether he is two feet from us or twelve. Until our attention is drawn to the facts, we are quite unconscious of the corrections that experience has led us to make in interpreting sensible appearances. There is a long journey from the child who draws two eyes in a profile to the physicist who talks of electrons and protons, but throughout this journey there is one constant purpose: to eliminate the subjectivity of sensation and substitute a kind of knowledge which can be the same for all percipients. Gradually the difference between what is sensed and what is believed to be objective grows greater; the child's profile with two eyes is still very like what is seen, but the electrons and protons have only a remote resemblance of logical structure. The electrons and protons, however, have the merit that they *may* be what actually exists where there are no sense organs, whereas our immediate visual data, owing to their subjectivity, are almost certainly not what takes place in the physical objects that we are said to see.

The electrons and protons—assuming it scientifically correct to believe in them—do not depend for their existence upon being perceived; on the contrary, there is every reason to believe that they existed for countless ages before there were any percipients in the universe. But although perception is not needed for their existence, it is needed to give us a reason for believing in their existence. Hundreds of thousands of years ago, a vast and remote region emitted incredible numbers of photons, which wandered through the universe in all directions. At last a very few of them hit a photographic plate, in which they caused chemical changes which made parts of the plate look black instead of white when examined by an astronomer. This tiny effect upon a minute but highly educated organism is our only reason for believing in the existence of a nebula comparable in size with the Milky Way. The order for knowledge is the inverse of the causal order. In the order for knowledge, what comes first is the brief subjective experience of the astronomer looking at a pattern of black and white, and what comes last is the nebula, vast, remote, and belonging to the distant past.

In considering the reasons for believing in any empirical statement, we cannot escape from perception with all its personal limitations. How far the information which we obtain from this tainted source can be purified in the filter of scientific method, and emerge resplendently godlike in its impartiality, is a difficult question, with which we shall be much concerned. But there is one thing that is obvious from the start: Only in so far as the initial perceptual datum is trustworthy can there be any reason for accepting the vast cosmic edifice of inference which is based upon it.

I am not suggesting that the initial perceptual datum must be accepted as indubitable; that is by no means the case. There are well-known methods of strengthening or weakening the force of individual testimony; certain methods are used in the law courts, somewhat different ones are used in science. But all depend upon the principle that *some* weight is to be attached to every piece of testimony, for it is only in virtue of this principle that a number of concordant testimonies are held to give a high probability. Individual percepts are the basis of all our knowledge, and no method exists by which we can begin with data which are public to many observers.

Stephen Leacock

Common Sense and the Universe

Stephen Leacock (1869-1944) was for many years a professor of political economy at McGill University in Montreal. Though he wrote extensively on the subject that he taught, he is best known as a humorist.

I

Speaking last December at the annual convention of the American Association for the Advancement of Science, and speaking, as it were, in the name of the great 100-inch telescope under his control, Professor Edwin Hubble, of the Mount Wilson Observatory, California, made the glad announcement that the universe is not expanding. This was good news indeed, if not to the general public who had no reason to suspect that it was expanding, at least to those of us who humbly attempt to "follow science." For some twenty-five years past, indeed ever since the promulgation of this terrific idea in a paper published by Professor W. de Sitter in 1917, we had lived as best we could in an expanding universe, one in which everything, at terrific speed, kept getting farther away from everything else. It suggested to us the disappointed lover in the romance who leaped on his horse and rode madly off in all directions. The idea was majestic in its sheer size, but it somehow gave an uncomfortable sensation.

Yet we had to believe it. Thus, for example, we had it on the authority of Dr. Spencer Jones, the Britist Astronomer Royal, in his new and fascinating book of 1940, *Life on Other Worlds*, that "a distant universe in the constellation of Boötes has been found to be receding with a velocity of 24,300 miles a second. We can infer that this nebula is at a distance of 230,000,000 light-years." I may perhaps remind my fellow followers of science that a light-year means the distance travelled in one year by light, moving at

186,000 miles a second. In other words, this "distant universe" is now 1,049,970,980,000,000,000,000 miles away!

"Some distance!" as Mr. Churchill would say.

But now it appears that that distant universe has *not* been receding at all; in fact, it isn't way out there. Heaven knows where it is. Bring it back. Yet not only did the astronomers assert the expansion, but they proved it from the behaviour of the red band in the spectrum, which blushed a deeper red at the revelation of it, like the conscious water that "saw its God and blushed" at Cana in Galilee long ago. One of the most distinguished and intelligible of our astronomers, Sir Arthur Eddington, had written a book about it, *The Expanding Universe,* to bring it down to our level. Astronomers at large accepted this universal explosion in all directions as calmly as they once accepted the universal fall of gravitation, or the universal death in the cold under Carnot's Second Law of Thermodynamics.

But the relief brought by Professor Hubble is tempered, on reflection, by certain doubts and afterthoughts. It is not that I venture any disbelief or disrespect toward science, for that is as atrocious in our day as disbelief in the Trinity was in the days of Isaac Newton. But we begin to doubt whether science can quite keep on believing in and respecting itself. If we expand today and contract tomorrow; if we undergo all the doubled-up agonies of the curvature of space, only to have the kink called off, as it has been; if we get reconciled to dying a martyr's death at one general, distributed temperature of 459 degrees below zero, the same for all, only to find that the world is perhaps unexpectedly warming up again— then we ask, where are we? To which, of course, Einstein answers, "Nowhere," since there is no place to be. So we must pick up our little book again, follow science, and wait for the next astronomical convention.

Let us take this case of the famous Second Law of Thermodynamics, that inexorable scroll of fate which condemned the universe—or at least all life in it—to die of cold. I look back now with regret to the needless tears I have wasted over that, the generous sympathy for the last little band of survivors, dying at 459 degrees below our zero − 273° centigrade); the absolute zero of cold when the molecules cease to move and heat ends. No stove will light at that, for the wood is as cold as the stove, and the match is as cold as both, and the dead fingers motionless.

I remember meeting this inexorable law for the first time in reading, as a little boy, a piece of "popular science" entitled *Our Great Timepiece Running Down*. It was by Richard Proctor, whose science-bogeys were as terrifying as Mrs. Crow's *Night Thoughts*, only slower in action. The sun, it appeared, was cooling; soon it would be all over. Lord Kelvin presently ratified this. Being Scotch, he didn't mind damnation and he gave the sun and the whole solar system only ninety million years more to live.

This famous law was first clearly enunciated in 1824 by the great French physicist, Nicolas Carnot. It showed that all bodies in the universe kept exchanging their temperature—hot things heated cold, and cold things chilled hot. Thus they pooled their temperature. Like the division of a rich estate among a flock of poor relations, it meant poverty for all. We must all share ultimately the cold of absolute space.

It is true that a gleam of hope came when Ernest Rutherford and others, working on radioactivity, discovered that there might be a contrary process of "stoking up." Atoms exploding into radioactivity would keep the home fires burning in the sun for a long time. This glad news meant that the sun was both much older and much younger than Lord Kelvin had ever thought it was. But even at that it was only a respite. The best they could offer was 1,500,000,000 years. After that we freeze.

And now what do you think! Here comes the new physics of the Quantum Theory and shatters the Second Law of Thermodynamics into gas—a word that is Dutch for chaos. The world may go on forever. All of this because of the final promulgation of the Law of the *Quantum*—or, shall we say, the Law of Just So Much—of which we shall presently speak. These physical people do not handle their Latin with the neat touch of those of us who knew our declensions as they know their dimensions. Of course they mean *Tantum*—but let it go at that. *Quantum* is drugstore Latin, *quantum sufficit*. *Tantum* is the real thing—*Virgilium vidi tantum* ("I saw something of Virgil").

At this point I may perhaps pause to explain that the purpose of this article is not to make fun of science, nor to express disbelief in it, but only to suggest its limits. What I want to say is that when the scientist steps out from recording phenomena and offers a general statement of the nature of what is called "reality," the ultimate nature of space, of time, of the beginning of things, of life, of a universe, then he stands exactly where you and I do, and the three of us stand where Plato did—and long before him Rodin's primitive thinker.

Consider this. Professor Hubble, like Joshua, has called upon the universe to be still. All is quiet. The universe rests, motionless, in the night sky. The mad rush is over. Every star in every galaxy, every island universe, is at least right where it is. But the old difficulty remains: Does it go forever, this world in the sky, or does it stop? Such an alternative has posed itself as a problem for every one of us, somewhere about the age of twelve. We cannot imagine that the stars go on forever. It's unthinkable. But we equally cannot imagine that they come to a stop and that beyond them is nothing, and then more nothing. Unending nothing is as incomprehensible as unending something. This alternative I cannot fathom, nor can Professor Hubble, nor can any one ever hope to.

Let me turn back in order to make my point of view a little clearer. I propose to traverse again the path along which modern science has dragged those who have tried to follow it for about a century past. It was, at first, a path singularly easy to tread, provided that one could throw aside the inherited burden of superstition, false belief, and prejudice. For the direction seemed verified and assured all along by the corroboration of science by actual physical results. Who could doubt electricity after the telegraph? Or doubt the theory of light after photography? Or the theory of electricity after reading under electric light? At every turn, each new advance of science unveiled new power, new mechanism of life—and of death. To "doubt science" was to be like the farmer at the circus who doubted the giraffe. Science, of course, had somehow to tuck into the same bed as Theology, but it was the theologian who protested. Science just said, "Lie over."

Let us follow then this path.

2

When the mediaeval superstition was replaced by the new learning, mathematics, astronomy, and physics were the first

sciences to get organized and definite. By the opening of the nineteenth century they were well set; the solar system was humming
away so drowsily that Laplace was able to assure Napoleon that
he didn't need God to watch over it. Gravitation worked
like clockwork, and clockwork worked like gravitation. Chemistry,
which, like electricity, was nothing but a set of experiments in Benjamin Franklin's time, turned into a science after Lavoisier had discovered that fire was not a thing but a process, something happening to things—an idea so far above the common thought that they
guillotined him for it in 1794. Dalton followed and showed that all
things could be broken up into a set of very, very small atoms,
grouped into molecules all acting according to plan. With Faraday
and Maxwell, electricity, which turned out to be the same as mag-
netism, or interchangeable with it, fell into its place in the new
order of science.

By about 1880 it seemed as if the world of science was fairly
well explained. Metaphysics still talked in its sleep. Theology
still preached sermons. It took issue with much of the new science,
especially with geology and the new evolutionary science of life
that went with the new physical world. But science paid little attention.

For the whole thing was so amazingly simple. There you had
your space and time, two things too obvious to explain. Here you
had your matter, made up of solid little atoms, infinitely small but
really just like birdseed. All this was set going by and with the
Law of Gravitation. Once started, the nebulous world condensed
into suns, the suns threw off planets, the planets cooled, life resulted and presently became conscious, conscious life got higher up
and higher up till you had apes, then Bishop Wilberforce, and then
Professor Huxley.

A few little mysteries remained, such as the question of what
space and matter and time and life and consciousness really were.
But all this was conveniently called by Herbert Spencer the *Unknowable,* and then locked in a cupboard and left there.

Everything was thus reduced to a sort of Dead Certainty. Just
one awkward skeleton remained in the cupboard. And that was the
peculiar, mysterious aspect of electricity, which was not exactly a
thing and yet was more than an idea. There was also, and
electricity only helped to make it worse, the old puzzle about "ac-

tion at a distance." How does gravitation pull all the way from here to the sun? And if there is *nothing* in space, how does light get across from the sun in eight minutes, and even all the way from Sirius in eight years?

Even the invention of "ether" as a sort of universal jelly that could have ripples shaken across it proved a little unconvincing.

Then, just at the turn of the century, the whole structure began to crumble.

The first note of warning that something was going wrong came with the discovery of X-rays. Sir William Crookes, accidentally leaving around tubes of rarefied gas, stumbled on "radiant matter," or "matter in the fourth state," as accidentally as Columbus discovered America. The British Government knighted him at once (1897), but it was too late. The thing had started. Then came Guglielmo Marconi with the revelation of more waves, and universal at that. Light, the world had learned to accept, because we can see it, but this was fun in the dark.

There followed the researches of the radioactivity school and, above all, those of Ernest Rutherford which revolutionized the theory of matter. I knew Rutherford well as we were colleagues at McGill for seven years. I am quite sure that he had no original intention of upsetting the foundations of the universe. Yet that is what he did, and he was in due course very properly raised to the peerage for it.

When Rutherford was done with the atom, all the solidity was pretty well knocked out of it.

Till these researches began, people commonly thought of atoms as something like birdseed—little round, solid particles, ever so little, billions to an inch. They were small. But they were there. You could weigh them. You could apply to them all the laws of Isaac Newton about weight and velocity and mass and gravitation —in other words, the whole of first-year physics.

Let us try to show what Rutherford did to the atom. Imagine to yourself an Irishman whirling a shillelagh around his head with the rapidity and dexterity known only in Tipperary or Donegal. If you come anywhere near, you'll get hit with the shillelagh. Now make it go faster; faster still; get it going so fast that you can't tell which is Irishman and which is shillelagh. The whole combination has turned into a green blur. If you shoot a bullet at it, it will probably go through, as there is mostly nothing there. Yet if you go up against it, it won't hit you now, because the shillelagh is going so fast that you will seem to come against a solid surface. Now make the Irishman smaller and the shillelagh longer. In fact, you don't need the Irishman at all; just his force, his Irish determination, so to speak. Just keep that, the *disturbance*. And you don't need the shillelagh either, just the *field of force* that it sweeps. There! Now put in two Irishmen and two shillelaghs and reduce them in the same way to one solid body—at least it seems solid but you can shoot bullets through it anywhere now. What you have now is a hydrogen atom—one proton and one electron flying around as a *disturbance* in space. Put in more Irishmen and more shillelaghs—or, rather, more protons and electrons—and you get other kinds of atoms. Put in a whole lot—eleven protons, eleven electrons; that is a sodium atom. Bunch the atoms together into combinations called molecules, themselves flying round—and there you are! That's solid matter, and nothing in it at all except disturbance. You're standing on it right now: the molecules are beating against your feet. But there is nothing there, and nothing in your feet. This may help you to understand how "waves," ripples of disturbance—for instance, the disturbance you call radio —go right through all matter, indeed right through *you*, as if you weren't there. You see, you aren't.

The peculiar thing about this atomic theory was that whatever the atoms were, birdseed or disturbance, it made no difference in the way they acted. They followed all the laws of mechanics and motion, or they seemed to. There was no need to change any idea of space or time because of them. Matter was their forte, like wax figures with Artemus Ward.

One must not confuse Rutherford's work on atoms with Einstein's theories of space and time. Rutherford worked all his life without reference to Einstein. Even in his later days at the Cavendish Laboratory at Cambridge when he began, ungratefully, to smash up the atom that had made him, he needed nothing from Einstein. I once asked Rutherford—it was at the height of the popular interest in Einstein in 1923—what he thought of Einstein's relativity. "Oh, that stuff!" he said. "We never bother with that in our work!" His admirable biographer, Professor A. S. Eve, tells us that when the German physicist, Wien, told Rutherford that no

Anglo-Saxon could understand relativity, Rutherford answered, "No, they have too much sense."

But it was Einstein who made the real trouble. He announced in 1905 that there was no such thing as absolute rest. After that there never was. But it was not till just after the Great War that the reading public caught on to Einstein and that little books on "Relativity" covered the bookstalls.

Einstein knocked out space and time, as Rutherford knocked out matter. The general viewpoint of relativity toward space is very simple. Einstein explains that there is no such place as *here*. "But," you answer, "I'm here; here is where I am right now." But you're moving, you're spinning around as the earth spins; and you and the earth are both spinning around the sun, and the sun is rushing through space toward a distant galaxy, and the galaxy itself is beating it away at 26,000 miles a second. Now, where is that spot that is here! How did you mark it? You remember the story of the two idiots who were out fishing, and one said, "We should have marked that place where we got all the fish," and the other said, "I did; I marked it on the boat." Well, that's it. That's *here*.

You can see it better still if you imagine the universe swept absolutely empty: nothing in it, not even *you*. Now put a *point* in it, just one point. Where is it? Why, obviously it's nowhere. If you say it's right there, where do you mean by there? In which direction is there? In *that* direction? Oh! Hold on, you're sticking yourself in to make a direction. It's in *no* direction; there aren't any directions. Now put in another point. Which is which? You can't tell. They *both* are. One is on the right, you say, and one on the left. You keep out of that space! There's no right and no left. Join the points with a line. Now you think you've got something, and I admit this is the nearest you have come to it. But is the line long or short? How long is it? Length soon vanishes into a purely relative term. One thing is longer than another: that's all.

There's no harm in all this, so far. To many people it's as obvious as it is harmless. But that's only the beginning. Leave space alone for a moment and take on time and then things begin to thicken. If there is no such place as here, a similar line of thought will show that there's no such time as now—not absolutely now. Empty the universe again as you did before, with not a speck in it, and now ask, What time is it? God bless me, how peculiar! It isn't any time. It can't be; there's nothing to tell the time by. You say you can feel it go; oh, but you're not there. There will be no *time* until you put something into space with dimensions to it—and then there'll be time, but only as connected somehow—no knowing how —with things in space. But just as there is no such thing as absolute top or bottom in space, so there is a similar difficulty as to time backward and time forward.

The relativity theory undertakes to explain both space and time by putting them together, since they are meaningless without one another, into a compound called "space-time continuum." Time thus becomes, they say, the fourth dimension of space. Until just recently it was claimed further that to fit these relationships together, to harmonize space and time, space must have a curve, or curvature. This was put over to the common mind by comparing what happens in space with what happens to a fly walking on a sphere (a globe). The fly walks and walks and never gets to the end. It's curved. The joke is on the fly. So was the joke long ago on the mediaeval people who thought the world was flat. "What happened to the theory of the earth," writes Eddington, "has happened also to the world of space and time."

The idea was made plainer for us by comparing space-time to an onion skin, or rather to an infinite number of onion skins. If you have enough, you can fill all space. The universe is your onion, as it was Shakespeare's oyster.

The discovery by Einstein of this curvature of space was greeted by the physicists with the burst of applause that greets a winning home run at baseball. That brilliant writer just mentioned, Sir Arthur Eddington, who can handle space and time with the imagery of a poet, and even infiltrate humour into gravitation—as when he says that a man in an elevator falling twenty stories has an ideal opportunity to study gravitation—is loud in his acclaim. Without this curve, it appears, things won't fit into their place. The fly on the globe, as long as he thinks it flat (like Mercator's map), finds things shifted, as by some unaccountable demon, to all sorts of wrong distances. Once he gets the idea of a sphere, everything comes straight. So with our space. The mystery of gravitation puzzles us, except those who have the luck to fall in an elevator, and even for them knowledge comes too late. They weren't falling at all: just curving. "Admit a curvature of the world," wrote Ed-

dington in his Gifford Lectures of 1927, "and the mysterious
agency disappears. Einstein has exorcised this demon."

But it appears now, fourteen years later, that Einstein doesn't
care if space is curved or not. He can take it either way. A prominent physicist of today, head of the department in one of the greatest universities of the world, wrote me on this point: "Einstein had
stronger hopes that a general theory which involved the assumption of a property of space, akin to what is ordinarily called
curvature, would be more useful than he now believes to be the
case." Plain talk for a professor. Most people just say Einstein has
given up curved space. It's as if Sir Isaac Newton years after had
said, with a yawn, "Oh, about that apple—perhaps it wasn't falling."

Now with the curve knocked out of it, the space-time continuum, with these so-called four dimensions, becomes really a
very simple matter; in fact, only a very pretentious name for a
very obvious fact. It just means that information about an occurrence is not complete unless we know both where it happened and
when it happened. It is no use telling me that Diogenes is dead if
I didn't know that he was alive.

Obviously "time-when" or "place-where" are bound together
and coexist with one another. If there were no space—just empti-
ness—there could be no time. It wouldn't count itself. And if there
were no time, there could be no space. Start it and it would flicker
out again in no time—like an electric bulb on a wobble-plug. Space-
time continuum is just a pretentious name for this consequence of
consciousness. We can't get behind it. We begin life with it, as the
chicken out of the egg begins with its cell memory. All the mathematics based on "space-time continuum" get no further, as far as
concerns the search for reality. It gets no further than the child's
arithmetic book that says, "If John walks two miles every day for
ten days," etc., etc. The child hooks space and time with a continuum as easily as the chicken picks up gravel.

3

But, unhappily, we can't get away from the new physics quite
as simply as that. Even if we beat them out on space and time,
there is far worse to come. That's only the start of it, for now, as
the fat boy in *Pickwick* said, "I'm going to make your flesh creep."

The next thing to go is cause and effect. You may think that one thing causes another. It appears that it doesn't. And, of course, when cause and effect go, the bottom is out of the universe, since you can't tell, literally can't, what's going to happen next. This is the consequence of the famous Quantum Theory, first hinted at by Professor Max Planck about forty years ago and since then scrambled for by the physicists like dogs after a bone. It changes so fast that when Sir Arthur Eddington gave the Gifford Lectures referred to, he said to his students that it might not be the same when they met next autumn.

But we cannot understand the full impact of the Quantum Theory in shattering the world we lived in, without turning back again to discuss time in a new relation, namely, the forward-and-backwardness of it, and to connect it up again with the Second Law of Thermodynamics—the law, it will be recalled, that condemns us to die of cold. Only we will now call it by its true name —which we had avoided before—as the Law of Entropy. All physicists sooner or later say, "Let us call it Entropy," just as a man says when you get to know him, "Call me Charlie."

So we make a new start.

I recall, as some other people still may, a thrilling melodrama called *The Silver King.* In this the hero, who thinks he has committed a murder (of course, he hasn't really), falls on his knees and cries, "Oh, God, turn back the universe and give me yesterday." The supposed reaction of the audience was, "Alas, you *can't* turn back the universe!"

But nowadays it would be very different. At the call, the Spirit of Time would appear—not Father Time, who is all wrong, being made old—but a young, radiant spirit in a silver frock made the same back and front. "Look," says the Spirit, "I'm going to turn back the universe. You see this wheel turning around? Presto! It's going the other way. You see this elastic ball falling to the floor? Presto! It's bouncing back. You see out of the window that star moving west? Presto! It's going east. Hence accordingly," continues the Spirit, now speaking like a professor, so that the Silver King looks up in apprehension, "time, as evidenced by any primary motion, is entirely reversible so that we cannot distinguish between future time and past time: indeed, if they move in a circle both are one."

The Silver King leaps up, shouts, "Innocent! Innocent!" and dashes off, thus anticipating Act V and spoiling the whole play. The musing Spirit, musing of course backwards, says, "Poor fellow, I hadn't the heart to tell him that this only applies to primary motion and not to Entropy. And murder, of course, is a plain case of Entropy."

And now let us try to explain. Entropy means the introduction into things that happen of a random element, as opposed to things that happen and "unhappen," like a turning wheel, good either way, or a ball falling and bouncing as high as it falls, or the earth going around the sun. These primary motions are "reversible." As far as they are concerned, time could just as well go backwards as forward. But now introduce the element of random chance. You remember how Humpty Dumpty fell off the wall? All the king's horses and all the king's men couldn't put Humpty together again. Of course not. It was a straight case of Entropy. But now consider a pack of cards fresh from the maker. Are they all in suits, all in order again? They might so arrange themselves, but they won't. Entropy. Take this case. You show a motion picture of a wheel spinning. You run it backwards; it spins the other way. That's time, the time of primary motion, both ways alike. Now show a motion picture of a waiter with a tray of teacups. He drops them; they roll in a hundred fragments. Now run it backwards; you see all the little fragments leap up in the air, join neatly into cups, and rest on the tray. Don't think that the waiter smiles with relief. He doesn't: He can't smile backwards: He just relaxes from horror to calm.

Here then is Entropy, the smashing down of our world by random forces that don't reverse. The heat and cold of Carnot's Second Law are just one case of it. This is the only way by which we can distinguish which of two events came first. It's our only clue as to which way time is going. If procrastination is the thief of time, Entropy is the detective.

The Quantum Theory begins with the idea that the quantities of disturbance in the atom, of which we spoke, are done up, at least they act that way, in little fixed quantities (each a Quantum —no more, no less), as if sugar only existed by the pound. The smallness of the Quantum is beyond comprehension. A Quantum is also peculiar. A Quantum in an atom flies around in an orbit. This orbit may be a smaller ring or a bigger ring. But when the Quantum shifts from orbit to orbit, it does not pass or drift or move *from one to the other*. No, sir. First, it's here and then it's there. Believe it or not, it has just shifted. Its change of place is random, and *not because of anything*. Now the things that we think of as matter and movements and events (things happening) are all based, infinitely far down, on this random dance of Quantums. Hence, since you can't ever tell what a Quantum will do, you can't ever say what will happen next. Cause and effect are all gone.

But as usual in this bright, new world of the new physics, the statement is no sooner made than it is taken back again. There are such a lot of Quantums that we can feel sure that one at least will turn up in the right place—by chance, not by cause.

The only difficulty about the Quantum Theory has been that to make the atomic "orbits" operate properly, and to put the Quantum *into two places at once*, it is necessary to have "more dimensions" in space. If they are not in one, they are in another. You ask next door. What this means I have no idea.

Nor does it tell us any ultimate truth about the real nature of things to keep on making equations about them. Suppose I wish to take a holiday trip and am selecting a place to go. I ask, "How far is it? How long does it take to get there? What does it cost?" These things all come into it. If I like I can call them "dimensions." It does no harm. If I like I can add other dimensions—how hot it is, how much gold it has, and what sort of women. I can say, if I wish, that the women are therefore found out to be the seventh dimension of locality. But I doubt if I can find anything sillier to say than the physicists' talk of ten and twelve dimensions added to space.

Let it be realized, I say, that making equations and functions about a thing does not tell us anything about its real nature. Suppose that I sometimes wonder just what sort of man Chipman, my fellow club member, is. While I am wondering, another fellow member, a mathematician, comes in. "Wondering about Chipman, were you?" he says. "Well, I can tell you all about him as I have computed his dimensions. I have here the statistics of the number of times he comes (t), the number of steps he takes before he sits down (s), his orbit in moving round (o), aberrations as affected by other bodies (ab), velocity (v), specific gravity (sp), and his saturation (S)." He is therefore a function of these things, or shall we say quite simply:

$$F \int \frac{s.v.o.sp.S}{t.ab}$$

Now this would be mathematically useful. With it I can calculate the likelihood of my friend's being at the Club at any particular time, and whether available for billiards. In other words, I've got him in what is called a "frame" in space-time. But just as all this tells me nothing of ultimate reality, neither do the super-dimensions of the new physics.

People who know nothing about the subject, or just less than I do, will tell you that science and philosophy and theology have nowadays all come together. So they have, in a sense. But the statement, like those above, is just a "statistical" one. They have come together as three people may come together in a picture theater, or three people happen to take apartments in the same building, or, to apply the simile that really fits, as three people come together at a funeral. The funeral is that of Dead Certainty. The interment is over, and the three turn away together.

"Incomprehensible," murmurs Theology reverently.

"What was that word?" asks Science.

"Incomprehensible; I often use it in my litanies."

"Ah, yes," murmurs Science, with almost equal reverence, "incomprehensible!"

"The comprehensibility of comprehension," begins Philosophy, staring straight in front of him.

"Poor fellow," says Theology, "he's wandering again; better lead him home."

"I haven't the least idea where he lives," says Science.

"Just below me," says Theology. "We're both above you."

V

Henry David Thoreau

The Battle of the Ants

Thoreau (1817-1862) is best known as the author of Walden, *a highly personal work, in which the author's idealism is constantly subjected to his scepticism.*

It is remarkable how many creatures live wild and free though secret in the woods, and still sustain themselves in the neighborhood of towns, suspected by hunters only. How retired the otter manages to live here! He grows to be four feet long, as big as a small boy, perhaps without any human being getting a glimpse of him. I formerly saw the raccoon in the woods behind where my house is built, and probably still heard their whinnering at night. Commonly I rested an hour or two in the shade at noon, after planting, and ate my lunch, and read a little by a spring which was the source of a swamp and of a brook, oozing from under Brister's Hill, half a mile from my field. The approach to this was through a succession of descending grassy hollows, full of young pitch-pines, into a larger wood about the swamp. There, in a very secluded and shaded spot, under a spreading white-pine, there was yet a clean firm sward to sit on. I had dug out the spring and made a well of clear gray water, where I could dip up a pailful without roiling it, and thither I went for this purpose almost every day in midsummer, when the pond was warmest. Thither too the woodcock led her brood, to probe the mud for worms, flying but a foot above them down the bank, while they ran in a troop beneath; but at last, spying me, she would leave her young and circle round and round me, nearer and nearer till within four or five feet, pretending broken wings and legs, to attract my attention, and get off her young, who would already have taken up their march, with

From *Walden, or Life in the Woods,* 1854.

faint wiry peep, single file through the swamp, as she directed. Or I heard the peep of the young when I could not see the parent bird. There too the turtle-doves sat over the spring, or fluttered from bough to bough of the soft white-pines over my head; or the red squirrel, coursing down the nearest bough, was particularly familiar and inquisitive. You only need sit still long enough in some attractive spot in the woods that all its inhabitants may exhibit themselves to you by turns.

I was witness to events of a less peaceful character. One day when I went out to my wood-pile, or rather my pile of stumps, I observed two large ants, the one red, the other much larger, nearly half an inch long, and black, fiercely contending with one another. Having once got hold they never let go, but struggled and wrestled and rolled on the chips incessantly. Looking farther, I was surprised to find that the chips were covered with such combatants, that it was not a *duellum*, but a *bellum*, a war between two races of ants, the red always pitted against the black, and frequently two red ones to one black. The legions of these Myrmidons covered all the hills and vales in my woodyard, and the ground was already strewn with the dead and dying, both red and black. It was the only battle which I have ever witnessed, the only battlefield I ever trod while the battle was raging; internecine war; the red republicans on the one hand, and the black imperialists on the other. On every side they were engaged in deadly combat, yet without any noise that I could hear, and human soldiers never fought so resolutely. I watched a couple that were fast locked in each other's embraces, in a little sunny valley amid the chips, now at noon-day prepared to fight till the sun went down, or life went out. The smaller red champion had fastened himself like a vice to his adversary's front, and through all the tumblings on that field never for an instant ceased to gnaw at one of his feelers near the root, having already caused the other to go by the board; while the stronger black one dashed him from side to side, and, as I saw on looking nearer, had already divested him of several of his members. They fought with more pertinacity than bulldogs. Neither manifested the least disposition to retreat. It was evident that their battle-cry was "Conquer or die." In the meanwhile there came along a single red ant on the hill-side of this valley, evidently

full of excitement, who either had despatched his foe, or had not
yet taken part in the battle; probably the latter, for he had lost
none of his limbs; whose mother had charged him to return with
his shield or upon it. Or perchance he was some Achilles, who had
nourished his wrath apart, and had now come to avenge or rescue
his Patroclus. He saw this unequal combat from afar,—for the
blacks were nearly twice the size of the red,—he drew near with
rapid pace till he stood on his guard within half an inch of the
combatants; then, watching his opportunity, he sprang upon the
black warrior, and commenced his operations near the root of his
right fore-leg, leaving the foe to select among his own members;
and so there were three united for life, as if a new kind of attraction had been invented which put all other locks and cements to
shame. I should not have wondered by this time to find that they
had their respective musical bands stationed on some eminent
chip, and playing their national airs the while, to excite the slow
and cheer the dying combatants. I was myself excited somewhat
even as if they had been men. The more you think of it, the less
the difference. And certainly there is not the fight recorded in
Concord history, at least, if in the history of America, that will
bear a moment's comparison with this, whether for the numbers
engaged in it, or for the patriotism and heroism displayed. For
numbers and for carnage it was an Austerlitz or Dresden. Concord
Fight! Two killed on the patriots' side, and Luther Blanchard
wounded! Why here every ant was a Buttrick,—"Fire! for God's
sake fire!"—and thousands shared the fate of Davis and Hosmer.
There was not one hireling there. I have no doubt that it was a
principle they fought for, as much as our ancestors, and not to
avoid a three-penny tax on their tea; and the results of this battle
will be as important and memorable to those whom it concerns as
those of the battle of Bunker Hill, at least.

I took up the chip on which the three I have particularly
described were struggling, carried it into my house, and placed it
under a tumbler on my window-sill, in order to see the issue.
Holding a microscope to the first-mentioned red ant, I saw that,
though he was assiduously gnawing at the near fore-leg of his
enemy, having severed his remaining feeler, his own breast was all
torn away, exposing what vitals he had there to the jaws of the

black warrior, whose breast-plate was apparently too thick for him to pierce; and the dark carbuncles of the sufferer's eyes shone with ferocity such as war only could excite. They struggled half an hour longer under the tumbler, and when I looked again the black soldier had severed the heads of his foes from their bodies, and the still living heads were hanging on either side of him like ghastly trophies at his saddle-bow, still apparently as firmly fastened as ever, and he was endeavoring with feeble struggles, being without feelers and with only the remnant of a leg, and I know not how many other wounds, to divest himself of them; which at length, after half an hour more, he accomplished. I raised the glass, and he went off over the window-sill in that crippled state. Whether he finally survived that combat, and spent the remainder of his days in some Hotel des Invalides, I do not know; but I thought that his industry would not be worth much thereafter. I never learned which party was victorious nor the cause of the war; but I felt for the rest of that day as if I had had my feelings excited and harrowed by witnessing the struggle, the ferocity and carnage, of a human battle before my door.

Kirby and Spence tell us that the battles of ants have long been celebrated and the date of them recorded, though they say that Huber is the only modern author who appears to have witnessed them. "Aeneas Sylvius," say they, "after giving a very circumstantial account of one contested with great obstinacy by a great and small species on the trunk of a pear tree," adds that " 'This action was fought in the pontificate of Eugenius the Fourth, in the presence of Nicholas Pistoriensis, an eminent lawyer, who related the whole history of the battle with the greatest fidelity.' A similar engagement between great and small ants is recorded by Olaus Magnus, in which the small ones, being victorious, are said to have buried the bodies of their own soldiers, but left those of their giant enemies a prey to the birds. This event happened previous to the expulsion of the tyrant Christiern the Second from Sweden." The battle which I witnessed took place in the Presidency of Polk, five years before the passage of Webster's Fugitive-Slave Bill.

Theodore Christian Schneirla and Gerard Piel

The Army Ant

T. C. Schneirla (1902-   ) is curator of the Department of Animal Behavior in the American Museum of Natural History in New York City and visiting professor in animal psychology at New York University. He has extensively studied the ways of the army ant on Barro Colorado Island, Panama Canal Zone. Gerard Piel (1915-   ) has been editor and publisher of The Scientific American *since 1947. This essay was first published in the* Scientific American, *June, 1948.*

> Wherever they pass, all the rest of the animal world is thrown into a state of alarm. They stream along the ground and climb to the summit of all the lower trees searching every leaf to its apex. Where booty is plentiful, they concentrate all their forces upon it, the dense phalanx of shining and quickly moving bodies, as it spreads over the surface, looking like a flood of dark-red liquid. All soft-bodied and inactive insects fall an easy prey to them, and they tear their victims in pieces for facility in carriage. Then, gathering together again in marching order, onward they move, the margins of the phalanx spread out at times like a cloud of skirmishers from the flanks of an army.

That is how Henry Walter Bates, a Victorian naturalist, described the characteristic field maneuvers of a tribe of army ants. His language is charged with martial metaphor, but it presents with restraint a spectacle which other eyewitnesses have compared to the predatory expeditions of Genghis Khan and Attila the Hun.

Army ants abound in the tropical rain forests of Hispanic America, Africa and Asia. They are classified taxonomically into more than 200 species and distinguished as a group chiefly by their peculiar mode of operation. Organized in colonies 100,000 to 150,000 strong, they live off their environment by systematic plun-

From *Scientific American*, June, 1948, and *Scientific American Reader*, 1952-1953. Reprinted by permission of the authors and the publisher, *Scientific American*.

der and pillage. They are true nomads, having no fixed abode. Their nest is a seething cylindrical cluster of themselves, ant hooked to ant, with queen and brood sequestered in a labyrinth of corridors and chambers within the ant mass. From these bivouacs they stream forth at dawn in tightly organized columns and swarms to raid the surrounding terrain. Their columns often advance as much as 35 meters an hour and may finally reach out 300 meters or more in an unbroken stream. For days at a time, they may keep their bivouacs fixed in a hollow tree or some other equally protected shelter. Then, for a restless period, they move on with every dusk. They swarm forth in a solemn, plodding procession, each ant holding to its place in line, its forward-directed antennae beating a hypnotic rhythm. At the rear come throngs of larvae-carriers and, at the very last, the big, wingless queen, buried under a melee of frenzied workers. Late at night they hang their new bivouac under a low branch or vine.

The army ant, observers are agreed, presents the most complex instance of organized mass behavior occurring regularly outside the homesite in any insect or, for that matter, in any subhuman animal. As such, it offers the student of animal psychology a subject rich in interest for itself. But it also provides an opportunity for original attack on some basic problems of psychology in general. The study here reported, covering the behavior of two of the Eciton species of army ants, was conducted by Schneirla over a 20-year period with extended field trips to the Biological Reservation on Barro Colorado Island in the Panama Canal Zone and to other ant haunts in Central America. In undertaking it, he had certain questions in mind. The central question, of course, was how such an essentially primitive creature as the ant manages such a highly organized and complex social existence. This bears on the more general consideration of organized group behavior as an adaptive device in natural selection. There was, finally, the neglected question of the nature of social organization. This is primarily a psychological problem because it concerns the contribution of individual behavior and relationships between individuals to the pattern of the group as a whole. It was expected that reliable data on these questions in the instance of the army ant might throw light on similar question about human societies.

The ant commends itself to study by man. Measured by the

dispassionate standard of survival, it stands as one of the most successful of nature's inventions. It is the most numerous of all land animals both in number of individuals and number of species (more than 3,500 at present count). It has occupied the whole surface of the globe between the margins of eternal frost.

The oldest of living families, the ant dates back more than 65 million years to the early Jurassic period. More significant, the societies of ants probably evolved to their present state of perfection no less than 50 million years ago. Man, by contrast, is a dubious experiment in evolution that has barely got under way.

Lord Avebury, a British myrmecologist, marveled at "the habits of ants, their large communities and elaborate habitations, their roadways, possession of domestic animals and, even, in some cases, of slaves!" He might have added that ants also cultivate agricultural crops and carry parasols. It is the social institutions of ants, however, that engender the greatest astonishment. The sight of an army ant bivouac put the British naturalist Thomas Belt in mind of Sir Thomas More's *Utopia*. The Swiss naturalist Auguste Forel urged the League of Nations to adopt the ant polity as the model for the world community.

The marvels of ant life have led some thinkers into giddy speculation on the nature of ant intelligence. Few have put themselves so quaintly on record as Lord Avebury, who declared: "The mental powers of ants differ from those of men not so much in kind as in degree." He ranked them ahead of the anthropoid apes. Maeterlinck was more cautious: "After all, we have not been present at the deliberations of the workers and we know hardly anything of what happens in the depths of the formicary." Others have categorically explained ant behavior as if the creatures could reason, exchange information, take purposeful action, and feel tender emotion.

Obviously anthropomorphism can explain little about ants, and it has largely disappeared from the current serious literature about ant behavior. Its place has been taken, however, by errors of a more sophisticated sort. One such is the concept of the "superorganism." This derives from a notion entertained by Plato and Aquinas that a social organization exhibits the attributes of a superior type of individual. Extended by certain modern biologists, the concept assumes that the biological organism, a society of cells, is the model for social organizations, whether ant or human. Plausible analogies are drawn between organisms and societies: division of function, internal communication, rhythmic periodicity of life processes, and the common cycle of birth, growth, senescence, and death. Pursuit of these analogies, according to the protagonists of the superorganism, will disclose that the same forces of natural selection have shaped the evolution of both organism and superorganism, and that the same fundamental laws govern their present existence.

This is a thoroughly attractive idea, but it possesses a weakness common to all Platonistic thinking. It erects a vague concept, "organism" or "organization," as an ultimate reality which defies explanation. The danger inherent in this arbitrary procedure is the bias it encourages in the investigator's approach to his problem. The social scientist must impose on his work the same rules of repetition, systematic variation, and control that prevail in the experimental sciences. Wherever possible he should subject his observations to experimental tests in the field and laboratory. In the area we are discussing this kind of work may at times seem more like a study of ants than an investigation of problems. But it yields dependable data.

The individual ant is not equipped for mammalian types of learning. By comparison with the sensitive perceptions of a human being, it is deaf and blind. Its hearing consists primarily in the perception of vibrations physically transmitted to it through the ground. In most species, its vision is limited to the discrimination of light and shadow. These deficiencies are partially compensated by the chemotactual perceptions of the ant, centered in its flitting antennae. Chiefly by means of its antennae, the army ant tells friend from foe, locates its booty, and, thanks to its habit of blazing its trail with organic products such as droplets from its anal gland, finds its way home to the nest. In any case, the ant has little need of learning when it crawls out of the cocoon. By far the greater part of its behavior pattern is already written in its genes.

How the essentially uncomplicated repertory of the individual ant contrives, when ants act in concert, to yield the exceedingly complex behavior of the tribe is one of the most intricate paradoxes in nature. This riddle has been fruitfully explored during the past generation under the guidance of the concept of "trophallaxis," originated by the late William Morton Wheeler of Harvard University, who ranks as the greatest of U. S. myrmecologists. Trophallaxis (from the Greek *trophe*, meaning food, and *allaxis*, exchange) is based upon the familiar observation that ants live in biological thrall to their nestmates. Their powerful mutual attraction can be seen in the constant turning of one ant toward another, the endless antennal caresses, the licking and nuzzling. In these exchanges they can be seen trading intimate substances— regurgitated food and glandular secretions. Most ants are dependent for their lives upon this biosocial intercourse with their fellows. There is strong evidence that an interchange of co-enzymes among larvae, workers, and queen is necessary to the survival of all three. Army ant queens unfailingly sicken and die after a few days of isolation.

The well-established concept of trophallaxis naturally suggests that clues to the complex behavior of the ant armies should be sought in the relationships among individuals within the tribe. Most investigators have looked elsewhere, with invariably mistaken results. In attempting to explain, for example, why an ant army alternates between periods of fixed bivouac and nomadic wandering, a half-dozen reputable scientists have jumped to the simplest and most disarmingly logical conclusion: food supply. The ants, they declared, stay in one place until they exhaust the local larder and then move on to new hunting grounds. Schneirla has shown, however, that the true explanation is quite different.

The migratory habits of the ant armies follow a rhythmically punctual cycle. The *Eciton hamatum* species, for example, wanders nomadically for a period of 17 days, then spends 19 or 20 days in fixed bivouac. This cycle coincides precisely with the reproductive cycle of the tribe. The army goes into bivouac when the larvae, hatched from the last clutch of eggs, spin their cocoons, and, now quiescent, approach the pupal stage. At the end of the first week in permanent camp, the queen, whose abdomen has swollen to more than five times its normal volume, begins a stupendous five- to seven-day labor and delivers the 20,000 to 30,000 eggs of the next generation. The daily foraging raids, which meanwhile have dwindled to a minimum, pick up again as the eggs hatch into a great mass of larvae. Then, on about the 20th day, the cocoons yield a new complement of callow workers, and the army sets off once more on its evening marches.

In determining this pattern of events Schneirla logged a dozen ant armies through one or more complete cycles, and upwards of 100 through partial cycles. Observations were set down in shorthand in the field. In the course of the last field trip, from February to July, 1953, broods of more than 80 colonies were sampled, most of them repeatedly at intervals of a few days.

A sentimentalist presented with this new picture of the army ant's domestic habits will perhaps decide that the ants stay in fixed bivouac to protect the queen and her helpless young through the time when they are most vulnerable. Doubtless this is the adaptive significance of the process. But the motivation which carries 100,000 to 150,000 individual ants through this precisely timed cycle of group behavior is not familial love and duty but the trophallactic relationship among the members of the tribe. A cocooned and slumberous pupa, for example, exerts a quieting influence upon the worker that clutches it in its mandible—somewhat as a thumb in the mouth pacifies an infant. But as it approaches maturity and quickens within its cocoon, the pupa produces precisely the reverse effect. Its stirring and twitching excite the workers to pick up the cocoon and snatch it from one another. As an incidental result, this manhandling effects the delivery of the cocoon's occupant.

The stimulus of the emerging brood is evident in a rising crescendo of excitement that seizes the whole community. Raiding operations increase in tempo as the hyperactive, newly delivered workers swarm out into the marching columns. After a day or two, the colony stages an exceptionally vigorous raid which ends in a night march. The bivouac site is left littered with empty cocoons. Later in the nomadic phase, as the stimulus of the callow workers wanes, the larvae of the next generation become the source of colony "drive." Fat and squirming, as big as an average worker, they establish an active trophallactic relationship with the rest of the tribe. Workers constantly stroke them with their antennae, lick them with their mouth parts, and carry them bodily from place to place. Since the larvae at this stage are usually well distributed throughout the corridors and the chambers of the overnight bivouac, their stimulus reaches directly a large number of the workers. This is reflected in the sustained vigor of the daily raids, which continue until the larvae spin their cocoons.

These observations are supported by a variety of experimental findings in the field and laboratory. The role of the callow workers in initiating the movement to break bivouac was confirmed by depriving a number of colonies of their callow broods. Invariably, the raiding operations of the colony failed to recover from the lethargic state that is characteristic of the statary phases. Some tribes even extended their stay in fixed bivouac until the larvae grew large and active enough to excite the necessary pitch of activity. To test the role of the larval brood, captured tribes were divided into part-colonies of comparable size. The group with larvae showed much greater activity than those that had no larvae or that had cocoons in the early pupal state.

The interrelationships among members of the colony thus provide a complete explanation for the behavior cycle of the army ant. It should be observed, in conclusion, that the whole complex process is carried out by individuals which do not themselves originate the basic motivations of their behavior.

Long before the intricacies of its domestic existence were suspected, the army ant's reputation as a social animal was firmly established by its martial conduct in external affairs. It does not require an overactive imagination to perceive the classic doctrines of offensive warfare in the action of an ant army in the field. The swarm carries through the maneuvers of wheeling, flanking and envelopment with a ruthless precision. But to find its motivations and explain its mechanics, one must consult the ant, not von Clausewitz.

Army ant raids fall into one of two major patterns. They are organized either in dense swarms which form at the head of the column or in a delicate tracery of capillary columns branching out at the forward end of the main raiding column. Both types of raiding are found in subgenera of each of the common species of Central American army ant. Two species of Eciton (*Eciton*) were selected for this study because they lead their life almost altogether on or above the forest floor and are thus accessible to continuous observation. Whether the army ants raid in swarm or column, however, the essential mechanics of their behavior are substantially the same.

The bivouac awakes in the early dawn. The stir of activity begins when the light (as measured by photometer) reaches .05 foot-candles, and it mounts steadily as the light increases. In strands and clusters, the workers tumble out of the bivouac into a churning throng on the ground. A crowding pressure builds up within this throng until, channeled by the path of least resistance, a raiding column suddenly bursts forth. The ants in the column are oriented rigidly along the line of travel blazed by the chemical trail of the leaders. The minims and medium-sized workers move in tight files in the center. The "workers major," displaced by the unstable footing afforded by the backs of their smaller fellows, travel along each side. This arrangement no doubt lends suggestive support to the major's legendary role of command. It has an adaptive significance in that it places the biggest and most formidable of the workers on the flanks. Unless disturbed, however, the majors hug the column as slavishly as the rest. The critical role of the tribal chemical in creating this drill sergeant's picture of order may be demonstrated by a simple field experiment. Removal of the chemically saturated litter from the trail brings the column to an abrupt halt. A traffic jam of ants piles up on the bivouac side of the break and is not relieved until enough ants have been pushed forward to re-establish the chemical trail.

Appearances are less ordered at the front of the column, where the "scouts" and "skirmishers" are most frequently observed. The timid individual behavior of the forward ants scarcely justifies such titles. The Eciton is a far from enterprising forager. It never ventures more than a few inches into the chemically-free area ahead. Even this modest pioneering is stimulated principally by physical impact from the rear. At the end of its brief sally, the Eciton rebounds quickly into the column. It is here that the critical difference between column and swarm raiding arises. The column-raiding ants are somewhat freer in their pioneering behavior and so open new pathways more readily. In the swarm raiders the comparatively reluctant progress of the forward elements creates a counterpressure against the progress of the column. This forces the head of the column into a broad elliptical swarm which arrays itself at right angles to the line of march. With ants pouring in from behind, the swarm grows steadily in size as it moves forward, often achieving a width of more than 15 meters.

The path of an ant army, whether in swarms or columns, shows no evidence of leadership. On the contrary, each individual makes substantially the same contribution to the group behavior pattern. The army's course is directed by such wholly chance factors as the stimulus of booty and the character of the terrain. On close inspection, .therefore, it appears that the field operations of ant armies approximate the principles of hydraulics even more closely than those of military tactics. This impression is confirmed by analysis of the flanking maneuver as executed by the swarm raiders. A shimmering pattern of whirls, eddies, and momentarily milling vortices of ants, the swarm advances with a peculiar rocking motion. First one and then the other end of the elliptical swarm surges forward. This action results in the outflanking of quarry, which is swiftly engulfed in the overriding horde of ants. It arises primarily, however, from an interplay of forces within the swarm. One of these forces is generated by the inrush of ants from the rear. Opposed by the hesitant progress of the swarm, the new arrivals are deflected laterally to the wing which offers least resistance. This wing moves forward in a wheeling motion until pressure from the slow advance of its frontal margins counterbalances the pressure from the rear. Pressure on the opposite wing has meanwhile been relieved by drainage of the ants into the flanking action. The cycle is therewith reversed, and a new flanking action gets under way from the other end. External factors, too, play a role in this cycle. The stimulus of booty will accelerate the advance of a flank. The capture of booty will halt it and bring ants stampeding in for a large-scale mopping-up party. But raiding activity as such is only incidental to the process. Its essential character is determined by the stereotyped behavior of the individual ant with its limited repertory of responses to external stimuli.

The profoundly simple nature of the beast is betrayed by an ironic catastrophe which occasionally overtakes a troop of army ants. It can happen only under certain very special conditions. But, when these are present, army ants are literally fated to organize themselves in a circular column and march themselves to death. Post-mortem evidence of this phenomenon has been found in nature; it may be arranged at will in the laboratory. Schneirla has had the good fortune to observe one such spectacle in nature almost from its inception to the bitter end.

The ants, numbering about 1,000, were discovered at 7:30 A.M. on a broad concrete sidewalk on the grounds of the Barro Colorado laboratories. They had apparently been caught by a cloudburst which washed away all traces of their colony trail. When first observed, most of the ants were gathered in a central cluster, with only a company or two plodding, counterclockwise, in a circle around the periphery. By noon all of the ants had joined the mill, which had now attained the diameter of a phonograph record and was rotating somewhat eccentrically at fair speed. By 10:00 P.M. the mill had divided into two smaller counterclockwise spinning discs. At dawn the next day the scene of action was strewn with dead and dying Ecitons. A scant three dozen survivors were still trekking in a ragged circle. By 7:30, 24 hours after the mill was first observed, the various small myrmicine and dolichoderine ants of the neighborhood were busy carting away the corpses.

This peculiarly Eciton calamity may be described as tragic in the classic meaning of the Greek drama. It arises, like Nemesis, out of the very aspects of the ant's nature which most plainly characterize its otherwise successful behavior. The general mechanics of the mill are fairly obvious. The circular track represents the vector of the individual ant's centrifugal impulse to resume the march and the centripetal force of trophallaxis which binds it to its group. Where no obstructions disturb the geometry of these forces, the organization of a suicide mill is almost inevitable. Fortunately for the army ant, the jungle terrain, with its random layout of roots and vines, leaves and stones, disarrays the symmetry of forces and liberates the ant from its propensity to destroy itself.

The army ant suicide mill provides an excellent occasion for considering the comparative nature of social behavior and organization at the various levels from ants to men. Other animals occasionally give themselves over to analogous types of mass action.

Circular mills are common among schools of herring. Stampeding cattle, sheep jumping fences blindly in column, and other instances of pellmell surging by a horde of animals are familiar phenomena. Experience tells us that men, too, can act as a mob. These analogies are the stock-in-trade of the "herd instinct" schools of sociology and politics.

We are required, however, to look beyond the analogy and study the relationship of the pattern to other factors of individual and group behavior in the same species. In the case of the army ant, the circular column really typifies the animal. Among mammals, such simplified mass behavior occupies a clearly subordinate role. Their group activity patterns are chiefly characterized by great plasticity and capacity to adjust to new situations. This observation applies with special force to the social potentialities of man. When human societies begin to march in circular columns, the cause is to be found in the strait-jacket influence of the man-made social institutions which foster such behavior.

As for "specialization of functions," that is determined in insect societies by specialization in the biological make-up of individuals. Mankind, in contrast, is biologically uniform and homogeneous. Class and caste distinctions among men are drawn on a psychological basis. They break down constantly before the energies and talents of particular individuals.

Finally, the concept of "organization" itself, as it is used by the superorganism theorists, obscures a critical distinction between the societies of ants and men. The social organizations of insects are fixed and transmitted by heredity. But members of each generation of men may, by exercise of the cerebral cortex, increase, change and even displace given aspects of their social heritage. This is a distinction which has high ethical value for men when they are moved to examine the conditions of their existence.

Alan Devoe

Our Enemy, the Cat

Alan Devoe (1909-1955) was an American naturalist who contributed widely to American periodicals on subjects of his special interest. Among other editorial tasks, he served as contributing editor to Audubon Magazine *and as consultant in natural history for* Reader's Digest. *The essay reprinted below first appeared in* The American Mercury.

I

We tie bright ribbons around their necks, and occasionally little tinkling bells, and we affect to think that they are as sweet and vapid as the coy name "kitty" by which we call them would imply. It is a curious illusion. For, purring beside our fireplaces and pattering along our back fences, we have got a wild beast as uncowed and uncorrupted as any under heaven.

It is five millenniums since we snared the wild horse and broke his spirit to our whim, and for centuries beyond counting we have been able to persuade the once-free dog to fawn and cringe and lick our hands. But a man must be singularly blind with vanity to fancy that in the three—ten?—thousand years during which we have harbored cats beneath our roof-trees, we have succeeded in reducing them to any such insipid estate. It is not a "pet" (that most degraded of creatures) that we have got in our house, whatever we may like to think. It is a wild beast; and there adheres to its sleek fur no smallest hint of the odor of humanity.

It would be a salutary thing if those who write our simpering verses and tales about "tabby-sit-by-the-fire" could bring themselves to see her honestly, to look into her life with eyes unblurred by wishful sentiment. It would be a good thing—to start at the beginning—to follow her abroad into the moonlight on one of those raw spring evenings when the first skunk-cabbages are thrusting their veined tips through the melting snow and when the loins of catdom are hot with lust.

The love-play of domestic creatures is mostly a rather comic thing, and loud are the superior guffaws of rustic humans to see the clumsy, fumbling antics that take place in the kennels and the stockpen. But the man had better not laugh who sees cats in their rut. He is looking upon something very like aboriginal passion, untainted by any of the overlaid refinements, suppressions, and modifications that have been acquired by most of mankind's beasts. The mating of cats has neither the bathetic clumsiness of dogs' nor the lumbering ponderousness of cattle's, but—conducted in a lonely secret place, away from human view—is marked by a quick concentrated intensity of lust that lies not far from the borderline of agony. The female, in the tense moment of the prelude, tears with her teeth at her mate's throat, and, as the climax of the creatures' frenzy comes, the lean silky-furred flanks quiver vibrantly as a taut wire. Then quietly, in the spring night, the two beasts go their ways.

It will be usually May before the kittens come; and that episode, too, will take place secretly, in its ancient feline fashion, where no maudlin human eye may see. Great is the pique in many a house when "pussy," with dragging belly and distended dugs, disappears one night—scorning the cushioned maternity-bed that has been prepared for her—and creeps on silent feet to the dankest cranny of the cellar, there in decent aloneness to void her blood and babies. She does not care, any more than a lynx does, or a puma, to be pried upon while she licks the birth-hoods from her squirming progeny and cleans away the membrane with her rough pink tongue.

A kitten is not a pretty thing at birth. For many days it is a wriggling mite of lumpy flesh and sinew, blind and unaware, making soft sucking noises with its wet, toothless mouth, and smelling of milk. Daily, hourly, the rough tongue of the tabby ministers to it in its helplessness, glossing the baby-fur with viscid spittle, licking away the uncontrolled dung, cleaning away the crumbly pellet of dried blood from its pointed ears. By that tenth or fourteenth day when its eyes wholly unseal, blue and weak in their newness, the infant cat is clean to immaculateness, and an inalienable fastidiousness is deep-lodged in its spirit.

It is now—when the kitten makes its first rushes and sallies from its birthplace, and, with extraordinary gymnastics of its chubby body, encounters chair-legs and human feet and other curious phenomena—that it elicits from man those particular expressions of gurgling delight which we reserve for very tiny fluffy creatures who act very comically. But the infant cat has no coy intent to be amusing. If he is comic, it is only because of the incongruity of so demure a look and so wild a heart. For in that furry head of his, grim and ancient urges are already dictating.

Hardly larger than a powder-puff, he crouches on the rug and watches a fleck of lint. His little blue eyes are bright, and presently his haunches tense and tremble. The tiny body shivers in an ague of excitement. He pounces, a little clumsily perhaps, and pinions the fleeting lint-fleck with his paws. In the fractional second of that lunge, the ten small needles of his claws have shot from their sheaths of flesh and muscle. It is a good game; but it is not an idle one. It is the kitten's introduction into the ancient ritual of the kill. Those queer little stiff-legged rushes and prancings are the heritage of an old death-dance, and those jerkings of his hind legs, as he rolls on his back, are the preparation for that day when—in desperate conflict with a bigger beast than himself —he will win the fight by the time-old feline technique of disembowelment. Even now, in his early infancy, he is wholly and inalienably a cat.

While he is still young he has already formulated his attitude toward the human race into whose midst he has been born. It is an attitude not easily described, but compounded of a great pride, a great reserve, a towering integrity. It is even to be fancied that there is something in it of a sort of bleak contempt. Solemnly the cat watches these great hulking two-legged creatures into whose strange tribe he has unaccountably been born—and who are so clumsy, so noisy, so vexing to his quiet spirit—and in his feline heart is neither love nor gratitude. He learns to take the food which they give him, to relish the warmth and the comfort and the caresses which they can offer, but these profferments do not persuade his wild mistrustful heart to surrender itself. He will not sell himself, as a dog will, for a scrap of meat; he will not enter into an allegiance. He is unchangeably and incorruptibly a cat, and he will accommodate himself to the ways and spirit of mankind no more than the stern necessity of his unnatural environment requires.

2

Quietly he dozes by the fire or on a lap, and purrs in his happiness because he loves the heat. But let him choose to move, and if any human hand tries to restrain him for more than a moment he will struggle and unsheath his claws and lash out with a furious hate. Let a whip touch him and he will slink off in a sullen fury, uncowed and outraged and unrepenting. For the things which man gives to him are not so precious or essential that he will trade them for his birth-right, which is the right to be himself—a furred four-footed being of ancient lineage, loving silence and aloneness and the night, and esteeming the smell of rat's blood above any possible human excellence.

He may live for perhaps ten years; occasionally even for twenty. Year after year he drinks the daily milk that is put faithfully before him, dozes in laps whose contours please him, accepts with casual pleasure the rubbing of human fingers under his chin —and withdraws, in every significant hour of his life, as far away from human society as he is able. Far from the house, in a meadow or a woods if he can find one, he crouches immobile for hours, his lithe body flattened concealingly in the grass or ferns, and waits for prey.

With a single pounce he can break a rabbit's spine as though it were a brittle twig. When he has caught a tawny meadow-mouse or a mole, he has, too, the ancient cat-ecstasy of toying and playing with it, letting it die slowly, in a long agony, for his amusement. Sometimes, in a dim remembrance from the remote past of his race, he may bring home his kill; but mostly he returns to the house as neat and demure as when he left, with his chops licked clean of blood.

Immaculate, unobtrusive, deep withdrawn into himself, he passes through the long years of his enforced companionship with humanity. He takes from his masters (how absurd a word it is) however much they may care to give him; of himself he surrenders nothing. However often he be decked with ribbons and cuddled and petted and made much over, his cold pride never grows less, and his grave calm gaze—tinged perhaps with a gentle distaste—is never lighted by adoration. To the end he adores only his own gods, the gods of mating, of hunting, and of the lonely darkness.

One day, often with no forewarning whatever, he is gone from the house and never returns. He has felt the presaging shadow of death, and he goes to meet it in the old unchanging way of the wild—alone. A cat does not want to die with the smell of humanity in his nostrils and the noise of humanity in his delicate peaked ears. Unless death strikes very quickly and suddenly, he creeps away to where it is proper that a proud wild beast should die—not on one of man's rugs or cushions, but in a lonely quiet place, with his muzzle pressed against the cold earth.

Hans Zinsser

Rats and Men

Hans Zinsser (1878-1940) was a bacteriologist who wrote Rats, Lice, and History *(1935), as he said in his preface, in "protest against the American attitude which tends to insist that a specialist should have no interests beyond his chosen field—unless it be golf, fishing, or contract bridge." He argued that "one type of intelligent occupation should, in all but exceptional cases, increase the capacity for comprehension in general; . . . and that art and sciences have much in common and both may profit by mutual appraisal." In his studies of typhus fever he was led to his speculations on the effect of plagues upon civilization and to his interest in the two principal characters in this story: the louse and the rat.*

Long before there could have been any knowledge concerning the dangerous character of rodents as carriers of disease, mankind dreaded and pursued these animals. Sticker has collected a great ·many references to this subject from ancient and mediaeval literature, and has found much evidence in the folklore of mediaeval Europe which points to the vague recognition of some connection between plague and rats. In ancient Palestine, the Jews considered all seven mouse varieties (akbar) unclean, and as unsuited for human nourishment as were pigs. The worshippers of Zoroaster hated water rats, and believed that the killing of rats was a service to God. It is also significant that Apollo Smintheus, the god who was supposed to protect against disease, was also spoken of as the killer of mice, and Saint Gertrude was besought by the bishops of the early Catholic Church to protect against plague and mice. The year 1498, Sticker tells us, was a severe plague year in Germany, and there were so many rats in Frankfurt that an attendant was stationed for several hours each day on a bridge in the town and directed to pay a pfennig for every rat brought in. The attendant cut off the tail of the rat—probably as a primitive method of accounting—and threw the bodies into the river. Heine, according to Sticker, speaks of a tax levied on the Jews of Frankfurt in the fifteenth century, which consisted of the annual delivery of five thousand rat tails. Folklore originating in a number of different parts of Europe during the great plague epidemics mentions cats and dogs, the hereditary enemies of rats and mice, as guardians against the plague.

Most scholars agree that there is no reliable mention of rats —as such—in classical literature. . . . Yet, in view of the probable ancient prevalence of rats in Eastern countries, and the close communications by sea between the Greeks and the Mediterranean coastal cities, as well as the regular grain traffic between Egypt and Rome, it is difficult to credit the complete absence of rats from the European littoral throughout antiquity.

In regard to mice and rats in the Near East, Herodotus tells us of Libya that "in this country there are three kinds of mice. One is called the 'two-legged' mouse; another the 'Zegeris' [a word that means a hill—possibly a sort of prairie dog]; a third, the 'prickly' mouse." Also he recounts that when Sanachrib, King of Arabia and Assyria, marched a great host against Egypt, on the night before the battle "there swarmed upon them mice of the fields, and ate up their quivers and their bows and the handles of their shields" so that, on the next day, they fled. This sounds much more like rats than like the timid field mouse. However, these things are hardly evidence.

It is quite impossible to make a case for the presence of true rats in Europe proper during classical times, much as this would clarify the epidemiological situation. It is conceivable that the manner of transmission of plague and typhus may have undergone modification since the Peloponnesian Wars by changed adaptations to hosts, both insect and rodent. But it would seem much more likely that the zoölogical differentiations between rodents so similar and closely related as mice and rats were inaccurate in ancient records, and that rats may have existed—though undomesticated. This would give us a wider latitude for speculation regarding the nature of epidemics, which, to be sure, were rarely, under the circumstances of ancient life, as widespread or deadly as they became with the later concentrations of population and of urban habits. At any rate, if rats had been present in those times in anything like the numbers in which they are found to-day, we should probably have reliable records. It may well be that the frugality of well-run households, like that of Penelope, gave little encouragement to house rats to become parasitic on man to the extent to which they have since.

All this is conjecture. According to the wisest students of the subject, there is no certain knowledge of rats in Europe, within historic periods, until shortly after the Crusades. In prehistoric days they certainly existed there—but later disappeared. Fossil remains of rats have been found in the Pliocene period of Lombardy (the Mastodon period of Europe) and in the later Pleistocene of Crete. They were present during the glacial period with the lake dwellers, whom they pestered in Mecklenburg and Western Germany. From that time on, there were either few or no rats until thousands of years later.

In regard to the reappearance of rats in Europe, our industrious colleagues, the zoölogists, have gathered an immense amount of information, much of which has been interestingly summarized by Barrett-Hamilton and Hinton in their *History of British Mammals*, and by Donaldson in his *Memoir on the Rat*. Before we proceed to this subject, however, it will be profitable to consider the striking analogy between rats and men. More than any other species of animal, the rat and mouse have become dependent on man, and in so doing they have developed characteristics which are amazingly human.

In the first place, like man, the rat has become practically omnivorous. It eats anything that lets it and—like man—devours its own kind, under stress. It breeds at all seasons and—again like man—it is most amorous in the springtime.[1] It hybridizes easily and, judging by the strained relationship between the black and the brown rat, develops social or racial prejudices against this practice. The sex proportions are like those among us. Inbreeding takes place readily. The males are larger, the females fatter. It adapts itself to all kinds of climates. It makes ferocious war upon its own kind, but has not, as yet, become nationalized. So far, it has still stuck to tribal wars—like man before nations were invented. If it continues to ape man as heretofore, we may, in a few centuries, have French rats eating German ones, or Nazi rats attacking Communist or Jewish rats; however, such a degree of civilization is probably not within the capacities of any mere animal. Also—like man—the rat is individualistic until it needs help. That is, it fights bravely alone against weaker rivals, for food or for love; but it knows how to organize armies and fight in hordes when necessary.

Donaldson, basing his calculations mainly on stages in the development of the nervous system, reckons three years of a rat life as ninety years for man. By this scale, the rat reaches puberty at about sixteen, and arrives at the menopause at the equivalent of forty-five. In following man about all over the earth, the rat has —more than any other living creature except man—been able to adapt itself to any conditions of seasonal changes or climate. . . .

A rat census is obviously impossible. It is quite certain, however, that they breed more rapidly than they are destroyed in

---

[1] On first sight, the fertility of rats would seem far to outstrip that of man; for rats reach adolescence when a little more than half grown, and produce one or two litters a year, averaging from five to ten in number. The difference from man, however, is not so striking if one remembers Donaldson's calculation that one rat year equals thirty years for man, and makes the comparison with human society of former years —in savage communities, or before the humane and sane practice of birth control had begun to weaken the inhibitions of religion in such matters. Many examples not too unlike conditions among rats could be cited— such as, for instance, the story of Samuel Wesley, father of John, which we take from a review by J. C. Minot of Laver's biography of Wesley. Samuel had fourteen children with his good Sukey before 1701, when he left her because she refused to pray for William III as the lawful King of England. On the accession of Queen Anne, he was reconciled and bestowed five more children upon the fortunate woman. The oldest of these pledges of reconciliation was the immortal John Wesley.

many places in the world. We can appraise the rat population only by the numbers that are killed in organized rat campaigns and by the amount of destruction they cause. In about 1860, Shipley tells us, there was a slaughterhouse for horses on Montfaucon, which it was planned to remove farther away from Paris. The carcasses of horses amounted to sometimes thirty-five a day, and were regularly cleaned up completely by rats in the following night. Dusaussois had the idea of trying to find out how many rats were engaged in this gruesome traffic. He set horse-meat bait in enclosures from which the exit of rats could be prevented, and in the course of the first night killed 2650. By the end of a month, he had killed over 16,000. Shipley estimates that there are about forty million rats in England at one time. In 1881 there was a rat plague in certain districts of India. The crops of the preceding two years were below average and a large part of them had been destroyed by rats. Rewards offered for rat destruction led to a killing of over 12,000,000 rats. Shipley estimates that a single rat does about 7s. 6d. worth of damage in a year, which makes a charge of £15,000,000 upon Great Britain and Ireland. It costs about sixty cents to two dollars a year to feed a rat on grain. Every rat on a farm costs about fifty cents a year. Lantz adds to this that hotel managers estimate five dollars a year as a low estimate of the loss inflicted by a rat. He thinks that in the thickly populated parts of the country an estimate of one rat per acre is not excessive, and that in most of our cities there are as many rats as people. He investigated, in 1909, the approximate total damage by rats in the cities of Washington and Baltimore. From the data he obtained, he calculated the annual damage in the two cities as amounting to $400,000 and $700,000 respectively—which, considering the populations, amounted to an average loss of $1.27 a year per person. On the same basis, the urban population of the United States, at that time 28,000,000 people, sustained an annual direct injury of $35,000,000 a year. In Denmark, the estimated rat cost is about $1.20 a person; in Germany, eighty-five cents a person; in France, a little over a dollar. Add to this the inestimable depreciation of property and the costs of protection.

All this has nothing to do with our main subject, but we were started on rats, and it is just as well to give thought to the problem of what rat extermination for sanitary purposes is likely to mean in other respects.

The tremendous speed with which rats swarmed over the continents of the world can be readily understood if one reads the observations of actual rat migrations made in modern times. The seasonal migration of rats from buildings to the open fields takes place with the coming of the warm weather and the growth of vegetation; and a return to shelter follows with the cold weather. Dr. Lantz tells us that in 1903 hordes of rats migrated over several counties in Western Illinois, suddenly appearing when for several years no abnormal numbers had been seen. An eyewitness stated to Lantz that, as he was returning to his home on a moonlight night, he heard a rustling in a near-by field, and saw a great army of rats cross the road in front of him. The army of rats stretched away as far as he could see in the moonlight. This, to be sure, was before the Eighteenth Amendment, but there must have been some fact behind it, since heavy damage was caused by rats in the entire surrounding country of farms and villages in the ensuing winter and summer. On one farm, in the month of April, about 3500 rats were caught in traps. Lantz himself saw a similar migration in the valley of the Kansas River, in 1904; and Lantz, being at that time an officer and gentleman of the United States Agricultural Service, cannot be under the suspicion that is aroused by accounts of armies of rats seen by moonshine. In England a general movement of rats inland from the coast occurs every October, and this migration is connected with the closing of the herring season. During the herring catch, rats swarm all over the coast, attracted by the food supply of herring cleaning; when it is over, they go back to their regular haunts. In South America, Lantz advises us, rat plagues are periodic in Paraná, in Brazil, and occur at intervals of about thirty years. In Chile, the same thing has been observed, at intervals of fifteen to twenty-five years. Studies of these migrations have shown that the rat plagues are associated with the ripening and decay of a dominant species of bamboo in each country. For a year or two, the ripening seed in the forests supplies a favorite food for the rats. They multiply enormously, and eventually, this food supply failing, they go back to the cultivated areas. A famine was caused in 1878 in the state of Paraná by the wholesale destruction of the corn, rice, and mandioca crops by rats. The invasion of Bermuda by rats in 1615, and their sudden disappearance, are as dramatic as the rise and fall of some of the short-lived Indian empires of Central and South America. Black rats appeared in that year, and within the two following ones increased with alarming rapidity. They devoured fruits, plants, and trees to such an extent that a famine resulted, and a law required every man in the islands to keep twelve traps set. Nothing, however, was of any use, until finally the rats disappeared with a suddenness that makes it almost necessary to assume that they died of a pestilence.

As we have indicated in a preceding paragraph, the natural history of the rat is tragically similar to that of man. Offspring of widely divergent evolutionary directions, men and rats reached present stages of physical development within a few hundred thousand years of each other—since remnants of both are found in the fossils of the glacial period.

Some of the more obvious qualities in which rats resemble men—ferocity, omnivorousness, and adaptability to all climates—have been mentioned above. We have also alluded to the irresponsible fecundity with which both species breed at all seasons of the year with a heedlessness of consequences which subjects them to wholesale disaster on the inevitable, occasional failure of the food supply. In this regard, it is only fair to state—in justice to man—that, as far as we can tell, the rat does this of its own free and stupid gluttony, while man has tradition, piety, and the duty of furnishing cannon fodder to contend with, in addition to his lower instincts. But these are, after all, phenomena of human biology, and man cannot be absolved of responsibility for his stupidities because they are the results of wrong-headedness rather than the consequences of pure instinct—certainly not if they result in identical disasters.

Neither rat nor man has achieved social, commercial, or economic stability. This has been, either perfectly or to some extent, achieved by ants and by bees, by some birds, and by some of the fishes in the sea. Man and the rat are merely, so far, the most successful animals of prey. They are utterly destructive of other forms of life. Neither of them is of the slightest earthly use to any other species of living things. Bacteria nourish plants; plants nourish man and beast. Insects, in their well-organized societies, are destructive of one form of living creature, but helpful to another. Most other animals are content to lead peaceful and adjusted lives, rejoicing in vigor, grateful for this gift of living, and doing the minimum of injury to obtain the things they require. Man and the rat are utterly destructive. All that nature offers is taken for their own purposes, plant or beast.

Gradually these two have spread across the earth, keeping pace with each other and unable to destroy each other, though continually hostile. They have wandered from East to West, driven by their physical needs, and—unlike any other species of living things—have made war upon their own kind. The gradual, relentless, progressive extermination of the black rat by the brown has no parallel in nature so close as that of the similar extermination of one race of man by another. Did the Danes conquer England; or the Normans the Saxon-Danes; or the Normans the Sicilian-Mohammedans; or the Moors the Latin-Iberians; or the Franks the Moors; or the Spanish the Aztecs and the Incas; or the Europeans in general the simple aborigines of the world by qualities other than those by which *Mus decumanus* has driven out *Mus rattus?* In both species, the battle has been pitilessly to the strong. And the strong have been pitiless. The physically weak have been driven before the strong—annihilated, or constrained to the slavery of doing without the bounties which were provided for all equally. Isolated colonies of black rats survive, as weaker nations survive until the stronger ones desire the little they still possess.

The rat has an excuse. As far as we know, it does not appear to have developed a soul, or that intangible quality of justice, mercy, and reason that psychic evolution has bestowed upon man. We must not expect too much. It takes a hundred thousand years to alter the protuberances on a bone, the direction of a muscle; much longer than this to develop a lung from a gill, or to atrophy a tail. It is only about twenty-five hundred years since Plato, Buddha, and Confucius; only two thousand years since Christ. In the meantime, we have had Homer and Saint Francis, Copernicus and Galileo; Shakespeare, Pascal, Newton, Goethe,

Bach, and Beethoven, and a great number of lesser men and women of genius who have demonstrated the evolutionary possibilities of the human spirit. If such minds have been rare, and spread thinly over three thousand years, after all, they still represent the sports that indicate the high possibilities of fortunate genetic combinations. And these must inevitably increase if the environment remains at all favorable. If no upward progress in spirit or intelligence seems apparent, let us say, between the best modern minds and that of Aristotle, we must remember that, in terms of evolutionary change, three thousand years are negligible. If, as in the last war and its subsequent imbecilities, mankind returns completely to the rat stage of civilization, this surely shows how very rudimentary an emergence from the Neanderthal our present civilization represents—how easily the thin, spiritual veneer is cracked under any strain that awakens the neolithic beast within. Nevertheless, for perhaps three or five thousand years, the beast has begun to ponder and grope. Isolated achievements have demonstrated of what the mind and spirit are capable when a happy combination of genes occurs under circumstances that permit the favored individual to mature. And the most incomprehensible but hopeful aspect of the matter is the fact that successive generations have always bred an adequate number of individuals sufficiently superior to the brutal mass to keep alive a reverence for these supreme achievements and make them a cumulative heritage. It is more than likely—biologically considered—that by reason of this progressive accumulation of the best that superior specimens of our species have produced, the evolution toward higher things may gain velocity with time, and that in another hundred thousand years the comparison of the race of men with that of rats may be less humiliatingly obvious.

Man and the rat will always be pitted against each other as implacable enemies. And the rat's most potent weapons against mankind have been its perpetual maintenance of the infectious agents of plague and of typhus fever.

James Thurber

The Cat in the Lifeboat

James Thurber (1894-   ), is one of America's best known essayists and cartoonists. Much of his work has appeared in The New Yorker, *with which he has been associated since 1926. The two selections that follow are included in* Further Fables For Our Time *(1956).*

A feline named William got a job as copy cat on a daily paper and was surprised to learn that every other cat on the paper was named Tom, Dick, or Harry. He soon found out that he was the only cat named William in town. The fact of his singularity went to his head, and he began confusing it with distinction. It got so that whenever he saw or heard the name William, he thought it referred to him. His fantasies grew wilder and wilder, and he came to believe that he was the Will of Last Will and Testament, and the Willy of Willy Nilly, and the cat who put the cat in catnip. He finally became convinced that Cadillacs were Catillacs because of him.

William became so lost in his daydreams that he no longer heard the editor of the paper when he shouted "Copy cat!" and he became not only a ne'er-do-well but a ne'er-do-anything. "You're fired," the editor told him one morning when he showed up for dreams.

"God will provide," said William jauntily.

"God has his eye on the sparrow," said the editor.

"So've I," said William smugly.

William went to live with a cat-crazy woman who had nineteen other cats, but they could not stand William's egotism or the tall tales of his mythical exploits, honors, blue ribbons, silver cups, and medals, and so they all left the woman's house and went to live happily in huts and hovels. The cat-crazy woman changed her will and made William her sole heir, which seemed only natural to him, since he believed that all wills were drawn in his favor. "I am eight feet tall," William told her one day, and she smiled and said, "I should say you are, and I am going to take you on a trip around the world and show you off to everybody."

William and his mistress sailed one bitter March day on the S.S. Forlorna, which ran into heavy weather, high seas, and hurricane. At midnight the cargo shifted in the towering seas, the ship listed menacingly, SOS calls were frantically sent out, rockets were fired into the sky, and the officers began running up and down companionways and corridors shouting, "Abandon ship!" And then another shout arose, which seemed only natural to the egotistical cat. It was, his vain ears told him, the loud repetition of "William and children first!" Since William figured no lifeboat would be launched until he was safe and sound, he dressed leisurely, putting on white tie and tails, and then sauntered out on deck. He leaped lightly into a lifeboat that was being lowered, and found himself in the company of a little boy named Johnny Green and another little boy named Tommy Trout, and their mothers, and other children and their mothers. "Toss that cat overboard!" cried the sailor in charge of the lifeboat, and Johnny Green threw him overboard, but Tommy Trout pulled him back in.

"Let *me* have that tomcat," said the sailor, and he took William in his big right hand and threw him, like a long incompleted forward pass, about forty yards from the tossing lifeboat.

When William came to in the icy water, he had gone down for the twenty-fourth time, and had thus lost eight of his lives, so he only had one left. With his remaining life and strength he swam and swam until at last he reached the sullen shore of a sombre island, inhabited by surly tigers, lions, and other great cats. As William lay drenched and panting on the shore, a jaguar and a lynx walked up to him and asked him who he was and where he came from. Alas, William's dreadful experience in the lifeboat and the sea had produced traumatic amnesia, and he could not remember who he was or where he came from. "We'll call him Nobody," said the jaguar. "Nobody from Nowhere," said the lynx. And so William lived among the great cats on the island until he lost his ninth life in a barroom brawl with a young panther who had

asked him what his name was and where he came from and had
got what he considered an uncivil answer. The great cats buried
William in an unmarked grave because, as the jaguar said, "What's
the good of putting up a stone reading 'Here lies Nobody from
Nowhere'?"

*Moral: Oh, why should the spirit of mortal be proud, in this
little voyage from swaddle to shroud?*

James Thurber

The Human Being and the Dinosaur

Ages ago in a wasteland of time and a wilderness of space,
Man, in upper case, and dinosaur, in lower, first came face to face.
They stood like stones for a long while, wary and watchful, taking
each other in. Something told the dinosaur that he beheld before
him the coming glory and terror of the world, and in the still air
of the young planet he seemed to catch the faint smell of his own
inevitable doom.

"Greetings, stupid," said Man. "Behold in me the artfully artic-
ulated architect of the future, the chosen species, the certain sur-
vivor, the indestructible one, the monarch of all you survey, and of
all that everyone else surveys, for that matter. On the other hand,
you are, curiously enough, for all your size, a member of the in-
consequent ephemera. You are one of God's moderately amusing
early experiments, a frail footnote to natural history, a contraption
in a museum for future Man to marvel at, an excellent example of
Jehovah's jejune juvenilia."

The dinosaur sighed with a sound like thunder.

"Perpetuating your species," Man continued, "would be foolish
and futile."

"The missing link is not lost," said the dinosaur sorrowfully.
"It's hiding."

Man paid the doomed dinosaur no mind. "If there were no

From *The New Yorker*, June 9, 1956. Permission the author. © 1956 The
New Yorker Magazine, Inc.

Man it would be necessary to create one," said Man, "for God moves in mysterious but inefficient ways, and He needs help. Man will go on forever, but you will be one with the mammoth and the mastodon, for monstrosity is the behemother of extinction."

"There are worse things than being extinct," said the dinosaur sourly, "and one of them is being you."

Man strutted a little pace and flexed his muscles. "You cannot even commit murder," he said, "for murder requires a mind. You are capable only of dinosaurslaughter. You and your ilk are incapable of devising increasingly effective methods of destroying your own species and, at the same time, increasingly miraculous methods of keeping it extant. You will never live to know the two-party system, the multi-party system, and the one-party system. You will be gone long before I have made this the best of all possible worlds, no matter how possible all other worlds may be. In your highest state of evolution you could not develop the brain cells to prove innocent men guilty even after their acquittal. You are all wrong in the crotch, and in the cranium, and in the cortex. But I have wasted enough time on you. I must use these fingers which God gave me, and now probably wishes He had kept for Himself, to begin writing those noble volumes about Me which will one day run to several hundred billion items, many of them about war, death, conquest, decline, fall, blood, sweat, tears, threats, warnings, boasts, hopelessness, hell, heels, and whores. There will be little enough about you and your ilk and your kith and your kin, for after all, who were you and your ilk and your kith and your kin? Good day and goodbye," said Man in conclusion. "I shall see to it that your species receives a decent burial, with some simple ceremony."

Man, as it turned out, was right. The dinosaur and his ilk and his kith and his kin died not long after, still in lower case, but with a curious smile of satisfaction, or something of the sort, on their ephemeral faces.

Moral: The noblest study of mankind is Man, says Man.

John Burdon Sanderson Haldane

On Being the Right Size

J. B. S. Haldane (1892-   ) is Professor of Genetics at the University of London. His eminence as a scientist is matched by the clarity with which he writes on science for the layman.

The most obvious differences between different animals are differences of size, but for some reason the zoölogists have paid singularly little attention to them. In a large text-book of zoölogy before me I find no indication that the eagle is larger than the sparrow, or the hippopotamus bigger than the hare, though some grudging admissions are made in the case of the mouse and the whale. But yet it is easy to show that a hare could not be as large as a hippopotamus, or a whale as small as a herring. For every type of animal there is a most convenient size, and a large change in size inevitably carries with it a change of form.

Let us take the most obvious of possible cases, and consider a giant man sixty feet high—about the height of Giant Pope and Giant Pagan in the illustrated *Pilgrim's Progress* of my childhood. These monsters were not only ten times as high as Christian, but ten times as wide and ten times as thick, so that their total weight was a thousand times his, or about eighty to ninety tons. Unfortunately, the cross sections of their bones were only a hundred times those of Christian, so that every square inch of giant bone had to support ten times the weight borne by a square inch of human bone. As the human thigh-bone breaks under about ten times the human weight, Pope and Pagan would have broken their thighs every time they took a step. This was doubtless why they were sitting down in the picture I remember. But it lessens one's respect for Christian and Jack the Giant Killer.

To turn to zoölogy, suppose that a gazelle, a graceful little creature with long thin legs, is to become large—it will break its bones unless it does one of two things. It may make its legs short and thick, like the rhinoceros, so that every pound of weight has still about the same area of bone to support it. Or it can compress its body and stretch out its legs obliquely to gain stability like the giraffe. I mention these two beasts because they happen to belong to the same order as the gazelle, and both are quite successful mechanically, being remarkably fast runners.

Gravity, a mere nuisance to Christian, was a terror to Pope, Pagan, and Despair. To the mouse and any smaller animal it presents practically no dangers. You can drop a mouse down a thousand-yard mine shaft and, on arriving at the bottom, it gets a slight shock and walks away, provided that the ground is fairly soft. A rat is killed, a man is broken, a horse splashes. For the resistance presented to movement by the air is proportional to the surface of the moving object. Divide an animal's length, breadth, and height each by ten; its weight is reduced to a thousandth, but its surface only to a hundredth. So the resistance to falling in the case of the small animal is relatively ten times greater than the driving force.

An insect, therefore, is not afraid of gravity; it can fall without danger, and can cling to the ceiling with remarkably little trouble. It can go in for elegant and fantastic forms of support like that of the daddy longlegs. But there is a force which is as formidable to an insect as gravitation to a mammal. This is surface tension. A man coming out of a bath carries with him a film of water of about one fiftieth of an inch in thickness. This weighs roughly a pound. A wet mouse has to carry about its own weight of water. A wet fly has to lift many times its own weight and, as everyone knows, a fly once wetted by water or any other liquid is in a very serious position indeed. An insect going for a drink is in as great danger as a man leaning out over a precipice in search of food. If it once falls into the grip of the surface tension of the water— that is to say, gets wet—it is likely to remain so until it drowns. A few insects, such as water beetles, contrive to be unwettable; the majority keep well away from their drink by means of a long proboscis.

Of course tall land animals have other difficulties. They have to pump their blood to greater heights than a man and, therefore, require a larger blood pressure and tougher blood vessels. A great many men die from burst arteries, especially in the brain, and this danger is presumably still greater for an elephant or a giraffe. But animals of all kinds find difficulties in size for the following reason. A typical small animal, say a microscopic worm or rotifer, has a smooth skin through which all the oxygen it requires can soak in, a straight gut with sufficient surface to absorb its food, and a single kidney. Increase its dimensions tenfold in every direction, and its weight is increased a thousand times, so that if it is to use its muscles as efficiently as its miniature counterpart, it will need a thousand times as much food and oxygen per day and will excrete a thousand times as much of waste products.

Now if its shape is unaltered, its surface will be increased only a hundred-fold, and ten times as much oxygen must enter per minute through each square millimetre of skin, ten times as much food through each square millimetre of intestine. When a limit is reached to their absorptive powers their surface has to be increased by some special device. For example, a part of the skin may be drawn out into tufts to make gills, or pushed in to make lungs, thus increasing the oxygen-absorbing surface in proportion to the animal's bulk. A man, for example, has a hundred square yards of lung. Similarly the gut, instead of being smooth and straight, becomes coiled and develops a velvety surface, and other organs increase in complication. The higher animals are not larger than the lower because they are more complicated. They are more complicated because they are larger. Just the same is true of plants. The simplest plants, such as the green algae growing in stagnant water or on the bark of trees, are mere round cells. The higher plants increase their surface by putting out leaves and roots. Comparative anatomy is largely the story of the struggle to increase surface in proportion to volume.

Some of the methods of increasing the surface are useful up to a point but not capable of a very wide adaptation. For example, while vertebrates carry the oxygen from the gills or lungs all over the body in the blood, insects take air directly to every part of their body by tiny blind tubes called tracheae which open to the surface at many different points. Now, although by their breathing movements they can renew the air in the outer part of the tracheal system, the oxygen has to penetrate the finer branches by means of diffusion. Gases can diffuse easily through very small distances, not many times larger than the average length traveled by a gas molecule between collisions with other molecules. But when such vast journeys—from the point of view of a molecule —as a quarter of an inch have to be made, the process becomes slow. So the portions of an insect's body more than a quarter of an inch from the air would always be short of oxygen. In consequence hardly any insects are much more than half an inch thick. Land crabs are built on the same general plan as insects, but are much clumsier. Yet, like ourselves, they carry oxygen around in their blood, and are therefore able to grow far larger than any insects. If the insects had hit on a plan for driving air through their tissues instead of letting it soak in, they might well have become as large as lobsters, though other considerations would have prevented them from becoming as large as man.

Exactly the same difficulties attach to flying. It is an elementary principle of aeronautics that the minimum speed needed to keep an airplane of a given shape in the air varies as the square root of its length. If its linear dimensions are increased four times, it must fly twice as fast. Now the power needed for the minimum speed increases more rapidly than the weight of the machine. So the larger airplane, which weighs sixty-four times as much as the smaller, needs one hundred and twenty-eight times its horsepower to keep up. Applying the same principles to the birds, we find that the limit to their size is soon reached. An angel whose muscles developed no more power, weight for weight, than those of an eagle or a pigeon would require a breast projecting for about four feet to house the muscles engaged in working its wings, while to economize in weight, its legs would have to be reduced to mere stilts. Actually a large bird such as an eagle or kite does not keep in the air mainly by moving its wings. It is generally to be seen soaring, that is to say balanced on a rising column of air. And even soaring becomes more and more difficult with increasing size. Were this not the case eagles might be as large as tigers and as formidable to man as hostile airplanes.

But it is time that we passed to some of the advantages of size. One of the most obvious is that it enables one to keep warm. All warm-blooded animals at rest lose the same amount of heat from a unit area of skin, for which purpose they need a food supply proportional to their surface and not to their weight. Five thousand mice weigh as much as a man. Their combined surface and food, or oxygen consumption, are about seventeen times a man's. In fact a mouse eats about one quarter of its weight of food every day, which is mainly used in keeping it warm. For the same reason small animals cannot live in cold countries. In the arctic regions there are no reptiles or amphibians, and no small mammals. The smallest mammal in Spitzbergen is the fox. The small birds fly away in the winter, while the insects die, though their eggs can survive six months or more of frost. The most successful mammals are bears, seals, and walruses.

Similarly, the eye is a rather inefficient organ until it reaches a large size. The back of the human eye on which an image of the outside world is thrown, and which corresponds to the film of a camera, is composed of a mosaic of "rods and cones" whose diameter is little more than a length of an average light wave. Each eye has about half a million, and for two objects to be distinguishable their images must fall on separate rods or cones. It is obvious that with fewer but larger rods and cones we should see less distinctly. If they were twice as broad, two points would have to be twice as far apart before we could distinguish them at a given distance. But if their size were diminished and their number increased, we should see no better. For it is impossible to form a definite image smaller than a wave length of light. Hence a mouse's eye is not a small-scale model of a human eye. Its rods and cones are not much smaller than ours, and therefore there are far fewer of them. A mouse could not distinguish one human face from another six feet away. In order that they should be of any use at all, the eyes of small animals have to be much larger in proportion to their bodies than our own. Large animals, on the other hand, only require relatively small eyes, and those of the whale and elephant are little larger than our own.

For rather more recondite reasons the same general principle holds true of the brain. If we compare the brain weights of a set of very similar animals such as the cat, cheetah, leopard, and tiger, we find that as we quadruple the body weight the brain weight is only doubled. The larger animal with proportionately larger bones can economize on brain, eyes, and certain other organs.

Such are a very few of the considerations which show that

for every type of animal there is an optimum size. Yet although Galileo demonstrated the contrary more than three hundred years ago, people still believe that if a flea were as large as a man it could jump a thousand feet into the air. As a matter of fact the height to which an animal can jump is more nearly independent of its size than proportional to it. A flea can jump about two feet, a man about five. To jump a given height, if we neglect the resistance of air, requires an expenditure of energy proportional to the jumper's weight. But if the jumping muscles form a constant fraction of the animal's body, the energy developed per ounce of muscle is independent of the size, provided it can be developed quickly enough in the small animal. As a matter of fact, an insect's muscles, although they can contract more quickly than our own, appear to be less efficient, as otherwise a flea or grasshopper could rise six feet into the air.

And just as there is a best size for every animal, so the same is true for every human institution. In the Greek type of democracy all the citizens could listen to a series of orators and vote directly on questions of legislation. Hence their philosophers held that a small city was the largest possible democratic state. The English invention of representative government made a democratic nation possible, and the possibility was first realized in the United States, and later elsewhere. With the development of broadcasting it has once more become possible for every citizen to listen to the political views of representative orators, and the future may perhaps see the return of the national state to the Greek form of democracy. Even the referendum has been made possible only by the institution of daily newspapers.

To the biologist the problem of socialism appears largely as a problem of size. The extreme socialists desire to run every nation as a single business concern. I do not suppose that Henry Ford would find much difficulty in running Andorra or Luxembourg on a socialistic basis. He has already more men on his pay roll than their population. It is conceivable that a syndicate of Fords, if we could find them, would make Belgium, Ltd., or Denmark, Inc., pay their way. But while nationalization of certain industries is an obvious possibility in the largest of states, I find it no easier to picture a completely socialized British Empire or United States than an elephant turning somersaults or a hippopotamus jumping a hedge.

VI

Joseph Wood Krutch

The Realm of Art

Joseph Wood Krutch (1893-   ) has recently retired as Brander Mathews Professor of Dramatic Literature at Columbia University. For many years he was an associate editor of The Nation. *He has written as a critic of drama and of literature and on many aspects of contemporary civilization.*

Philosophy commonly distinguishes between what we may conveniently call "Experience" and "Nature." In the first of these categories is included the whole realm of human perception; in the second the whole realm of phenomena which occur outside of man; and philosophy is concerned with the traffic which goes on between them.

Though this traffic appears to be both constant and intimate, yet our knowledge of the external world remains purely inferential. Because of the imperfection of our senses and the faultiness of our deductions we are never in perfect or unambiguous contact with anything outside ourselves and we can never hope to form a conception of Nature identical with Nature herself. But neither, on the other hand, can we ever—as dreamers wish—detach ourselves wholly from the influence of this outside world concerning which we know nothing with surety, and that sense of uncertainty inseparable from the process of living arises out of the necessity of dealing with an imperfectly known reality. We grope through a universe filled with looming shapes and we cannot always distinguish those made of shadow from others more substantial. Life is partly a dream, but it is not *merely* a dream because we are constantly awakened out of that dream into which we tend to fall by contacts, often rude enough, with realities independent of our consciousness.

For the purposes of discourse it is usually assumed that man has to do with nothing which is neither Nature nor his Experience with it, but in this essay we shall discuss a third realm which is called the realm of Art. Moreover, though this realm includes far more than the sum of the books which have been written, the pictures which have been painted, and the musical scores which have been composed, we may, by considering them alone, get some idea both of the important part played in our lives by our contact with it and of the characteristics which distinguish it from the realm of Nature.

The latter never ceases to be in some sense alien. Natural objects and natural events being independent of the human will, exist or take place in accordance with laws which we neither fully comprehend nor fully approve. But in the realm of Art everything exists because of the activity of this same will. The realm itself was created out of desire and though it may here and there imitate the forms assumed by Nature it is controllable by its creators who thus mold it as they will and constitute themselves the architects of a universe independent of the universe of Nature. In this one respect it obviously resembles the insubstantial creations of mere reverie, and obviously also it is related to dream; but the thing dreamed becomes Art, properly so called, only when it assumes something like an independent existence, only when it ceases to be valid for the creator alone and becomes, like Nature, capable of being experienced by various individuals for whom a book, a statue, or a picture has become an objective fact—like a natural phenomenon in so far as, existing outside the self, it is capable of being perceived and reacted to; unlike a natural phenomenon in so far as it was created, not by Nature, but by a mind which resembles the spectators' own.

Thus the world of art is a mimic world, superficially resembling the natural one but fundamentally quite different. For even when it seems most literally imitative, even when it is most determinedly realistic, it is conceived in accordance with the laws and the limitations of the human mind. In it the emphasis is the emphasis of an unescapable human prejudice; the very order of events is an order logical according to the system of human logic; and the meaning is a meaning humanly comprehensible instead of being, as the meaning of Nature may very well be, quite beyond the understanding of man, who is only one of Nature's innumerable children. Nor can even the most desperately "naturalistic" art escape from this fact, for it is, at its most literal, nature passed through a human mind, nature probably distorted by desire and nature certainly modified to whatever extent is necessary in order that it may be comprehended by a reason which can operate only within its own limitations. Philosophers may dispute concerning the extent to which the actual universe is a *thinkable* one, but the distinguishing feature of the Universe of Art is just the fact that it is perfectly and readily thinkable—for the very reason that it came into existence by being thought, that it is everywhere molded by the human mind.

Now if the distinguishing features of the realm of Art be those which have just been mentioned, it is evident that the realm is far more extensive than it would seem to be to those who have thought of it as including no more than literature, music, and the plastic arts, for it includes, as a matter of fact, whatever is not found in Nature and yet is treated as real. Even the most ardent disciple of any particular religion must admit that all religions except his own are, by the definition just made, works of art; and the most zealous defender of the absolute validity of any particular code of morals must be the first to affirm that all other codes are, in similar fashion, part of the realm of Art. All philosophies—including the religious and the moral—are Art in the sense that they are interpretations of Nature in terms, if not of human desire, then at least of human logic. They are efforts to substitute for her imperfectly perceived and imperfectly comprehended phenomena a humanly understandable and humanly satisfactory conception of them, just as all stories are an attempt to substitute for events an understandable and satisfactory account of them.

Hence it is obvious that any man living in a civilized society has experiences with Art which affect the course of his life hardly less than do his experiences with Nature. It is not merely that he is exalted by tragedies and stirred by songs. He is also rendered obedient to creeds. In his world the laws of Nature count for little more than do the laws of those various works of art which constitute the social customs, the economic institutions, and the conceptions of justice accepted in his community. A law of his society is to be violated with no greater impunity than a law of Nature. Fire burns and adultery is punished by some specific penalty ordained by his group. Unless the victim is a philosopher he hardly needs to distinguish between the foundations upon which these two facts rest, for Art and Nature have become for him practically indistinguishable. Indeed, he may not unlikely submit himself to the former with less of inward resentment than he feels toward the latter. He may rail against disease or death while accepting the punishment meted out by man, for the very reason that he feels that the logic of law is his logic in a sense that the logic of Nature is not. And this, to be sure, suggests one of the chief distinctions between man and the other animals, since man is the animal who can not only create Art, but live by it as well.

In this essay we shall be concerned chiefly with literature alone, but in passing we must remark that if esthetics is that department of philosophy which deals with man's experience with Art, then various branches of it should be concerned with the study of his relation to the various fictions called law, morality, justice, etc., since they are, quite as clearly as books or pictures, part of the universe he creates rather than part of the universe which is created for him. But even within the narrow field of our speculations the point of view adopted has certain advantages. Thanks to it we see the creative artist inevitably reshaping the world in his very effort to form an image of it and thanks to it also we realize that from the character of his reformations may be deduced the nature of his humanity. . . .

If, then, our terms be broadly understood, our scheme very easily accommodates—not merely the tales of the nursery and not merely a Poe or a Stendhal—but also and at least those poets like Lucretius, Virgil, Dante, and Milton who have so appropriately been described as "philosophical." In the case of them there is obvious (as there is not, for example, in the case of Shakespeare) a consistent intention to interpret the world in terms of a scheme clearly human by virtue of its logical simplicity. And without unduly straining a point it might be said that Lucretius *wanted* to banish the terrors of superstition by reducing life to the level of a mechanical accident, or that Dante *wanted* to construct a cosmology in accord with a conception of justice which had been formed to answer the needs of his particular human temperament. Nor can there be any objection—however incomplete the statement may be—to going the one step further necessary to add that the philosophical poets found the universes they had made more satisfactory to themselves than the universe which was made for them.

As for us, their audience, we enter their world, we experience it for a time, and we share to some extent, at least, their delight in it. Doubtless it is not quite so real for us as it was for them and neither is it so wholly delightful, for the very reason that the desires which it satisfies were in part peculiar to them as well as in part universally human. And yet (at the very least) so great is the inevitable relief when we exchange the confused world of phenomena for one in which everything is part of an understandable pattern, that we feel in the world made for Dante or the world made for Lucretius a certain sense of being at home which we never feel in the world of Nature. We may be very different men from either of them—our experiences, our tastes, and our desires may be poles asunder—but we are, nevertheless, *men*, and to that extent we are far more like them than like that force (whatever it may be) which rules the external universe. At least the categories of our minds are the same and we can understand one another as no mind can ever understand Nature.

Now the very fact that such poets as these explain themselves, the very fact that they state the laws of their universes in explicit terms, has led certain critics to accord them the highest place in the hierarchy of literature and to dismiss as relatively barbarous certain others whose intellectual scheme is less distinctly formulated. Like those eighteenth century commentators who found much "Nature" but little "Art" in Shakespeare, they tend to estimate the importance of a work of literature in accordance with the extent to which it proclaims the principle of its selection and modification and to relegate to the lowest level those poets who are not philosophical.

Yet there is an instinct which rebels against such summary evaluations, an instinct which refuses to accept the demonstration that Shakespeare is merely "Natural" or barbarous. And that instinct is sound for if it is difficult to deduce a philosophy from his works or from those, let us say, of Chaucer, it is obvious that neither works are, for that reason, not Art.

Certainly the world of Hamlet is quite as distinct and quite as easily recognizable as the world of the Divine Comedy, even if it be, as it certainly is, less easy to define. Entering it we feel—quite as conspicuously as in entering the world of Dante—the sense of entering a harmonious universe, of having escaped into a realm where events are not only understandable but somehow consistent one with another. Nothing happens but what, in some obscure way, ought to happen; and there is implied some system of values which does not need to be defined in order that it may be joyfully accepted. In our experiences with Nature we discover that the mood evoked by one incident is generally outraged by the next, but in Hamlet—as in any great work of art—emotional anticipations are always satisfied and each hunger we are led to feel is immediately fed.

It is by facts such as these that the central mystery of Art is suggested, and perhaps the poets like Shakespeare and Chaucer are, not lesser than Lucretius and Dante, but greater, for the very reason that they achieve a subtly ordered universe without recourse to an obvious schematization; for the very reason that their worlds retain a suggestion of the rich variety of Nature while maintaining some sort of harmony which Nature perpetually violates. Certainly it is with them that the critic, as distinguished from either the pure psychologist or the pure philosopher, has to deal, and certainly an esthetic theory must meet its final test in attempting to deal fruitfully with them.

Art, as we have already insisted, is readily thinkable. Thanks to the fact that it has been conceived by a human mind it has been conceived in accordance with the categories of that mind and is interpretable in the terms of its logic. But this same human mind is not merely a thinking machine. It can rarely analyze or reflect without being at the same time compelled to feel, and it is almost as difficult for it to vary the norms of its feeling as to transcend the categories of its understanding. An event may seem to us amusing or pathetic. It may arouse our anger or our pity. But the number of our possible emotions is limited and we feel ill at ease in the presence of any phenomenon which, without leaving us perfectly indifferent, does not evoke any one of the feelings of which we are capable.

The world of Nature is replete with such phenomena. Most

of the events which take place in it are as emotionally unsatisfactory as they are intellectually incomprehensible. They do not seem either directed toward any rational end or calculated to provoke any unified emotion, and we are tempted to conclude that if any power directs them, then that power must be alien to both our feelings and our understanding. But in the world of Art such phenomena do not exist. Since every work of art came into existence by being thought and by being felt every such work is, by consequence, not only readily thinkable but readily feelable as well.

Edward Morgan Forster

Homo Fictus

E. M. Forster (1879-   ), one of the most distinguished English novelists, author of A Passage to India, *wrote the following essay as part of the Clark lectures, delivered at his alma mater, Cambridge University, in 1927.*

Having discussed the story—that simple and fundamental aspect of the novel—we can turn to a more interesting topic: the actors. We need not ask what happened next, but to whom did it happen; the novelist will be appealing to our intelligence and imagination, not merely to our curiosity. A new emphasis enters his voice: emphasis upon value.

Since the actors in a story are usually human, it seemed convenient to entitle this aspect People. Other animals have been introduced, but with limited success, for we know too little so far about their psychology. There may be, probably will be, an alteration here in the future, comparable to the alteration in the novelist's rendering of savages in the past. The gulf that separates Man Friday from Batouala may be paralleled by the gulf that will separate Kipling's wolves from their literary descendants two hundred years hence, and we shall have animals who are neither symbolic, nor little men disguised, nor as four-legged tables moving, nor as painted scraps of paper that fly. It is one of the ways where science may enlarge the novel, by giving it fresh subject matter. But the help has not been given yet, and until it comes we may say that the actors in a story are, or pretend to be, human beings.

Since the novelist is himself a human being, there is an affinity between him and his subject matter which is absent in many other forms of art. The historian is also linked, though, as we shall see, less intimately. The painter and sculptor need not be linked: that is to say they need not represent human beings unless they wish, no more need the poet, while the musician cannot represent them even if he wishes, without the help of a programme. The novelist, unlike many of his colleagues, makes up a number of word-masses roughly describing himself (roughly: niceties shall come later), gives them names and sex, assigns them plausible gestures, and causes them to speak by the use of inverted commas, and perhaps to behave consistently. These word-masses are his characters. They do not come thus coldly to his mind, they may be created in delirious excitement, still, their nature is conditioned by what he guesses about other people, and about himself, and is further modified by the other aspects of his work. This last point—the relation of characters to the other aspects of the novel—will form the subject of a future enquiry. At present we are occupied with their relation to actual life. What is the difference between people in a novel and people like the novelist or like you, or like me, or Queen Victoria?

There is bound to be a difference. If a character in a novel is exactly like Queen Victoria—not rather like but exactly like—then it actually is Queen Victoria, and the novel, or all of it that the character touches, becomes a memoir. A memoir is history, it is based on evidence. A novel is based on evidence + or − x, the unknown quantity being the temperament of the novelist, and the unknown quantity always modifies the effect of the evidence, and sometimes transforms it entirely.

The historian deals with actions, and with the characters of men only so far as he can deduce them from their actions. He is quite as much concerned with character as the novelist, but he can only know of its existence when it shows on the surface. If Queen

Victoria had not said, "We are not amused," her neighbours at table would not have known she was not amused, and her ennui
could never have been announced to the public. She might have
frowned, so that they would have deduced her state from that—
looks and gestures are also historical evidence. But if she remained
impassive—what would any one know? The hidden life is, by definition, hidden. The hidden life that appears in external signs is
hidden no longer, has entered the realm of action. And it is the
function of the novelist to reveal the hidden life at its source: to
tell us more about Queen Victoria than could be known, and thus
to produce a character who is not the Queen Victoria of history.

The interesting and sensitive French critic, who writes under
the name of Alain, has some helpful if slightly fantastic remarks on
this point. He gets a little out of his depth, but not as much as I
feel myself out of mine, and perhaps together we may move toward the shore. Alain examines in turn the various forms of
æsthetic activity, and coming in time to the novel (le roman) he
asserts that each human being has two sides, appropriate to history and fiction. All that is observable in a man—that is to say his
actions and such of his spiritual existence as can be deduced from
his actions—falls into the domain of history. But his romanceful or
romantic side (sa partie romanesque ou romantique) includes "the
pure passions, that is to say the dreams, joys, sorrows and self-
communings which politeness or shame prevent him from mention-
ing"; and to express this side of human nature is one of the chief
functions of the novel. "What is fictitious in a novel is not so much
the story as the method by which thought develops into action, a
method which never occurs in daily life. . . . History, with its
emphasis on external causes, is dominated by the notion of fatality,
whereas there is no fatality in the novel; there, everything is
founded on human nature, and the dominating feeling is of an
existence where everything is intentional, even passions and crimes,
even misery."[1]

This is perhaps a roundabout way of saying what every British
schoolboy knew, that the historian records whereas the novelist
must create. Still, it is a profitable roundabout, for it brings out
the fundamental difference between people in daily life and people

[1] Paraphrased from *Système des Beaux Arts,* pp. 314-315. I am indebted
to M. André Maurois for introducing me to this stimulating essay.

in books. In daily life we never understand each other; neither complete clairvoyance nor complete confessional exists. We know each other approximately, by external signs, and these serve well enough as a basis for society and even for intimacy. But people in a novel can be understood completely by the reader, if the novelist wishes; their inner as well as their outer life can be exposed. And this is why they often seem more definite than characters in history, or even our own friends; we have been told all about them that can be told; even if they are imperfect or unreal they do not contain any secrets, whereas our friends do and must, mutual secrecy being one of the conditions of life upon this globe.

Now let us restate the problem in a more schoolboyish way. You and I are people. Had not we better glance through the main facts in our own lives—not in our individual careers but in our make-up as human beings? Then we shall have something definite to start from.

The main facts in human life are five: birth, food, sleep, love, and death. One could increase the number—add breathing for instance—but these five are the mose obvious. Let us briefly ask ourselves what part they play in our lives, and what in novels. Does the novelist tend to reproduce them accurately or does he tend to exaggerate, minimize, ignore, and to exhibit his characters going through processes which are not the same through which you and I go, though they bear the same names?

To consider the two strangest first: birth and death; strange because they are at the same time experiences and not experiences. We only know of them by report. We were all born, but we cannot remember what it was like. And death is coming even as birth has come, but, similarly, we do not know what it is like. Our final experience, like our first, is conjectural. We move between two darknesses. Certain people pretend to tell us what birth and death are like: a mother, for instance, has her point of view about birth, a doctor, a religious, have their points of view about both. But it is all from the outside, and the two entities who might enlighten us, the baby and the corpse, cannot do so, because their apparatus for communicating their experiences is not attuned to our apparatus for reception.

So let us think of people as starting life with an experience they forget and ending it with one which they anticipate but cannot understand. These are the creatures whom the novelist proposes to introduce as characters into books; these, or creatures plausibly like them. The novelist is allowed to remember and understand everything, if it suits him. He knows all the hidden life. How soon will he pick up his characters after birth, how close to the grave will he follow them? And what will he say, or cause to be felt, about these two queer experiences?

Then food, the stoking up process, the keeping alive of an individual flame, the process that begins before birth and is continued after it by the mother, and finally taken over by the individual himself, who goes on day after day putting an assortment of objects into a hole in his face without becoming surprised or bored: food is a link between the known and the forgotten; closely connected with birth, which none of us remembers, and coming down to this morning's breakfast. Like sleep—which in many ways it resembles—food does not merely restore our strength, it has also an æsthetic side, it can taste good or bad. What will happen to this double-faced commodity in books?

And fourthly, sleep. On the average, about a third of our time is not spent in society or civilization or even in what is usually called solitude. We enter a world of which little is known and which seems to us after leaving it to have been partly oblivion, partly a caricature of this world and partly a revelation. "I dreamt of nothing" or "I dreamt of a ladder" or "I dreamt of heaven" we say when we wake. I do not want to discuss the nature of sleep and dreams—only to point out that they occupy much time and that what is called "History" only busies itself with about two-thirds of the human cycle, and theorizes accordingly. Does fiction take up a similar attitude?

And lastly, love. I am using this celebrated word in its widest and dullest sense. Let me be very dry and brief about sex in the first place. Some years after a human being is born, certain changes occur in it, as in other animals, which changes often lead to union with another human being, and to the production of more human beings. And our race goes on. Sex begins before adolescence, and survives sterility; it is indeed coeval with our lives, although at the mating age its effects are more obvious to society. And besides sex, there are other emotions, also strengthening towards maturity: the various upliftings of the spirit, such as affection, friendship, patriotism, mysticism—and as soon as we try to determine the relation between sex and these other emotions we shall of course begin to quarrel as violently as we ever could about Walter Scott, perhaps even more violently. Let me only tabulate the various points of view. Some people say that sex is basic and underlies all these other loves —love of friends, of God, of country. Others say that it is connected with them, but laterally, it is not their root. Others say that it is not connected at all. All I suggest is that we call the whole bundle of emotions love, and regard them as the fifth great experience through which human beings have to pass. When human beings love they try to get something. They also try to give something, and this double aim makes love more complicated than food or sleep. It is selfish and altruistic at the same time, and no amount of specialization in one direction quite atrophies the other. How much time does love take? This question sounds gross but it must be asked because it bears on our present enquiry. Sleep takes about eight hours out of the twenty-four, food about two more. Shall we put down love for another two? Surely that is a handsome allowance. Love may weave itself into our other activities—so may drowsiness and hunger. Love may start various secondary activities: for instance, a man's love for his family may cause him to spend a good deal of time on the Stock Exchange, or his love for God a good deal of time in church. But that he has emotional communion with any beloved object for more than two hours a day may be gravely doubted, and it is this emotional communion, this desire to give and to get, this mixture of generosity and expectation, that distinguishes love from the other experiences on our list.

That is the human make-up—or part of it. Made up like this himself, the novelist takes his pen in his hand, gets into the abnormal state which it is convenient to call "inspiration," and tries to create characters. Perhaps the characters have to fall in with something else in his novel: this often happens (the books of Henry James are an extreme case), and then the characters have, of course, to modify the make-up accordingly. However, we are considering now the more simple case of the novelist whose main passion is human beings and who will sacrifice a great deal to their convenience—story, plot, form, incidental beauty.

Well, in what senses do the nations of fiction differ from those of the earth? One cannot generalize about them, because they have nothing in common in the scientific sense; they need not have glands, for example, whereas all human beings have glands. Nevertheless, though incapable of strict definition, they tend to behave along the same lines.

In the first place, they come into the world more like parcels than human beings. When a baby arrives in a novel it usually has the air of having been posted. It is delivered "off"; one of the elder characters goes and picks it up and shows it to the reader, after which it is usually laid in cold storage until it can talk or otherwise assist in the action. There is both a good and a bad reason for this and for all other deviations from earthly practice; these we will note in a minute, but do just observe in what a very perfunctory way the population of noveldom is recruited. Between Sterne and James Joyce, scarcely any writer has tried either to use the facts of birth or to invent a new set of facts, and no one, except in a sort of auntish wistful way, has tried to work back towards the psychology of the baby's mind and to utilize the literary wealth that must lie there. Perhaps it cannot be done. We shall decide in a moment.

Death. The treatment of death, on the other hand, is nourished much more on observation, and has a variety about it which suggests that the novelist finds it congenial. He does, for the reason that death ends a book neatly, and for the less obvious reason that working as he does in time he finds it easier to work from the known towards the darkness rather than from the darkness of birth towards the known. By the time his characters die, he understands them, he can be both appropriate and imaginative about them—strongest of combinations. Take a little death—the death of Mrs. Proudie in the *Last Chronicle of Barset*. All is in keeping, yet the effect is terrifying, because Trollope has ambled Mrs. Proudie down many a diocesan bypath, showing her paces, making her snap, accustoming us, even to boredom, to her character and tricks, to her "Bishop, consider the souls of the people," and then she has a heart attack by the edge of her bed, she has ambled far enough,—end of Mrs. Proudie. There is scarcely anything that the novelist cannot borrow from "daily death"; scarcely anything he may not profitably invent. The doors of that darkness lie open to him and he can even follow his characters through it, provided he is shod with imagination and does not try to bring us back scraps of séance information about the "life beyond."

What of food, the third fact upon our list? Food in fiction is mainly social. It draws characters together, but they seldom require it physiologically, seldom enjoy it, and never digest it unless specially asked to do so. They hunger for each other, as we do in life, but our equally constant longing for breakfast and lunch does not get reflected. Even poetry has made more of it—at least of its æsthetic side. Milton and Keats have both come nearer to the sensuousness of swallowing than George Meredith.

Sleep. Also perfunctory. No attempt to indicate oblivion or the actual dream world. Dreams are either logical or else mosaics made out of hard little fragments of the past and future. They are introduced with a purpose and that purpose is not the character's life as a whole, but that part of it he lives while awake. He is never conceived as a creature a third of whose time is spent in the darkness. It is the limited daylight vision of the historian, which the novelist elsewhere avoids. Why should he not understand or reconstruct sleep? For remember, he has the right to invent, and we know when he is inventing truly, because his passion floats us over improbabilities. Yet he has neither copied sleep nor created it. It is just an amalgam.

Love. You all know how enormously love bulks in novels, and will probably agree with me that it has done them harm and made them monotonous. Why has this particular experience, especially in its sex form, been transplanted in such generous quantities? If you think of a novel in the vague you think of a love interest—of a man and woman who want to be united and perhaps succeed. If you think of your own life in the vague, or of a group of lives, you are left with a very different and a more complex impression.

There would seem to be two reasons why love, even in good sincere novels, is unduly prominent.

Firstly, when the novelist ceases to design his characters and begins to create them—"love" in any or all of its aspects becomes important in his mind, and without intending to do so he makes his characters unduly sensitive to it—unduly in the sense that they would not trouble so much in life. The constant sensitiveness of characters for each other—even in writers called robust like Fielding—is remarkable, and has no parallel in life, except among people who have plenty of leisure. Passion, intensity at moments—yes, but not this constant awareness, this endless readjusting, this ceaseless hunger. I believe that these are the reflections of the novelist's own state of mind while he composes, and that the predominance of love in novels is partly because of this.

A second reason; which logically comes into another part of our enquiry, but it shall be noted here. Love, like death, is congenial to a novelist because it ends a book conveniently. He can make it a permanency, and his readers easily acquiesce, because one of the illusions attached to love is that it will be permanent. Not has been—will be. All history, all our experience, teaches us that no human relationship is constant, it is as unstable as the living beings who compose it, and they must balance like jugglers if it is to remain; if it is constant it is no longer a human relationship but a social habit, the emphasis in it has passed from love to marriage. All this we know, yet we cannot bear to apply our bitter knowledge to the future; the future is to be so different; the perfect person is to come along, or the person we know already is to become perfect. There are to be no changes, no necessity for alertness. We are to be happy or even perhaps miserable for ever and ever. Any strong emotion brings with it the illusion of permanence, and the novelists have seized upon this. They usually end their books with marriage, and we do not object because we lend them our dreams.

Here we must conclude our comparison of those two allied species, Homo Sapiens and Homo Fictus. Homo Fictus is more elusive than his cousin. He is created in the minds of hundreds of different novelists, who have conflicting methods of gestation, so one must not generalize. Still, one can say a little about him. He is generally born off, he is capable of dying on, he wants little food or sleep, he is tirelessly occupied with human relationships. And—most important—we can know more about him than we can know about any of our fellow creatures, because his creator and narrator are one. Were we equipped for hyperbole we might exclaim at this point: "If God could tell the story of the Universe, the Universe would become fictitious."

For this is the principle involved.

Arnold Hauser

Can Movies Be "Profound"?

Arnold Hauser is a German writer who now lives in London. He contributed the essay that follows to Partisan Review.

The novel is the only major art form that has come down to us from the nineteenth century in a viable condition. No other genre was capable of expressing modern man with his complexities, contradictions, and approximations. Only the novel could do justice to the multiplicity and atomization of his mind, his unfettered spirit of experimentation, his ambivalent morality and divided emotions. The drama by comparison seemed obsolete, having lost its social function and moral significance. By the turn of the century, society had ceased to create new dramatic conflicts and the old ones were withering away. This, and not the competition of the movies, was the danger facing the theater; actually the film owed its success to the precarious situation of the theater, or, more accurately, the decline of the theater and the rise of the film can both be attributed to a new sense of solidarity with the objective world. The novel in this respect only prepared the way for the film.

The dramatic form was too narrow for the labyrinthine ways of modern psychology; within its limitations a character living in the twilight between the white and the black of stage conceptions could not be made credible. In the era of bourgeois tolerance, in which to understand was to forgive, the drama which interpreted character in terms of a single action and identified the whole man with his act, could not be the representative art form, but inevitably gave way to a genre capable of showing that the act, as often as not, is a mere mask behind which the actor hides. The drama of this period dealt with the hereditary themes either

From *Partisan Review,* January, 1948. Reprinted by permission of Partisan Review and the author.

in the manner of a semi-serious, playfully ironic puppet show, or else in the style of a philosophical essay, closer to the modern intellectual novel than to traditional drama which gathered all problems into a single conflict and cut the knot with one bold stroke. The sense of modern reality was present only in the novel. Respect for the drama was a mere left-over from Puritan classicism, a flirtation with the poverty of a form that had been spiritually outgrown.

The novel was the representative literary form of the previous century, if only because it was the psychological genre par excellence. For, just as in the Middle Ages theology was master over all other intellectual disciplines, now psychology was becoming the central science and the epitome of all wisdom. Every significant achievement in literature and the humane sciences opened new access to the human psyche, every important work of philosophy or history constituted a new contribution to the analysis and interpretation of man. The French, English, and Russian novel, the new social sciences, modern psychology, and psychoanalysis, all strove toward an understanding of the man who had risen out of the turmoil of the industrial revolution and, in modern bourgeois society, fallen out with himself. The basic trait of the picture they revealed was inner conflict, the disintegration of the personality. The findings of historical research are perhaps best summed up in the words of Ortega y Gasset: "Man has no nature, he has only a history." And in literature, a hero's disunity and alienation actually became the touchstone of his significance. The psychology that failed to see the strange, the dangerous, the abysmal in man, that did not state at the outset: "You are not what you seem," came to be regarded as hopelessly idyllic and simplistic. To be sure, at the time of the First World War when the film art was coming into being, certain signs (such as the works of Franz Kafka, which departed from a purely psychological vision of man) pointed to a change in this attitude. Nevertheless the film was, and is increasingly, judged by the standards of psychological analysis, a type of expression for which it is not equipped, and from this inadequate standpoint it appears superficial and meaningless. A conception which can only subject the problems of metaphysics and ethics, the symbols of religion and mythology to pyschological interpretation, and which, instead of creating such ideas, religions, myths, can only produce a psychology of man's struggle with them, cannot do justice to the drama or to the film, and will inevitably appraise the film in particular as intrinsically unintellectual and unprofound. The profundity that resides in the multiplicity and shadings of psychological analysis will fit neither into the three acts of a drama nor into the three hundred scenes of a film. In a certain sense Thomas Mann is right in saying that the novel is more profound than the drama, and he even seems to be more or less justified in remarking elsewhere that the film has nothing in common with art. It assuredly has little in common with the art that fathoms psychological depths.

However, all art is not "profound"; there is also an art which, though lacking the dimension of depth, can boast some very great works. Raphael, Rossini, Victor Hugo—to take the most disparate examples—cannot but be regarded as great masters, but no one will claim that their works offer an insight into the depths of man's soul or destiny. The euphony, the balance, the harmonious lines of their works are pleasing without being profound, and the impression conveyed by these works is one of perfect artistry, although they exist in a world that is without mystery, fully deciphered and unveiled.

In addition to this unprofound art, there is an art whose profundity is *not* psychological, that is to say, it is not accomplished by analysis and interpretation of the individual traits of psychological being. The great tragedies of Aeschylus and Sophocles are profound without psychological depth, because their *form*, the form of tragedy itself is profound. Their profundity consists in the unveiling of the intelligible, free personality turned essence and in the revelation of a substantial being that is ordinarily covered over. The characters of tragedy can, in a certain sense they must, be uncomplicated, schematic, flat-surfaced; the tragedy itself is never flat, for every successful work participates in the depth of the genre.

And literature offers other forms of depth that are not psychological and do not derive from dark, mysterious characters. There can be depth in the relations between unprofound, undifferentiated, summarily sketched characters, as for example between Aunt Betsey and Mr. Dick in *David Copperfield*. The earthly paradise of these two fools is beyond a doubt one of the most beautiful and most profound daydreams in literature; the idea that in life's important moments a fool aways says "the right thing," because in such moments all of us are fools, and because Betsey Trotwood knows how to find the right thing, the best thing, in the words of a fool—or perhaps even in the twittering of a bird—*is* profound and cannot be called anything but profound. And this picture of a world in which the words of fools and the twittering of birds have a meaning that cannot be expressed in the language of intelligence, has a depth of its own which—as the Mr. Dick scenes in the film version of *David Copperfield* amply show—is quite accessible to the film.

There are not only manifest forms of depth in art, there is also a latent form: a hint of depth, which reveals only the gap where a link in the chain is missing and there is meaning to be filled in; an intimation of the breach in the edifice and the blind spot in our own eye; an indirect representation of depth, or in other words, a circling round the mystery, an admission of our incompetence even to inquire into it (see Ernst Bloch's variations on this theme of *"docta ignorantia"* in his *Geist der Utopie* [Spirit of Utopia], 1923). Art possesses in the symbol an instrument which in spite or perhaps indeed because of its emphasis on the meaning-less torso of things, conveys some sense of its participation in an-other world, its bond with the original mystery. And the more indirect, stammering, recalcitrant the form through which art suggests the meaning beneath and destroys the surface mean-ing, the closer it comes to the mystery of things. The strange, inarticulate wisdom of the witches in *Macbeth*, the Mothers in Goethe's *Faust*, Hölderlin's flags that "clatter in the wind," the ghost in Gogol's "The Overcoat," the eerie "I-piti-piti-ti-ti-ti" of the telegraph in Andrey Bolkonsky's delirious dream, are all such intrinsically meaningless messages from the depths. Or the old legend related by Tolstoy in his *Popular Tales:* Long, long ago there was a saintly hermit who lived on a desert island. One day some fishermen landed near his hut, among them an old man who was so simple-minded that he could barely talk and was unable to pray at all. Such ignorance filled the hermit with consternation, and with great trouble and pains he taught the old man the Lord's Prayer. The old man thanked him kindly and left the island with the other fishermen. Some time later, after the boat had vanished in the distance, the hermit suddenly saw a human shape on the horizon, walking on the surface of the water and approaching the island. Soon he recognized the old man, his pupil, and when the old man set foot on the island, the hermit, silent and abashed, came out to meet him. The old man stammered: "I have forgotten the prayer." "*You* don't have to pray," the hermit replied, and sent him away. Striding over the waters, the old man hurried after his boat.

Here depth is expressed without psychological complexity. Another such surface symbol occurs in the story of the conversion of the Indian saint, Rama Krishna. One day when he was still hardly more than a boy, he saw a flock of white cranes flying over the fields of his native village, high in the air, close to the blue heavens. He was so affected by the sight that he fell into a dead faint. When he recovered his senses, he was a changed man, awakened and converted.

Such depths are not closed to the film. The gulls and sailboats that swarm around the mutinous cruiser in *Potemkin* have no less symbolic power than the cranes in the story of Rama Krishna. As these little sailing craft, bringing gifts of bread and cigarettes to the rebels in their helpless ship, glide weightless over the wide dark waters with billowing sails, white and innocent as the sea-gulls and the woolly sheep in the sky, are they not a symbol and a promise of human brotherhood?

Robert Warshow

The Gangster as Tragic Hero

Robert Warshow (1917-1955) was managing editor of Commentary *at the time of his death. He frequently contributed thoughtful criticism of the movies to* Partisan Review.

America, as a social and political organization, is committed to a cheerful view of life. It could not be otherwise. The sense of

From *Partisan Review*, February, 1948. Reprinted by permission of Partisan Review and Martin Greenberg and Sherry Abel, literary executors of Robert Warshow.

tragedy is a luxury of aristocratic societies, where the fate of the individual is not conceived of as having a direct and legitimate political importance, being determined by a fixed and supra-political —that is, non-controversial—moral order or fate. Modern equalitarian societies, however, whether democratic or authoritarian in their political forms, always base themselves on the claim that they are making life happier; the avowed function of the modern state, at least in its ultimate terms, is not only to regulate social relations, but also to determine the quality and the possibilities of human life in general. Happiness thus becomes the chief political issue—in a sense, the only political issue—and for that reason it can never be treated as an issue at all. If an American or a Russian is unhappy, it implies a certain reprobation of his society, and therefore, by a logic of which we can all recognize the necessity, it becomes an obligation of citizenship to be cheerful; if the authorities find it necessary, the citizen may even be compelled to make a public display of his cheerfulness on important occasions, just as he may be conscripted into the army in time of war.

Naturally, this civic responsibility rests most strongly upon the organs of mass culture. The individual citizen may still be permitted his private unhappiness so long as it does not take on political significance, the extent of this tolerance being determined by how large an area of private life the society can accommodate. But every production of mass culture is a public act and must conform with accepted notions of the public good. Nobody seriously questions the principle that it is the function of mass culture to maintain public morale, and certainly nobody in the mass audience objects to having his morale maintained.[1] At a time when the normal condition of the citizen is a state of anxiety, euphoria spreads over our culture like the broad smile of an idiot. In terms of attitudes towards life, there is very little difference between a "happy" movie like *Good News*, which ignores death and suffering, and a "sad" movie like *A Tree Grows in Brooklyn*, which

[1] In her testimony before the House Committee on Un-American Activities, Mrs. Leila Rogers said that the movie *None But the Lonely Heart* was un-American because it was gloomy. Like so much else that was said during the unhappy investigation of Hollywood, this statement was at once stupid and illuminating. One knew immediately what Mrs. Rogers was talking about; she had simply been insensitive enough to carry her philistinism to its conclusion.

uses death and suffering as incidents in the service of a higher optimism.

But, whatever its effectiveness as a source of consolation and a means of pressure for maintaining "positive" social attitudes, this optimism is fundamentally satisfying to no one, not even to those who would be most disoriented without its support. Even within the area of mass culture, there always exists a current of opposition, seeking to express by whatever means are available to it that sense of desperation and inevitable failure which optimism itself helps to create. Most often, this opposition is confined to rudimentary or semi-literate forms: in mob politics and journalism, for example, or in certain kinds of religious enthusiasm. When it does enter the field of art, it is likely to be disguised or attenuated: in an unspecific form of expression like jazz, in the basically harmless nihilism of the Marx Brothers, in the continually reasserted strain of hopelessness that often seems to be the real meaning of the soap opera. The gangster film is remarkable in that it fills the need for disguise (though not sufficiently to avoid arousing uneasiness) without requiring any serious distortion. From its beginnings, it has been a consistent and astonishingly complete presentation of the modern sense of tragedy.[2]

In its initial character, the gangster film is simply one example of the movies' constant tendency to create fixed dramatic patterns that can be repeated indefinitely with a reasonable expectation of profit. One gangster film follows another as one musical or one Western follows another. But this rigidity is not necessarily opposed to the requirements of art. There have been very successful types of art in the past which developed such specific and detailed conventions as almost to make individual examples of the type interchangeable. This is true, for example, of Elizabethan revenge tragedy and Restoration comedy.

For such a type to be successful means that its conventions have imposed themselves upon the general consciousness and become the accepted vehicles of a particular set of attitudes and a

[2] Efforts have been made from time to time to bring the gangster film into line with the prevailing optimism and social constructiveness of our culture; *Kiss of Death* is a recent example. These efforts are usually unsuccessful; the reasons for their lack of success are interesting in themselves, but I shall not be able to discuss them here.

particular aesthetic effect. One goes to any individual example of the type with very definite expectations, and originality is to be welcomed only in the degree that it intensifies the expected experience without fundamentally altering it. Moreover, the relationship between the conventions which go to make up such a type and the real experience of its audience or the real facts of whatever situation it pretends to describe is of only secondary importance and does not determine its aesthetic force. It is only in an ultimate sense that the type appeals to its audience's experience of reality; much more immediately, it appeals to previous experience of the type itself: it creates its own field of reference.

Thus the importance of the gangster film, and the nature and intensity of its emotional and aesthetic impact, cannot be measured in terms of the place of the gangster himself or the importance of the problem of crime in American life. Those European movie-goers who think there is a gangster on every corner in New York are certainly deceived, but defenders of the "positive" side of American culture are equally deceived if they think it relevant to point out that most Americans have never seen a gangster. What matters is that the experience of the gangster *as an experience of art* is universal to Americans. There is almost nothing we understand better or react to more readily or with quicker intelligence. The Western film, though it seems never to diminish in popularity, is for most of us no more than the folklore of the past, familiar and understandable only because it has been repeated so often. The gangster film comes much closer. In ways that we do not easily or willingly define, the gangster speaks for us, expressing that part of the American psyche which rejects the qualities and the demands of modern life, which rejects "Americanism" itself.

The gangster is the man of the city, with the city's language and knowledge, with its queer and dishonest skills and its terrible daring, carrying his life in his hands like a placard, like a club. For everyone else, there is at least the theoretical possibility of another world—in that happier American culture which the gangster denies, the city does not really exist; it is only a more crowded and more brightly lit country—but for the gangster there is only the city; he must inhabit it in order to personify it: not the real

city, but that dangerous and sad city of the imagination which is
so much more important, which is the modern world. And the
gangster—though there are real gangsters—is also, and primarily,
a creature of the imagination. The real city, one might say, produces only criminals; the imaginary city produces the gangster: he
is what we want to be and what we are afraid we may become.

Thrown into the crowd without background or advantages,
with only those ambiguous skills which the rest of us—the real
people of the real city—can only pretend to have, the gangster is
required to make his way, to make his life and impose it on others.
Usually, when we come upon him, he has already made his choice
or the choice has already been made for him, it doesn't matter
which: we are not permitted to ask whether at some point he
could have chosen to be something else than what he is.

The gangster's activity is actually a form of rational enterprise, involving fairly definite goals and various techniques for
achieving them. But this rationality is usually no more than a vague
background; we know, perhaps, that the gangster sells liquor or
that he operates a numbers racket; often we are not given even
that much information. So his activity becomes a kind of pure
criminality: he hurts people. Certainly our response to the gangster film is most consistently and most universally a response to
sadism; we gain the double satisfaction of participating vicariously
in the gangster's sadism and then seeing it turned against the
gangster himself.

But on another level the quality of irrational brutality and
the quality of rational enterprise become one. Since we do not
see the rational and routine aspects of the gangster's behavior, the
practice of brutality—the quality of unmixed criminality—becomes the totality of his career. At the same time, we are always
conscious that the whole meaning of this career is a drive for success: the typical gangster film presents a steady upward progress
followed by a very precipitate fall. Thus brutality itself becomes at once the means to success and the content of success—a
success that is defined in its most general terms, not as accomplishment or specific gain, but simply as the unlimited possibility
of aggression. (In the same way, film presentations of businessmen
tend to make it appear that they achieve their success by talking

on the telephone and holding conferences and that success *is* talking on the telephone and holding conferences.)

From this point of view, the initial contact between the film and its audience is an agreed conception of human life: that man is a being with the possibilities of success or failure. This principle, too, belongs to the city; one must emerge from the crowd or else one is nothing. On that basis the necessity of the action is established, and it progresses by inalterable paths to the point where the gangster lies dead and the principle has been modified: there is really only one possibility—failure. The final meaning of the city is anonymity and death.

In the opening scene of *Scarface*, we are shown a successful man; we know he is successful because he has just given a party of opulent proportions and because he is called Big Louie. Through some monstrous lack of caution, he permits himself to be alone for a few moments. We understand from this immediately that he is about to be killed. No convention of the gangster film is more strongly established than this: it is dangerous to be alone. And yet the very conditions of success make it impossible not to be alone, for success is always the establishment of an *individual* pre-eminence that must be imposed on others, in whom it automatically arouses hatred; the successful man is an outlaw. The gangster's whole life is an effort to assert himself as an individual, to draw himself out of the crowd, and he always dies *because* he is an individual; the final bullet thrusts him back, makes him, after all, a failure. "Mother of God," says the dying Little Caesar, "is this the end of Rico?"—speaking of himself thus in the third person because what has been brought low is not the undifferentiated *man*, but the individual with a name, the gangster, the success; even to himself he is a creature of the imagination. (T. S. Eliot has pointed out that a number of Shakespeare's tragic heroes have this trick of looking at themselves dramatically; their true identity, the thing that is destroyed when they die, is something outside themselves—not a man, but a style of life, a kind of meaning.)

At bottom, the gangster is doomed because he is under the obligation to succeed, not because the means he employs are unlawful. In the deeper layers of the modern consciousness, *all* means are unlawful, every attempt to succeed is an act of aggression, leaving one alone and guilty and defenseless among enemies: one is *punished* for success. This is our intolerable dilemma: that failure is a kind of death and success is evil and dangerous, is—ultimately—impossible. The effect of the gangster film is to embody this dilemma in the person of the gangster and resolve it by his death. The dilemma is resolved because it is *his* death, not ours. We are safe; for the moment, we can acquiesce in our failure, we can choose to fail.

VII

Henry Bamford Parkes

The New Man

Henry B. Parkes (1904-   ) was born in England, studied at Oxford, and came to the United States in 1927. Since 1930 he has taught history at New York University. This essay is the first chapter of his interpretative history of the character and civilization of the American people, published under the title of The American Experience, *1947.*

The central theme in the history of the Americas can be stated very simply. During the four and a half centuries that have elapsed since the first voyage of Columbus, a stream of migration has been flowing from Europe westward across the Atlantic and into the two American continents. Relatively small during the first three hundred years, it increased during the nineteenth century and did not reach its peak until shortly before the First World War. In all, between fifty and sixty million persons left their European homes and established themselves in the New World. During the same period another five or ten millions were brought to the Americas by force from Africa. This is by far the largest movement of peoples in all history. There was no comparable process at any earlier epoch, and nothing like it is likely to happen again in the future. Whether one judges it by the number of individuals involved in it or by its results and implications, it is the most important single factor in the recent history of the human race.

This Atlantic migration was not the first invasion of the American hemisphere. Some twenty thousand years earlier, peoples of a different ethnic group, originating in northeastern Asia, had crossed into America by way of the Bering Strait. But it was only in Mexico and along the plateaus of the Andes that these "Indian" races succeeded in creating well-integrated societies that did not dissolve before the onset of the Europeans. In these two areas, which were among the first to pass under white control, the Indian masses, though subjugated and exploited by the newcomers, have retained their racial identity and many of their traditional characteristics. But elsewhere the hemisphere has become the undisputed property of the white man or of the Negro whom he brought with him.

In the southern continent the main lines of European settlement were marked out within fifty years of the first voyages of discovery. This rapid initial attack was followed by a long period of quiescence, during which there was relatively little new exploration or settlement. In the late nineteenth century, with a revival of energy and a new flow of migration into South America from Europe, the process was resumed. In the north the advance of the Europeans was more gradual but more consistent. Beginning more than a hundred years later than in the south, it covered only a few hundred miles from the Atlantic seacoast during the first century and a half, but gathered momentum quickly during the century that followed. The progress of white colonization reached its climax in the two continents almost simultaneously. The peoples of Argentina and Chile were imposing white rule over the hitherto unconquered Indians of the far south during the same two or three decades in which the people of the United States subjugated the Indians of the great plains and completed the settlement of the West.

That this movement of the European races into the New World should be regarded as the essential substance of American history is not difficult to understand. The explorer, the conquistador, the pioneer, and the liberator are the primary symbols of the American cultures. But the full implications, political and psychological, of this migration are not so easy to define. Establishing himself in the New World, the American repudiated a part of his European inheritance. In certain respects, though not in all, he ceased to be a European and became a new subspecies of humanity. It is only by understanding the qualities of this new man, the American, that we can interpret much that may other-

wise seem puzzling or disturbing in his achievements and his behavior. We must, above all, avoid the error of regarding the civilization of America as a mere extension, without essential changes,
of that of Europe. The differences between them should, in fact,
be emphasized, since otherwise the American peoples will be unable either to form a sound evaluation of their own institutions or
to avoid misunderstandings with those European nations with
whom they must be associated.

This volume is concerned with the evolution of civilization
in the United States, and here the divergence from European
traditions was sharper than in the Spanish-speaking countries. Both
the North and the South Americans have displayed certain common American characteristics, but these developed more fully in
the north. The imprint of European institutions, of monarchy,
aristocracy, and clericalism, and of the view of life and habits of
thought associated with them, was much deeper and more lasting
in the southern countries than it was in the United States. This
was owing partly to the authoritarian policies of Spanish imperialism and partly to the presence of large Indian populations
who could be reduced to a servitude resembling that of the peasants of feudal Europe. To a large degree Latin America became an
extension of Latin Europe. The migration to the United States, on
the other hand, created a new way of life that quickly acquired
certain unique qualities.

The impulse of migration may be described, negatively, as an
impulse of escape. The American fled from a Europe where he
could find no satisfying fulfillment of his energies and was confronted by conflicts and dilemmas that had no easy solution. The
groups who came to all parts of the New World were, in general,
those who were most acutely discontented with their status in
European society and who had the least hope of being able to improve it. The Hispanic colonies were settled mainly by impover-
ished members of the lower nobility and by adventurers from the
lower classes. Unable to achieve aristocratic status at home, they
hoped to win riches, land, and glory for themselves in America.
Most of the early immigrants to the United States came from the
petty bourgeoisie in the English cities or from the yeoman farmers;
a few were motivated primarily by the desire to put into practice
novel religious or political ideas, but the majority expected to im-

prove their economic condition. The later migration from the other European countries into both North and South America was similar in character, including some religious and political refugees, but consisting mainly of ambitious younger sons of the bourgeoisie and of oppressed and land-hungry peasants from Ireland, Germany, Scandinavia, Italy, and the Austrian and Russian empires. All sought in the New World an environment where they could act more freely, without being restricted by traditional forms of authority and discipline or by a scarcity of land and natural resources.

Of the various factors that caused men to come to America, the economic was no doubt the most important. Throughout the period of the migrations, there was no free land in Europe; natural resources were limited; and the population was always in danger of increasing faster than the means of subsistence. Migration always occurred chiefly from areas of Europe where agriculture was still the chief occupation and where (owing to the growth of big estates or to genuine overcrowding) the demand for land was in excess of the supply. This was true of Spain in the sixteenth century, of England in the early seventeenth, and of Ireland, Germany, Scandinavia, Italy, and the Slavic countries of the east in the nineteenth.

An almost equally influential stimulus to migration was the European class system. This was, in fact, perhaps the chief cause of European economic privation, since the big estates of the aristocracy diminished the supply of land available for the peasants. Before the discovery of America, European society had been molded by feudalism into a tightly knit organic structure in which every individual, from the king at the top to the humblest peasant at the bottom, was expected to know his place and to perform the duties appropriate to it. These class differences had originated with the barbarian invasions during the fall of the Roman Empire, or even earlier, and for a thousand years they had been a deeply rooted part of the European consciousness. Ambitious and enterprising members of the middle and lower classes could sometimes improve their position, either individually or in groups, but the battle against aristocratic privilege was always difficult, and never reached a conclusion. For such persons the opening of the

New World beyond the Atlantic promised an easier escape from frustration and the sense of inferiority.

Privation and inequality weighed upon all underprivileged persons in Europe, but did not cause all of them to come to America. Human behavior is conditioned by economic and social factors in the sense that these establish the problems to be solved, but it is not determined by them: how particular individuals choose to act in a given situation depends upon deeper, more intangible, and more mysterious forces. Confronted by the same difficulties, some individuals preferred to submit to them or to continue struggling with them, while others, generally the more restless and adventurous, decided to come to the New World. Thus the settlement of America was a selective process that attracted those members of the European middle and lower classes who had the appropriate bent and disposition; it appealed not necessarily to the ablest or the strongest, but usually to the most enterprising. In a sense it may be said that America was from the beginning a state of mind and not merely a place.

In the New World, at least during the earlier period of colonization, this selective process continued. Those who had the requisite energy, adaptability, and capacity for endurance survived and prospered; others died of starvation or in battle with the Indians. In the course of centuries certain qualities became established as suitable to the new environment and as characteristically American. Men born in the New World were disposed, both by inheritance and by conditioning, to develop them, and later immigrant groups found it necessary to acquire them. Thus the civilizations of the New World promoted certain special psychic configurations that differentiated the American from the European.

In the Hispanic countries the presence of Indian labor and the importation of Negro slaves enabled many of the early immigrants to achieve the aristocratic status to which they aspired. But in the United States there were no Indian peoples who could be made to work for white overlords; and though the institution of Negro slavery was adopted during the colonial period, its influence was restricted to one section of the country. There were in the United States, on the other hand, enormous stretches of fertile land and vast mineral resources of all kinds. Immigrants could find, in this undeveloped and almost empty country, opportunities for self-advancement that have never been equaled in the whole of human history. The individual had to display industry, courage, and resourcefulness; but if he possessed these qualities, then security, independence, and prosperity were within his reach. This unexampled abundance of land and resources was the cardinal factor in the development of American civilization. It molded the character of the American people, and was the chief reason for the unique qualities of their way of life. It facilitated the growth of individual freedom and social equality, and it promoted attitudes of optimism and self-assurance.

The society that developed under these conditions differed from that of Europe not only in its political and economic characteristics but also in its animating beliefs and view of life. The American acquired new attitudes and learned to see the world in a new way. And the nationality he created became a vast experiment in new social principles and new modes of living.

The European mind had been dominated by a hierarchical sense of order. This sense was embodied most completely in the philosophical and political theory of the Middle Ages; but even after the breakdown of feudalism and the repudiation of the scholastic philosophy, it continued, in one form or another, to permeate the consciousness of most Europeans. Human society was regarded as the reflection of an ideal order derived from the will of God and fully embodied in the cosmos. And the life of the individual acquired meaning and value insofar as he conformed with the order of the society to which he belonged. Yet the Europeans believed also that the attempt to realize this ideal order in concrete forms must always be incomplete. Evil was an inherent element in human experience, and both in nature and in the human spirit there were anarchical and rebellious forces that conflicted with the ideal order and that could never be wholly controlled. This belief in the reality of evil led to the European doctrine of original sin and was the basis of the European sense of tragedy.

The first immigrants to America brought with them this sense of order, but in the American world it gradually grew weaker; it did not remain a permanent part of the American con-

sciousness. Coming to a country where there was no elaborate
social organization, and where the individual must constantly do
battle with the forces of nature, the American came to see life not
as an attempt to realize an ideal order, but as a struggle between
the human will and the environment. And he believed that if men
were victorious in this struggle, they could hope that evil might
gradually be conquered and eliminated. What appeared as evil was
not a fundamental and permanent element in the nature of things,
but should be regarded merely as a problem to which the correct solution would one day be discovered. The American was
therefore a voluntarist and an optimist. He did not believe in the
devil, nor did he accept the dogma of original sin.

The most obvious result of this American attitude was the
fostering of an extraordinary energy and confidence of will. The
American came to believe that nothing was beyond his power to
accomplish, provided that he could muster the necessary moral
and material resources, and that any obstacle could be mastered by
means of the appropriate methods and technology. A failure was
the result either of weakness or of an incorrect technique. By
contrast with the European, the American was more extroverted,
quicker and more spontaneous in action, more self-confident, and
psychologically simpler. His character was molded not by the
complex moral and social obligations of an ordered hierarchical
system, but by the struggle to achieve victory over nature.

Rejecting both the belief in a fixed social order and the belief
in the depravity of human beings, the American created a society
whose special characteristic was the freedom enjoyed by its individual members. Respect for the freedom of every individual
and confidence that he would use his freedom wisely and con-
structively became the formative principles of the new American
nationality. By crossing the Atlantic, the American had asserted
a demand to be himself; he had repudiated the disciplines of the
class hierarchy, of long-established tradition, and of authoritarian religion. And in the society that took shape in the New World
it was by his natural and inherent quality that the individual was
measured, rather than by rank or status or conformity to convention. To a much greater degree than elsewhere, society in
America was based on the natural man rather than on man as
molded by social rituals and restraints. The mores of America

were less rigid and less formalized than those of any earlier community, and the individual was less inhibited. The American did
not believe that men needed to be coerced, intimidated, or indoc-
trinated into good behavior.

By European standards this American attitude often seemed
unrealistic, Utopian, and naïve. The American appeared to be
deficient in the recognition of evil and in the sense of tragedy. Yet
as long as he was engaged primarily in the conquest of the wilderness, he had good reasons for his optimism. His naïveté was, in
fact, an expression of a genuine innocence. He was simpler than
the European because his life was freer, more spontaneous, and
less frustrated. In Europe, with its economic privation, its hierarchy of classes, and its traditional disciplines and rituals, emotional
drives were more inhibited; and it is when aggressive energies are
thrown back upon themselves and can find no satisfying outlet in
action that they become evil. The European was psychologically
much more complex than the American, and therefore capable of
deeper and more subtle insights and of profounder spiritual and
æsthetic achievements; but he was also more corrupt, with a
greater propensity toward the negative emotions of fear and
avarice and hatred. He believed in the depravity of human nature
because he knew it in his own experience.

In social organization and in practical activity the American
confidence in human nature was abundantly justified by its results.
The tone of American society was more generous and hospitable,
more warmhearted and more genuinely kindly, than that of other
peoples. And by encouraging individuals to develop latent talents
and to prefer versatility and adaptability to professional specialization, it promoted an astonishing activity and ingenuity. The genius
of American life lay in its unprecedented capacity to release for
constructive purposes the energies and abilities of common men
and women. In consequence, the material achievements of the
Americans were stupendous. And though they hated the authoritarian discipline of warfare, they displayed when they went to war
an inventiveness and a resourcefulness that no other people could
equal.

Yet though the civilization of the Americans had remarkable virtues, it also had grave deficiencies. The conditions that
produced their material achievements did not result in any cor-

responding intellectual efflorescence. Their bent was toward the conquest of nature rather than toward metaphysical speculation or æsthetic creation. And though their suspicion of professional pretensions and their trust in the abilities of the common man had astonishing results in politics, technology, and warfare, the effect upon intellectual life was less desirable; for the common man has usually valued material progress above the difficult and apparently useless disciplines of abstract thought. In consequence, the more formal intellectual activities of the Americans often appeared to be timid, conventional, and derivative. They frequently used ideas that had been borrowed from Europe, and that had little relevance or vital connection with their own society. Their practice was usually bolder and more original than their theory. Outside the fields of practical activity, America developed no living system of general ideas and no continuing intellectual tradition, so that each generation of writers and thinkers had a tendency to start afresh, with little guidance or encouragement from the past.

Whether the American civilization was capable not only of rapid material growth but also of stability was, moreover, open to question. For the conditions under which it had acquired its unique qualities were transitory and not permanent. The land and the natural resources of the New World were not inexhaustible. Before the end of the nineteenth century every part of the United States had been settled; and most of its resources had become the private property of individuals. There was no longer an open frontier inviting the restless, the dissatisfied, and the ambitious. And though an expanding capitalism continued to offer opportunities for the exercise of initiative, it was only the exceptionally enterprising and the exceptionally lucky, not the average American citizen, who could take advantage of them. Under such circumstances, certain contradictions that had always been inherent in the American view of life became more manifest and more dangerous. For while the Americans had believed in a universal freedom and equality, they had also encouraged and applauded the competitive drive of individuals toward wealth and power. And in a complex industrial society this drive was directed less against nature and more against other human beings. Those individuals who succeeded in acquiring economic privileges did so by restricting the freedom of others; and the competitive struggle for power and prestige threatened to destroy the human warmth and openheartedness that had hitherto been the special virtues of American society.

How far and by what methods could the qualities of the American way of life be preserved after the conditions under which they first developed had disappeared? These questions began to confront the American people in the twentieth century. As long as they had been engaged in conquering and settling an empty continent, material conditions had in themselves promoted freedom, equality, and a spirit of co-operation. But after this process had been completed, the Americans could remain a democratic people only by conscious choice and deliberate effort. If they wished to remain American, they must now acquire a more critical understanding of their way of life, of the historical experience by which it had been shaped, and of the contradictions within it which must be eliminated or transcended. They had to establish a cultural and intellectual tradition matching their material achievements and growing out of the American experience instead of being borrowed from Europe. Otherwise the American experiment in democracy could have no happy outcome.

And upon the results of this American experiment depended, in large measure, the future not only of the Americans themselves but of the whole human race. For the movement toward individual liberation and toward the mastery of nature, which was represented in its purest and completest form in the United States, was of world-wide extent, so that the whole world seemed to be gradually becoming Americanized. During the entire period from the voyage of Columbus to the present day, while some persons sought a greater freedom by crossing the Atlantic, others fought for it at home; the same forces of social protest that caused the Atlantic migration brought about profound changes in the society, first of Europe, and afterwards of the Orient; and the rise, first of the bourgeoisie, and afterwards of the proletariat, caused a slow disintegration of traditional concepts of social hierarchy. During the nineteenth century the rapid expansion of capitalism in Europe and Asia created opportunities comparable to those existing in America, while the achievements of American democracy exerted a magnetic influence and attraction upon the peoples of other countries. Thus the civilizations of the Old World were moving in the same direction as the new civilization of America. There was no complete transformation of European society, and still less of the society of the Orient. Europe never forgot the feudal emphasis on rank, status, and authority or the belief in individual subordination to the order of the whole; nor did the European acquire the simplicity and the optimism characteristic of the American. In Europe the struggle between the principles of freedom and those of authority was unending and reached no decisive conclusion. Yet the problem that confronted the Americans—the problem of reconciling the freedom of individuals with the welfare and stability of society—had universal implications. Would the achievements of American civilization continue to attract the peoples of other countries? Or would the Americans themselves end by abandoning American principles and reverting to European traditions of authority and social hierarchy?

For these reasons the history of America, considered as a state of mind and not merely as a place, presented a series of problems of immense spiritual and practical importance.

Carl Lotus Becker

Democracy: The Reality

Carl Becker. See page 79. This essay is a part of a series of lectures delivered at the University of Virginia in 1940. In the first lecture Becker presented the theory of the democratic state. In this, the second lecture, he contrasted "The Reality" with "The Ideal."

> Men mistook the pernicious channels in which selfish propensities had been flowing for the propensities themselves, which were sure to find new channels when the old had been destroyed.   JAMES BRYCE

> Those who own the country ought to govern it.
>   JOHN JAY

I

In the preceding lecture we were concerned with the ideal
form of democracy. It is obvious that the reality does not strictly
conform to this ideal. There is nothing remarkable in that. The
ideal is always better than the real—otherwise there would be no
need for ideals. We have been told, as if it were a surprising thing,
that in Russia the Revolution has been betrayed. But it was bound
to be betrayed. It is in the nature of revolutions to be betrayed,
since life and history have an inveterate habit of betraying the
ideal aspirations of men. In this sense the liberal-democratic revolution was likewise bound to be betrayed—men were sure to be
neither so rational nor so well-intentioned as the ideology conceived them to be. But while a little betrayal is a normal thing, too
much is something that calls for explanation. The liberal-democratic revolution has been so far betrayed, the ideal so imperfectly
portrayed in the course of events, that its characteristic features
cannot easily be recognized in any democratic society today. In
this lecture I shall attempt to disclose some of the essential reasons
for the profound discord between democracy as it was ideally
projected and democracy as a going concern.

Stated in general terms the essential reason is that the idea of
liberty, as formulated in the eighteenth century, although valid
enough for that time, has in one fundamental respect ceased to be
applicable to the situation in which we find ourselves. In the eighteenth century the most obvious oppressions from which men suffered derived from governmental restraints on the free activity of
the individual. Liberty was therefore naturally conceived in terms
of the emancipation of the individual from such restraints. In the
economic realm this meant the elimination of governmental restraints on the individual in choosing his occupation, in contract-
ing for the acquisition and disposal of property, and the purchase
and sale of personal services. But in our time, as a result of the
growing complexities of a technological society, the emancipation of the individual from governmental restraint in his economic activities has created new oppressions, so that for the
majority of men liberty can be achieved only by an extension of

governmental regulation of competitive business enterprise. It is in the economic realm that the traditional idea of liberty is no longer applicable; in the economic realm, accordingly, that the discord between democracy as an ideal and democracy as a going concern is most flagrant, most disillusioning, and most dangerous.

In order to elaborate this statement it will be well, first of all, to note the chief characteristics of the social situation in the eighteenth century—the situation against which the liberal-democratic revolution was directed, and from which the eighteenth-century conception of liberty emerged as an obvious and valid rationalization.

From the twelfth to the seventeenth century the cardinal economic fact in western Europe was the rise of an industrial capitalist class in the towns; the cardinal political fact was the consolidation of royal power over all classes and corporations within definite territorial limits. The chief obstacles encountered by kings in this political process were two: first, the feudal vassals who claimed, and often exercised, virtual independence within their domains; second, the Roman Church, which claimed to be superior to the civil power, was in large part a self-governing institution, and exercised in fact over the king's subjects an authority independent of, and often in conflict with, the authority of the king.

In this three-cornered struggle for power, kings were sometimes supported by the church against the nobles, sometimes by the nobles against the church; but the persistent and effective support against both church and nobility came from the rising industrial class. Merchants and traders always found the turbulence of the nobility bad for business, and were usually willing, however painful it may have been, to supply the king with some of the money he needed to establish orderly government. Thus in the course of centuries, chiefly with the aid of the industrial bourgeois class, kings gradually reduced the nobles to the status of landed proprietors who retained, as the price of submission, the distinctions and prerogatives of a superior social class.

Meantime, the long struggle for the subordination of the church to royal power was virtually completed by the upheaval known as the Protestant Reformation, and it was the growing power and heretical ideas of the industrial classes that made the Reformation successful. Everywhere stronger in the towns than in the country, stronger in industrialized than in nonindustrialized countries, the Protestant Reformation was in effect a revolt of the middle classes against a church which, being controlled by a landed aristocracy, enforced ethical standards and religious practices unsuited to the temper and contrary to the interests of an industrial society. The chief political result of the Reformation was that by breaking the power of Rome it enhanced the power of kings, and by enhancing the power of kings it subordinated the church to the state, and thereby reduced the clergy, like the nobility, to the status of a privileged social class.

Thus in the seventeenth century, as a result of the rise of an industrial capitalist class, the consolidation of royal power, and the survival of nobles and clergy as privileged classes within the state, there emerged in western Europe a social system that was everywhere much the same. The prevailing form of government was absolute monarchy. In theory the power of the king rested upon the doctrine of divine right, supplemented by the Roman Law precept "What the Prince wills has the force of law." In practice the power of the king rested upon the support of nobles, clergy, and the rich bourgeois industrialists and financiers, and functioned for the most part to their advantage by exploiting an underlying population of peasants and workers.

It was what we should call a highly regimented system—a system in which the rights and obligations of the individual, always subject to the arbitrary will of the king, were normally determined by the rights and obligations appertaining to the class in which he was born. Generally speaking, there was for the individual neither freedom of occupation, nor of opinion or religion, nor any recognized method by which he might initiate or modify the law and custom by which his thought and conduct were controlled. The character of the liberal-democratic revolution which occurred from the seventeenth to the nineteenth centuries was conditioned by this fact. Dispensing with verbal refinements, all revolutions are made in behalf of liberty—freedom from some sort of real or fancied oppression; and in a social situation in which the individual was so obviously restrained and oppressed by law and custom not of his own making, it was inevitable that liberty should be conceived in terms of the emancipation of the individual from social and political control.

The revolution was initiated and directed, not by those who were most oppressed, but by those who were most aware of oppression and most competent to denounce and resist it—that is to say, not by the brutalized and ignorant peasants and workers, but by the educated and well-to-do middle classes. The bourgeoisie derived their power neither from birth nor office, but from money, that abstract and supple measure of the material value of all things. They acquired the education, cultivated the virtues, and developed the mentality appropriate to the occupations that engaged them. Occupied with practical affairs, with defined and determinable relations, with concrete things and their disposal and calculable cash value, they cultivated the virtues of thrift and prudence, dependability and sound judgment, and developed a pragmatic and skeptical temper, averse to the mystical and otherworldly, little disposed to slavish adherence to tradition, easily adaptable to the new and the experimental.

In every country the liberal-democratic revolution developed, with occasional violent upheavals, in the measure that the bourgeoisie acquired power and became class conscious—became aware, that is to say, of their peculiar class interests and virtues; and of the frustration of their interests and virtues by rococo class distinctions, and by arbitrary royal decrees which hampered business enterprise and deprived them of their property for the benefit of an aristocracy which they regarded as less intelligent, less moral, and less socially useful than themselves. The central, dramatic episode in the rise of liberal-democracy was the French Revolution; and it was in connection with this episode that there appeared in western Europe an exceptionally able group of intellectuals who rationalized the social situation by identifying the middle-class interests and virtues with the rights of all men—the right of all men to equality of status and of opportunity, to freedom of occupation and of economic enterprise, to freedom of opinion and of religion, and to freedom from arbitrary political authority.

2

Fortunately for the bourgeoisie and for the revolution, the interests of the middle classes were, in one respect, identical with the interests of the great majority. The liberal-democratic revolution could not have been won if it had been fought on behalf of bourgeois class interests alone. Of all the liberties demanded, freedom of economic enterprise was the one least stressed by the Philosophers and of least importance for the purposes of revolutionary propaganda. The liberty which could be demanded with most assurance and denied with least grace was liberty of person and of opinion—freedom of religion, freedom of speech and the press, freedom of learning and of teaching, freedom from the insane brutalities practiced in the civil and ecclesiastical administration of justice and in the punishment of crimes. In proclaiming the worth and dignity of the individual, in demanding the emancipation of men from the inhumanity of man to man, the bourgeois spokesmen were appealing to interests transcending all class lines. They were appealing to the spirit of Christianity against its practices, and espousing the cause with which all the saints and sages of the world had been identified. In doing so they injected into the liberal-democratic revolution the quality of a religious crusade, and thereby enlisted the widespread support which alone could assure its success.

The political and economic interests of the bourgeoisie could not, unfortunately, be thus identified with the interests of all. On the contrary, the interests of the bourgeoisie, both in the political and the economic realm, proved in the long run to be in sharp conflict with the interests of the masses. It was the interest of the bourgeoisie to deny to the masses the political privileges which they demanded for themselves; while the freedom of economic enterprise which enriched bourgeois employers turned out to be, for the proletarian peasants and workers, no more than the old subjection under new forms. As liberal-democracy emerged into the light of day, this conflict of class interests became more obvious and more disastrous; and it is this conflict which in our time has created those profound social discords which so largely nullify the theory and threaten to undermine the stability of democratic institutions.

In the earlier stages of the revolution, when the chief task was to deprive kings and aristocrats of political power and social privilege, this latent conflict between middle- and lower-class interests was not apparent. For the time being, indeed, it did not exist. The tyranny of kings and aristocrats, so effectively denounced by the Philosophers, was real enough, and so long as it existed all the unprivileged, bourgeois and people alike, had a common interest in resisting it. The doctrine that all men had a natural right to govern themselves seemed then but a simple truth, and the bourgeoisie could accept it without bothering too much about its practical application, all the more so since only by accepting it could they enlist the support of the people in destroying absolute monarchy and class privilege. In all the great "revolutionary days"—the English civil wars in the seventeenth century, the American and the French revolutions at the close of the eighteenth, the South American wars of independence, the revolutions of 1830 and 1848—in all these crucial struggles in which the tyranny of kings and aristocrats was still the central issue, the bourgeoisie and the people are found united in the effort to win political freedom by overthrowing the existing regime. They differed only in the respective parts which they played in the struggle: the function of the bourgeoisie was to take the initiative and supply the ideas; the function of the people was to erect the barricades and supply the necessary force.

It is always easier for diverse groups to unite for the destruction of an existing regime than it is to unite for the construction of a new one. Having united to destroy the tyranny of kings and aristocrats, the bourgeoisie and the people were divided on the question of what political liberty should mean in practice. The doctrine that all men had a natural right to govern themselves was interpreted by the people to mean that all adult male citizens should share in choosing the magistrates and shaping the laws by which the community was governed. By the bourgeoisie it was interpreted to mean, as John Jay put it, that "those who own the country ought to govern it." In this respect the first result of the revolution was everywhere essentially a victory for the bourgeoisie. Kings lost their absolute power, aristocrats lost their special privileges, or most of them; but political liberty—the right to choose the magistrates and enact the laws by which the community was governed—was limited to the people of property; the masses, having served their purpose by erecting the barricades, found themselves still excluded from what Guizot called "the political country."

Having thus, with the aid of the people, elbowed kings and aristocrats out of the seats of power, the bourgeoisie promptly united with the aristocrats to control the state. They had a common interest in excluding the people from political privilege, but in the competition for votes and power within the political country their interests were opposed. There accordingly emerged, for the promotion of their respective interests, two political parties which, although known by different names in different countries, we may call conservative and liberal. Conservative parties were composed for the most part of the landed aristocracy, the clergy of the established churches, high-placed bureaucrats, and hangers-on of royal courts. In some countries, more royalist than the king, they at first entertained the vain hope of restoring the ancient regime; but in any case they defended the interests of land against capital, the established church against dissenting religions, and old social distinctions and aristocratic prestige against the leveling influence of democratic customs. Liberal parties were composed of the educated and well-to-do middle classes—businessmen, professional people, middle-class intellectuals, perhaps a few liberalized aristocrats. Occupying a middle position, the liberal parties fought on two fronts: equally opposed to absolutism and democracy, they were defenders of liberty against kings and aristocrats, but defenders of their own newly acquired privilege against the people.

In this situation, there emerged a third political party—variously called republican, progressive liberal, radical—which for convenience we may call democratic. The democratic party represented those who were still excluded from the political country —at first more particularly the industrial workers, who were most oppressed and the first to become class conscious. They were commonly led by middle-class intellectuals, who formulated for them a doctrine and a program. The doctrine was the pure liberal-democratic ideology which middle-class liberals professed in theory but denied in practice—the doctrine that all men had a natural right to govern themselves, and the chief point in the program was accordingly the extension of the suffrage to all adult male citizens, in the confident belief that the workers, once possessed of the right to vote for those who made the laws, could correct by legislation the economic inequalities that oppressed them.

In the course of time, after much fruitless effort and some abortive uprisings, the people were admitted to the political country—in the United States during the period from about 1830 to 1840, in European countries for the most part during the last three decades of the century. To this result both logic and political tactics contributed. In point of logic, it was difficult for middle-class Liberals, who had won political privilege by advocating the right of all men to govern themselves, to refute the argument that the masses as well as the classes should enjoy that right. But it was less the logic of the ideology than of political strategy that determined the outcome. As the fear of kings declined and the revolution was accepted as an accomplished fact, the opposition between upper-class Liberal and Conservative parties declined also. Agreeing upon fundamentals, they were chiefly divided by the competitive struggle for votes; and it seemed obvious that the party which first pleased the masses by giving them the right to vote would stand the best chance of winning their support at the polls. Generally speaking, therefore, at least so far as European countries are concerned, it can hardly be said that the people forced their way into the political country. Quite as often as not they were admitted by Conservative or Liberal party governments, each of which, in the particular instance, hoped to increase its voting strength by enlarging the electorate.

The adoption of universal manhood suffrage was thought at the time to be a signal triumph for democracy. And it did in fact add something to the power of the people, since it compelled upper-class parties to take account of popular opinion in formulating policies and devising measures that would appeal to the mass of the voters. But on the whole, the admission of the people to the political country did very little to increase their power or improve the conditions under which they lived. Political control remained, as before, essentially in the hands of upper-class political parties.

Many reasons may be advanced for the failure of the people

to profit by their apparent victory. When they entered the political country they found the upper classes intrenched in all the strategic positions. The forms and procedure of representative institutions were already established; political parties, representing for the most part the upper classes, were well organized; and the technique for selecting candidates and manipulating elections was such that politics was a profession only men of property and social position could enter with much chance of success. In theory the masses were free to present to the electorate the measures that seemed to them desirable for the public good; in fact the means of propaganda were freely available only to the educated and well-to-do. In theory the poor man could vote for candidates of his own choosing; in fact his choice was limited to candidates who represented the dominant upper-class parties. It is true that in the course of time the people organized working-class socialist parties of their own; but while such parties often obtained from conservative or liberal governments measures designed to protect the interests of the poor, effective political control still remained in the hands of those who could easily afford the expensive luxury of self-government.

These are the superficial reasons for the failure of political equality to safeguard the interests of the people. The more fundamental reason is to be found in the economic structure of the society that emerged from the liberal-democratic revolution. Individual liberty in the political realm proved inadequate because individual liberty in the economic realm failed to bring about even that minimum degree of equality of possessions and of opportunity without which political equality is scarcely more than an empty form. This point, since it is fundamental, calls for some elaboration.

3

The principle of individual freedom in the economic realm, although not much stressed in the propaganda of the great crusading days, was always an integral part of the liberal-democratic ideology. For the needed emancipation of industry from the hampering restraints of monopolistic privilege and petty governmental regulation, it was a sound working principle; but applied without qualifications it could only benefit the industrial bourgeoisie at the expense of the underlying population of peasants and workers. As set forth in the *Wealth of Nations,* and in the more rigorous and apparently more scientific works of the English classical economists, the principle was indeed scarcely more than pure rationalization of the business interests of capitalist employers; but this ominous fact was long concealed because the principle was formulated in terms of the word liberty, the magic of which was sufficient at that time to give a general sanction even to the brutalities of cutthroat competition and the systematic degradation of women and children. The present misery of the workers could be more easily contemplated and dismissed because it could be regarded as a necessary but temporary phase in the operation of a divinely ordained law of progress. The average humane middle-class man, whether employer or not, could therefore accept the principle of individual freedom in the economic realm, along with the other great freedoms, since it so happily enabled him to reconcile his selfish with his altruistic impulses by assuring him that he could best serve God and his neighbor by doing as he pleased. "Private advantage a public benefit"—such was the succinct formula by which the prosperous middle classes justified their amiable expectation that when everyone was free all would presently be equal, when all were equal everyone would presently have enough, when all had enough no one would any longer be unjust or inhumane.

The expectation was surely naïve, in no sort of harmony with the relevant facts of social experience. Even under the most favorable circumstances, a society of uprooted and freely competing individuals must have functioned to the advantage of the few who by good fortune, intelligence, or lack of scruple were able to acquire wealth and employ it to advance their interests through the mechanism of politics: the times would always be ripe for a sufficient number of not-too-good men to come to the aid of the party. But this result was greatly accelerated and intensified by those changes in the economic and material conditions of life which, effected without blare of trumpets and scarcely perceived at the time, are now known as the industrial or technological revolution of modern times.

Technological is the better term. Industrial is wholly inadequate to denote one of the two or three major revolutions in the history of the human race. Man is a tool-using animal, and all civilization is conditioned by the sources of natural power known to him and the mechanical appliances he can invent to make such power available for use. The first great epoch of discovery and invention takes us back before the time of recorded history. All the more obvious sources of natural power—gravitation, fire, wind and water, domesticated animals, the fertility of the soil— and the simple hand tools, weapons, utensils, and appliances for making such power available were known to primitive man. From the time of the invention of writing, some five or six thousand years ago, until comparatively recent times few if any new sources of natural power, except crude explosives and magnetic force, were discovered; and during all that long time the mechanical appliances available, although more numerous and greatly perfected, were essentially of the same order as those employed from time immemorial.

But we are now living in the second great epoch of discovery and invention. Since the seventeenth century, the discovery of steam power, gas, electricity, and radiation have made possible those innumerable tools and appliances, those complicated and powerful machines, and those delicate instruments of precision which elicit our wonder and our admiration. The result has been that the new technology, by giving men unprecedented control over material things, has transformed the relatively simple agricultural communities of the eighteenth century into societies far more complex and impersonal than anything the prophets of liberal-democracy could have imagined—mechanized Leviathans which Thomas Jefferson at least would have regarded as unreal and fantastic and altogether unsuited to the principles of liberty and equality as he understood them.

I need not say that the influence of the technological revolution has not been confined to any particular aspect of social life. On the contrary, it has exerted and still exerts a decisive influence in modifying all the habitual patterns of thought and conduct. But I am here concerned with the influence of the technological revolution in accelerating and intensifying that concentration of wealth and power in the hands of a few which the principles of individual freedom in the economic realm would in any case have tended to bring about.

The first and most obvious result of the technological revolution has been to increase the amount of wealth in the form of material things which can be produced in a given time by a given population. For example, in 1913 there was produced in Great Britain seven billion yards of cotton cloth for export alone. In 1750 the total population of Great Britain, working with the mechanical appliances then available, could have produced only a small fraction of that amount. A second result of the technological revolution is that, as machines are perfected and become more automatic, man power plays a relatively less important part in the production of a given amount of wealth in a given time. Fifty years ago, when all type was set by hand, the labor of several men was required to print, fold, and arrange in piles the signatures of a book. Today machines can do it all, and far more rapidly; little man power is required, except that a mechanic, who may pass the time sitting in a chair, must be present in case anything goes wrong with the machine. And finally, a third result of the technological revolution is that, under the system of private property in the means of production and the price system as a method of distributing wealth, the greater part of the wealth produced, since it is produced by the machines, goes to those who own or control the machines, while those who work the machines receive that part only which can be exacted by selling their services in a market where wages are impersonally adjusted to the necessities of the machine process.

I use the phrase "own *or* control the machines" for the reason that, as a result of modern technology and business organization, those who own private property in the means of production do not necessarily control it. The ownership of property is now a highly intangible and illusive concept. Mass production calls for enormous industrial plants which are commonly managed by corporations and financed by selling corporation stock to the investing public. If I buy ten shares of General Motors I may be said to own that amount of General Motors property, but I have no control of it. The property is controlled by those who own a majority of the stock, and the majority of the stock is commonly owned by a few persons. Ownership, as far as I am concerned, consists in the possession of a slip of paper which gives me a lively hope that those who control the property will periodically send me a check for a certain sum of money: if they fail to do so there is nothing I can do about it. By the intricate device of the holding company, control may be still further concentrated and still further divorced from ownership: several corporations may be controlled by a few persons who have little or no interest in the operating companies except to manipulate and exploit them for financial gain. Thus it happens that while the ownership of private property in the means of production may be widely distributed, the effective control of that property is likely to be concentrated in the hands of a few.

If the concept of ownership is intangible and illusive, the concept of property is no less so. The value of General Motors property resides, not in the physical plant and the financial assets alone, but essentially in the business as a going concern. To be a prosperous going concern, the corporation must be able to purchase labor and supplies at a cost that will enable it to sell its products throughout the entire community at a profit. For this reason General Motors cannot live or die to itself alone. Its prosperity, and therefore the value of its property, conditions and is conditioned by the prosperity of innumerable individuals and business enterprises—the enterprises, large and small throughout the community and even throughout the world, which sell its cars and supply it with raw material, fuel, and equipment; the individuals who, as laborers or stockholders, are associated with General Motors and with the many enterprises that are integrated with it.

The value of private property in the means of production is thus not a private matter. It is both cause and effect in the functioning of a highly integrated and delicately adjusted industrial structure that touches the public interest at every point. That the few who control private property in the means of production should be wealthy men is no great matter. What matters is that their control of the means of production gives them an indeterminate and impersonal power over the lives and fortunes of millions of people unknown to them—power which they are sometimes unwilling but far more often quite unable to use for the public good.

In any society there is bound to be a close connection between economic and political power. In any society those who possess economic power, like other people, are disposed to identify their economic interests with the general good, and to promote their interests through the mechanism of politics and propaganda. But in modern industrial societies, based upon democratic political control and the principle of free economic enterprise, the beneficiaries of private property in the means of production are in a peculiarly advantageous position for molding opinion and shaping legislation. Their advantage arises less from the fact that they can and do spend money freely for those purposes, than from the fact that political procedure and the instruments of propaganda are so integrated with the industrial system that legislation and opinion more or less automatically respond to the pressure of the system of free enterprise from which their economic power is derived.

In democratic societies political power is mediated through political parties organized primarily for the purpose of obtaining control of the government by winning elections. To win elections a political party must of course formulate a program of legislation that will appeal to the voters. But elections are not won on the merits of a program alone. The winning of an election is a practical business enterprise, which calls for a capital investment in the form of a campaign fund, and for an intricate organization of employees—a political machine managed by professional politicians whose business it is to deliver the vote. Contributions to the campaign fund may be made from interested or disinterested motives; but the largest contributions will commonly be made by wealthy men or corporations expecting in return that the party will not, at the very least, be altogether indifferent to the kind of legislation they desire.

The professional politician, whose business it is to deliver the vote, is concerned primarily with the vote of those whose loyalty to the party is determined less by the merits of the party program than by the disposition of the party to confer tangible benefits upon them. The function of the highest species of politician is to handle the patronage, to distribute appointive offices to those who can best serve the party. The function of the lowest species of politician—the *déclassé* ward heeler—is to do what respectable statesmen know must be done but are prevented by the mores from doing themselves, namely, to see to it that the poor and dispossessed are provided with a minimum of subsistence, and not too much hampered in their private enterprises, even sometimes if they happen to be on the wrong side of the fence, by the majesty of the law. In delivering the vote, the ward heeler is the henchman of the political boss, the political boss has the necessary contacts with the party leaders who hold elective or appointive offices, and the political leaders have the necessary personal and social contacts with the businessmen who contribute so generously to the campaign fund. In every community, large or small, there is this unavowed, undercover integration of economic and political power; and apart from some unanticipated ethical disturbance in the climate of opinion, legislation, always defended by statesmen in terms of the common good, is always insensibly influenced by the pressure of the predominant industrial interest.

In molding opinion, no less than in shaping legislation, those who possess economic power have a great advantage over the general run of citizens. This is not to say that freedom of speech and the press does not exist in democratic societies. One has only to compare nondemocratic with democratic societies to realize that, in a very real and important sense, it does exist. In democratic societies any man may freely express his opinion without first looking furtively over his shoulder to see if a government spy is in the offing; any man may publish a book or a newspaper without first submitting it to an official censor. This is the fundamentally important privilege; and no cataloguing of incidental violations of civil liberties, serious and deplorable as they are, can obscure the fact that through the press and the radio detailed information about events, and the most diverse opinions, are with little let or hindrance daily and hourly presented to the people.

Nevertheless, the average individual, although free to express his ideas, plays a distinctly minor role in the molding of opinion: his role is not to initiate, but passively to receive information and ideas presented to him by others. The propaganda of social or political opinion, to be effective under modern conditions, must be organized; and its promoters will have an indifferent success unless they resort to mass production and distribution of their wares. The chief instruments of propaganda—the press and broadcasting stations—are not readily available to the average individual for conveying his ideas: they can be effectively used only by the government, political parties and party leaders, prominent organizations, wealthy men and business corporations, associations organized for specific purposes, and the writers of books which publishing houses find it worth while to publish.

Even more important is the fact that the instruments of propaganda are themselves business corporations organized and financed for profit, and as such subject to those influences that condition and are conditioned by the system of free economic enterprise. Newspapers are free to print all the news that's fit to print; but they cannot consistently propagate ideas that will alienate the business interests whose paid advertisements enable them to distribute profits to the stockholders. Broadcasting corporations are free from government censorship, or reasonably so, reasonably free to broadcast what they will; but in the last analysis they will not broadcast that which seriously offends the prevailing mores, or the business enterprises which, in this country at least, sponsor and finance their programs of entertainment. In democratic societies free and impartial discussion, from which the truth is supposed to emerge, is permitted and does occur. But the thinking of the average man is largely shaped by a wealth of factual information and the conflicting opinions which the selective process of competitive business enterprise presents to him for consideration: information, the truth of which he cannot verify; ideas, formulated by persons he does not know, and too often inspired by private economic interests that are never avowed.

Such, in broad outline, are the circumstances that may serve to explain the profound discord between democracy as an ideal and as a reality. In terms of the ideal there should have emerged from the liberal-democratic revolution a relatively simple society of free, equal, and prosperous citizens, fraternally coöperating to effect, by rational discussion and mutual concession, the common good. In fact there emerged an extremely complex society in which highly intricate and impersonal economic forces, stronger than good will or deliberate intention or rational direction, brought about an increasing concentration of wealth and power in the hands of the fortunate few, and thereby nullified, for the majority of the people, many of those essential liberties which provide both the theoretical justification and the necessary conditions for the practical success of democratic institutions.

This discord, long since perceived by the discerning, has in our time become so flagrant that in many countries the ideal has been abandoned as an illusion. In these countries new social philosophies now prevail which maintain that the attempt to apply the principles of individual liberty, not only in the economic but in the political and the intellectual realm, was a fundamental error, and is responsible for the social and international conflicts which now bewilder and distress the world.

To accept this view implies the end of democratic institutions as we know them, and the renunciation of that faith in the worth and dignity of the individual which we have cherished even if we have not always justified it in action. I do not accept this view. I believe that in the long run it will prove mistaken—fatal to any way of life that can rightly be called civilized. But I also believe that if the democratic way of life is to survive we must give to the traditional concept of freedom a more positive content. The traditional concept of individual liberty is essentially negative. The freedom it emphasizes is freedom from constraint, and indeed from a particular kind of constraint, that is to say, governmental constraint. In the economic realm the result of freeing the individual from governmental constraint is that today far too many people are always in danger of losing those positive goods without which freedom from governmental constraint is of no value. What the average man now needs is the opportunity to acquire by his own effort, in an occupation for which he is fitted, the economic security which is essential to decent and independent living. This opportunity has now disappeared for something like a quarter of the working population. In my opinion it can only be restored, if at all, by such governmental regulations of our economy as may be necessary to enable private economic enterprise to function effectively and for the common good.

If then the democratic way of life is to survive we must distinguish the kinds of individual freedom that are essential to it from those that are unessential or disastrous. Broadly speaking, the kinds that are essential are those which the individual enjoys in his intellectual and political activities; the kinds that are unessential are the relatively unrestrained liberties he has hitherto enjoyed in his economic activities. The distinction is comparatively easy to make in theory, but will be extremely difficult to effect in practice. Not the least of the difficulties arises from the fact that in the traditional ideology the freedom of the individual in the

political, the intellectual, and the economic realms are so intimately associated that they seem to stand or fall together. The
result is that any proposal to regulate by governmental authority
the system of free economic enterprise is sure to be opposed on
the ground that if the system of free economic enterprise cannot
be maintained the other freedoms of democracy, freedom of
thought and political freedom, must in the end be abandoned also.
Whether this is true can only be determined by the event. Whatever the event may be, the difficult but essential task which com-
fronts all democratic societies today may be formulated as follows:
how in practice to curtail the freedom of the individual in economic enterprise sufficiently to effect that equality of opportunity
and of possessions without which democracy is an empty form,
and at the same time to preserve that measure of individual freedom in intellectual and political life without which it cannot exist.

Gerald White Johnson

Our Heritage of the Common Law

*Gerald Johnson (1890-   ) is an American newspaperman who
was associated with the Baltimore* Evening Sun *from 1926 to 1939
and with* The Sun *until 1943. After this date he became a free-lance
writer and has written a number of books, generally on political
subjects. Part III of this chapter from* Our English Heritage *has
been omitted.*

I

Every American who has listened to a Fourth of July oration
must be more or less vaguely aware of the existence of something called "the common law" that was imported from England
in colonial times and that is supposed to be highly meritorious.
But not every American has taken the trouble to find out what it
is, or in what its merit consists.

A layman, indeed, runs into difficulties as soon as he undertakes to examine the subject because the term "common law" may mean any of several different things, depending upon whether it is used by counsel in a bigamy case, a jurisconsult writing a dissertation on legal principles, a historian discussing the rise of monarchy in England, or a Silver Tongue whipping up the enthusiasm of precinct workers at a political clambake. Counsel, for instance, would mean unwritten law based on decided cases with some reference to custom; the jurisconsult would mean that body of law which is distinguished from civil law and the law of equity; the historian would mean—or might mean—that law which is unmistakably English in origin and cannot be traced back to the *Pandects* of Justinian, or any other Roman authority; while the Silver Tongue, in all probability, would mean something that is not the common law by any definition, but a hodge-podge of all historical theories of the Rights of Man, with overtones of *Magna Carta*, trial by jury and the writ of *habeas corpus*.

Yet it is what the orator has in mind that is best worth examining in a study of English influence on the pattern of American life, for the heritage that most people think of when they refer to our possession of the English common law is certainly not any specific compilation of statutes, nor that body of law which is apart from civil law, canon law and equity. It is something much vaguer and more elusive—less actual law than an attitude toward the law developed both by the officers of the court and by the people of England.

It began far back when the theory of monarchy was as yet relatively undeveloped and the King was not regarded as a divinely appointed sovereign but merely as the first among the peers. The right to rule belonged to the barons, but experience and, no doubt, an innate sense of order convinced them that someone had to lead; so they agreed in principle to follow one of their number. But it was a long time before they admitted that any special sanctity attached to the King's person or to his lineage, except as they were all committed to support of the principle of inheritance.

The affair at Runnymede, for example, was an illustration of the reluctance of the barons to permit any broadening of the gap between royalty and nobility. It was a later generation that construed it as a fight to establish the liberty of the subject. To the barons themselves that liberty was not in question. It was already established, and the operation was designed merely to cut John, the King, down to what they regarded as nearer his proper size. *Magna Carta* was simply a promise in writing, since his oral promise had proved worthless, to stick strictly to his own business and let theirs alone.

More than eighty years after Runnymede Roger Bigod, earl of Norfolk, and perhaps the most powerful noble in the realm, was so little disposed to take orders from the King that their altercation has become historical and is enshrined in the *Encyclopaedia Britannica*. Bigod, ordered to carry war into Gascony, flatly refused. "By God, earl," exploded the King, "you shall either go or hang." "By that same oath, O King," responded the earl, "I shall neither go nor hang." The record shows that he did not go and he did not hang. The King dared not press the issue, for he knew that he would not be supported by the majority of the nobles.

Yet even then it was admitted that by virtue of his position as first of the peers the King did have certain rights more general than those held by any of the rest. He was not permitted to interfere between a lord and his lieges except where his own interests were concerned. Local law was made and administered by the local lord, and an act that was a capital crime on one demesne might be no crime at all a few miles away in the territory of another lord.

But there were certain acts that touched the King's rights, as well as the lord's. Murder, for example, deprived the King of a subject. If one lord's servant robbed the servant of another lord, that was a breach of the King's peace. Such crimes, therefore, were crimes anywhere, regardless of whims of the baron on whose estate they occurred, and the laws against them were valid everywhere, that is to say, they were common to the whole realm. Judges representing the King, therefore, were said to administer the common law, while judges representing the baron administered only the local law.

But in view of the relative weakness of the King's power the common law could be enforced only with the assistance, or at

least the consent, of the baron. Therefore, in the beginning, the
common law applied only to acts that all men, everywhere, admitted were flagitious. That is to say, the common law had to be
so obviously right that no man could seriously maintain that it was
anything but just. By degrees this idea took hold so firmly upon
the popular imagination that it overshadowed its origin and men
came to believe that conduct revolting to the moral sense was a
violation of the common law, whether or not any legislative body
had dealt with it in specific terms. In case after case judges so
ruled, and their rulings became precedents with the force of law.
So by 1607, when the English settlement of America began, England had a tremendous body of law that Parliament had never
seen.

Yet, although its formal basis was precedents set by courts,
it is somewhat misleading to call it judge-made law. That term
today connotes an assumption by the judiciary of the legislative
power without the consent of the people or their representatives.
The common law of England is better described as law made by
common consent. A decision approved by the consciences of fair-
minded men became a precedent with the force of law; one not
so approved was over-ruled, evaded, or undermined by subsequent
decisions and did not survive.

It was a muddled, illogical and haphazard method of building
up a body of law, but it suited the English and served their purposes sufficiently well. It was familiar to the colonists and accepted
by them, even though it was the despair of legal scholars on the
continent of Europe, accustomed to the definite precision of the
Roman system. But when the colonists broke away from the
empire in 1776 a problem suddenly arose. They had formally repudiated all political bonds with Great Britain; but was not the
law a political bond, in fact, the most important of all? If all the
laws of England were repealed by the act of separation, what was
to take their place? For a legislature to create at one sitting an
entire code was a labor too enormous for human capacity, but
something had to be done to avoid anarchy.

In most of the colonies the difficulty was met by a simple
enactment that while the authority of Parliament was ended and
its acts of no force in America, the common law of England
should remain the law of the new State until such time as its legis-

lature should provide otherwise. The legislatures went at the task with great assiduity, and much of the common law was swiftly replaced by specific statutes, usually embodying the same principles, but sometimes repudiating them. A case in point is the Virginia Statute of Religious Freedom, the drafting of which Thomas Jefferson considered one of his three great achievements, the other two being the writing of the Declaration of Independence and the founding of the University of Virginia—not his Governorship, his ambassadorship, his Secretaryship of State, or the Presidency.

Others were the laws, also fathered by Jefferson, disestablishing the Church of England and abolishing primogeniture in Virginia, both of which were eventually adopted by all the thirteen States. But the great body of the early legislation following the Revolution simply wrote into the statute books the legal principles gradually and often painfully evolved by the development of the English common law. It is therefore broadly true to say that American law is formal enactment of the law that grew up in England haphazardly.

There are exceptions. The law of Louisiana, for instance, is based on the *Code Napoléon*. Recent federal legislation permitting husband and wife to file for taxation each a report of half their joint income was forced because Californians enjoyed an advantage over the rest of the country by reason of the fact that their law of joint property is based on Spanish, not English, principles. But the exceptions are minor. In the main, the pattern of life represented by the law was set by the English and to this day remains largely English.

2

But what the orators have in mind when they refer to the heritage of the common law has little reference to either accumulated precedents or statutory enactments. They mean, rather, the attitude toward the law that was fostered by the way in which the common law came into existence. This attitude was stated formally by Edward Coke in the dictum, "Reason is the life of the law; nay, the Common Law itself is nothing but reason."

Americans have drawn from this the obvious inference that if it isn't reasonable, it can't be good law. Legislatures may legislate until they are black in the face, but if their legislation doesn't meet the standards of common sense and common decency, it simply isn't good law and neither Congress nor the courts can make it good.

This was first exemplified strikingly by the Alien and Sedition laws, which were never approved by the masses of the people and for that reason brought destruction upon the party that enacted them.

It was exemplified again in the various Fugitive Slave laws of the years immediately preceding the Civil War. From the strictly legalistic standpoint, these laws were perfectly sound. Not much federal legislation has been more firmly based on Constitutional authority nor more logically constructed than the acts requiring law officers and citizens of the so-called Free States to detain and return to bondage a slave who might escape into their territory.

But such laws did not seem either reasonable or right to the people of the Free States; hence these people could never be convinced that such statutes had the force and effect of real law. In England the common law had to be right in the eyes of a majority of the people before it was recognized as law. The fact that American legislatures had enacted the common law into statute law did not eradicate from the minds of the people the notion that the law acquires its validity through its reasonableness. Jefferson expressed this attitude in his First Inaugural: "though the will of the majority is in all cases to prevail, that will to be rightful must be reasonable." Unreasonable legislation he branded as oppression, and resistance to oppression he always regarded as a sacred duty.

The most recent demonstration of the survival of this attitude for more than three hundred years was the incident of the adoption and subsequent repeal of the Eighteenth Amendment to the Constitution of the United States, prohibiting the manufacture and sale of intoxicating beverages. This legislation, from the legalistic standpoint, was as sound as the Fugitive Slave laws; indeed, if repeated sanction by constituted authority had any effect, it might be called sounder, for it was cast in the form of an addition to the organic law, regularly submitted to the several States and ratified by more than three-fourths of them. Nevertheless, over large areas it was regarded as utterly unreasonable, therefore null and void.

The approval of Congress, of State legislatures and of the courts, up to and including the Supreme Court of the United States, could not make it reasonable and thus, in the opinion of millions, could not make it good law. After fourteen years this opinion became so strong that the law became in itself a menace to all laws, even the most necessary, and therefore had to be abandoned.

Repeated instances of this sort have created a widespread opinion in other countries, and even among the over-educated in this one, that the American is essentially lawless. Englishmen, in particular, seem to hold to this view with great tenacity; Kipling's reference to "the cynic devil in his blood," the impulse

> That bids him flout the Law he makes,
> That bids him make the Law he flouts,

is typical. Apparently it never crossed the mind of the poet that this "cynic devil" is a profound respect for the spirit of the English common law, expressed differently, because the situation is different, but identical at bottom with the Briton's firm belief that if it isn't reasonable it isn't sound law.

The difference in the situation is that much of the English common law is the result of defiance of acts of Parliament by judges, rather than by the people. The massive array of technicalities created by the English courts prior to the last century was, in effect, the judges' way of invalidating foolish statutes. When there were three hundred crimes punishable by death in England the law was unreasonable, and every honest judge knew it. The law said that a man convicted of stealing goods to the value of thirteen pence should be hanged; but generations before the law was changed judges knew that it was bad law; therefore they sought eagerly for some technicality, were it only a misplaced comma in a bill of indictment, that would give them an excuse to refuse to convict. By skillful use of precedent and of tortuous reasoning, the judges contrived to nullify the more idiotic acts of Parliament.

But most of them were convinced of the extreme fragility of public order, which they thought would be swiftly undermined by any outward show of disrespect for constituted authority. Under no circumstances, therefore, would they say brusquely that the law was idiotic; instead they managed somehow, without questioning its righteousness, to find an excuse to say that the law did not apply to the instant case and to let the defendant go.

American judges have had no such convenient recourse. American law is relatively new and highly explicit, and there exists no immeasurable labyrinth of precedent and custom in which the courts can conveniently lose themselves in order to avoid rendering an iniquitous judgment. With no avenue of escape American judges have had to enforce to the letter statutes that were, in the opinion of a large minority, sometimes a majority, of the people unjust, unrighteous and unworthy of the respect of honest men.

There is no royal authority in the United States that must be protected from the merest breath of disrespect by such fictions as the dictum that the King can do no wrong. The highest legislative authority in the land is Congress, and Americans are of the opinion that Congress can do wrong and feel no hesitation about saying so with emphasis. They are, therefore, no respectors of the acts of Congress; but to assume that this means that they are no respectors of law is to assume that the statutes are necessarily good law, which is flatly contrary to the opinion that Englishmen have maintained stubbornly for many centuries.

This has greatly perturbed legalists in both countries ever since efforts began to be made to reduce law within the bounds of logic. Whole libraries have been written to defend the indefensible thesis that disrespect for a disreputable statute is disrespect for law. Logicians have insisted that any other theory leads straight to anarchy, for a man who feels no obligation to do anything save what is right in his own eyes is an anarchist. But these logicians will not admit the statistical factor that nevertheless enters the equation, whether they like it or not. A man who does what is right only in his own eyes may be an anarchist; but a man who does what is right in his own eyes and also in the eyes of nine-tenths of his neighbors is not an anarchist, and cannot be transformed into one by any sort of dialectic, no matter how subtle.

The English, committed to the thesis that the King can do no wrong, but confronted by the stubborn fact that wrong was obviously being done, had recourse to the theory that all wrong is attributable to the King's ministers who are quite capable of putting through Parliament legislation of the most villainous kind.

But no Englishman regards such legislation as good law. It violates the British constitution and binds no man's conscience, however it may bind his acts. Only one generation ago the famous Dr. John Clifford, the Nonconformist clergyman, regularly suffered his household goods to be seized and sold by officers of the law rather than obey the statute that taxed him for the support of the Church of England. Yet a description of Dr. Clifford as having a "cynic devil in his blood" would have been regarded, even by Rudyard Kipling, as singular indeed.

The existence of frontier conditions did, of course, make inevitable a certain amount of genuine lawlessness, lawlessness in the literal sense. On any frontier the establishment of adequate and efficient agencies of law enforcement is a slow, laborious process and until such agencies are established there is, in fact, no law. The United States government announced the closing of the last frontier on this continent in 1893; so from 1607 to 1893, a period of two hundred and eighty-six years, there was an area where the edge of civilization was cutting into the wilderness, which is to say an area without law.

Since Frederick Jackson Turner made his famous study of the effect of the frontier on the civilization behind it, many writers have attributed the so-called lawlessness of America to habits acquired on the frontier. It is a questionable thesis. The spirit of the frontier was not one of contempt for all law; on the contrary, it was one of such strong, even fanatical, belief in the common law that offenses against it were suppressed with great violence. The Vigilantes of the West were frankly contemptuous of the forms of law, but in their own eyes they were enforcing the spirit of the law, which doubtless convicts them of disrespect for legalism, but strongly emphasizes their respect for law.

The man who created the legendary West confected a literary marshmallow[1] but it had some flavor of truth in its central tragedy, that of a man who hanged his best friend for stealing cattle. A more staggering proof of respect for law can hardly be imagined, yet things of that kind did happen on the frontier.

---

[1] Owen Wister's novel, *The Virginian*, which today seems no more than a monument of honeycomb tripe, but which was a sensational success when it was published in 1902 and became the precursor of the "westerns" that still enthrall the minds of small boys from nine to ninety.

An intellectual stereotype of recent years is the assumption that the essential lawlessness of the American people is proved by the obsolescent crime of lynching.[2] Yet the fact is that lynching in its heydey, some sixty years ago, flourished mainly in the West and in the South, one a region in which no firm social order had been established, the other a region in which the existing order had been blasted by a four years' war followed by conquest and ten years' military rule by an army of occupation. In the one case there were no forms of law; in the other, the forms of law imposed by a military conqueror were regarded by the majority of the people as iniquitous. But in both cases the ancient English idea of the common law, that is, law approved by the consciences of all honest men whether or not it had been approved by Congress, was not only accepted but was supported vigorously and violently.

It is frequently asserted that the point at which the English and the Americans diverge most widely is the point of the latter's disrespect for law. Yet it may be argued plausibly that this apparent disrespect is itself a part of the pattern of American life set by the English, because it stems from the ancient English belief that acts of Parliament or of the King himself are not true law unless they are just and righteous.[3]

4

The heritage of American life brought by the importation of English law is remarkable, therefore, first of all for a certain

[2] In the first five years of this century lynchings, according to the Tuskegee Institute records, averaged about 104 annually; in the last five years for which figures are available (1941-6) they averaged a fraction under four annually. Even of these some are doubtful cases, bearing more resemblance to private vendettas than to true mob violence.

[3] If some critical reader cites against this description of the American notion of the common law the famous dictum of Mr. Justice Holmes, "The Common Law is not a brooding omnipresence in the sky but the articulate voice of some sovereign or quasi-sovereign that can be identified" (O. W. Holmes, dissent in *Southern Pacific Company vs. Jensen*, 1916), the answer is that Mr. Justice Holmes was a jurisconsult, speaking for and to the courts and the bar. In that, his voice is authoritative. But to the common man, unskilled in legal science, the common law *is* "a brooding omnipresence in the sky" or something akin to it—his own inner conviction of what is reasonable and right. In spite of the multiplicity of lawyers among us, the mass of the American people consists of common folk, and their ideas, not professional definitions, establish the manner of American thought and American life.

vagueness of outline. There is no point at which the law is sharply and definitely supreme; certain rights of the citizen always take precedence. In theory, at least, the officers of the law are always accountable; they may in no case detain a citizen without being forced by a writ of *habeas corpus* to show cause, and if their excuse is patently not reasonable it is the duty of the court to free the prisoner.

This is true, of course, only when men's minds are relatively serene. When we are terrified, there will always be a Lincoln to suspend the writ of *habeas corpus*, whether or not he has the right to do so; and if we are sufficiently terrified, there will always be an Un-American Activities Committee or its equivalent to sentence men to pains and penalties without convicting them, trying them, or even indicting them. There is only one legal dictum that frightened men have ever held immutable and inviolate, and that is *Inter arma silent leges*. Even a "cold war," as recent events have amply demonstrated, can strike the law dumb.

But when we are not afraid, it is a deep American conviction that the law "to be rightful must be reasonable," for no legislature by passing statutes can convert wrong into right. This part of the pattern was set for us by the English and its importance in the pattern is denied by none.

Some decry it, and they are by no means always representatives of other nations who have come to this country since England obtained dominance over the continent. There are those of English origin who deplore the American reluctance to admit the existence of any absolute authority save the authority of the moral law or, if you prefer, the law of God. To their logical minds the absence of any unquestionable earthly authority is an invitation to anarchy. Some very eminent Americans have belonged to this school. John Adams was one; so was John Marshall; so was John C. Calhoun; and, to dispense with the Johns, so were Adams' remote descendants, Henry and Brooks Adams.

But more sanguine men, less perturbed by *lacunae* in logical thinking, and observing that the English spirit has not led us into anarchy in three hundred and forty-odd years, are persuaded that it will never do so. They may even go as far as Jefferson, who hoped for a slight rebellion about every twenty years merely to keep authority reminded that it is, after all, accountable, and that

if its acts do not square with what the common man believes is
right, they are not legal and cannot be made legal.

To the authoritarian this may be the very essence of anarchy.
But to the libertarian it is the best hope of the survival of human
freedom. For the gift of this idea he holds himself more deeply in
debt to the English than he is for all the rest that they have added
unto it.

Walter Lippmann

The Indispensable Opposition

Walter Lippmann (*1889-*   ) *was an associate editor of the* New
Republic *and editor of the New York* World *until 1931. He is now
a special writer for the New York* Herald Tribune *and other newspapers. His writing constantly reflects his well-informed and
thoughtful mind.*

I

Were they pressed hard enough, most men would probably
confess that political freedom—that is to say, the right to speak
freely and to act in opposition—is a noble ideal rather than a practical necessity. As the case for freedom is generally put to-day, the
argument lends itself to this feeling. It is made to appear that,
whereas each man claims his freedom as a matter of right, the freedom he accords to other men is a matter of toleration. Thus, the
defense of freedom of opinion tends to rest not on its substantial,
beneficial, and indispensable consequences, but on a somewhat eccentric, a rather vaguely benevolent, attachment to an abstraction.

It is all very well to say with Voltaire, "I wholly disapprove of
what you say, will defend to the death your right to say it,"
but as a matter of fact most men will not defend to the death the

rights of other men: if they disapprove sufficiently what other men say, they will somehow suppress those men if they can.

So, if this is the best that can be said for liberty of opinion, that a man must tolerate his opponents because everyone has a "right" to say what he pleases, then we shall find that liberty of opinion is a luxury, safe only in pleasant times when men can be tolerant because they are not deeply and vitally concerned.

Yet actually, as a matter of historic fact, there is a much stronger foundation for the great constitutional right of freedom of speech, and as a matter of practical human experience there is a much more compelling reason for cultivating the habits of free men. We take, it seems to me, a naïvely self-righteous view when we argue as if the right of our opponents to speak were something that we protect because we are magnanimous, noble, and un-selfish. The compelling reason why, if liberty of opinion did not exist, we should have to invent it, why it will eventually have to be restored in all civilized countries where it is now suppressed, is that we must protect the right of our opponents to speak because we must hear what they have to say.

We miss the whole point when we imagine that we tolerate the freedom of our political opponents as we tolerate a howling baby next door, as we put up with the blasts from our neighbor's radio because we are too peaceable to heave a brick through the window. If this were all there is to freedom of opinion, that we are too good-natured or too timid to do anything about our opponents and our critics except to let them talk, it would be difficult to say whether we are tolerant because we are magnanimous or because we are lazy, because we have strong principles or because we lack serious convictions, whether we have the hospitality of an inquiring mind or the indifference of an empty mind. And so, if we truly wish to understand why freedom is necessary in a civilized society, we must begin by realizing that, because freedom of discussion improves our own opinions, the liberties of other men are our own vital necessity.

We are much closer to the essence of the matter, not when we quote Voltaire, but when we go to the doctor and pay him to ask us the most embarrassing questions and to prescribe the most dis-agreeable diet. When we pay the doctor to exercise complete freedom of speech about the cause and cure of our stomachache, we do not look upon ourselves as tolerant and magnanimous, and worthy to be admired by ourselves. We have enough common sense to know that if we threaten to put the doctor in jail because we do not like the diagnosis and the prescription it will be unpleasant for the doctor, to be sure, but equally unpleasant for our own stomachache. That is why even the most ferocious dictator would rather be treated by a doctor who was free to think and speak the truth than by his own Minister of Propaganda. For there is a point, the point at which things really matter, where the freedom of others is no longer a question of their right but of our own need.

The point at which we recognize this need is much higher in some men than in others. The totalitarian rulers think they do not need the freedom of an opposition: they exile, imprison, or shoot their opponents. We have concluded on the basis of practical experience, which goes back to Magna Carta and beyond, that we need the opposition. We pay the opposition salaries out of the public treasury.

In so far as the usual apology for freedom of speech ignores this experience, it becomes abstract and eccentric rather than concrete and human. The emphasis is generally put on the right to speak, as if all that mattered were that the doctor should be free to go out into the park and explain to the vacant air why I have a stomachache. Surely that is a miserable caricature of the great civic right which men have bled and died for. What really matters is that the doctor should tell *me* what ails me, that I should listen to him; that if I do not like what he says I should be free to call in another doctor; and that then the first doctor should have to listen to the second doctor; and that out of all the speaking and listening, the give-and-take of opinions, the truth should be arrived at.

This is the creative principle of freedom of speech, not that it is a system for the tolerating of error, but that it is a system for finding the truth. It may not produce the truth, or the whole truth all the time, or often, or in some cases ever. But if the truth can be found, there is no other system which will normally and habitually find so much truth. Until we have thoroughly understood this principle, we shall not know why we must value our liberty, or how we can protect and develop it.

2

Let us apply this principle to the system of public speech in a totalitarian state. We may, without any serious falsification, picture a condition of affairs in which the mass of the people are being addressed through one broadcasting system by one man and his chosen subordinates. The orators speak. The audience listens but cannot and dare not speak back. It is a system of one-way communication; the opinions of the rulers are broadcast outwardly to the mass of the people. But nothing comes back to the rulers from the people except the cheers; nothing returns in the way of knowledge of forgotten facts, hidden feelings, neglected truths, and practical suggestions.

But even a dictator cannot govern by his own one-way inspiration alone. In practice, therefore, the totalitarian rulers get back the reports of the secret police and of their party henchmen down among the crowd. If these reports are competent, the rulers may manage to remain in touch with public sentiment. Yet that is not enough to know what the audience feels. The rulers have also to make great decisions that have enormous consequences, and here their system provides virtually no help from the give-and-take of opinion in the nation. So they must either rely on their own intuition, which cannot be permanently and continually inspired, or, if they are intelligent despots, encourage their trusted advisers and their technicians to speak and debate freely in their presence.

On the walls of the houses of Italian peasants one may see inscribed in large letters the legend, "Mussolini is always right." But if that legend is taken seriously by Italian ambassadors, by the Italian General Staff, and by the Ministry of Finance, then all one can say is heaven help Mussolini, heaven help Italy, and the new Emperor of Ethiopia.

For at some point, even in a totalitarian state, it is indispensable that there should exist the freedom of opinion which causes opposing opinions to be debated. As time goes on, that is less and less easy under a despotism; critical discussion disappears as the internal opposition is liquidated in favor of men who think and feel alike. That is why the early successes of despots, of Napoleon I and of Napoleon III, have usually been followed by an irreparable mistake. For in listening only to his yes men—the others being in exile or in concentration camps, or terrified—the despot shuts himself off from the truth that no man can dispense with.

We know all this well enough when we contemplate the dictatorships. But when we try to picture our own system, by way of contrast, what picture do we have in our minds? It is, is it not, that anyone may stand up on his own soapbox and say anything he pleases, like the individuals in Kipling's poem who sit each in his separate star and draw the Thing as they see it for the God of Things as they are. Kipling, perhaps, could do this, since he was a poet. But the ordinary mortal isolated on his separate star will have an hallucination, and a citizenry declaiming from separate soapboxes will poison the air with hot and nonsensical confusion.

If the democratic alternative to the totalitarian one-way broadcasts is a row of separate soapboxes, then I submit that the alternative is unworkable, is unreasonable, and is humanly unattractive. It is above all a false alternative. It is not true that liberty has developed among civilized men when anyone is free to set up a soapbox, is free to hire a hall where he may expound his opinions to those who are willing to listen. On the contrary, freedom of speech is established to achieve its essential purpose only when different opinions are expounded in the same hall to the same audience.

For, while the right to talk may be the beginning of freedom, the necessity of listening is what makes the right important. Even in Russia and Germany a man may still stand in an open field and speak his mind. What matters is not the utterance of opinions. What matters is the confrontation of opinions in debate. No man can care profoundly that every fool should say what he likes. Nothing has been accomplished if the wisest man proclaims his wisdom in the middle of the Sahara Desert. This is the shadow. We have the substance of liberty when the fool is compelled to listen to the wise man and learn; when the wise man is compelled to take account of the fool, and to instruct him; when the wise man can increase his wisdom by hearing the judgment of his peers.

That is why civilized men must cherish liberty—as a means of promoting the discovery of truth. So we must not fix our whole attention on the right of anyone to hire his own hall, to rent his own broadcasting station, to distribute his own pamphlets. These rights are incidental; and though they must be preserved, they can be preserved only by regarding them as incidental, as auxiliary to the substance of liberty that must be cherished and cultivated.

Freedom of speech is best conceived, therefore, by having in mind the picture of a place like the American Congress, an assembly where opposing views are represented, where ideas are not merely uttered but debated, or the British Parliament, where men who are free to speak are also compelled to answer. We may picture the true condition of freedom as existing in a place like a court of law, where witnesses testify and are cross-examined, where the lawyer argues against the opposing lawyer before the same judge and in the presence of one jury. We may picture freedom as existing in a forum where the speaker must respond to questions; in a gathering of scientists where the data, the hypothesis, and the conclusion are submitted to men competent to judge them; in a reputable newspaper which not only will publish the opinions of those who disagree but will reëxamine its own opinion in the light of what they say.

Thus the essence of freedom of opinion is not in mere toleration as such, but in the debate which toleration provides: it is not in the venting of opinion, but in the confrontation of opinion. That this is the practical substance can readily be understood when we remember how differently we feel and act about the censorship and regulation of opinion purveyed by different media of communication. We find then that, in so far as the medium makes difficult the confrontation of opinion in debate, we are driven towards censorship and regulation.

There is, for example, the whispering campaign, the circulation of anonymous rumors by men who cannot be compelled to prove what they say. They put the utmost strain on our tolerance, and there are few who do not rejoice when the anonymous slanderer is caught, exposed, and punished. At a higher level there is the moving picture, a most powerful medium for conveying ideas, but a medium which does not permit debate. A moving picture cannot be answered effectively by another moving picture; in all free countries there is some censorship of the movies, and there would be more if the producers did not recognize their limitations by avoiding political controversy. There is then the radio. Here debate is difficult: it is not easy to make sure that the speaker is being answered in the presence of the same audience. Inevitably, there is some regulation of the radio.

When we reach the newspaper press, the opportunity for debate is so considerable that discontent cannot grow to the point where under normal conditions there is any disposition to regulate the press. But when newspapers abuse their power by injuring people who have no means of replying, a disposition to regulate the press appears. When we arrive at Congress we find that, because the membership of the House is so large, full debate is impracticable. So there are restrictive rules. On the other hand, in the Senate, where the conditions of full debate exist, there is almost absolute freedom of speech.

This shows us that the preservation and development of freedom of opinion are not only a matter of adhering to abstract legal rights, but also, and very urgently, a matter of organizing and arranging sufficient debate. Once we have a firm hold on the central principle, there are many practical conclusions to be drawn. We then realize that the defense of freedom of opinion consists primarily in perfecting the opportunity for an adequate give-and-take of opinion; it consists also in regulating the freedom of those revolutionists who cannot or will not permit or maintain debate when it does not suit their purposes.

We must insist that free oratory is only the beginning of free speech; it is not the end, but a means to an end. The end is to find the truth. The practical justification of civil liberty is not that self-expression is one of the rights of man. It is that the examination of opinion is one of the necessities of man. For experience tells us that it is only when freedom of opinion becomes the compulsion to debate that the seed which our fathers planted has produced its fruit. When that is understood, freedom will be cherished not because it is a vent for our opinions but because it is the surest method of correcting them.

The unexamined life, said Socrates, is unfit to be lived by man. This is the virtue of liberty, and the ground on which we may best justify our belief in it, that it tolerates error in order to serve the truth. When men are brought face to face with their opponents, forced to listen and learn and mend their ideas, they cease to be children and savages and begin to live like civilized men. Then only is freedom a reality, when men may voice their opinions because they must examine their opinions.

3

The only reason for dwelling on all this is that if we are to preserve democracy we must understand its principles. And the principle which distinguishes it from all other forms of government is that in a democracy the opposition not only is tolerated as constitutional but must be maintained because it is in fact indispensable.

The democratic system cannot be operated without effective opposition. For, in making the great experiment of governing people by consent rather than by coercion, it is not sufficient that the party in power should have a majority. It is just as necessary that the party in power should never outrage the minority. That means that it must listen to the minority and be moved by the criticisms of the minority. That means that its measures must take account of the minority's objections, and that in administering measures it must remember that the minority may become the majority.

The opposition is indispensable. A good statesman, like any other sensible human being, always learns more from his opponents than from his fervent supporters. For his supporters will push him to disaster unless his opponents show him where the dangers are. So if he is wise he will often pray to be delivered from his friends, because they will ruin him. But, though it hurts, he ought also to pray never to be left without opponents; for they keep him on the path of reason and good sense.

The national unity of a free people depends upon a sufficiently even balance of political power to make it impracticable for the administration to be arbitrary and for the opposition to be revolutionary and irreconcilable. Where that balance no longer exists, democracy perishes. For unless all the citizens of a state are forced by circumstances to compromise, unless they feel that they can affect policy but that no one can wholly dominate it, unless by habit and necessity they have to give and take, freedom cannot be maintained.

Thomas Reed Powell

Constitutional Metaphors

Thomas Reed Powell (1880-1955), a native of Vermont, graduated from the Law School of Harvard University in 1904 and was admitted to the Vermont Bar, but remained only a few years in active practice. In 1907 he became a member of the faculty of Columbia University, later taught at the University of Illinois, and in 1925 returned to Harvard and the faculty of its Law School. His major interest was constitutional law. The essay that follows is a review of James M. Beck's The Constitution of the United States.

Even before the eighteenth amendment, books about the United States Constitution were apt to be pretty dry. They usually tell what the Supreme Court says in a lot of cases and try to show how what it says in one case will jibe all right with what it says in the other cases. After the writers tell what happens in each case, then they try to forget it and to put all the cases together and make up a set of rules to show what the Supreme Court has been up to and what it is going to do next. This is a very hard thing to do, and it is very hard to read after it has been done. You have to think very hard all the time, and even then you get all mixed up. This kind of book makes you tired because you have to try so hard to think, and so you usually stop trying to read it.

The new book which Mr. Beck has written about the Constitution is a very different kind of book. You can read it without thinking. If you have got tired trying to read the other kind of books, you will be glad of the nice restful book that Mr. Beck has written. It runs along like a story in a very interesting way. Most of the story is about how the Constitution got made. This is really history, but it is written in a very lively way like a novel, with a great many characters, almost all male, and plenty of conversation and a very exciting plot. Many of the chapters have names like

From the *New Republic*, February 11, 1925. Reprinted by permission of the publishers.

those in a novel, such as "The Opening of the Battle," "The Crisis," "The Dawn," "Nearing the End," "The Curtain Falls," and others. Besides the story there are many quotations from Shakespeare, Beethoven, Horace, Isaiah, Euripides, Beard, and other famous men. Many of these quotations are quite old, but some of them seem fairly new. They help to make the book a really high-class book. There is not much more to say about the part of the book that tells how the Constitution got made, except that it is fun and easy to read and seems pretty true to life.

The rest of the book is about what a good Constitution it is and how bad it is to make changes in it. The main reason why it is so good is because it was made by such good men. Mr. Beck says very nice things about them. He calls them "a group of gentlemen of substance and honor," and he thinks that "all apparently were inspired by a fine spirit of self-effacement." They kept their ears a good way from the ground, as gentlemen of substance and honor should, for Mr. Beck says that "they represented the spirit of representative government at its best in avoiding the cowardice of time-servers and the low cunning of demagogues." This means that they were the kind of men who would do what they thought was best for all the people without trying to find out what the people thought was best for themselves. Some of the people in those days who were not gentlemen of substance and honor had been trying to do very foolish things, and it was partly to stop such foolishness that these good men came together to make the Constitution.

It was this foolishness of the men who didn't make the Constitution that made the men who made it make it such a good Constitution. This was the second main reason why it is so good. It is what Mr. Beck has in his mind when he speaks of "the anterior necessity of those who had property interests to protect themselves against that spirit of social revolt which we today call 'Bolshevism.'" If these men who made the Constitution had not been so full of their "fine spirit of self-effacement," they might not have seen so clearly what was the best thing to do. But they did. Mr. Beck says that it was because of the hard times that we got such a good Constitution. This was the third main reason. Of course the hard times couldn't give us a good Constitution all by themselves, but you can see how much they helped when you read Mr. Beck's book where it says:

It is therefore true that the Constitution was born of an economic travail, and that its merits were largely determined by the commercial necessities of the American people. It was largely the work of men of affairs; for most of the members of the Convention were influential and, for the times, well-to-do professional and business men, who felt that, if their property interests were to be safeguarded and prosperity were to return after the panic of 1785, there must be, not merely freer commercial intercourse between the States, but also greater security to the rights of property against the disintegrating social tendencies, due to the distress among the masses, which, then as now, inevitably follows a depreciated currency.

I never knew what the Constitution really is until I read Mr. Beck's book. He says that "it is something more than a written formula of government—it is a great spirit. It is a high and noble assertion, and, indeed, vindication, of the morality of government." It is splendid to have a Constitution like that and to know, as Mr. Beck tells us, that "to the succeeding ages, the Constitution will be a flaming beacon." This is not all that it is, for Mr. Beck says also:

I have elsewhere likened the Constitution to a Gothic cathedral, like that of Rheims. Its foundations seem secure, even though some of its buttresses may be weakened and its statuary mutilated. Nevertheless it remains a noble and serviceable temple of Liberty and Justice. Let us hope that, with the present indifference of the masses to the Constitution and the spirit of innovation of this restless and impatient age, the time will not come that the Constitution will be as the Cathedral of Rheims when the author saw it in the summer of 1916. Rheims was a noble but pitiful ruin. Its high altar had been overthrown, and its glorious rose windows hopelessly shattered.

The high altar of the Constitution is the self-restraint which the American people of 1787 were wise enough to impose upon themselves and their posterity, and the rose windows are those great traditions of Liberty which we have gained at an infinite sacrifice of treasure and life from our English-speaking ancestry.

It helps us to know what the Constitution is if we know what it is not. It is a beacon and a Gothic cathedral, but it is not a rock and it is not a beach. Instead of these things, it is a floating dock. Mr. Beck puts it very beautifully when he says:

The Constitution is neither, on the one hand, a Gibraltar rock, which wholly resists the ceaseless washing of time and circumstances, nor is it, on the other hand, a sandy beach, which is slowly destroyed by the erosion of the waves. It is rather to be likened to a floating dock, which, while firmly attached to its moorings, and not therefore at the caprice of the waves, yet rises and falls with the tide of time and circumstance.

You might think that a Constitution which is all these wonderful things would be sure to last forever without any help from anything else. But this is not so. Mr. Beck says that it would not have lasted so long as it has if it had not been for the Supreme Court, which he says is "the balance wheel of the Constitution." He has a whole chapter which he calls "The Balance Wheel," and this chapter ends up by saying:

But always the Supreme Court stands as a great lighthouse, and even when the waves beat upon it with terrific violence (as in the Civil War, when it was shaken to its very foundation), yet after they have spent their fury, the great lamp of the Constitution—as that of another Pharos—illumines the troubled face of the waters with the benignant rays of those immutable principles of liberty and justice, which alone can make a nation free as well as strong.

It makes you see how marvelous the Supreme Court really is when it can be a balance wheel at the beginning of a chapter and a lighthouse at the end.

Even if you are not interested in the Constitution for its own sake, you will like to read what Mr. Beck says about it because he is such a lovely writer. He is the kind of writer who likes to write just for the sake of writing. He shows how he loves his work. He is not one of those writers who have to stop in their writing while they are making up their minds what to say. You can read him right along because he is so simple in his thoughts. He does not get you all mixed up the way so many writers do, but he brings up in your mind beautiful pictures of the Constitution as a temple and a beacon and a floating dock, and he lets you see the Supreme Court shining and balancing in a very wonderful way. I have read a great many books about the Constitution, but there is no other book that has given me just the same kind of pleasure that this one has.

You will have a very happy feeling while you are reading Mr. Beck's book, until you come to the last three chapters. Then you will begin to feel sad. The ending is not a happy ending. It tells of dangers that will hurt our country if we do not look out. It is not enough to have a Gothic cathedral with a balance wheel. We must all be wise and good men who will not make changes. This is

like so many books that have a moral lesson at the end. On his
very last page Mr. Beck tells us what we should do. He says that
when the Constitution came out of the safe in the State Department a few years ago, "the ink, in which it had been engrossed
nearly one hundred and thirty-seven years ago, was found to have
faded." He hopes that this is not a bad sign. This is what he means
when he says that "all who believe in constitutional government
must hope that this is not a portentous symbol." Just hoping will
not help any, and it would not do any good to put fresh ink on top
of the ink that is fading. We must do something different from
that. Mr. Beck tells us very plainly what we should do when he
says that "the American people must write the compact, not with
ink upon a parchment, but with 'letters of living light'—to use Webster's phrase—upon their hearts." That must be a very hard way to
write, and I should think it would be a good thing to write the ink
letters as well as the light letters, because the light might go out
before the ink had all faded.

Alexander Woollcott

The Archer-Shee Case

*Alexander Woollcott (1887-1943), a graduate of Hamilton College,
was best known as a New York dramatic critic and as the Town
Crier in his radio program. "The Archer-Shee Case," originally published in* The Atlantic Monthly, *February, 1939, is Woollcott's
version of an actual lawsuit, in which the accused was acquitted
many years before Woollcott was attracted by its dramatic and
political significance. Seven years after Woollcott's essay, Terence
Ratigan turned to the same material for a play,* The Winslow Boy,
produced in London in 1946 and in New York in 1948.

From time to time, since the turn of the century, there has
issued from the press of a publishing house in London and Edin-
burgh a series of volumes called the *Notable British Trials*, each
volume dedicated to some case in the criminal annals of England

or Scotland. Each would contain not only the testimony of witnesses, the photographs of exhibits, the arguments of counsel, the
dicta from the bench, and the verdict of the jury, but also an in-
troductory essay nicely calculated to enthrall those readers who
collect such instances of human violence, much as other madmen
collect coins or autographs or stamps.

The cases thus made available range all the way from the trials
of the mutineers aboard the *Bounty* to the libel action which, in
the twilight of the Victorian era, grew out of a charge of cheating
during a card game at a place called Tranby Croft, a gaudy lawsuit which agitated the entire Empire because it dragged into the
witness box no less a personage, a bit ruffled and breathing heavily,
than H.R.H. the Prince of Wales, who was later to rule and con-
solidate that empire as Edward VII. But for the most part, of
course, the cases thus edited have had their origin in murder most
foul, and they constitute not only an indispensable part of every
law library but a tempting pastime to all of us whose telltale interest in poison and throat-cutting is revealed in no other aspect of
our humdrum, blameless lives.

Now, as an avid subscriber to the series, I have long been both
exasperated and puzzled by the fact that it contained no tran-
script of that trial which, more and more in recent years, has taken
definite shape in my own mind as one of the most notable and certainly the most British of them all. Nowhere in England or America is there available in any library a record of the Archer-Shee
case. The student eager to master its details must depend on such
scattered odds and ends as he can dredge up from contemporary
memoirs and from the woefully incomplete reports in newspaper
files which already moulder to dust at the touch.

But within recent months, by a series of curious chances too
fantastic to have been foreseen, a complete private record of the
entire case has come into my possession, and it is my present plan,
before another year has passed, to put it into print for the use
of anyone who needs it as a light or craves it as a tonic. For the
Archer-Shee case is a short, sharp, illuminating chapter in the long
history of human liberty, and a study of it might, it seems to me,
stiffen the purpose of all those who in our own day are freshly
resolved that that liberty shall not perish from the earth.

In the fall of 1908, Mr. Martin Archer-Shee, a bank manager

in Liverpool, received word, through the commandant of the Royal Naval College at Osborne, that the Lords Commissioners of the Admiralty had decided to dismiss his thirteen-year-old son George, who had been proudly entered as a cadet only a few months before. It seems that a five-shilling postal order had been stolen from the locker of one of the boys—stolen, forged, and cashed—and, after a sifting of all the available evidence, the authorities felt unable to escape the conclusion that young Archer-Shee was the culprit. Out of such damaged and unpromising material the Admiralty could scarcely be expected to fashion an officer for His Majesty's Navy. "My Lords deeply regret," the letter went on to say, "that they must therefore request you to withdraw your son from the College." This devastating and puzzling news brought the family hurrying to Osborne. Was it true? No, Father. Then why did the authorities accuse him? What had made them think him guilty? The bewildered boy had no idea. "Well," said the father in effect, "we'll have to see about this," little guessing then, as he was to learn through many a bitter and discouraging month, that that would be easier said than done.

What had made them think the boy a thief? The offish captain could only refer him to the Admiralty, and the Lords of the Admiralty—by not answering letters, evading direct questions, and all the familiar technique of bureaucratic delay—retired behind the tradition that the Navy must be the sole judge of material suitable for the making of a British officer. If once they allowed their dismissal of a cadet to be reviewed by an inevitably outraged family, they would be establishing a costly and regrettable precedent.

What the elder Archer-Shee found blocking the path was no personal devil, no vindictive enemy of his son, no malignant spirit. But he was faced with an opponent as maddening, as cruel, and as destructive. He was entering the lists against the massive, complacent inertia of a government department which is not used to being questioned and does not like to be bothered. He was girding his loins for the kind of combat that takes all the courage and patience and will power a man can summon to his aid. He was challenging a bureaucracy to battle.

At a dozen points in the ensuing struggle, in which he was

backed up every day by his first-born, who was a Major and an M.P. and a D.S.O., a less resolute fighter might have been willing to give up, and one of smaller means would have had to. After all, the boy's former teachers and classmates at Stonyhurst, the Catholic college where he was prepared for Osborne, had welcomed him back with open arms, and, as allusions to the episode began to find their way into print, there were plenty of comfortable old men in clubs who opined loudly that this man Archer-Shee was making a bloody nuisance of himself. But you may also be sure that there were those among the neighbors who implied by their manner that the Navy must know what it was doing, that where there was so much smoke there must be some fire, that if the whole story could be told, and so forth and so forth. I think the father knew in his heart, as surely as anyone can know anything in this world, that his son was innocent. While there was a breath left in his body and a pound in his bank account, he could not let the youngster go out into the world with that stain on his name. He would not give up. Probably he was strengthened by his memory of how bitterly his little boy had wept on the day they took him away from Osborne. The father lived—by no more than a few months—to see the fight through.

The first great step was the retaining of Sir Edward Carson, then at the zenith of his incomparable reputation as an advocate. In his day, Carson was to hold high office—Attorney-General, Solicitor-General—to assume political leadership in the Ulster crisis—leader of the Irish Unionists in the House—to be rewarded with a peerage. It was part of the manifold irony of that crowded and stormy life, which ended in his death at eighty-one in 1935, that probably he will be longest remembered because of that hour of merciless cross-examination, in a libel suit at the Old Bailey, which brought down in ruins the towering and shaky edifice known as Oscar Wilde. But some there are who, when all else is forgotten, will rather hold Carson in highest honor for the good turn he once did to a small boy in trouble. He put all his tremendous power and implacable persistence and passionate hatred of tyranny at the service of Master Archer-Shee.

It was only after he had heard the boy's own story (and raked him with such a bracketing fire of questions as he was famous for

directing against a witness) that he agreed to take the case at all.
From that interview he rose, saying in effect, "This boy did not
steal that postal order. Now, let's get at the facts."

This took a bit of doing. It was the nub of the difficulty that
the small embryo officer had, by becoming a cadet, lost the rights
of an ordinary citizen without yet reaching that status which
would have entitled him to a court-martial. To be sure, the Admiralty by this time had resentfully bestirred itself to make several supplementary inquiries, but these were all *ex parte* proceedings, with the boy unrepresented by counsel, the witnesses unsub-
jected to the often clarifying fire of cross-examination. Even when
the badgered authorities went so far as to submit their findings to
the Judge Advocate General for review, they still kept the Archer-
Shees cooling their heels in the anteroom.

I am commanded by the Lords Commissioners of the Admiralty
to acknowledge receipt of your letter relative to the case of George
Archer-Shee, and my Lords desire me to say that the further enquiry
is not one at which a representative of your side in the sense in which
you use the word would be appropriate.

Well, even at the horrid risk of following a procedure which
might be described as "inappropriate," Carson was determined to
get the case into court, to make those witnesses tell their story
not to a biased and perhaps comatose representative of the Admiralty but to a jury of ordinary men—above all, to tell it with
the public listening. Resisting him in this was Sir Rufus Isaacs, later
to become, as Lord Reading, Chief Justice of England, but then
—in 1909 and 1910, this was—Solicitor-General and, unbecoming
as was the posture into which it threw him, mysteriously compelled by professional tradition to defend the Admiralty's action at
every step.

How to get the case into court? Carson finally had recourse
to an antique and long-neglected device known as the Petition of
Right. First he had to establish the notion that there had been a
violation of contract—a failure of the Crown to keep its part of the
bargain implied when, at some considerable expense to his folks
and with a binding agreement on his own part to serve as an officer
in the Navy once he had been trained for the job, the boy matric-
ulated. But, contract or no contract, a subject may sue the King
only under certain circumstances. If he approach the throne with

a Petition of Right and the King consent to write across it "Let right be done," His Majesty can, in that instance and on that issue, be sued like any commoner.

Instead of welcoming such a course as the quickest way of settling the original controversy and even of finding out what really had happened to that fateful postal order, the Admiralty, perhaps from sheer force of habit, resorted to legal technicalities as a means of delay. Indeed, it was only the human impatience of the justices, to whom a demurrer was carried on appeal, that finally cut through the red tape. They would eventually have to decide whether or not a Petition of Right was the suitable remedy, but in the meantime, they asked, why not let them have the facts? Why not, indeed? It was all Carson was contending for. It was all the Archer-Shees had ever asked for. Later in the House of Commons, where he was to hear the intervention of the demurrer denounced as a tragic error, Sir Rufus took considerable credit to himself for having bowed to this call for the facts, but he was making a virtue of something that had been very like necessity.

Anyway, the trial was ordered. So at long last, on a hot day in July 1910—nearly two years after the postal order was stolen and too late for any hope of finding out who really had stolen it —the case came before a jury in the King's Bench Division, and the witnesses whose stories in the first place had convinced the Osborne authorities that young Archer-Shee was a thief must, with Sir Rufus vigilant to protect them, submit themselves to cross-examination by the most alarming advocate of the English bar.

By this time the case had ceased to be a local squabble, reported as a matter of professional interest in various service journals but showing up in the ordinary newspapers only in an occasional paragraph. Now it was being treated by the press, column after column, as a *cause célèbre*, and all the Empire was following it with bated breath. Carson was on his feet in open court speaking for the Suppliant:

His son was branded as a thief and as a forger, a boy thirteen years old was labeled and ticketed, and has been since labeled and ticketed for all his future life, as a thief and a forger, and in such investigation as led to that disastrous result, neither his father nor any friend was ever there to hear what was said against a boy of thirteen, who by that one letter, and by that one determination was absolutely deprived of the possibility of any future career either in His Majesty's Service, or indeed in any other Service. Gentlemen, I protest against the injustice to a little boy, a child thirteen years of age, without communication with his parents, without his case ever being put, or an opportunity of its ever being put forward by those on his behalf—I protest against that boy at that early stage, a boy of that character, being branded for the rest of his life by that one act, an irretrievable act that I venture to think could never be got over. That little boy from that day, and from the day that he was first charged, up to this moment, whether it was in the ordeal of being called in before his Commander and his Captain, or whether it was under the softer influences of the persuasion of his own loving parents, has never faltered in the statement that he is an innocent boy.

But these reverberant words had overtones which all English-men could hear. Now the case was being followed with painful attention by plain men and women slowly come to the realization that here was no minor rumpus over the discipline and punctilio of the service, indeed no mere matter of a five-shilling theft and a youngster's reputation, but a microcosm in which was summed up all the long history of British liberty. Here in the small visible compass of one boy's fate was the entire issue of the inviolable sovereignty of the individual.

The Archer-Shees had as their advantageous starting point the inherent improbability of the boy's guilt. There seemed no good reason why he *should* steal five shillings when he was in ample funds on which he could lay his hands at will by the simple process of writing a chit. But if, for good measure or out of sheer deviltry, he *had* stolen his classmate's postal order, it seemed odd that instead of cashing it furtively he would not only openly get permission to go to the post office, which was out of bounds, but first loiter about for some time in an effort to get a schoolmate to go along with him for company. But this inherent improbability, so visible from this distance, quite escaped the attention of the college authorities who, by the sheer momentum of prosecution, had hastily reached their own conclusion by another route.

When young Terence Back dolefully reported to the Cadet Gunner that the postal order which had arrived that very morning as a present from some doting relative was missing from his locker, the Chief Petty Officer at once telephoned the post office to find out if it had already been cashed. It had. Oh!

There followed a rush of officialdom to the post office and much questioning of the chief clerk, Miss Anna Clara Tucker, first there and later at the college by Commander Cotton, the officer in charge of the investigation. Now, Miss Tucker, had there been any cadets at the post office that day? Yes, two—one to buy a 15s. 6d. postal order, the other to buy two totaling 14s. 9d. And was it one of them who had cashed the stolen order? Yes, it was. Would the postmistress be able to pick him out? No. They all looked so alike, in their uniforms, that she wouldn't know one from the other. But this she could tell, this she *did* remember—the stolen order was cashed by the boy who had bought the postal order for fifteen and six. And which one was that? Well, her records could answer that question. It was Cadet Archer-Shee. (He had needed that order, by the way, to send for a model engine on which his heart was set, and to purchase the order he had that morning drawn sixteen shillings from his funds on deposit with the Chief Petty Officer, a sum which would not only buy the order but pay for the necessary postage and leave in his pocket some small change for emergencies.)

Thus to Commander Cotton—Richard Greville Arthur Wellington Stapleton Cotton, who, oddly enough, was later to command H.M.S. *Terrible*—thus to Commander Cotton, who reported accordingly to the Captain, and he, through Portsmouth, to the Admiralty, it seemed satisfactorily evident that the postmistress was ineluctably identifying Archer-Shee as the thief, or at least as the villain who had converted the stolen goods into cash.

On her testimony the authorities acted—innocently, if you like, and not without later taking the precaution to support it by the dubious opinion of a handwriting expert. But so muddle-headed was this investigation, and such is the momentum of prosecution the world around, that the very first *précis* of that testimony filed with the Admiralty was careful to omit, as perhaps weakening the evidence against the boy—so swiftly do departmental investigators change from men seeking the truth into men trying to prove a hasty conclusion—was careful to omit the crucial fact that at the college next morning, when six or seven of the cadets were herded past her for inspection, the postmistress had been unable, either by the look of his face or by the sound of his voice, to pick out Archer-Shee. This failure became patently crucial when, two years later on that sweltering July day, Carson, with artfully deceptive gentleness, took over Miss Tucker for cross-examination.

The cashing of the stolen order and the issuing of the order for fifteen and six had taken place at the same time? Well, one transaction after the other. Her records showed that? No, but she remembered. The two took place within what space of time? Well, there might have been interruptions. After all, she was in sole charge of the office at the time? Yes. There was the telephone to answer, telegrams to take down as they came over the wire? Yes, and the mail to sort. These matters often took her away from the window? Yes. Even into the back room? Sometimes. So sometimes, if one cadet should go away from the window and another step into his place during any one of the interruptions, she might not notice the exchange? That was true. And, since they all looked alike to her, one cadet in this very instance *could* have taken the place of another without her realizing, when she returned to the window, that she had not been dealing throughout with the same boy? Possibly. So that now she couldn't say it was Archer-Shee who had cashed the stolen order? She had never said that exactly. Nor could she even be sure, now that she came to think of it, that the stolen order had, in fact, been cashed by the same cadet who bought the order for fifteen and six? Not absolutely sure. That, in effect—here oversimplified in condensation, but in effect—was her testimony.

Well, there it was—a gap in her story wide enough to drive a coach through. As soon as he saw it—it would strike a mere onlooking layman that the Admiralty might well have asked these same questions two years before—Sir Rufus knew the jig was up. Wherefore, when court opened on the fourth day, he was soon on his feet announcing that he no longer wished to proceed with any question of fact. It takes no great feat of imagination to guess at the breathlessness in that courtroom as the Solicitor-General came to the point:

As a result of the evidence that has been given during the trial that has been going on now for some days, and the investigation that has taken place, I say now, on behalf of the Admiralty, that I accept the statement of George Archer-Shee that he did not write the name on the postal order, and did not cash it, and consequently that he is innocent of the charge. I say further, in order that there may be no misapprehension about it, that I make that statement without any reserve of any description, intending that it shall be a complete justification of the statement of the boy and the evidence he has given before the Court.

In return—perhaps a fair exchange haggled for behind the scenes—Carson went on record as holding the belief that the responsible persons at Osborne and at the Admiralty had acted in good faith and that not even the disastrous Miss Tucker had been wanting in honesty. He had merely sought to show that she was mistaken.

Then, while the jury swarmed out of the box to shake hands with Carson and with the boy's father, the exhausted advocate turned to congratulate the boy himself, only to find that he wasn't even in court. Indeed, the case was over and court had adjourned before he got the news. When, blushing and grinning from ear to ear and falling all over himself, he went to Carson's room in the Law Courts to thank him, the great advocate ventured to ask how in his hour of triumph the boy had happened to be missing. Well, sir, he got up late. It seems he went to the theater the night before and so had overslept. Overslept! For weeks Carson himself had hardly been able to get any sleep. Overslept! Good God! Hadn't he even been anxious? Oh, no, sir. He had known all along that once the case got into court the truth would come out. Carson mopped his brow. Then he laughed. Perhaps that *was* the best way to take such things.

Thereafter, of course, the boy's was not the only attention that wandered. All England may have been watching, but, after all, other current topics were not without their elements of public interest. For one thing, a new King was on the throne. The Edward who had written "Let right be done" across the Archer-Shee petition now lay in his tomb at Windsor, and his son George was only just beginning the reign which was to prove so unforeseeably eventful. Then, even as the case came to an end, another was ready to overshadow it. Indeed, on the very day when, on behalf of the Admiralty, Sir Rufus acknowledged the boy's innocence, Inspector Dew arrived in Quebec to wait for the incoming *Montrose* and arrest two of her passengers, a fugitive medico named Crippen and his dream-girl, Ethel Le Neve. Even so, thanks to the sounding board known as the House of Commons, neither the public nor the Admiralty was allowed to forget the Archer-Shee case. Indeed, news of its conclusion had hardly reached the House when several members were on their feet giving notice—due notice that England would expect some specific assurance that the lesson had been learned, that never again would a boy be thus cavalierly dismissed from Osborne without notice to his folks or a chance for adequate defense.

In this instance, of course, it was too late for anything but apology and indemnification. "This," one speaker said with apparently unconscious humor, "could be left to the generosity of the Admiralty." Another speaker—the honorable member for the Universities of Glasgow and Aberdeen—put it this way: "I am quite sure the Admiralty will do all in their power to redress the very terrible and almost irreparable wrong done to the boy, on such a wrong being brought to their knowledge." But this confidence proved to be naïve. Month followed month with no word of apology, no word even of regret, and, as for indemnification, no offer to pay more than a fraction of what the boy's father had already spent in his defense. Indeed, in the fitful discussion on this point, the Admiralty had even introduced the pretty suggestion that the nipping of young Archer-Shee's naval career in the bud had not been so very injurious, because he was not a promising student anyway. It looks, at this distance, like a bad case of bureaucratic sulks.

So in March and April of the following year the attack was renewed. By the quaint but familiar device of moving that the salary of the First Lord of the Admiralty (Mr. Reginald McKenna) be reduced by one hundred pounds, the honorable member for Kingston (Mr. Cave) started the ball rolling. Although the honorable member for Leicester, Mr. Ramsay MacDonald, was so far out of key as to call the motion an attempt to blackmail the Treasury (cries of "Shame! Shame!"), the resulting debate went to the heart of the matter and put in memorable and satisfying words just what many decent and inarticulate men had been wanting to have said about the case all along.

The relative passages in *Hansard* make good reading to this day, because all those who moved to the attack spoke as if nothing in the world could matter more than the question of justice to one small unimportant boy. The wretched legalism of the Admiralty's evasions received its just meed of contempt, with the wits of Sir

Rufus Isaacs matched (and a bit more) by the same F. E. Smith
who was later to become Lord Birkenhead and who, by the way,
was at the time fresh from the defense of Ethel Le Neve at the
Old Bailey. These members, together with Lord Charles Beresford
and others, firmly jockeyed the unhappy First Lord into the position where he not only gave assurance that thereafter no boy at
Osborne would ever be so dealt with—this he had come prepared
to do—but went on record, at long reluctant last, as expressing in
this case his unqualified regrets. He even consented to pay to the
boy's father whatever sum a committee of three (including Carson himself) should deem proper. This ended in a payment of
£7120, and with that payment the case may be said to have come
to an end.

The case—but not the story. That has an epilogue. The characters? Most of them are gone. I don't know whatever became of
poor Miss Tucker, but the elder Archer-Shee is gone, and Isaacs
and Carson. Even Osborne is gone—Osborne where Victoria
walked with Albert and one day plucked the primroses for Disraeli. At least its Naval College has gone out of existence, swallowed up in Dartmouth.

And the boy himself? Well, when it came to him, the author
of the epilogue dipped his pen in irony. To say that much is tantamount to a synopsis. If you will remember that the boy was
thirteen when they threw him out of Osborne and fifteen when
his good name was re-established, you will realize that when the
Great War began he was old enough to die for King and Country.
And did he? Of course. As a soldier, mind you. The lost two
years had rather discouraged his ambitions with regard to the
Navy. August 1914 found him in America, working in the Wall
Street firm of Fisk & Robinson. Somehow he managed to get back
to England, join up with the Second Battalion of the South Staf-
fordshire Regiment, win a commission as Second Lieutenant, and
get over to France in time to be killed—at Ypres—in the first
October of the War.

So that is the story of Archer-Shee, whose years in the land,
all told, were nineteen. To me his has always been a deeply moving
story, and more and more, as the years have gone by, a significant
one. Indeed, I should like to go up and down our own land telling
it to young people not yet born when Archer-Shee kept his ren-

dezvous with death. You see, I know no easier way of saying something that is much on my mind. For this can be said about the Archer-Shee case: that it could not happen in any totalitarian state. It is so peculiarly English, this story of a whole people getting worked up about a little matter of principle; above all, the story of the foremost men of the land taking up the cudgels—taking up the cudgels against the state, mind you—because a youngster had been unfairly treated. It would have been difficult to imagine it in the Germany of Bismarck and the Wilhelms. It is impossible to imagine it in the Germany of Adolf Hitler.

George Orwell

Shooting an Elephant

George Orwell is the pesudonym of Eric Blair (1903-1950); his Animal Farm *and* Nineteen Eighty-Four *firmly established his reputation as a vigorous and original satirist. He was born in India and served for five years (1922-1927) in the Indian Imperial Police in Burma, an experience which provided him with, among other material, the incident that he describes in the essay that follows.*

In Moulmein, in Lower Burma, I was hated by large numbers of people—the only time in my life that I have been important enough for this to happen to me. I was sub-divisional police officer of the town, and in an aimless, petty kind of way anti-European feeling was very bitter. No one had the guts to raise a riot, but if a European woman went through the bazaars alone somebody would probably spit betel juice over her dress. As a police officer I was an obvious target and was baited whenever it seemed safe to do so. When a nimble Burman tripped me up on the football field and the referee (another Burman) looked the other way, the crowd yelled with hideous laughter. This happened more than once. In the end the sneering yellow faces of young men that met me everywhere, the insults hooted after me when I was at a safe distance, got badly on my nerves. The young Buddhist priests were the worst of all. There were several thousands of them in the town and none of them seemed to have anything to do except stand on street corners and jeer at Europeans.

All this was perplexing and upsetting. For at that time I had already made up my mind that imperialism was an evil thing and the sooner I chucked up my job and got out of it the better. Theoretically—and secretly, of course—I was all for the Burmese and all against their oppressors, the British. As for the job I was doing, I hated it more bitterly than I can perhaps make clear. In a job like that you see the dirty work of Empire at close quarters. The wretched prisoners huddling in the stinking cages of the lock-ups, the grey, cowed faces of the long-term convicts, the scarred buttocks of the men who had been flogged with bamboos—all these oppressed me with an intolerable sense of guilt. But I could get nothing into perspective. I was young and ill-educated and I had had to think out my problems in the utter silence that is imposed on every Englishman in the East. I did not even know that the British Empire is dying, still less did I know that it is a great deal better than the younger empires that are going to supplant it. All I knew was that I was stuck between my hatred of the empire I served and my rage against the evil-spirited little beasts who tried to make my job impossible. With one part of my mind I thought of the British Raj as an unbreakable tyranny, as something clamped down, in *saecula saeculorum*, upon the will of prostrate peoples; with another part I thought that the greatest joy in the world would be to drive a bayonet into a Buddhist priest's guts. Feelings like these are the normal by-products of imperialism; ask any Anglo-Indian official, if you can catch him off duty.

One day something happened which in a roundabout way was enlightening. It was a tiny incident in itself, but it gave me a better glimpse than I had had before of the real nature of imperialism—the real motives for which despotic governments act. Early one morning the sub-inspector at a police station the other end of the town rang me up on the 'phone and said that an elephant was ravaging the bazaar. Would I please come and do something about it? I did not know what I could do, but I wanted to see what was happening and I got on to a pony and started out. I took my rifle, an old .44 Winchester and much too small to kill an elephant, but I thought the noise might be useful *in terrorem*. Various Burmans stopped me on the way and told me about the elephant's doings. It was not, of course, a wild elephant, but a tame one which had gone "must." It had been chained up, as tame elephants always are when their attack of "must" is due, but on the previous night it had broken its chain and escaped. Its mahout, the only person who could manage it when it was in that state, had set out in pursuit, but had taken the wrong direction and was now twelve hours' journey away, and in the morning the elephant had suddenly reappeared in the town. The Burmese population had no weapons and were quite helpless against it. It had already destroyed somebody's bamboo hut, killed a cow, and raided some fruit-stalls and devoured the stock; also it had met the municipal rubbish van and, when the driver jumped out and took to his heels, had turned the van over and inflicted violences upon it.

The Burmese sub-inspector and some Indian constables were waiting for me in the quarter where the elephant had been seen. It was a very poor quarter, a labyrinth of squalid bamboo huts, thatched with palm-leaf, winding all over a steep hillside. I re- member that it was a cloudy, stuffy morning at the beginning of the rains. We began questioning the people as to where the ele- phant had gone and, as usual, failed to get any definite information. That is invariably the case in the East; a story always sounds clear enough at a distance, but the nearer you get to the scene of events the vaguer it becomes. Some of the people said that the ele- phant had gone in one direction, some said that he had gone in another, some professed not even to have heard of any elephant. I had almost made up my mind that the whole story was a pack of lies, when we heard yells a little distance away. There was a loud, scandalized cry of "Go away, child! Go away this instant!" and an old woman with a switch in her hand came round the corner of a hut, violently shooing away a crowd of naked children. Some more women followed, clicking their tongues and exclaiming; evidently there was something that the children ought not to have seen. I rounded the hut and saw a man's dead body sprawling in the mud. He was an Indian, a black Dravidian coolie, almost naked, and he could not have been dead many minutes. The people said that the elephant had come suddenly upon him round the corner of the hut, caught him with its trunk, put its foot on his back and ground him into the earth. This was the rainy season and the ground was soft, and his face had scored a trench a foot deep and a couple of yards long. He was lying on his belly with arms crucified and head sharply twisted to one side. His face was coated with mud, the eyes wide open, the teeth bared and grinning with an expression of unendurable agony. (Never tell me, by the way, that the dead look peaceful. Most of the corpses I have seen looked devilish.) The friction of the great beast's foot had stripped the skin from his back as neatly as one skins a rabbit. As soon as I saw the dead man I sent an orderly to a friend's house nearby to borrow an elephant rifle. I had already sent back the pony, not wanting it to go mad with fright and throw me if it smelt the elephant.

The orderly came back in a few minutes with a rifle and five cartridges, and meanwhile some Burmans had arrived and told us that the elephant was in the paddy fields below, only a few hundred yards away. As I started forward practically the whole population of the quarter flocked out of the houses and followed me. They had seen the rifle and were all shouting excitedly that I was going to shoot the elephant. They had not shown much interest in the elephant when he was merely ravaging their homes, but it was different now that he was going to be shot. It was a bit of fun to them, as it would be to an English crowd; besides they wanted the meat. It made me vaguely uneasy. I had no intention of shooting the elephant—I had merely sent for the rifle to defend myself if necessary—and it is always unnerving to have a crowd following you. I marched down the hill, looking and feeling a fool, with the rifle over my shoulder and an ever-growing army of people jostling at my heels. At the bottom, when you got away from the huts, there was a metalled road and beyond that a miry waste of paddy fields a thousand yards across, not yet ploughed but soggy from the first rains and dotted with coarse grass. The elephant was standing eight yards from the road, his left side towards us. He took not the slightest notice of the crowd's approach. He was tearing up bunches of grass, beating them against his knees to clean them and stuffing them into his mouth.

I had halted on the road. As soon as I saw the elephant I knew with perfect certainty that I ought not to shoot him. It is a serious matter to shoot a working elephant—it is comparable to destroying a huge and costly piece of machinery—and obviously one ought not to do it if it can possibly be avoided. And at that distance, peacefully eating, the elephant looked no more dangerous than a cow. I thought then and I think now that his attack of "must" was already passing off; in which case he would merely wander harmlessly about until the mahout came back and caught him. Moreover, I did not in the least want to shoot him. I decided that I would watch him for a little while to make sure that he did not turn savage again, and then go home.

But at that moment I glanced round at the crowd that had followed me. It was an immense crowd, two thousand at the least and growing every minute. It blocked the road for a long distance on either side. I looked at the sea of yellow faces above the garish clothes—faces all happy and excited over this bit of fun, all certain that the elephant was going to be shot. They were watching me as they would watch a conjurer about to perform a trick. They did not like me, but with the magical rifle in my hands I was momentarily worth watching. And suddenly I realized that I should have to shoot the elephant after all. The people expected it of me and I had got to do it; I could feel their two thousand wills pressing me forward, irresistibly. And it was at this moment, as I stood there with the rifle in my hands, that I first grasped the hollowness, the futility of the white man's dominion in the East. Here was I, the white man with his gun, standing in front of the unarmed native crowd—seemingly the leading actor of the piece; but in reality I was only an absurd puppet pushed to and fro by the will of those yellow faces behind. I perceived in this moment that when the white man turns tyrant it is his own freedom that he destroys. He becomes a sort of hollow, posing dummy, the conventionalized figure of a sahib. For it is the condition of his rule that he shall spend his life in trying to impress the "natives," and so in every crisis he has got to do what the "natives" expect of him. He wears a mask, and his face grows to fit it. I had got to shoot the elephant. I had committed myself to doing it when I sent for the rifle. A sahib has got to act like a sahib; he has got to appear resolute, to know his own mind and do definite things. To come all that way, rifle in hand, with two thousand people marching at my heels, an then to trail feebly away, having done nothing—no, that was impossible. The crowd would laugh at me. And my whole life, every white man's life in the East, was one long struggle not to be laughed at.

But I did not want to shoot the elephant. I watched him beating his bunch of grass against his knees, with that preoccupied grandmotherly air that elephants have. It seemed to me that it would be murder to shoot him. At that age I was not squeamish about killing animals, but I had never shot an elephant and never wanted to. (Somehow it always seems worse to kill a *large* animal.) Besides, there was the beast's owner to be considered. Alive, the elephant was worth at least a hundred pounds; dead, he would only be worth the value of his tusks, five pounds, possibly. But I had got to act quickly. I turned to some experienced-looking Burmans who had been there when we arrived, and asked them how the elephant had been behaving. They all said the same thing: he took no notice of you if you left him alone, but he might charge if you went too close to him.

It was perfectly clear to me what I ought to do. I ought to walk up to within, say, twenty-five yards of the elephant and test his behavior. If he charged, I could shoot; if he took no notice of me, it would be safe to leave him until the mahout came back. But also I knew that I was going to do no such thing. I was a poor shot with a rifle and the ground was soft mud into which one would sink at every step. If the elephant charged and I missed him, I should have about as much chance as a toad under a steam-roller. But even then I was not thinking particularly of my own skin, only of the watchful yellow faces behind. For at that moment, with the crowd watching me, I was not afraid in the ordinary sense, as I would have been if I had been alone. A white man musn't be frightened in front of "natives"; and so, in general, he isn't frightened. The sole thought in my mind was that if anything went wrong those two thousand Burmans would see me pursued, caught, trampled on, and reduced to a grinning corpse like that Indian up the hill. And if that happened it was quite probable that some of them would laugh. That would never do. There was only one alternative. I shoved the cartridges into the magazine and lay down on the road to get a better aim.

The crowd grew very still, and a deep, low, happy sigh, as of people who see the theatre curtain go up at last, breathed from innumerable throats. They were going to have their bit of fun after all. The rifle was a beautiful German thing with cross-hair sights. I did not then know that in shooting an elephant one would shoot to cut an imaginary bar running from ear-hole to ear-hole. I ought, therefore, as the elephant was sideways on, to have aimed straight at his ear-hole; actually I aimed several inches in front of this, thinking the brain would be further forward.

When I pulled the trigger I did not hear the bang or feel the kick—one never does when a shot goes home—but I heard the devilish roar of glee that went up from the crowd. In that instant, in too short a time, one would have thought, even for the bullet to get there, a mysterious, terrible change had come over the elephant. He neither stirred nor fell, but every line of his body had altered. He looked suddenly stricken, shrunken, immensely old, as though the frightful impact of the bullet had paralysed him without knocking him down. At last, after what seemed a long time— it might have been five seconds, I dare say—he sagged flabbily to his knees. His mouth slobbered. An enormous senility seemed to have settled upon him. One could have imagined him thousands of years old. I fired again into the same spot. At the second shot he did not collapse but climbed with desperate slowness to his feet and stood weakly upright, with legs sagging and head drooping. I fired a third time. That was the shot that did for him. You could see the agony of it jolt his whole body and knock the last remnant of strength from his legs. But in falling he seemed for a moment to rise, for as his hind legs collapsed beneath him he seemed to tower upward like a huge rock toppling, his trunk reaching sky-wards like a tree. He trumpeted, for the first and only time. And then down he came, his belly towards me, with a crash that seemed to shake the ground even where I lay.

I got up. The Burmans were already racing past me across the mud. It was obvious that the elephant would never rise again, but he was not dead. He was breathing very rhythmically with long rattling gasps, his great mound of a side painfully rising and falling. His mouth was wide open—I could see far down into caverns of pale pink throat. I waited a long time for him to die, but his breathing did not weaken. Finally I fired my two remaining shots into the spot where I thought his heart must be. The thick blood welled out of him like red velvet, but still he did not die.

His body did not even jerk when the shots hit him, the tortured breathing continued without a pause. He was dying, very slowly and in great agony, but in some world remote from me where not even a bullet could damage him further. I felt that I had got to put an end to that dreadful noise. It seemed dreadful to see the great beast lying there, powerless to move and yet powerless to die, and not even to be able to finish him. I sent back for my small rifle and poured shot after shot into his heart and down his throat. They seemed to make no impression. The tortured gasps continued as steadily as the ticking of a clock.

In the end I could not stand it any longer and went away. I heard later that it took him half an hour to die. Burmans were bringing dahs and baskets even before I left, and I was told they had stripped his body almost to the bones by the afternoon.

Afterwards, of course, there were endless discussions about the shooting of the elephant. The owner was furious, but he was only an Indian and could do nothing. Besides, legally I had done the right thing, for a mad elephant has to be killed, like a mad dog, if its owner fails to control it. Among the Europeans opinion was divided. The older men said I was right, the younger men said it was a damn shame to shoot an elephant for killing a coolie, because an elephant was worth more than any damn Coringhee coolie. And afterwards I was very glad that the coolie had been killed; it put me legally in the right and it gave me a sufficient pretext for shooting the elephant. I often wondered whether any of the others grasped that I had done it solely to avoid looking a fool.

VIII

Herbert Joseph Muller

The Adventure of Civilization

Herbert Muller. See page 96. Part 3 of this selection has been omitted.

I THE COSTS OF CIVILIZATION

We have been dealing with history as a branch of knowledge. As we turn to the past itself, the subject of that knowledge, we might well begin with a pious tribute to our nameless prehistoric ancestors, who by inconceivably arduous and ingenious effort succeeded in establishing a human race. They made the crucial discoveries and inventions, such as the tool, the seed, and the domesticated animal; their development of agriculture, the "neolithic revolution" that introduced a settled economy, was perhaps the greatest stride forward that man has ever taken. They created the marvelous instrument of language, which enabled man to discover his humanity, and eventually to disguise it. They laid the foundations of civilization: its economic, political, and social life, and its artistic, ethical, and religious traditions. Indeed, our "savage" ancestors are still very near to us, and not merely in our capacity for savagery. Although the primitive survives most obviously in the superstitions and fetishes of simple men, it survives as well in quite respectable customs, such as the tabooed word, the initiation ceremony, and the national totem. Our everyday language is alive with its animism: skies still "threaten," seas and fires "rage," forests "murmur," and "Mother Earth" beckons us to rest. Our literature, religion, philosophy, and science all retain elements of the myth and magic out of which they grew.

For such reasons men have looked to primitive societies to

discover human nature in its "pure" state. In fact, however, we cannot find such a universal state of nature. We find instead a fantastic diversity in designs for living, with often an outrageous disregard of the reputed laws of human nature. And this common-place of modern anthropology is pertinent because first of all we have to deal with primitivism—the familiar idea that civilization is a disease, and that the only possible cure for it is a return to nature and the simple life. Although this idea is commonly identified with Jean Jacques Rousseau, it is an ancient and universal one. The myth of the noble savage is at least as old as Homer, who mentions "the noble mare-milkers and the mild-drinking Abieo, the most righteous of men" (an apparent reference to the Scythians); while later Greek and Roman literature is full of homilies on the happier, more virtuous life of rude peoples. Every-where we find civilized man troubled by misgivings about his most remarkable achievement, pining for a lost Eden. Such misgivings are natural, given the inevitable complications of civilized life, and may be salutary. Simple peoples can often teach us simple les-sons in good will and good sense. (So the dictators might take a lesson in wit from the Ashanti in Africa, who have an annual cere-mony during which the people are not only permitted but re-quired to ridicule and upbraid their rulers.) But with all respect for primitive cultures, primitivism is a shallow, sentimental atti-tude.

Usually it is based on a misunderstanding of primitive life, whose apparent simplicity is complicated by rigid taboos and black magic. At best, however, the primitivists cherish an impossible desire. They wish to appreciate the simple life with all the self-consciousness and sensitivity that only civilization makes possible; they wish to be children of nature and also poets and philosophers celebrating nature. Above all, they fail to make clear why civil-ization is "unnatural"—why a stone axe, say, is according to nature, but a power-driven saw is not. They evade the basic issue of just what is the natural life for man—the issue that is the final concern of all philosophy and religion, and that is constantly confused by the ambiguities of the term *nature*. If the term is taken to mean the entire universe, with all its phenomena, then everything that goes on is bound to be natural, and it is meaningless to tell man to fol-low nature. If the term is taken to mean the entire universe apart from man, then it is inhuman to tell man to follow the ways of other animals, and to discourage his efforts to understand and control nature. Or if the term is taken to mean native or essential character, as in "human nature," then the distinctively human lies in consciousness, and the civilized effort to widen, clarify, and enrich consciousness would seem quite natural.

We cannot absolutely prove that it is better to be a civilized man than a caveman, or even that it is worth being a human being. We can say that if conscious life has no value, nothing has value and all thought is meaningless. No man in his senses really wishes to change places with a contented imbecile or a pig in his sty. But then we have to pay for our knowledge of good and evil. The price of conscious life is discontent, fear, and pain unknown to other animals. The conditions of civilized life are richer values and higher costs. By its more elaborate, complex organization of life a civilization provides more goods, both material and spiritual, than a primitive society can; and it thereby creates more tension, friction, instability, insecurity.

Adventure, as Whitehead maintained, is quite literally the key to civilization. This highest achievement of man is a "program for discontent." Likewise Toynbee suggests that the terms of the adventure may be summed up in Faust's wager with the Devil:

> If ever time should flow so calmly on
> Soothing my spirits in such oblivion
> That in the pleasant trance I would arrest
> And hail the happy moment in its course,
> Bidding it linger with me . . .
> Then willingly do I consent to perish.

By the grace of Goethe, Faust was saved, as civilizations have not been; but unlike them he stuck to the terms of the bargain. They have typically succumbed to complacency or conservatism, losing their creative energy or readiness for adventure; and only in stagnation and death can they approach the stable equilibrium they seek. The stablest element in human history is precisely the most primitive and formless—the peasant masses that have no real history. The great creative ages, on the other hand, have been conspicuously unstable. When bookmen celebrate the golden ages, now changeless, composed, and serene in splendor, they are apt to falsify the spirit of these ages; for no man who craves security and peace of mind would have been happy in Periclean Athens, Renaissance Italy, or Elizabethan England. When Henry Adams concluded his *Education* with the faint hope that the future might see "a world that sensitive and timid natures could regard without a shudder," he was even fainter than he thought. Such natures are doomed to shudder in any civilized world.

Today, at any rate, there is no mistaking the necessity of adventure. The pace of revolution is strictly unprecedented; centuries in Egypt, China, and India, or even in Greece and Rome, brought less radical change than a lifetime today. We are all too aware of the risks, the costs we pay for the goods of our kind of civilization. For this reason, however, we are apt to magnify the costs, or to regard any costs as unprecedented. We forget that men have always had to live dangerously, above all when they were living near the height of their powers. So we might do well to review the distinctive means and ends of civilization, the main articles of its program for discontent.

The adventure begins with some improvement in technology that enables a surplus of material goods, and a release of energy for other purposes than a mere livelihood; thus men illustrated the value of adversity by developing the irrigation systems of the Nile and the Euphrates, creating their own Garden of Eden in a desert. Then rises the city, which is the first clear sign of civilization. In the city the economic surplus is collected and managed, or squandered, and energy is further stimulated by close association, division of labor, and the pursuit of more wealth or the competition for a larger share of the existing wealth. One result of this stimulus is the invention of writing. Apparently developed for the practical purpose of keeping accounts, writing turns out to have immense, unforeseen consequences, in the growth of learning, literature, holy scriptures, and all forms of culture. And from all this activity emerges the self-conscious individual, the creator who is nevertheless the product of civilization; for in primitive societies a potential Shakespeare, Michelangelo, or Newton would have no chance of discovering his genius, much less of cultivating it.

These distinctive achievements of civilization are real gains, real goods. Only in a civilized society can man contemplate his inability to live on bread alone, and dream of better ways of living.

The material surplus provides the leisure of cultivating spiritual interests; the city is the main center of creative activity, the spiritual as well as the commercial and political capital; writing is indispensable to the transmission of a high culture; the self-conscious individual at his best is the glory of civilization, or even the only justification of the whole enterprise. At the same time, these creative achievements automatically create new problems or new evils. The surplus wealth breeds inequality and injustice; the city becomes Babylon, the central source of babble, disorder, corruption, and decay; literate learning sanctifies and perpetuates the superstitions, prejudices, and injustices of the past; the self-conscious individual is always a threat to the security of the group, or a victim of it. The freedom that has been gained not only permits the familiar abuses of freedom but heightens the awareness of the limits to human freedom, and raises the ultimate problem—freedom for what? Having learned his strength, man rediscovers his weakness.

The conclusion of all this is not a fatalistic acceptance of inevitable evil. Evil will always be with us, to be sure; but the specific forms of evil are not static, absolute, and irremediable. In creating them, civilization likewise creates the standards by which we judge them, and stimulates the effort to eradicate them. In deploring the limited success of this effort, we may forget that we have set higher standards and goals, that we seek to do away with conditions (such as slavery) once accepted as inevitable or even proper —that in this way too we make evils by making good. My immediate conclusion, again, is that the adventure of civilization is necessarily inconclusive; or at least that its issues call for further complication before we jump to conclusions.

2   THE MATERIAL BASIS OF CIVILIZATION

It would seem obvious that material wealth and power are the essential basis of civilization, and that they are essentially only the basis, the means to other ends. No high civilization, no golden age, has been poor and weak. The creation and transmission of the spiritual achievements of a society depend upon its material achievements; its monuments testify to both its artistic and its technological power, its ideals and its wealth. Yet the values of the mind or spirit remain the "higher" values, the ends of civilized life. Although the great writers and thinkers do not agree on precisely what they are, almost all describe the good life by such terms as wisdom, virtue, love, beauty, peace, and holiness; their disagreements come down to different versions of the abiding trinity—the Good, the True and the Beautiful. Although simple men think in terms of happiness and are likely to identify it with material success, they too know at heart that wealth is no guarantee of happiness; and almost all pay at least lip service to "the finer things of life."

I begin with these platitudes because it seems very hard for men to see their material progress steadily and whole, in its necessity and its insufficiency, its values and its evils. The ruling classes of former societies evidently enjoyed their wealth but were generally contemptuous of the artisans and merchants who provided it for them; the high cultural tradition found an honorable place for war and aristocratic sport but not for practical, useful activities. In the last century, however, business and technology have been honored above all other activities; most Americans pay only lip service to the "higher" values as they boast shamelessly of their high standard of living. This gross materialism has in turn driven many intellectuals into a corner, where they cry out a shallow, futile scorn of material progress. Even the hardy Thoreau took civilization with him when he turned his back on it and went to the woods; he still needed its tools and materials, to live and to record his protest against it. Critics of modern industrialism make far more liberal use of its products and services, with as little acknowledgment. We cannot in any event do away with business, or call a halt to technology. If we hope to humanize them we need to recognize their human value, as indispensable means to civilized life and as creative activities in their own right. It might be good strategy to begin with a reverent view of the material achievements of man, and an ironic view of his spiritual achievements.

To judge by all the available evidence, the rise of civilization was not a gift of the gods or a tribute to them. It was a technological affair, an economic enterprise inspired by practical motives. Through inventions and discoveries, men were able to take care of their physical wants more efficiently; in the leisure, comfort, and relative security thus achieved, they were able to develop social graces, fine arts, literate learning, and higher religions. In all civilizations before our own, agriculture remained the chief source of wealth; because most aristocracies were landed aristocracies, agriculture had more prestige than commerce—as it still does among literary devotees of the ancient cultural tradition. Nevertheless civilization flourished with the growth of industry and trade, which were far more extensive in antiquity than is commonly realized. The great adventure of Greek civilization in particular began as an adventure in trade, or specifically with the exploitation of the humble grape and olive; the production of wine and olive oil enabled the enterprising Greeks to enter the world market and compete with the Phoenicians (one of the few known peoples whose brilliant culture was frankly identified with commerce, and organized to promote commerce). The first notable achievements in Greek poetry, philosophy, and science were contributed by Ionia, the colonial cities in Asia Minor that were the first to develop a thriving commerce. The glory of Greece reached its zenith in Athens, at the zenith of the Athenian adventure in economic imperialism.

Whitehead declared that commerce is the beginning of civilization and freedom in that it is intercourse by persuasion instead of force. For all the loose talk about free private enterprise, it does in fact promote enterprise, initiative, personal independence—the adventurous spirit on which a flourishing civilization depends; arrested commerce is one of the surest signs of a civilization in decay. For all the sordid motives involved in commerce, it inspires daring adventures such as no merely practical man would embark upon. Thus the commercial Phoenicians led the way for the Greeks, exploring the whole Mediterranean, exploring even the whole coast of Africa (a feat that no Greek or Roman dared to attempt); thus Marco Polo ventured across a vast unknown continent, Columbus discovered a new continent, Magellan circled the world. Commerce also acts as a major stimulus to civilization by promoting commerce in ideas, an exchange of spiritual as well as material goods. Thus the acquisitive Greeks in Ionia acquired knowledge of older civilizations, and speculation in business led to speculation in thought, which is another gamble.

Commerce in turn is but one example of the division and diversification of labor resulting from the advance of technology and the accumulation of an economic surplus. Men are apt to underrate the very great gains this has made possible. Resenting their confinement to a particular task or regretting their dependence, they are fond of cultivating the illusion of being as self-sufficient as their pioneering ancestors by hunting their own game, building their own shacks. Yet specialization—by the individual and by the community—is the clearest index of human development. The self-sufficient man has little to contribute to the community, the self-sufficient community has little to contribute to other communities. Both may still be found—in the most primitive parts of the world. (One may even find "natural" economies so close to a bare subsistence that they cannot afford such specialists as the priest or witch-doctor.) Specialization alone has enabled the extraordinary man to discover and develop his genius, and the ordinary man to discover and develop his individuality.

As plainly, however, it may narrow, warp, and impoverish individuality. In our own world specialization has produced the machine-tender and the bookkeeper, the technician and the academician—the hordes of cultural illiterates and expert ignoramuses. It denies millions the opportunity of really creative work, the elemental satisfaction of saying, "I made this." Even the wealth of opportunities it affords is a wealth of square holes for round pegs; in a civilization there are many more possibilities of going wrong, or—as bad—of restless doubts that one has made the best choice. We have innumerable educational agencies for guiding choices of occupation, or for intensifying the confusion by multiplying the possible choices; but we are only beginning to educate for the all-important problem, of co-ordinating and humanizing our specialized knowledge, bringing our experts together, teaching our technicians to speak a common civilized language. In short, division of labor naturally leads to excessive division, or sharp separation; and it brings us back to the familiar complex of good-and-evil. So too with commerce. All the energy, initiative, and daring that go into it help to promote the indolence and conservatism of privileged classes. Still plainer, commerce breeds fraud, greed, strife, war.

And so with the major problem, the everlasting problem, raised by the surplus wealth that made civilization possible. It posed the question who was to own the surplus, and for what purposes was it to be used. The historic answer has invariably been the creation of a hierarchy of classes, more or less rigid. In every civilization the wealth and the power that goes with it have been concentrated in the hands of a few. Among the early specialists were experts in consumption—a class whose chief functions included what Veblen called conspicuous consumption, or vicarious consumption for the edification of the producing classes.[1] We may assume that the rise of privileged classes was largely unconscious, not a deliberate plot by greedy men. We may also assume that the problem of sharing the wealth, or approaching equity, will plague even the "classless society," since power has to be exercised by a few and is always liable to abuse. But the basic paradox remains that for great masses of men civilization has always meant less material well-being than primitive men usually enjoy. It has meant a man-made misery, which was aggravated by increasing inequality as in time the privileged came to exploit the masses more deliberately and systematically. And with the Industrial Revolution came still more glaring contradictions, of more wretched poverty and impotence amidst vastly increased wealth and power. An astounding triumph of technological efficiency created unemployment and want, bringing on periodic depressions and panics by producing more goods than could be sold, while millions needed those goods. For the first time in history, society has been plagued by abundance rather than scarcity.

To this whole problem we shall keep recurring. Meanwhile we may note another fundamental difference between modern civilization and its predecessors. The historic result of the material surplus has not been the constant class struggle pictured by Marxists, between the few who have and the many who have not. Although such class wars have broken out occasionally, as in ancient Greece and Rome, the significant struggles have usually been within the upper classes, involving kings, priests, warrior nobles, and in time wealthy merchants. Throughout most of history the peasant masses accepted their lowly status. Their infrequent rebellions, in times of extreme want or oppression, were blind up-

---

[1] That this can still be a humane function is apparent from the crowds that gather at the entrance of the Metropolitan Opera House when the season opens. Few of the hangers-on seem bitter or resentful as they watch the wealthy ladies enter in their furs and jewels. Most appear to be happy, even grateful to these ladies who so arduously perform the duty of consuming for them.

risings, not planned revolutions in the name of democratic rights, and had no profound, lasting results. With the rise of democracy, however, the masses have become a real factor in the problem of sharing the wealth. Despite the marked inequalities, the advanced democracies have unquestionably raised the standard of living of the great majority of their citizens. The ordinary man now has opportunities for a richer life than he dreamed of in the past. What he does with these opportunities, how he conceives the rich life, is another problem, to which we shall also recur. But it would seem dishonest as well as futile for well-fed, well-clothed, well-housed intellectuals merely to deplore the common desire for material well-being. . . .

4 THE AMBIGUITIES OF THE SPIRITUAL ACHIEVEMENT

I have said that as we share the venerable faith in the Good, the True, and the Beautiful, as the ends of civilization, we should do well to begin with an ironic view of the spiritual achievements of man. For this faith is strictly a faith: one that is always vulnerable to the taunts of practical men, who may seem to get along well enough with their material wealth and coarse pleasures, and as vulnerable to the analysis of skeptics and cynics, who may ask what good has come of all this spiritual achievement, and how we know that it is good. The faith is always threatened as well by the falsities and absurdities of its disciples: the pursuit of virtue, truth, and beauty has inspired egregious evil, error, and ugliness. We should not be surprised to find that the highest manifestations of civilization have involved the deepest contradictions.

The historic source of these contradictions, Ralph Turner points out, was the invention of writing. Literate learning, the major means to intellectual growth and creative achievement, has also been a major aid to the conservative forces that resist growth and adventure. From the outset it encouraged a purely verbal kind of learning that was confused with natural knowledge, and a liturgical kind that discouraged free inquiry. It helped to standardize and sanctify the codes, classics, and scriptures that embalmed the ignorance and prejudice as well as the wisdom of the ancestors. As the possession of a privileged few—especially the priestly class —it consolidated the power of the upper classes, raising them still higher above the illiterate masses, who were condemned to blind obedience and blind worship.

One result of this aristocratic monopoly on learning has been an inevitable distortion of history. The records of the past, which reflect chiefly the interests of the upper classes, give only an incidental or indirect view of the life of the masses, the everyday business of hewing and hauling. Thus Gibbon wrote his celebrated description of the Roman Empire under Trajan, Hadrian, and the Antonines, as the period in the history of the world during which "the condition of the human race was most happy and prosperous"; but he was not actually talking about the "human race." He was describing the condition of the prosperous upper classes. There is some evidence that the great majority of the population—the peasants, the city proletarians, and the slaves—were not especially happy or prosperous at this time. The main point, however, is simply that we do not know and cannot know much about their lot. And so with all the other great empires. When the anonymous masses enter history it is chiefly to be slaughtered in battle, to die of famine or privation—to illustrate the failures of their betters; apart from these calamities we can only conjecture how contented they were under their priests and kings, and whether they enjoyed the golden ages. We have the mighty pyramids, but no first-hand account of the feelings of the wretches who built them. We have the sublime *Meditations* of Marcus Aurelius, but no diaries of his countless subjects who had greater need of his stoicism. Or when we can make out the best and the worst in past societies, we still cannot be sure of the balance, the average, the quality of the commonplace, the level of everyday life—the proportions of pomp and misery, fine art and dirty work, high endeavor and petty concern. We have the exalted tragedies of Aeschylus, but we do not know to what extent they exalted the citizens of Athens, or could compete with such attractions as the Olympic games.

A related effect of the aristocratic monopoly was the cultivation of knowledge for decorative, honorific, esoteric, or sacred purposes, rather than practical or productive ones. Invented to facilitate business transactions, writing soon became the medium for transactions with the gods or the god-kings, and those who carried on this elevated business naturally looked down on the lowly business of the world, the vulgar doing and making of artisans, merchants, and slaves. Applied knowledge was not merely degraded but divorced from the higher learning; the "useful" was opposed to the philosophical and the spiritual. Hence the advance of science in the Western world was not a clear gain but a constant "problem": it jeopardized traditional beliefs that had been cut off from natural knowledge. Since the last century, to be sure, the tables have been turned. Now useful knowledge has become almost sacred, as the means to our wealth and power; our "institutions of higher learning" have been specializing in a practical training that is neither high nor learned. But the ancient aristocratic bias still persists. The immense visions of modern physics and astronomy are considered less imaginative than the most tortured imaginings of modern poets, less spiritual than the mildewed metaphors of conventional churchmen. In general, the limitations of modern culture are due not only to the narrowness of scientists and technicians, and the grossness of businessmen, but to the fastidious exclusiveness of literary and learned men, jealous of their traditional prerogatives as custodians of a higher or holier kind of truth.

Apart from the classiness of the classical, however, the glorious accomplishments of the mind and spirit have always had inglorious consequences. Today the conspicuous example is science. Its enormous extension of knowledge has meant not only a narrowing of consciousness for many specialists but an impoverishment of consciousness for the many others who have regarded its severely limited descriptions as complete explanations, the whole truth about the world. Its triumphant advance in the understanding and control of nature has weakened man's belief in his own importance in the cosmic scheme, or even in the reality of his spiritual values; many thinkers concluded that man is a mere mechanism whose behavior is blindly determined. More recently, the triumphs have culminated in discoveries about the subatomic world that appear to undermine the basic assumptions of uniformity and causality on which science has rested, and that give man a power which conceivably may destroy science and all its work. Altogether, the most successful instrument of human reason has shaken the faith in reason that has been the mainspring of Western civilization.

But the humanities have also been inhuman, or all too human, in their conceit. Religion everywhere has exhibited the paradoxes of St. Sophia. The higher religions have commonly grown out of the failures of civilization, bringing promises of eternal life to dying societies. Although they survive these societies they bear the marks of their defeatist origins; the most characteristic sign of their loftiness is the abasement of man and this earth, an otherworldly or life-denying spirit. They are therefore always liable to conflict with the creative forces of a flourishing society, and thence to profound inconsistencies or ignoble concessions. Above all, they are invariably corrupted by their worldly success. As they become popular their revolutionary spiritual ideals are translated into popular hopes, fears, and desires; the loftier they are, the wider is the gap between the idealism of their founders and the practice and belief of most of their followers. As they become institutionalized they suffer the fate of all other worldly institutions. A priesthood ceases to propagate new values and devotes itself primarily to conserving the old ones, piously reducing them to routine rituals and dead dogmas. An established church also tends to ally itself with other vested interests, and thus to become infected with the worldly pride it was born to combat. And the periodic reactions that follow—the efforts to reinterpret the original revelation or recapture the original purity—revitalize the faith at the cost of splintering it into more sects and further confusing the nature of the original revelation.

All such perversions of high tradition are intensified by traditionalism, the occupational disease of guardians of culture. The guardians tend to forget that tradition has always been the great enemy of the founders of great traditions: that Socrates was a radical who did corrupt the youth of Athens by impiously urging them to question the time-honored ways; or that the teachings of Christ were an outrage to precisely the most cultivated, respectable, God-fearing people of his time; or that the American Revolution was strictly a revolution, illegal, violent, and bloody. In particular, the traditionalists abuse our Western heritage by singling out some one school of thought as the "essential" or "true" tradition; whereas diversity and nonconformity are the very soul of this heritage. It is the richest tradition that man has ever known simply because it includes so many disparate elements from diverse sources, and has never been at rest.[2]

Yet the last word must be spoken in piety. We have said enough about the abuses of the higher values to enable us, in realism and in honor, to declare their supreme value. While man is immensely indebted to the past for practical knowledge and skills, he cherishes the past for its contributions to the life of the mind or spirit. Ultimately he has never really honored the material wealth and power he has always sought. Reverently he recalls the great failures, ironically the mere conquests or triumphs of power. Assyria was a mighty empire, Sparta succeeded in dominating all Greece, the Mongols under the extraordinary Jenghiz Khan swept out of nowhere to conquer most of the known world. But who mourns the fall of Nineveh and Sparta, or the disappearance of the Mongols into the obscurity whence they came? Athens, Jerusalem, and Rome exemplified the limitations and excesses of great cultural achievement, all the paradoxes of glory and grandeur. But who rejoices at their fall?

Since the higher values are usually given a high metaphysical or religious sanction, it is worth observing that they require no such sanction. Like the simple goods of physical well-being, they are intrinsic goods, good for their own sake. And since, as capitalized abstractions, the Good, the True, and the Beautiful are apt to seem highfalutin' in an age of business and technology, it is well to stress their homely origins. The Good is rooted in the fact that man is a social animal, naturally gregarious, whose "soul" may come from God but in any event can come simply from his relations with his fellows, and his natural desire for their esteem; his very self is a social product, or itself a society, which becomes self-conscious only as it becomes aware of other selves. The True is rooted in natural curiosity, the desire of all men to know something about whatever they are interested in, whether the work-

[2] T. S. Eliot, perhaps the most famous of contemporary traditionalists, is one of the most exclusive, rejecting a great deal of the political, philosophical, and religious heritage of the Western world. For all his subtlety and sincerity, Eliot argues much like the politicians and businessmen who maintain their power and prestige by laying claim to the true American tradition, of Jefferson or of Lincoln, and denouncing their opponents as enemies of the American Way.

ings of an engine or of a universe; the most abstruse concepts of science and philosophy grow out of a simple fondness for observing the out-of-doors. The Beautiful is rooted in the esthetic sense and creative impulse common to all men, and apparent even in the hard-headed man who thinks Art is effeminate; when he admires his new tool or gadget he says, "It's a beauty." The "higher" values may be considered simply a fuller development of these natural human impulses, a fuller realization of the distinctive but natural possibilities of being a human being.

Harrison Scott Brown

Patterns of the Future

Harrison Brown (1917-   ) has been a Professor of Geochemistry at the California Institute of Technology since 1951. He was at Oak Ridge from 1943 to 1946.

> Ah Love! could you and I with Him conspire
> To grasp this sorry Scheme of Things entire,
>   Would not we shatter it to bits—and then
> Re-mould it nearer to the Heart's Desire!
>   OMAR KHAYYAM

I

We have seen that the resources available to man are being rapidly consumed, but that, at the same time, new resources are being made available by our increased knowledge and improved technology. Given adequate supplies of energy, man can, in principle, extract everything that he needs for his existence at a high standard of living from substances which exist abundantly on the earth's surface—air, seawater, and ordinary rock. We have seen that within the rock itself there is sufficient energy to carry out the processing and also to provide power for the operation of industrial machinery. At the same time, man can extract energy from sunlight and use it to operate his factories. When we look at the situation solely from the point of view of technological and energetic feasibility, we must conclude that the resources available to man permit him, in principle, to provide adequately for a very large population for a very long period of time.

There are, of course, physical limitations of some sort which will determine the maximum number of human beings who can live on the earth's surface. But at the present time we are far from the ultimate limit of the number of persons who could be provided for. If we were willing to be crowded together closely enough, to eat foods which would bear little resemblance to the foods we eat today, and to be deprived of simple but satisfying luxuries such as fireplaces, gardens, and lawns, a world population of 50 billion persons would not be out of the question. And if we really put our minds to the problem we could construct floating islands where people might live and where algae farms could function, and perhaps 100 billion persons could be provided for. If we set strict limits to physical activities so that caloric requirements could be kept at very low levels, perhaps we could provide for 200 billion persons.

At this point the reader is probably saying to himself that he would have little desire to live in such a world, and he can rest assured that the author is thinking exactly the same thing. But a substantial fraction of humanity today is behaving as if it would like to create such a world. It is behaving as if it were engaged in a contest to test nature's willingness to support humanity and, if it had its way, it would not rest content until the earth is covered completely and to a considerable depth with a writhing mass of human beings, much as a dead cow is covered with a pulsating mass of maggots.

For population densities to reach levels much higher than those which exist in present-day agrarian cultures, a great deal of technology is required. India, for example, could not possibly support her existing high population density without the benefit of the knowledge and materials she obtains from the industrialized society of the West. Without the existence of an industrialized society somewhere in the world, disease could not be effectively controlled and transportation would not be in existence which would permit shipment of food from areas of surplus to areas of deficiency. In the absence of the availability of the products of industrialization, the population of the Indian sub-continent would probably not exceed about 100 million persons. Similarly, if industrialization should for some reason cease to exist in the world, and human life were to be supported entirely by intensive agriculture, the population of human beings would probably never exceed about 5 billion persons. This represents about the maximum number that could be supported on a bare subsistence basis in the absence of the means to construct elaborate transportation and irrigation systems, and provide artificial fertilizers and chemicals and other weapons for combating animals and insects which compete with man for food.

2

As is indicated in an earlier chapter, within a period of time which is very short compared with the total span of human history, supplies of fossil fuels will almost certainly be exhausted. This loss will make man completely dependent upon waterpower, atomic energy, and solar energy—including that made available by burning vegetation—for driving his machines. There are no fundamental physical laws which prevent such a transition, and it is quite possible that society will be able to make the change smoothly. But it is a transition that will happen only once during the lifetime of the human species. We are quickly approaching the point where, if machine civilization should, because of some catastrophe, stop functioning, it will probably never again come into existence.

It is not difficult to see why this should be so if we compare the resources and procedures of the past with those of the present.

Our ancestors had available large resources of high-grade ores and fuels that could be processed by the most primitive technology—crystals of copper and pieces of coal that lay on the surface of the earth, easily mined iron, and petroleum in generous pools reached by shallow drilling. Now we must dig huge caverns and follow seams ever further underground, drill oil wells thousands of feet deep, many of them under the bed of the ocean, and find ways of extracting elements from the leanest of ores—procedures that are possible only because of our highly complex modern techniques, and practical only to an intricately mechanized culture which could not have been developed without the high-grade resources that are so rapidly vanishing.

As our dependence shifts to such resources as low-grade ores, rock, seawater, and the sun, the conversion of energy into useful work will require ever more intricate technical activity, which would be impossible in the absence of a variety of complex machines and their products—all of which are the result of our intricate industrial civilization, and which would be impossible without it. Thus, if a machine civilization were to stop functioning as the result of some catastrophe, it is difficult to see how man would again be able to start along the path of industrialization with the resources that would then be available to him.

The situation is a little like that of a child who has been given a set of simple blocks—all the blocks of one type which exist— with which to learn to build, and to make the foundation for a structure, the upper reaches of which must consist of more intricate, more difficult-to-handle forms, themselves quite unsuited for the base. If, when the foundation was built, he conserved it, he could go on building. But if he wasted and destroyed the foundation blocks, he would have "had it," as the British Royal Air Force would say. His one chance would have been wasted, his structure of the future would be a vanished dream, because there would be nothing left with which to rebuild the foundation.

Our present industrialization, itself the result of a combination of no longer existent circumstances, is the only foundation on which it seems possible that a future civilization capable of utilizing the vast resources of energy now hidden in rocks and seawater, and unutilized in the sun, can be built. If this foundation is destroyed, in all probability the human race has "had it." Perhaps there is possible a sort of halfway station, in which retrogression stops short of a complete extinction of civilization, but even this is not pleasant to contemplate.

Once a machine civilization has been in operation for some time, the lives of the people within the society become dependent upon the machines. The vast interlocking industrial network provides them with food, vaccines, antibiotics, and hospitals. If such a population should suddenly be deprived of a substantial fraction of its machines and forced to revert to an agrarian society, the resultant havoc would be enormous. Indeed, it is quite possible that a society within which there has been little natural selection based upon disease resistance for several generations, a society in which the people have come to depend increasingly upon surgery for repairs during early life and where there is little natural selection operating among women, relative to the ability to bear children—such a society could easily become extinct in a relatively short time following the disruption of the machine network.

Should a great catastrophe strike mankind, the agrarian cultures which exist at the time will clearly stand the greatest chance of survival and will probably inherit the earth. Indeed, the less a given society has been influenced by machine civilization, the greater will be the probability of its survival. Although agrarian societies offer little security to the individual, they are nevertheless far more stable than industrial ones from a long-range point of view.

Is it possible to visualize a catastrophe of sufficient magnitude to obliterate industrial civilization? Here the answer must clearly be in the affirmative, for, in 1954, it takes no extraordinary imagination to foresee such a situation. Practically all major industrial countries are now aligned on one side or the other of a major dispute. Weapons of such power that whole cities can be destroyed in a few minutes are in the hands of the disputants, and, should a major war break out, those weapons, which become more powerful every year, will almost certainly be used. It is clearly within the realm of possibility that another war would so disrupt existing industrial societies that recovery would be impossible and the societies would either revert to agrarian cultures or become extinct. Indications of the possibilities that confront us are offered by the catastrophe which paralyzed Western Europe in World War II, and the slow process of its postwar recovery—a process which would have been very much slower had the highly industrialized United States not been in existence, relatively unscarred and prepared to give aid. And the damage and disruption of industrial activity we witnessed then are insignificant when compared with the disruption that might be suffered by all participants in an "atomic" war.

It is quite possible that a war fought at the present time, even with existing powerful weapons of mass destruction, would not bring industrial civilization to an end. With America and Europe prostrate, the people of Asia would have room into which they could expand and thus accelerate the evolution of their own industrial society. It is also quite possible that the West would recover from a major war, although admittedly recovery would be a far slower process than it was after World War II. But with each passing year, as populations become larger, as the industrial network becomes more complex, and as high-grade resources dwindle, recovery from a major war will become increasingly difficult.

It must be emphasized, however, that industrial civilization can come to an end even in the absence of a major catastrophe. Continuance of vigorous machine culture beyond another century or so is clearly dependent upon the development and utilization of atomic or solar power. If these sources of newly applied energy are to be available in time, the basic research and development must be pursued actively during the coming decades. And even if the knowledge is available soon enough, it is quite possible that the political and economic situation in the world at the time the new transition becomes necessary will be of such a nature that the transition will be effectively hindered. Time and again during the course of human history we have seen advance halted by unfavorable political and economic conditions. We have seen societies in which technical knowledge and resources were both present, but where adequate capital and organization were not in existence and could not be accumulated sufficiently rapidly.

3

At the present time a part of the world is agrarian and another part is either already industrialized or in the process of industrialization. It appears most unlikely that these two greatly different ways of life can co-exist for long. A world containing two major patterns of existence is fundamentally unstable—either the agrarian regions of the world will industrialize or, in the long run, the industrial regions will revert to agrarian existence.

That the agrarian regions of the world will attempt to industrialize is unquestionable. We see about us today signs of revolution, of reorganization, and of reorientation of goals leading toward the creation of local counterparts of Western machine culture. The reasons underlying the trend are obvious. It is in the nature of man not to want to die early and to look enviously at his neighbor who possesses greater wealth than his. A longer life, greater personal security, and more material comforts are looked upon as harbingers of greater happiness, and although this premise is by no means necessarily true, the fact that the individual believes it to be true is the important consideration that confronts us.

The search for greater personal security, longer life, and more material possessions will force the agrarian regions of the world to attempt to industrialize. But, as is indicated here, the probability of their succeeding in the absence of a major world catastrophe in the near future is small. There are clearly paths that could be taken which would lead to a successful transition in the world as a whole. But the nature of man makes remote the possibility that the steps necessary for complete transition will be taken. The picture would change considerably if Western machine civilization were to collapse, thus giving the present agrarian cultures room into which they could expand. But the collapse of Western culture would have to come well in advance of the time when high-grade ore and fuel deposits disappear. We have seen that a collapse of machine civilization after the disappearance of high-grade ore deposits would probably be irreversible, and the world as a whole would be covered with people living an agrarian existence.

It is clear that machine civilization as it is organized at the present time may revert to agrarian culture. In view of this possibility, the most probable pattern for the future of mankind is that sooner or later the entire world will become an agrarian one. This could come about in one of several ways. The status quo could be maintained with abortive attempts on the part of agrarian regions to industrialize, leading eventually to depletion of ore deposits, followed by the decline and eventual decay of machine culture. The regions of advanced machine culture might fight one another and so disrupt the elaborate machine network that recovery would be impossible. The greater part of the world might actually succeed in industrializing, but a catastrophe could bring about reversion to agrarian existence.

Collapse of machine civilization would be accompanied by starvation, disease, and death on a scale difficult to comprehend.

In the absence of adequate sanitation facilities, the ability to inoculate against disease, facilities for food transportation and storage, factories for producing items which are essential for the maintenance of life, the death rate would reduce the population to a level far below that which could be supported by a stable agrarian society which practices intensive agricultural techniques. There would be such violent competition for food that savagery would be the heritage of the survivors. Human life would be confined once again to those areas which can be most easily cultivated, watered, and fertilized, and the principles enunciated by Malthus would once again become the major force operating upon human populations. Only very slowly would the number of persons climb to the level which could be supported by a world-wide agrarian culture—about 5 billion.

The characteristics of the agrarian society of the future would probably be very much like those of most parts of China today or like those of societies which existed in Europe as late as the early eighteenth century. The ratio of available food to total population would be low. There would be no large-scale industries, for metals would be practically non-existent and the only sources of energy would be wood and waterpower. Lack of adequate supplies of metals would prevent the widespread use of electricity. Although parts of society would benefit from accumulated knowledge concerning public health and human biology, death rates would be high. Antibiotics and vaccines would be non-existent. Birth rates would almost certainly lie close to the biological maximum.

In the agrarian world of the future, as in the world prior to 1750, there would be very little difference in the manner of life of all civilized people. This fact is vividly illustrated by a story told recently by a well-known demographer:

I remember walking down a street in Nanking, China, one afternoon nearly twenty years ago with the eminent English economic historian, R. H. Tawney, and remarking to him that Chinese cities often reminded me of his description of early eighteenth-century English economic life. He replied in effect: "I was just thinking that the English workmen of that age would have been very much at home in the economy as well as in the living conditions we have just been observing, but so also would the Frenchman from Paris or the Italian from Florence. The farmers would have wondered at some of the crops raised here, but they would have understood the Chinese methods of cultivation and the care given the soil." [1]

Although the world as a whole would be predominantly agrarian, it is possible that small pockets of semi-industrialized society would survive. These would be centered largely around areas where waterpower is available and limited quantities of metals such as magnesium from seawater could be produced. But in the absence of a broader industrial base, per capita production of such materials would be extremely small. These semi-industrial areas, centered around regions of waterpower, might well become the wealthiest regions of the world, and it is in such regions that we might expect the traditions of the arts and the sciences to be perpetuated. But in such a world the sciences almost certainly would not flourish to the extent to which they do today or even to that which distinguished the ancient empires. Material wealth would be too rare and the struggle for food too intense to permit many persons to engage in such activities.

Much of the knowledge existing at the time when industrial civilization reached its peak would probably be preserved, taught in schools, and passed on from generation to generation. But much of it would be valueless and, as time went on, would be lost. We know from observations of past societies that knowledge and techniques can be lost rather quickly. In order to appreciate this, we have only to contrast the superb engineering techniques of the Romans with those of the residents of the Italian peninsula early in the Renaissance.

It is of course possible that, starting from a base of knowledge accumulated by previous society, and the abilities to utilize waterpower and to extract magnesium from seawater, man might once again learn to process rock, harness solar power, and extract energy from uranium. In such an eventuality a world-wide industrial civilization would arise once again and cover the earth, perhaps later to crumble under pressures similar to those which now confront humanity. But the probabilities of a second emergence would be remote. The advantages gained by the existence of previously accumulated knowledge would probably be offset by the scarcity

[1] Warren R. Thompson, "Population," in *Scientific American*, February 1950, p. 11

of the number of raw materials necessary for the smooth functioning of an industrial society.

4

Although machine civilization as it exists at the present time is
unstable and may revert to agrarian culture, it is important that
we examine ways and means whereby stability in a world industrial society might be achieved. Can we imagine a sequence of
events that might lead eventually to industrialization of all peoples
of the world? And can we further imagine political, economic,
and social structures that would permit the resultant society to
maintain a long-range stability? When we enumerate all the difficulties in which the human species can become embroiled, it
would appear *a priori* that the probability of successful transition
along any path would be extremely small. Yet the fact that we
are able to imagine patterns that might lead to successful transition is, in itself, significant. If stability is possible, it is achievable,
although the probability of achievement may be small.

Perhaps the most immediate danger to confront machine civilization is war. A world filled solely by agrarian cultures is a stable
one, and in such a world the various groups can fight among themselves as much as they please without endangering human population as a whole to any great extent. War in an agrarian world
decreases individual security, and in like manner it decreases national security. But the world is so large that in the absence of
machines that permit both rapid transportation over long distances
and truly large-scale destruction, the existence of war would constitute no great danger to humanity. As in the past, nations, empires, and universal states would rise only to fall as new ones rose
in turn.

But, as we can see, industrial society as a whole is extremely
vulnerable to disruption by war, and the vulnerability is increasing
rapidly as weapons become more effective, as the range of warfare
increases, as the people become more dependent upon the smooth
functioning of the industrial network, and as the reservoir of
easily obtainable resources decreases. It is clear that industrial
civilization cannot afford the luxury of many more wars. It is
conceivable that the next war could so shatter it that it would
be unable to recover. On the other hand, it is also conceivable

that it could survive two or three more. But in any case, the number which can be tolerated is finite, and each conflict will decrease further the probability that industrial civilization will continue to exist.

Wars in the past have been fought for varieties of causes, for resources such as water, agricultural land, and ore deposits, for outlets to markets, to discard yokes of enslavement and to sever colonial bonds, to further religious, economic, and political creeds, to obtain power for power's sake. They have been fought over the pursuit of military security and over real or imagined threats to security. The causes of past wars have indeed been manifold, and the potential causes of future wars are equally numerous.

An agrarian region cannot wage a successful major war by itself against an industrial region; the weapons in the hands of the latter are too powerful to permit this. To be sure, agrarians can be trained and armed by industrialists and thus enabled to prosecute a war, as was the case with Russian-armed Chinese Communists fighting in Korea. But in a partially industrialized world the main dangers of war spring from the areas which are already industrialized and from those which have undergone partial transition.

History shows that wars between cities, states, and geographic regions cease once the originally independent units have amalgamated under the leadership of a single government with the power of making and enforcing laws that are binding upon individuals. One might reason on this basis that if all of the industrialized and semi-industrialized regions of the world were to federate under a common government, the probability of another war would be greatly decreased. It seems likely that this conclusion would be valid if the resultant federation were as complete as was the federation formed by the original thirteen colonies in America. On the other hand, it is extremely unlikely that such a highly centralized federation could come into existence at the present time; nationalistic feelings of individual men and groups of men, and conflicts of economic interests, are too strong to permit rapid transition. Also, those nations which have high per capita reserves of resources and high per capita production would be most reluctant to delegate their sovereignties to higher authority and to abandon the economic barriers that now exist.

It is possible that a federation possessing jurisdiction only over those features of society that determine the immediate ability of a nation to engage in war—the production of munitions and the creation and deployment of armed forces, for example—would decrease the probability of war. But it is extremely doubtful that such a system would really eliminate war as an instrument of national policy. Just as the existence of the United Nations decreases somewhat the probability of war today, so a universal government with jurisdiction limited solely to matters connected with armament and armed forces might decrease the probability of war still further. But it seems highly likely that nothing short of complete federation—of the creation of a true universal state possessed of the power to make and enforce laws dealing with a wide range of international economic and social matters—can really eliminate war in the long run.

The factors which increase the probability of war among industrialized and semi-industrialized areas are, in the main, the factors which prevent federation—desires on the part of the "haves" to maintain the status quo; desires on the part of the "have nots" to improve their position; enthusiasm for a particular economic or political creed; desire for power. As time goes on the effects of increasing population, decreasing resources, disappearing markets, and waning possibilities of importing food and raw materials from abroad should produce leveling effects that will simultaneously decrease the probability of war and increase the possibility of obtaining federation. A century ago the creation of a federation of the nations of Western Europe by means other than force would have been unthinkable. Today the fact that the predicaments of the nations involved are very nearly the same makes possible serious discussion of the subject.

Thus far we have spoken in terms of federation of those areas which are industrialized. The first reason for speaking in such terms is that the major danger of war springs directly from the war-making potential of industrialized countries. Secondly, true federation between countries of high population growth potentials and those of low is extremely difficult to imagine if abolishment of economic barriers is to be an integral feature of federation. For example, although a federation between the United States and Canada would produce relatively little dislocation in either social structure or economy and could possibly be consummated easily should both countries agree, a federation between the United States and Mexico at the present time could have disastrous consequences. Although the standards of living in Mexico would probably be improved by such a move, at least temporarily, the standard of living in the United States would almost certainly be lowered, and, far more important, the sudden incorporation in our society of a major group possessed of high growth potential would lead to an accelerated rate of population increase, together with the numerous difficulties associated with an accelerated rate of increase. Examination of the Puerto Rican situation provides an excellent clue to the difficulties which could be created by federation of areas of high and low growth potentials. Fortunately Puerto Rico is small, but even so the difficulties she creates are out of all proportion to her size. To take but one example, the high growth potential of Puerto Rico swells the relief rolls of the city of New York, largely as a result of the steady emigration from the island to the city and of the difficulties encountered by the Puerto Ricans when they attempt to support themselves in their new environment.

The creation of a true federation of the world, containing no economic barriers, indeed appears to be remote at the present time, but at least a pathway can be discerned which might lead eventually to this goal. One of the first steps might be the creation of a broad federation, including elimination of economic barriers between industrialized areas whose growth potentials are low. Concurrently, the United Nations could be strengthened and given adequate powers to control the production of armaments and sizes and locations of armed forces. Simultaneously, the industrialized areas of the world could take concerted action to help the unindustrialized areas build factories, increase crop yields, lower birth rates and death rates, and generally improve their standards of living. Once the net reproduction rates of such areas reach unity within a framework of low birth rates and low death rates, the areas would become eligible for admission to the broad federation of industrialized areas, and economic barriers would be removed. Continuation of this process could lead eventually to a completely industrialized world under a common government.

It should be emphasized again at this point that the author does not suffer from the illusion that there is much probability that a pattern of evolution such as is described in the preceding paragraph might actually come into existence. But, as is stressed earlier, that which can be imagined by man becomes possible, provided the achievement of what is imagined does not require violation of fundamental physical and biological laws. Time and again during the history of man major changes have taken place that would have been considered impossible during earlier times. Human beings have demonstrated frequently that they can unite against common threats to their existence and against common threats to their ways of life. And battles against common dangers have frequently created strange bedfellows.